A Guest in the House of Israel

Also by Clark M. Williamson
with Ronald J. Allen
Published by Westminster/John Knox Press

The Teaching Minister

A Guest in the House of Israel

Post-Holocaust Church Theology

—·—·—·—·—·—

Clark M. Williamson

Westminster/John Knox Press
Louisville, Kentucky

Book design by Drew Stevens

First edition

Published by Westminster/John Knox Press
Louisville, Kentucky

This book is printed on acid-free paper that meets
the American National Standards Institute Z39.48 standard. ∞

PRINTED IN THE UNITED STATES OF AMERICA
2 4 6 8 9 7 5 3 1

Library of Congress Cataloging-in-Publication Data

Williamson, Clark M.
    A guest in the house of Israel : post-Holocaust church theology /
Clark M. Williamson. — 1st ed.
       p.   cm.
Includes bibliographical references and index.
ISBN 0-664-25454-3 (alk. paper)

    1. Theology, Doctrinal—20th century. 2. Judaism (Christian theology) 3. Holocaust, Jewish (1939–1945)—Influence. 4. Christianity and other religions—Judaism—1945– 5. Judaism—Relations—Christianity—1945– I. Title.
BT78.W585 1993
231.7'6—dc20
                                                      93–3261

Contents

and seek to help the church understand who it is given and called to be, not *sub specie aeternitatis*, but in this time and place, the time and place of peoples and groups whose voices have otherwise been shut out of the theological conversation. Post-Holocaust theology pursues this same task on behalf of the Israel of God and various members of the Israel of God whom we have seldom if ever heard in the one context—that of the covenant between the God of Israel and the Israel of God—in which they can be understood. What post-Holocaust theology seeks to do is to criticize and revise Christian self-understanding in ways appropriate to the radically free grace and total claim of the God who redeems the ungodly, hence in ways that do not "nullify the faithfulness of God" (Rom. 3:3) to the Israel of God.

This post-Holocaust theology is a "church theology" in the sense that it is done in and on behalf of the church and in the sense that it is done under the guidance of the church. Since the Holocaust, various churches have issued numerous statements on Jewish-Christian relations and Christian self-understanding and practice. I take these statements as the churches' attempt to articulate a new *regula fidei* (rule of faith) by which the interpretation of the Christian faith is to be guided. Hence, every chapter articulates a thesis already propounded in and by one of the post-Holocaust teaching documents issued by the churches. This theology is done in, with, and on behalf of the church, not calling it to anything that it does not already know, but calling it to confront its own teachings and their implications.

No finality of expression is presumed here. This work seeks to add a voice and a concern to the ongoing theological discussion. What I hope for this volume is that it succeeds in getting its question taken seriously. That its answer or answers to this question will be debated is expected and anticipated.

There are a number of people without whose assistance this volume would be diminished. They are Ed Towne, Chuck Blaisdell, Ron Allen, Michael Kinnamon, Susannah Heschel, Gerry Janzen, Calvin L. Porter, Paul M. van Buren, and the members of two theological discussion groups: the Christian Study Group on Judaism and the Association of Disciples for Theological Discussion. Their critical and constructive reactions to various chapters have been of enormous help. I also want to thank the late Dick Doolen, a librarian at Christian Theological Seminary, for his helpfulness in running down information, and Ed Steele for seeing to it that the flow of literature never stops.

This book is dedicated to Barbara Williamson, consummate person, whose companionship graces my life and whose spirit lights up the dark places.

C. W.

1

Theology After the *Shoah*

We acknowledge in repentance the church's long and deep complicity in the proliferation of anti-Jewish attitudes and actions through its "teaching of contempt" for the Jews. Such teaching we now repudiate, together with the acts and attitudes which it generates.

—*General Assembly of the Presbyterian Church (U.S.A.)*

Why should we still be concerned, almost fifty years after the end of the *Shoah*[1] (the Nazi attempt to destroy the Jewish people, to leave planet earth *Judenrein,* "clean of Jews"), with the question of the church's "teaching of contempt" for Jews and Judaism? Surely this matter is history by now—if not ancient, at least no longer pertinent, not when there are so many pressing items on the theological agenda, such as women's issues, ecological issues, African-American issues, and the pursuit of liberation from poverty and dependence on the part of third-world peoples. Why should we still be concerned with relations between Christians and Jews? Particularly, why should we be theologically concerned with them?

The Continuing Life of Anti-Judaism

There are two answers to this question, one theological and the other more immediately practical. As to the first, anti-Judaism remains a strong force in much highly influential recent and contemporary theology.[2] This is not to say that theologians in whose work anti-Judaism remains efficacious harbor personal feelings of hostility toward Jews, but that anti-Judaism is an inherited ideology of which Christians tend to be unconscious until it is brought to their attention. Because such an awareness has not been widely experienced, this ideology can be found in much current work.

1

As to the second, anti-Judaism is an old practice of the church and remains so, even when the ideological rationale supporting it may have been long forgotten. To illustrate the point, let me describe three events that happened on one day in the life of a post-*Shoah* theologian. The day was Ash Wednesday. In the morning mail was a press release from a seminary advertising an M.A. degree in missiology "with a concentration in Judaic Studies and Jewish Evangelism." Estimating that there are in excess of forty thousand Jews in North America "who confess Jesus as their Messiah," it claimed that not since the first generation of the church's history have Jewish people been as receptive to the gospel. The degree offered would prepare students "for this demanding ministry so close to the heart of our Lord Jesus Christ." Shelves of books on the history of Christian anti-Judaism and volumes of church statements on relations between Jews and Christians have failed to overcome the assumption that the chief responsibility Christians have toward Jews is to convert them.

That, one might respond, may be, but the example is from "evangelical" Protestantism. "Mainline Christians," one can almost hear the rejoinder, "would not mount a campaign to evangelize Jews." Perhaps not, although whether they would refrain out of fear of not being "nice" or out of theological conviction is a good question. In the next event of Ash Wednesday, I perused the recent issue of a denominational monthly and found the commentaries on the lectionary readings for the upcoming Sundays. One reading was John 18:28–40, the story of Jesus' appearance before Pilate. The commentary opened with this paragraph:

> The Jews [sic] hatred for Jesus caused them to lose all sense of proportion
> for justice and truth. They were so righteous in observing their religious
> law while they demonically pursued the death of Jesus. They accused him
> of blasphemy, contempt for God (Matthew 26:65), but they twisted the
> charge to political insurrection (John 19:12) in order to get the death
> penalty from Pilate. At the same time, they violated their own beliefs when
> they said, "We have no king but Caesar" (John 19:15). The Jews had al-
> ways proclaimed that God alone was their king.[3]

In spite of the author's language about "the Jews," she tries to back out of the corner into which she paints herself by saying that we should not blame "all Jews for the act of a few." But what she gives back she takes away again, explaining that Pilate wanted to release Jesus to "the people," but they, instead, "chose Barabbas." The author (1) writes as if no historical-critical scholarship could be brought to bear on the passage, (2) applies no hermeneutic of suspicion to it, and (3) is oblivious to the fact that Christians project onto their Jewish neighbors attitudes and beliefs that they are taught concerning Jews in the biblical story.[4] Whatever her intent, she reinforces anti-Jewish attitudes among Christians.

The third event of Ash Wednesday was a worship service in which the reading was from Matthew. As it was read, references to human beings were paraphrased and made inclusive, and "your Father in heaven" became "your God." However, the strongly negative attitudes Matthew expresses toward Jews were left intact; they remained "the hypocrites in the synagogue." A university president was once asked why he did not censor the student newspaper. He answered that if he changed some items in it, that would imply that he approved the rest. Thus, one might draw the implication from this reading of Matthew that it is morally acceptable to refer to Jews as "hypocrites."[5]

These latter two cases are small matters, but it is in such small ways that Christian anti-Judaism is continually reinforced by the churches. The first step the church can take with regard to any significant problem is to accept responsibility for its language, for how it talks, in this case of Jews and Judaism. The use of inclusive language, indeed the preparation of an entire inclusive language lectionary, shows that the church can take this kind of responsibility with regard to women. But both the church and the lectionary-makers have by and large failed to do so with regard to Jews (about half of whom are women). As long as we uncritically refer to "the Jews' hatred of Jesus" or to Jews as "hypocrites," churchgoers will hear these remarks not only about Jews of long ago but about their neighbors across the street. The primary business of theology is to bring the church to self-understanding and self-criticism and thereby to change its practice, which means, first, to change its speech. Attitudes and actions also need changing, but speech is itself a form of human behavior in need of correction.

Even when scripture readings are rendered into inclusive language, the anti-Judaism of those same readings is left untouched. Even after the *Shoah* and the Second Vatican Council, church publications carry columns decrying "the Jews' hatred of Jesus." Even after numerous teaching bodies of the church have affirmed that both Jews and Christians share a common responsibility to be "a light to the nations" on behalf of the God of Israel, a theological seminary initiates a program for the evangelization of Jews. Dealing with Christian anti-Judaism by articulating an alternative theological understanding of the Christian faith remains a pertinent endeavor.

Being Suspicious of Pre-*Shoah* Theology

Much theology has been done since the *Shoah*, but not much by theologians who are critically aware that they do their thinking "after Auschwitz."[6] Liberal theology, chiefly associated with the work of Albrecht

Ritschl, was still important in the American Midwest in the 1950s, although Ritschl's major works were published between 1870 and 1874. The social gospel theologian Walter Rauschenbusch died in 1918. Neo-Reformation theology, associated with Karl Barth and Emil Brunner, arose in response to the crisis in the church unveiled by World War I and the problem of "culture-religion." Barth's decisive commentary on *Romans* appeared in 1919 and the first volume of the *Church Dogmatics* in 1932, a year before Hitler came to power. Paul Tillich's major theological breakthrough came while he was at Marburg in the 1920s. Consequently, none of these theologians puts to the Christian tradition the hard questions that come from a post-*Shoah* awareness of that tradition's complicity in the Nazi policy of *Judenvernichtung* (destruction of the Jews). Nor is anti-Judaism overcome in these theologians.[7]

Hence, we cannot simply adopt one of these theologies and apply its approach to the subject of Christian theology after Auschwitz. Rather, we must heed the warning given us by the Roman Catholic theologian Johann-Baptist Metz: "Ask yourselves if the theology you are learning is such that it could remain unchanged before and after Auschwitz. If this is the case, be on your guard."[8] Metz is not proposing an absolute ban on every theological statement made before the *Shoah*, but is suggesting that we test them to determine if they express a supersessionist ideology vis-à-vis Jews and Judaism.[9] Metz's rule is to be taken seriously because of two features of traditional Christian theology. First, its claim that the church displaced the Israel of God in the covenant with God also signified that Jews were religiously out of business, that they should cease being Jews and become Christians. Second, this supersessionist ideology, which inspired and reinforced an anti-Jewish practice embodied in preaching, teaching, and identity-formation, was expressed in both legislation and acts of violence.

As Rosemary Ruether analyzes the anti-Jewish ideology of the church, it turns upon two major themes: rejection/election and inferiority/superiority. According to the first, in rejecting Jesus Christ the Jews are rejected by God, and in accepting Jesus Christ the Gentiles are elected. The price of the election of the Gentiles is the rejection of the Jews. Gentile believers displace them in the economy of salvation and in God's favor. This motif pays a lot of attention to the "two peoples" allegory, the elder/younger brother stories in the Bible, and the claim that Jewish history is a "trail of crimes" culminating in deicide. According to the second theme, everything about Jewish faith and life is inferior to Christian faith and life, which is, in all respects, better. Christian ethics, worship, and biblical interpretation improve upon Jewish "law," worship, and exegesis. The Christian way of doing things "fulfills" biblical promises, which Jews, being blind to the meaning of their own scriptures, misunderstand. Only

Christians can rightly interpret the Hebrew Bible, which they make over into an "Old Testament." Jews fail to recognize that their covenant has been superseded and continue to pursue patently invalid modes of commitment to it.[10]

David P. Efroymson's somewhat different analysis looks upon anti-Judaism as a double-edged model, a model *of* and a model *for*. First, it is a model *of* Judaism, on which Judaism is a system and Jews a people "rejected by God, unfaithful to God, opposed to Christianity, and caught up in the crimes appropriate to their carnality, hardness, blindness and *vetustas* [obdurate commitment to what is past and gone, oldness]." Jews are a people of oldness, Judaism a religion of oldness. On the same model, Christians, by contrast, are "a people and a system of newness, of fidelity, of spirituality, of moral vigor, and of universality." At the same time, anti-Judaism is a model *for* how Christians are to be Christians. It is

> a model for action, for acting "ethically," for praying or worshiping "spiritually," for reading the Bible accurately—all in specific and clearly focused distinction from the Jewish way of acting, praying, and of reading the Bible.[11]

If we ask what Christianity is, the anti-Jewish answer is: everything new, good, spiritual, and universal that the old, bad, carnal, and ethnocentric Jews can never be.

Every Christian doctrine can be and was interpreted through the lens of this anti-Jewish hermeneutic. God is the God who displaces Jews and replaces them with Christians. Christ is the mediator on behalf of Christians who cut a displacement deal with God. The church is the replacement people who displace Jews in the covenant. The covenant is a new covenant, replacing the old. The scriptures and their interpretation warrant these understandings. In order to examine the ideological deformation of our tradition, the discussion of each Christian doctrine in this book will begin with a description of the way anti-Judaism distorted it.[12]

Anti-Judaism was never mere theorizing without significant practical implications. To say that something is mere theory is itself mere theory, and bad theory at that. Theory or interpretation always is momentously practical, and practice is always theory-laden. Anti-Judaism was never academic theorizing but a part of preaching, pastoral care, and community formation. It functioned in the early and medieval church in two ways. First, it served to answer the questions that religion must answer: Who are we? Who is God? (Or how is ultimate reality to be characterized?) What are we to do? It answered: We are the new, gentile, universal, spiritual people with whom God replaces the Jews in the covenant. God is the God who effects such a payoff in our behalf and to our benefit.

What are we to do? Nothing that Jews do, but those things that are required of a morally and spiritually superior people. The most significant contribution of anti-Judaism was to shape Christian identity over time. This shaping has gone on for so long that it and its language escape the notice of most Christians, indicating that the identity runs deep in the Christian psyche.

Second, with the shift of Christianity from illegitimacy in the Roman Empire to establishment under Emperor Theodosius came the enacting of canon and state laws that gave anti-Judaism legal force in church and state. The purpose of these laws, in Ruether's fine phrase, was "the social incorporation of the myth of Jews in the fabric of Christendom."[13] If Jews are a people and Judaism a religion of "oldness," they should be made to look the part. Hence, canon and state laws were passed forbidding the building of new synagogues and the repair of old ones. The bishops at the 1222 Council of Oxford felt it necessary to reenact this statute.[14] Nor was it just in religion, but in every way, that Jewish life was to reflect Christian ideology. Jews were forbidden from owning slaves, not out of any concern for slaves, but to prevent Jews from competing with Christians in farming and small manufacturing. Christians could own slaves. Jews were barred from serving as judges or tax collectors, from holding public office, from giving evidence in suits against Christians except in behalf of other Christians, and could hold no position of authority over a Christian in the army, civil administration, law, or economy. They were required by the 1215 Fourth Lateran Council to wear distinctive dress (a rule to which Hitler's lawyers appealed as a precedent for requiring all Jews in the Third Reich to wear the Star of David).

As a rule, Jews were stateless and without rights, forced to live in ghettos sanctioned by councils of the church and by popes, the 1267 Synod of Breslau and Pope Paul IV (1555–1559) having declared ghettos compulsory for Jews. Each of Hitler's Nuremberg laws found its precedent in a piece of canon law. In Augustine's theology, the role of Jews in history was to bear "the strange witness of unbelief." In their homelessness and poverty, Jews witness to the fate of those who reject Christ. Said Augustine: "So to the end of the seven days of time, the continued preservation of the Jews will be a proof to believing Christians of the subjection merited by those who . . . put the Lord to death."[15] According to Augustine, Jews are to be *preserved* in a state of *subjection*. (One wonders if Augustine realized that he was proposing a ban on efforts to convert Jews. They can hardly be both converted and preserved "to the end of the seven days of time.") His views became official church policy in the Middle Ages, with the papacy seeking both to protect Jews and to keep them in a marginalized position in the society, polity, and economy. Yet from the time of the Crusades, this double-handed policy proved unable to prevent violence, with the result that pogrom after pogrom was unleashed against Jews by Christians on all manner of fantastic charges such as the blood libel, well-poisoning, and desecration of the host.[16]

Such actions, which mounted in scope and intensity through the nineteenth-century pogroms in Czarist Russia, indicate a sickness at the heart of Christendom, a sickness rooted in the teaching of contempt for Jews and Judaism. They indicate that ideas have consequences, that people tend to live by the story they tell of themselves, that if the telling of that story is defective, so will be the living-out of it; that both anti-Jewish action and the anti-Jewish story or set of beliefs stand in need of fundamental theological criticism and revision.

The purpose of this brief review of anti-Jewish practice has not been to provide a full description of such matters, but to indicate that the church's theological understanding of itself in relation to Jews and Judaism was never mere theorizing. Theory, interpretation, *always* has a practical moment. The church's anti-Judaism reflects and reinforces anti-Jewish practice, whether that practice is internal to the church in how it talks about Jews and Judaism and itself, in the ideas and attitudes that people adopt toward Jews, or whether it finds its ramification in more visible and public forms, such as legislation or a willingness to tolerate violence or discrimination against Jews.

Post-*Shoah* theology takes as its task critical reflection on the historical anti-Jewish praxis of the church, and to liberate the church's witness and theology from its inherited *adversus Judaeos* ideology. Post-*Shoah* theology is a form of liberation theology in two senses: it criticizes the church's supersessionist ideology toward Jews and Judaism, an ideology that has sanctioned oppression, and it does so in solidarity with the victims of that oppression, namely, with Jews. It expresses this solidarity by the simple means of speaking up, within the church, on behalf of those who have no voice in the church.[17]

Linkage with Other Forms of Oppression

Anti-Judaism is not a problem unto itself, boxed off in its own category, unrelated to other forms of oppression. When we examine early Christian anti-Judaism, we find that its representatives were not opposed to Jews only. The Gnostic movement and its docetic Christologies spurned this material, earthly world in which we live, the human body, and the inferior God who made this world and who was made known to the Jewish people through the law and the prophets. Jews, the law, the "Old Testament," the body, this world, the God of Genesis, all were detested by the Gnostics. Although the church formally rejected the Gnostic doctrine, materially it was deeply shaped by Gnostic attitudes. "Accordingly," points out Peter von der Osten-Sacken, "salvation is to be found in a rejection of all three—Israel's Bible, Israel's God, and the creation brought about by that God—and hence, once again, of the people of Israel."[18] Earthiness is distasteful to Christian anti-Judaism. Women, thought to be earthy and carnal, were looked upon as less than fully human and, later, as associated with Jews in the "witches' sabbath."[19]

Nor is racism unrelated to anti-Judaism. Gnosticism divided human beings into three classes, with the lowest designated "physical" and the highest "spiritual," and an intermediate class termed the "psychical." Salvation, guaranteed to members of the spiritual class, was impossible to members of the physical class. It was to the intermediate class that Gnosticism appealed, because souls of this class, trapped in bodies, had to learn the secret *gnosis* if they were to achieve salvation. Salvation was very difficult for women, being more physical, which is why in the Gnostic *Gospel of Mary* Mary herself says: "Let us praise his greatness, for he has prepared us [and] made us into men."[20] Gnosticism shares with racism an elitism based on presumed inherent characteristics. In the transition from the Middle Ages to the modern era, anti-Judaism figures in the development of modern racism. After Ferdinand and Isabella had reunited Spain under Christian auspices in 1492, they required that all Jews in Spain be baptized or expelled from the country. Thus began the Diaspora of Sephardic Jewry. All Jews who stayed in Spain were baptized and thus were no longer Jews, but Christians. Spanish Christians then had a new problem, how to prevent "Jewish-Christians" from rising to prominence in the state and the church. Spanish Christians created the "purity of blood" statutes, which they introduced to provide a new basis for discriminating against Jews.[21]

"What contemporary ideology criticism has uncovered," says Sandra Schneiders, "is the intrinsic connection among all forms of systemic domination."[22] Schneiders' thesis is that patriarchy is the nerve of classism, racism, sexism, and clericalism. Whether that is so or whether the situation is more complex need not concern us here. What commands our attention is that all forms of domination are interconnected and inseparable, including anti-Judaism, which Schneiders fails to mention. Certainly, throughout Christendom Jewish women would have to be listed as suffering heavy oppression from racism, sexism, classism, and clericalism.

Hence all major contemporary forms of the drive for liberation from oppression are interrelated and inseparable. Questions as to the proper Christian relationship to African Americans, women, the ecology, and Jews are distinguishable but indivisible. Some people who struggle to be liberated from oppression have to fight on more than one front at a time. African-American women have to struggle against racism *and* sexism. Jewish women have to contend with sexism *and* anti-Judaism. Oppression does not come in discrete packages. African-American and Jewish women face double jeopardy. Many African-American women also must deal with poverty, and thus the triple jeopardy of sexism, racism, and classism. There are even African-American women who are Jewish, reminding us that sexism, racism, and anti-Judaism "cannot always be differentiated."[23] James Cone points out that Eldridge Cleaver saw the necessity for Black power when he understood what happened to Jews during the *Shoah*, that we cannot live without the power to resist tyranny.[24] Therefore, the focus in this book on anti-Judaism and its overcoming in Christian theology does not mean that other forms of oppression are unimportant.[25] It is a great tragedy when and if those who struggle against oppression also struggle against each other.

Doing Theology in Conversation with Jews

Metz alerts us to a danger facing Christian theology: if we are not mindful of what we are doing, we may repeat after the *Shoah* the very theological attitudes that preceded it and made it possible. Like every hermeneutic of suspicion, a critique of the anti-Judaism of the Christian tradition has a negative and a constructive pole. If we accept Metz's warning, we will remove Christian anti-Judaism from our theology. But with what shall we replace it? The constructive pole of the hermeneutic comes into play in answer to this question. Here we suggest some preliminary rules for how theology should be done post-*Shoah*.

First, we must finally learn a lesson that we neglected as long ago as the latter part of the first century—that Christians cannot give theological shape to their self-understanding as Christians without engaging in conversation with Jews. This rule does *not* say that Christians need not engage in other conversations as well. The different "religions" of the world are all candidates for conversation partners in our increasingly pluralistic age. It does say that the conversation with Jews is indispensable to understanding Christian faith; that the historical evidence massively attests to the fact that apart from listening to and talking with Jews, we will misunderstand the Christian faith and act on our misunderstandings. With very few exceptions, most of them recent, few Christian theologians have taken Jews seriously as a living people and Judaism seriously as a living faith in the God of Israel. For almost two thousand years, Paul the apostle was virtually the last, or only, theologian to do so. Seldom do theologians in articulating Christian doctrine think to ask how Jews understand that doctrine. Yet anti-Judaism had a profound effect on how Christian doctrines were framed, and no doctrine escaped its baleful influence. Metz's caution prompts us to converse with Jews as we set out to propose a revisionist understanding of a range of Christian teachings.

Two of the Jewish thinkers with whom we will seek to become acquainted and by whom we will allow theology to be corrected are *Yeshua ha Notsri*, a wandering first-century Galilean teacher more widely known as Jesus of Nazareth, whose very Jewish name, *Yeshua*, means "Yahweh is salvation," and Paul the apostle, who was in his self-description "circumcised on the eighth day, a member of the people of Israel, of the tribe of Benjamin, a Hebrew born of Hebrews; as to the law, a Pharisee; as to zeal, a persecutor of the church; as to righteousness under the law, blameless" (Phil. 3:5–6). Each of these Jewish teachers will be the subject of a separate chapter (Chapters 3 and 4) in which, after delineating and dismissing the traditional anti-Jewish way of construing Jesus or Paul, we will try to make clear how each should be understood in the context of the covenant between the Israel of God and the God of Israel.

Reconstructing either figure is a life's work for any scholar. All that a theologian can do with such large undertakings is make what sense is possible out of a sampling of recent scholarly literature. The purpose of the chapters on Jesus and Paul is not to produce versions of them that will warrant and support what we today want to do. As the Christology chapter (7) will argue, it is a mistake to assume that the Jesus of historical-critical reconstruction is the norm of Christian faith and practice or the subject of Christology. Scholars and theologians who take Jesus as such a norm typically are forced to produce a version of him that will support what they are most convinced we ought to be and do. They reconstruct the figure of Jesus in a way that will allow and/or require them to do what they have already decided to do in any case.[26] What we seek from the empirical-historical Jesus here, as well as from an understanding of Paul, is something else—to let them serve as correctives to theology.[27] Also, as the Christology chapter (7) will argue, Jesus Christ stands to Christians as their savior and, hence, more than any mere norm. To claim him as a norm is to claim far too little. Yet it is the case, as John Bowden puts it, that "time and again the church (and the Christ it has worshipped) has been challenged in the name of Jesus."[28] That is what the discussion of Jesus and Paul here intends to enable—to let these two members of the Israel of God call us back to the God of Israel.

Historically and still to a great extent, Christians have felt no need to consult Jews prior to describing Judaism. Any description of Jews that served Christian ideological purposes was acceptable.[29] Theology today has been challenged by Jeffrey Stout's comment that Christianity can no longer put every other voice in the conversation in its place. Rather, "it must take its place among the other voices, as often to be corrected as to correct."[30] We will risk taking seriously a possibility suggested by Charles Hartshorne, "that it just might be that the Jews, in their differences from Christians, have been more right all along on some issues."[31] Hartshorne correctly notes that readiness to engage in conversation implies that one's conversation partner *might sometimes* be right.

This "conversational" approach to theology recognizes that a genuine conversation is one in which no party to it seeks to dominate the other party or parties involved. Relationships of domination and seeking domination were the main goal of traditional Christian ways of talking to or about Jews. Both approaches are oppressive of the other partner and inappropriate to the Christian faith, which should apply its commandment of loving the neighbor as oneself to the way in which it approaches conversation. George Lakoff and Mark Johnson show that "one [metaphor] that we live by" in our culture describes argument or conversation as "war." They provide a variety of expressions ordinarily used to describe argument: "Your claims are *indefensible.* He *attacked every weak point* in my argument. His criticisms were *right on target.* I *demolished* his argument."[32] If we approach conversation as war, every conversation is a win-lose proposition. If Christianity wins, Judaism loses; if Judaism wins, Christianity loses. Some Christians and Jews still assume just this as they enter conversation with each other. This assumption derives from the prior supposition by each party that *it* must achieve mastery over the conversation-partner. The ideology of Christian anti-Judaism, which requires Christianity to "win" every discussion with or about Judaism, reflects the church's will-to-power over Jews and Judaism. A conversation so approached is no conversation at all, because it is motivated by Christianity's tendency to put every other voice in the conversation in its place.

A better approach is one in which each party at least attempts to let the subject of the conversation dominate. What Henry Nelson Wieman called "creative interchange" provides a constructive alternative to the understanding of conversation as war. In the social event of creative interchange, he argued, four discernible subevents take place. First, the individuals involved are open to and aware of the qualitative meanings that others in the conversation try to communicate to them. One is receptive, aware that the first moral responsibility in conversation is to listen. Second, lest one's mind become a garbage-heap of accumulated meanings deposited there by one's conversation partners, one must critically integrate these meanings with the values and perspective that one brought to the conversation. Commitment to a more supreme and embracing good facilitates this kind of integration. Third, if one has been receptive and critical of the shared meanings donated by others, then one has an expanded and enriched "appreciable world" and enjoys a "new structure of interrelatedness."[33] Paul Tillich describes this as the power of the divine

Spirit experienced as "the power of breaking through the walls of self-seclusion." It is God calling us "toward a mature relatedness."[34] It is a growing communion among participants in the conversation and a commitment to the further extension of mature relatedness, aware that our very being is a being-in-community. Fourth, the new structure of interrelatedness transforms not only the person and his or her appreciable world but the person's relations "with those who have participated with him [or her] in this occurrence." One shares in a broader and deeper companionship with one's fellow human beings. Although I do not concur with Wieman's identification of creative interchange with his functional doctrine of God, I do find it a helpful model for approaching conversation.[35] It is far better that conversations be characterized by a willingness to listen, to integrate critically, to broaden one's perspective, and to engage in a deeper companionship than that they be a verbal substitute for war.

Conversation has its own morality, according to which the participants must yield to the back-and-forth movement of questions worth probing. David Tracy suggests that an interpreter's relation to a text (for example, a biblical text) should be conversational, in which neither the text nor the interpreter dominates the other but in which each cedes control to the question or theme at the heart of the conversation.[36] If we cannot converse, we cannot understand. Understanding will always be creative, will yield a new interpretation of the subject of discussion. To approach conversation as creative interchange does not mean that we will avoid conflict, argument, and criticism. The attempt to understand and be understood will require a willingness to suffer conflict, to defend, to argue, to correct, as well as a willingness to be corrected, to say "yes," to change one's mind when it is obvious that one should. Conversation must be authentically critical to be genuine or for those in the conversation to sense that they are taken seriously. But conversation motivated by the urge to win generates more heat than light.

We will also enter into conversation with the Christian tradition, critically engaging it on the question of the appropriateness, credibility, and morality of its self-understanding in relationship to the God of Israel and the Israel of God. Karl Barth taught us that in dealing with theologians of the past, we have to recognize that they are not dead. "'In Him they all have life,' in the greatness and within the limitations in which they once lived."[37] Hence, we cannot follow the rule *De mortuis nihil nisi bene* (speak only well of the dead), but will treat the theological voices of the tradition, canonical or postcanonical, as living conversation partners and engage them in the give-and-take involved in understanding the Christian faith. When they quit conversing and give voice to anti-Jewish ideology, we will suspend the conversation and describe the ideology. To describe it is to criticize it.

Second, we will allow the *Shoah* to put an end to all theological talk that cannot meet the test of Auschwitz. We will accept Irving Greenberg's working principle: "No statement, theological or otherwise, should be made that would not be credible in the presence of the burning children."[38] Greenberg refers to the roughly one and a half million Jewish children who were killed in the *Shoah*, some without the "benefit" of poison gas so that the Nazis could save one-half *pfennig* per death.

Greenberg's working principle has at least two meanings. It is a *moral* criterion that any theological statement that contributed to creating the *adversus Judaeos* tradition that made the *Shoah* possible may not be repeated. The "teaching of contempt" for Jews and Judaism was a necessary but not sufficient cause of the Holocaust. Now that we see the complicity of that teaching in making possible the Holocaust, we may not morally repeat it. It is a standard for *credibility* in that it disallows statements that cannot stand as plausible in the presence of the burning children. Certain ways of talking about the power of God, for example, that imply either that God committed the Holocaust or allowed it to happen but could have prevented it are ruled out by one's inability so to speak of God's love and justice in the presence of the burning children. The living God of the Bible is the Lord who "loves justice" (Ps. 37:28) and of whom we must speak justly.

Not only are statements that would allow for Auschwitz morally reprehensible. Those that cannot stand as credible prove inadequate as well to dealing with every other problem we face in this nuclear-ecological age. Christian doctrines of God have not only been as deeply shaped by anti-Judaism as have other doctrines, but few such doctrines are formulated in response to Elie Wiesel's question from his experience in Auschwitz: "Where is God?"[39] No doctrine of God and God's providence can be framed in the light of the fires of Auschwitz that does not seek to be credible in the presence of the burning children.

Third, a Christian theology developed in conversation with Jews will lay heavy stress on faith as discipleship, as a Way of life. The primary lesson we can learn from Jews and Judaism is the importance of faith as a Way given us by God to walk in the world and through history and, paradoxically, as a Way that we are responsible for determining while we walk it. Road maps stretch out in space, but not over time. The route ahead is uncharted, but the singular promise and singular command of God disclosed in the law and the prophets and re-presented in the gospel of Jesus Christ constitute a lamp to our feet and a light to our path (Ps. 119:105). Jewish faith never loses sight of the fact that God's people are called and claimed to be a "light to the nations," nor are Jesus' followers to forget that they are called to be "the light of the world" (Matt. 5:14), to let people see their good works that they may glorify God (Matt. 5:15–16; Luke 11:33; Mark 4:21). What Jews call *Halakah*, that practical-moral reflection on the dual *torah* (written and oral), means "way." *Halakah* is the decisions Jews make about questions that arise as they walk the Way of God, conscious that the covenant is given to them not for their private benefit but to enable them to be a light to the world. Some parts of the early church regarded themselves as people of "the Way" (Acts 9:2) following the Way of God (Acts 18:26). Hence, Christian theology can inculcate no merely private understanding of faith but one that calls for willingness to resist powerful social prejudices in the name of justice. A theology done after Auschwitz and in conversation with Jews will share with other liberation theologies a sense of the unredeemedness of the world and of the brokenness of the church. It will seek to "re-Judaize" itself, not in the sense of playing at being Jewish, but in yearning and working for the actualization of the divine promises in history.[40] Christian theology has to go beyond the emphasis on historical consciousness and historicity as those were stressed in the Liberal and Neo-Reformation eras. It must move into the actual history of suffering and oppression, which it cannot do without facing the awful ways in which it has contributed to that history, particularly in the case of the praxis of the teaching of contempt for Jews and Judaism and the reality of the *Shoah*.

The Inadequacy of "Pure Narrative Theology"[41]

Narrative theology is distinctive for its argument that our ability to know God, God's character, and God's characteristic actions depends on a prior ability to identify God as an agent whose individualizing behavior patterns unfold in the biblical narrative. As such, narrative theology is associated with the postliberal theologies that define the task of theology as "Christian self-description."[42] On the pure narrative model, the task of theology is not to engage the Christian tradition in a correlation with what Paul Tillich called "the situation," but to describe how matters look from the (or a) Christian perspective, to tell the Christian story. The connection between narrative theology and Lindbeck's postliberal theology is found in Lindbeck's "cultural-linguistic model" of religion, according to which a religion defines a language and a practice that together make possible certain kinds of experience, including the experience or knowledge of God. Hence, the task of theology is Christian self-description, not correlation with the situation. The latter approach, the postliberals argue, risks reducing Christian faith to what modern, eighteenth-century models of credibility will allow as well as reducing the distinctiveness of Christian faith to one more form "of a single commodity needed for transcendent self-expression and self-realization."[43] Postliberal theology does not seek to be credible in relation to the situation in which human beings live but, instead, seeks to be "truthful" to the Christian story.[44]

If the postliberals would not mind my putting it this way, there is much truth in their position. A post-*Shoah* Christian theology can only welcome a rigorous insistence on truthfulness to the Christian story, on understanding how language shapes experience and behavior, and on accurately telling the story. Yet that story has for long been told in an anti-Jewish way, a way that is false to the God characterized in the biblical story as the God of steadfast love (*hesed*). That the story thus told has resulted in innumerable untruthful forms of behavior toward Jews cannot be denied.

Yet difficulties remain. First, post-*Shoah* theologians go about their business aware that they do theology *after* Auschwitz and in the light thrown by Auschwitz on the way the church has told its story for two millennia. Such theologians wish to criticize and revise the telling of the story in the light of the situation. They also want to criticize the situation in the light of what the Christian faith, appropriately understood, is all about. They want to call into judgment both the teaching of contempt and the *Shoah*, to which the teaching of contempt contributed. As a conversational theology, post-*Shoah* theology will try to effect a two-way conversation between the situation in which it does its theologizing and the Christian tradition.

Second, a post-*Shoah* theology is at best an "impure narrative" theology. Gary L. Comstock claims that for the pure narrative theologians, "narrative is an autonomous literary form particularly suited to the work of theology," whereas for the impure narrative theologians, narrative is a significant "genre in which important religious truths and practices are communicated." A post-Holocaust theology is, at best, an impure narrative theology, because it must deny to narrative a unique theological status. Post-*Shoah* theologians are aware that Christian narratives are "irreducibly infected with historical, philosophical and psychological concerns." As a result, we apply to narrative various hermeneutical methods, including that of a hermeneutics of suspicion or ideology critique, and regard narrative as "neither pure nor autonomous."[45] Post-Holocaust theologians share with other theologians concerned to liberate theology from its inherited ideologies an awareness that it is not just "that scripture has been used to legitimate oppression (although this is a continuing problem), but that the Bible itself is both a product and a producer of oppression, that some of its *content* is oppressive."[46] We are concerned not only to retrieve the Christian tradition but also to submit it to a hermeneutic of suspicion, to de-ideologize it by disengaging it from the political, social, economic, and cultural injustices that it has been used to condone.[47] Taking ideology to mean "the deformation of truth for the sake of social interest,"[48] post-Holocaust theology criticizes the anti-Judaism in the Christian narrative with which the church promoted the oppression of the Jewish people, those Jewish neighbors who were outside the arena of the church's moral responsibility.

Let me provide two illustrations of this point. The first will set up a critical relationship between a Christian narrative theologian and a Jewish commentator on his work. The Christian narrative theologian is Ronald F. Thiemann, whose *Revelation and Theology: The Gospel as Narrated Promise* stresses that when we are interested in *who* a person is, we are often told a story that exhibits that person's character.[49] When we can compile enough "story-bound" character traits, we can individuate a character and evaluate the character's behavior. The biblical narrative enables us to do this with God, to come to know who God is as a character in the persistent patterns of whose storied behavior over time there is no inconstancy. As Rabbi Michael Goldberg rightly describes Thiemann's narrative theology of Matthew, the intent of the gospel is to provide "an increasingly specific identity description of Jesus, thereby revealing his acts to be enactments of God's intentions for Israel and the world." The description and the justification of the Christian belief that "God is identifiable in Jesus Christ" are made possible only by close attention to the narrative that gives rise to it.[50]

At this point, Rabbi Goldberg asks whether the God identifiable in Jesus Christ is the God of Israel. As he sees it, Thiemann neglects to inquire into the story of God with Israel, which Jews and Christians have in common. Thiemann links Jesus to the Davidic and Abrahamic covenants that God made with Israel, but ignores the third significant covenantal promise, "the one associated with Israel's becoming *a people* in the first place: Sinai." Hence, the major motif in Israel's story is expunged from the Christian story. There results a major discrepancy in the two story-bound attempts to render the character of God. In the Abrahamic and Davidic covenants, God acts unilaterally out of sheer grace; in the Sinai covenant, a bilateral treaty, "the parties to the pact must *all* faithfully fulfill its mutually binding stipulations." In the light of the Exodus story, "God might well be *unrecognizable* in Jesus Christ." Further, if God acted in the way Thiemann described, a deep inconstancy would be introduced into God's character, thus nullifying the narrative attempt to individuate God *over time* as demonstrating "no inconstancy in action," as the covenantally faithful One.[51]

Goldberg, a Jewish narrative theologian, is keenly aware of the whole story of the Israel of God and the God of Israel up to the time of Matthew, Matthew's anti-Jewish bias, and of the contemporary, post-*Shoah* situation (to which the church's even more anti-Jewish use of Matthew contributed). All these he takes into account in attempting his own narrative theology. He finds it exceedingly important that both Christians and Jews tell the story straight, that they critically revise past ways of telling the story, even canonical ones. Goldberg's work illustrates why a pure narrative theology is not particularly helpful to us after Auschwitz.

The second illustration comes from the work of Jack Dean Kingsbury, who seeks to "set forth the thought of Matthew as it finds expression in the story of Jesus being narrated." Kingsbury finds the theme of conflict "central to the plot of Matthew." Matthew turns on the conflict between Jesus and Israel, whose leaders are Jesus' "implacable adversaries." Between him and them the tension in the story sharply heightens. Their and Israel's repudiation of Jesus "rapidly escalates to the point of irreconcilable hostility." Once its acme is reached, the tension between Jesus, the Jewish leaders, and Israel "abates no more." The "whole gamut of Jewish officialdom" repudiates Jesus, and he in turn excoriates them "in a scathing speech of woes." The conflict is resolved by Jesus' death, and God "ultimately decides the conflict between Jesus and Israel" by vindicating Jesus in the resurrection. Furthermore, in Matthew's story, Jesus and the disciples count as "round" characters; they are "real people." In contrast, the Jewish leaders and crowds "prove to be flat characters, highly predictable in their behavior."[52]

God and Jesus are the only two characters in the story "whom Matthew always puts in the right." Matthew's Jewish leaders all represent a united front against Jesus who, in turn, views them as "evil," a "brood of vipers," headed for Gehenna. Their "root traits" are "evilness" and "hypocrisy." Matthew's list of pejorative adjectives for describing them is *very* long. Kingsbury departs from his literary-critical approach at the end of his book and turns to historical-criticism to describe the social climate in which Matthew was written. This climate was one "of intense conflict," partly with "a vigorous Jewish community." Matthew's community is "outside" the synagogue, and he mounts a "massive apology against it [Judaism] in his Gospel."[53]

Kingsbury's work starts out as narrative theology, but resorts to historical criticism to explain how Matthew's anti-Jewish apology shapes his narrative. If the conflict theme is as central to Matthew as Kingsbury claims, then we must ask how this theme shapes the story-bound character traits of Jesus and God as Matthew's narrative yields them. Both characters are shaped by anti-Judaism. Jesus' life is lived in conflict with Jews and Judaism, his teachings are set forth as against Jews and Judaism, his death is at the hands of Jews and Judaism, and God vindicates him against Jews and Judaism. Because Matthew several times redacts a supersessionist interpretation into the parables of Jesus ("Therefore I tell you, the kingdom of God will be taken away from you and given to a people that produces the fruits of the kingdom" [21:43]), are we to conclude that God according to Matthew is God the displacer of the Jews and Jesus the agent through whom the displacement was effected?

All this is not to say that the pure narrativists are simply wrong. In the final analysis, it may well be that a good description constitutes a very large part, if not the whole, of an adequate explanation. However, we are a long way from offering that description. The anti-Judaism in the tradition, including the parts of the tradition defined as canonical, must be eliminated and a new interpretation offered that seeks both to be more appropriate to the tradition and more plausible in a post-*Shoah* situation. Then we may have arrived at something that can be offered, if not as a good description, at least as a contribution to the discussion of what would constitute a good description.

The Gospel—A Norm of Appropriateness

Because a post-*Shoah* revisionist theology risks subjecting the tradition to criticism as well as offering a new interpretation of the Christian faith, it has to deal with the question of its authority for doing these things. What authorizes a new interpretation of the significance of Jesus Christ or of who Jesus Christ is and what he does? Christian theology often has difficulty in developing a new interpretation because it frequently takes the Apostolic Age as the definitive period of Christian history. Robert Wilken observes: "Christians have prized as values tradition, antiquity, apostolicity, uniformity, and permanence, and they have spurned change, innovation, novelty, and diversity." By selecting and interpreting, we have made the Apostolic Age "an ideal expression of Christianity," "the model for all later generations."[54] The gravest accusation made against heretics was that they were innovators.

All this, argues Wilken, is a myth: "There never was a Golden Age when the church was whole, perfect, pure—virginal. The faith was not purer, the Christians were not braver, the church was not one and undivided." The fallacy of taking the Apostolic Age or the New Testament straightforwardly as the norm for Christian life and thought is that it allows us to escape serious historical criticism. "We must learn . . . to live with the unpleasant fact that anti-Semitism is part of what it has meant historically to be a Christian, and is still part of what it means to be Christian."[55] Idealizing that past age inverts the order of our historical experience and tempts us to avoid dealing with our own theological and ethical questions. Even if the early witness had not been anti-Jewish, that still would not allow us to dismiss the criticism directed at the Christian tradition by a post-Holocaust hermeneutics of suspicion.

Why the church in the second through the fourth centuries defined apostolicity as "earliest" is a good question. In the Roman world, the notion that truth is always older than error, that if we can get back to the most primeval of days we are more likely to find truth there than in recent times, was itself a traditional Roman understanding of truth and authority. "What is older is better: 'the real thing always exists before the representation of it; the copy comes later,' wrote Tertullian." Eusebius of Caesarea felt it necessary to respond to critics who charged Jesus Christ with being a newcomer.[56] To Romans, "new" connoted "faddish" or "belated," not "fresh and innovative."

Christian theologians who seek new responses to new questions find that this traditional Christian understanding of authority thwarts their efforts. As a result, Delwin Brown contends that the nature of theological authority has been misinterpreted,[57] charging that the church uncritically adopted a Roman model of authority. This Roman model presupposed an understanding of ancestors as "permanent parents . . . who under all circumstances represent the example of greatness for each successive age."[58] What Hannah Arendt termed "the sacredness of foundation," "that once something had been founded it remains binding for all future generations," became the cornerstone of Roman life. The Roman understanding of religion as *religare*, "to be tied back," meant that the authority of the living was "tied back" to that of the founders.[59] This patriarchal Roman model of authority grants the power to authorize what happens in the present to those who were fathers (*pateres*) in the beginning and who still govern.

In contrast to this Roman model of authority stands the suppleness of Jewish understandings of authority, which manifest a "dynamic interplay between authoritative Torah-teaching and biblical midrash [interpretation], both within the Pentateuch and between the Pentateuch and later materials." Here we have a creative appropriation of tradition, which suggests a distinction between the "authorizing" model of authority derived from the Roman tradition, and an "authoring" model of authority, according to which the author grants life and freedom to the author's characters; "the creatures, given life, become creators." What gives a religious tradition life is this dialectical interplay between the limitation imposed by a canon of scripture and the ingenuity of interpreters who reappropriate and reinterpret it in and for new situations. Brown is not simply arguing that what authors the Christian tradition authors our creativity. What he argues for is well expressed in his analogy of the relation between a conductor (the interpreter) and the score (the canon): "A conductor cannot give to a score an interpretation it does not already possess as possible, but a score can give to a conductor a musical possibility that for him or her is genuinely new."[60]

Judith Plaskow, a Jewish feminist, struggles with the same issue. The problem for feminists is that although they have contributed to the undermining of biblical authoritarianism "by pointing to the patriarchal origins and development of so-called normative texts, they have also tried to develop alternatives to patriarchal religion which are themselves in need of some authoritative grounding." Some feminists, in spite of their awareness of the patriarchal character of texts and traditions, still try to get back to the "origins" and find a nonpatriarchal beginning point that can function as a norm for today. Such an effort runs afoul of the observation that the purity of the earliest period is a myth and of the insight that the very notion of such authority is borrowed from Roman patriarchy. Nonetheless, a number of Christian feminists "have sought to find a 'real' (that is, nonsexist) Paul or a 'feminist' Jesus who can function as models for Christians today." Other feminists, Jewish and Christian, appeal to the prophetic yearning for justice, to the minority voices in scripture, or to the equality of women and men in Genesis 1. Such efforts to warrant contemporary convictions by appeal to biblical underpinnings *"disguise or deny the authority of the reader."* Plaskow does not wish to invest authority in the single reader, but in a "community of interpreters that seeks to understand texts and/or experience in ways that give meaning and structure to human life." "We are," she holds, "to be our own authorities—not against God, not without God, but also not in such a way that we dodge our responsibilities to create the structures we need to live our lives."[61]

Christian post-*Shoah* theologians appreciate the problem with which Plaskow struggles, but are reluctant to agree that "we are our own authorities." We have seen in Christianity what can happen when those who arrogate authority unto themselves go badly astray. The fault of the "German Christians," who supported the Nazi effort to create a new "folk" Christianity for Germany, was that they allowed themselves to be their own authorities. They effectively and tacitly rejected any and all critical principles in the light of which their new proposals could have been, at least in principle, criticized.[62] Post-*Shoah* theology must negotiate an alternative that avoids granting authoritarian status to texts and traditions deeply flawed by anti-Judaism and allows contemporary Christians to usurp authority unto themselves. Hence it is necessary to nuance Plaskow's point and maintain that we must take *responsibility* for formulating a theological understanding of authority, but that this responsibility requires of us the formulation of an understanding of authority by which we can be called into question.

Already we have stipulated one set of rules for doing Christian theology after Auschwitz: that we will beware any theological statement made after the *Shoah* that is unchanged from how it was made before, that we will do theology in conversation with Jews, that we will say nothing that we could not say in the presence of the burning children, and that a post-*Shoah* theology will stress discipleship. What has not been done is to set these rules in a perspective which illustrates that they are appropriate to biblical faith, and which permits and requires the kind of rethinking that our situation makes urgent.

We begin with a simple distinction used by many theologians, between the work of the church and the work of the theologian done in the church and on its behalf. The task of the church is to *make* the Christian witness to the gospel of Jesus Christ; the task of the theologian is to *criticize* the way in which the church makes its witness. Karl Barth makes such a distinction when he differentiates between the church's *language* and the way the church *tests* its language.[63] This distinction is not a separation; we cannot make the witness of faith without thinking about what we are doing, and we cannot think about it without also making it, even if indirectly.[64] Rather, it is a matter of emphasis, with the stress of the church being more on making the Christian witness than on criticizing how it is made, that of the theologian more on criticizing how witness is made than on making it. In some moments, we are more intent on the one than on the other.

When we ask from where we derive the norm of appropriateness in the light of which we can test both the Christian witness and theological efforts to understand it, we find that canonical criticism is helpful.[65] It stresses that at whatever historical juncture we encounter the biblical community of faith, we find it *reinterpreting* its faith. We never find Israel or the later church wallowing in uninterpreted experience. "If we desire a record of uninterpreted experience, we must ask a stone to record its autobiography."[66] We also find the community encountering a new situation that it must interpret in the light of its tradition in order to understand it. The situation poses new questions, to which the community must find new answers by reinterpreting its tradition. The community's difficulty is that it must reinterpret its tradition in order to include and make sense of the new situation. The community is under no compunction to say things in exactly the same way in which they were previously said. Sometimes its reinterpretations will deny what had previously been affirmed: "As I live, says the Lord GOD, this proverb shall no more be used by you in Israel" (Ezek. 18:3). The view of scripture found in canonical criticism accords with Rowan D. Williams' claim that the world of scripture "is an *historical* world in which meanings are discovered and recovered in action and encounter. To challenge the church to immerse itself in its 'text' is to encourage it to engage with a history of such actions and encounters." The church's commitment to interpret the world in terms of its foundational narratives "affects the narratives as well as the world."[67]

When we ask by what standards Israel reinterpreted its faith, we are led to its hermeneutical principles, those axioms that guided its reinterpretation. They provide us a way of formulating a norm of appropriateness for use in our task of interpreting the Christian faith. They are (1) The Bible is a monotheizing (not merely a monotheistic) literature that, in every new context, finds itself struggling "within and against polytheistic contexts to affirm God's oneness."[68] It reflects a broad theocentric hermeneutic expressed in two further axioms: (2) the prophetic and (3) the constitutive. The prophetic axiom stipulates that God is the God of *all*. The constitutive stresses that God is the particular redeemer of Israel or the church. It says: God loves *you*. The prophetic axiom says: God loves *all*, therefore do justice to them and do not think too highly of yourselves. The constitutive axiom bespeaks *promise;* the prophetic gives voice to *challenge*, demand.[69] Each expresses the gracious love of God, love freely extended to *all* God's beloved, on the one hand, and *particularly* to us, on the other. In the history of the biblical community, in moments of desperation, the community was reminded of God's love for it; in more prosperous moments, when the community failed to reflect justice in its own life and to be a light to the nations, it was reminded that God is the God of *all*, for whom God demands justice.

We can organize these three hermeneutical emphases into one statement of a norm of appropriateness for interpreting the Christian faith. The *theocentric* emphasis of the biblical axioms reminds us that, whatever the topic with which we are dealing, ultimately it is God with whom we have to deal. So, we must do all our witnessing and theologizing "to the greater glory of God" (*ad maiorem Dei gloriam*). We are well advised to remember that the God to whose greater glory we do our theologizing is the God of Israel, Maker and Redeemer of heaven and earth. The constitutive axiom re-presents to us God's special love for us, for each of us in the community and for this community, whereas the prophetic recalls to us God's love for all God's creatures as well as God's commandment that we do justice to them. The constitutive promise and the prophetic command are wrapped up with the theocentric emphasis in this way. The good news is that God is the God of a singular promise and a singular command: the promise is that God's love is freely, graciously, offered to each and all, and the command is the twofold requirement that we are to love God with our whole selves and to love and do justice to our neighbors as ourselves.

What makes this norm of appropriateness specifically Christian is that we find our sources of it and access to it in the testified-to Jesus and Paul. The earliest witness to Jesus is inclusive, picturing him as going to *all* the sheep of the house of Israel, particularly to its *lost* sheep. He confronts them with the God of Israel, presenting a message of promise and command, call and claim, requiring response, decision, and total commitment.[70] Paul is a theocentric thinker convinced of God's faithfulness, struggling in Romans 9–11 with the question of the relation between Christians and (non-Christian) Jews. Discussions of Jesus and Paul will be found in subsequent chapters. Here it must suffice to say that each can only be understood in the context of Israel's understanding of its Way with God, an understanding articulated in Israel's hermeneutical axioms.

This statement of the gospel I take as the standard of appropriateness in the light of which all interpretations of the Christian faith can be critically scrutinized. The argument underlying this claim is straightforward: (1) the process of interpretation and reinterpretation from context to context did not cease in the Apostolic Age but continues and will continue throughout the history of the church; and (2) it is appropriate to interpret the tradition (including the canon) in the way in which it interpreted itself. We should always ask whether the way we want to make the Christian witness truly testifies to the gospel of Jesus Christ. The first question is whether this or that piece of Christian witness or interpretation is *appropriate*, whether it is authentically Christian. We have to ask, for example, whether this or that construal of the historical Jesus or of the meaning of a biblical text is appropriate to the gospel.

Also, this way of formulating the norm of appropriateness (the gracious promise of God's love freely offered to each and all and therefore the command of God that in turn we love God with all our selves and do justice to, that is, love, the neighbor as ourselves) is not a circle with one center, but an ellipse with two foci: God's radically free, empowering grace and God's command of justice. When Christians forget the first, they invariably fall into works-righteousness and a reward, payoff (win/lose) mentality. Works-righteousness has nothing to do with the issue of whether faith requires good works. It does, beyond question. Rather, works-righteousness takes the free gift of God's unconditional love and turns it into a condition apart from which God is not free to be gracious. Anti-Judaism is a works-righteousness. When Christians forget the second, they fall into cheap grace, grace that asks nothing, commands nothing—grace that, in the final analysis, is not even interesting. We should note also that the emphasis on God's radically free grace affirms the truth of the Reformation principles *sola gratia, sola fide* (by grace alone, by faith alone). That even the Reformers themselves sometimes forgot these principles and at other times failed to see their radical implication, that *nothing* and *no one* can be set up as a condition that must be met if God's love is to be available, is a tragedy that dogs Christian history. Our justification is *by* God's grace, apprehended *through* our response of faith. At the same time, the emphasis on God's command that justice be done reminds us that our lives are to be radically transformed by God's liberating grace and put at the service of "the least of these."

Canonical criticism also alerts us to the fact that the community of faith was frequently in the position of having to make sense of its tradition in relation to a new historical situation and to make sense of this new situation in relation to its tradition. The biblical tradition is a sense-making tradition; a concern for intelligibility is at the heart of biblical faith. The biblical literature was produced over a period of 1,500–1,800 years and across five different culture eras.[71] In such a long span of time, historical circumstances underwent major changes, and the fortunes of the people altered dramatically. Consequently, the people of God "needed to know ever anew *who they were and what they should do*."[72] Struggling in and against polytheistic contexts, they also needed to know who God is. The question of who we are is an *existential* question, and human beings are the beings who have to ask and answer this question. The answer that comes back from the hermeneutical axioms of the biblical community is a *theological-existential-moral* one: we are a people who can understand themselves in any ultimate sense in terms of and only in terms of the singular promise and the singular command of the God of Israel; that is, we are a people who are freely and unmeritedly loved by God and who, in turn, are to love God and the neighbor. What that means, particularly as it bears on the question of what we are to do, how we are to flesh out the general command to love the neighbor, will change from situation to situation, as the neighbor's need changes; and our response to it must also change if it is to be adequate to the neighbor's situation. Intelligibility is existential (it helps us know *who* we are in this context), practical/moral (it helps us figure out *what* we are to do in this context), and theological (it tells us who *God* is and what God gives to and demands of us). The quest for intelligibility in every period of church history, and particularly in a post-*Shoah* time, is entirely appropriate. Who do we understand ourselves to be, post-Holocaust, as Christians and inheritors of a tradition deeply flawed by anti-Judaism? What are we to do in relationship to our neighbors, particularly our Jewish neighbors, in light both of our tragic history together and of the new, pluralistic and post-Holocaust situation in which we find ourselves? Whom do we Christians worship as God? This book cannot respond to these questions in anything like the scope and profundity required, but it proposes that we are called by God to understand ourselves differently from ways in which we have previously understood ourselves and that we are to act differently toward our Jewish neighbors. One of the first things we can do in this regard is change how we talk about the Christian faith and about ourselves; in the long run, that may prove to be the most important thing we can do.

We may trust the tradition, because the tradition was and remains a self-critical, self-correcting, reinterpreting tradition. We may be suspicious of the tradition, because the tradition exercised suspicion on itself. In a traditional Christian prayer for the church, God is asked to purify the church where it is corrupt, to direct it where it is in error, to reform it where in anything it is amiss. That the church may never cease being self-critical and self-reforming is entirely congruent with its deepest self-understanding.

Alfred North Whitehead once remarked of what he called "rational religion" (by which he really meant biblical faith) that "it appeals to the direct intuition of special occasions, and to the eludicatory power of its concepts for all occasions." Such a religion, he said, is one "whose beliefs and rituals have been reorganized with the aim of making it the central element in a coherent ordering of life—an ordering which shall be coherent both in respect to the elucidation of thought, and in respect to the direction of conduct towards a unified purpose commanding ethical approval."[73] He implies that such a religion continually reinterprets itself in light of new events so as to make sense in a new context and indicate how we ought to live in that context. H. Richard Niebuhr quoted and paraphrased Whitehead's definition of "rational religion" to provide his influential understanding of revelation:

> The special occasion to which we appeal in the Christian church is called Jesus Christ, in whom we see the righteousness of God, his power and wisdom. But from that special occasion we also derive the concepts which make possible the elucidation of all the events in our history. Revelation means this intelligible event which makes all other events intelligible. . . . Revelation means the point at which we can begin to think and act as members of an intelligible and intelligent world of persons.[74]

The revelatory event upon which all else turns in the Christian faith is that of Jesus Christ. It is an orienting event, from which we take our bearings as we "begin to think and act as members of an intelligible and intelligent world of persons." It makes possible and requires that we interpret intelligibly the faith we receive and the situation we confront in relation to each other, and that we converse about what it means to act morally in this situation. To do theology conversationally and post-Holocaust, in light of this understanding of our orienting event and norm of appropriateness, is not to take our bearings from "the world." We are trying to work out how things look from within a Christian tradition that interprets and reinterprets itself in relation to changing circumstances. We recognize that the more drastic the change in our context, the more radical the reinterpretation that is required. What a norm of appropriateness derived from canonical criticism does for us is to require us to look critically at our own tradition and engage in conversation with a post-*Shoah* situation. It allows for new interpretations of the Christian faith at the same time that it provides a standard against which to test those interpretations.

The Ecclesial Character of Post-*Shoah* Theology

Theologians sometimes make the mistake of being idiosyncratic, as if each one could single-handedly reconstruct how the Christian faith ought to be understood. When theology is done properly, it is done in and on behalf of the church, even if by a theologian whose major mode of relating to the church is that of having a lover's quarrel with it. Whether or not all Christian theology is "church theology," theology ought to be "churchly." Friedrich Schleiermacher argued that it was as much a requirement of theology to be churchly (*kirchlich*) as it was to be disciplined (*wissenschaftlich*).[75] For him this meant that theology should take its cues from the most recent church confessions, and he began his treatment of every doctrine by consulting the church's most recent confessions on the point. Schleiermacher may have been the first to develop a "church dogmatics." Also for Schleiermacher, for theology to be churchly meant that it would be ecumenical. He wrote his *Christian Faith* for an emerging union of the Reformed and Lutheran churches in Germany, and he consulted all Evangelical (Protestant) confessions in framing his theology.

Whereas Schleiermacher argued that all dogmatic propositions had to "approve themselves . . . by appeal to Evangelical confessional documents,"[76] we will appeal to both Roman Catholic and Protestant documents issued since the *Shoah* and particularly since the Second Vatican Council. To do so is to take steps in the direction of a post-Holocaust *church* theology, which seeks to be churchly in Schleiermacher's sense of the word, but in our situation. We will take our cues for the development of every doctrine from the post-Holocaust teaching documents of the churches, a wide-ranging body of confessional literature from Roman Catholic and Protestant churches (to my knowledge, no Eastern Orthodox church has issued a post-*Shoah* teaching document). Thereby we will also seek to be ecumenical, availing ourselves of the considered deliberations of numerous churches. This does not mean that this theology will be without any edge to it. It means that its purpose is not to speak down to the churches with regard to what they should be saying, but to confront them with their own teachings and the implications of those teachings. The next chapter provides a discussion of the post-Holocaust teaching documents of the churches.

2

The Church and the Jewish People: Revolutionary Confessions

———·—·—·—·—·—·—

> There is little doubt that the Spirit of God is once again
> moving over the waters. From every direction there are
> reports of a new awareness, a new consciousness, a new
> understanding between Jews and Christians.
>
> —*The Texas Conference of Churches, 1982*

The recent teaching documents of the churches on how Christians are to understand Jews and Judaism and their relationship to Jews and Judaism are "revolutionary confessions." What justifies using the word *revolution* for what the churches are saying? The answer lies in the contrast between what the churches now say and what they said in the past. Historically, anti-Jewish teaching was left to bishops, pastors, and theologians; the church in its confessions (as at Nicaea) did not explicitly articulate anti-Judaism. Rather, the church councils enacted into canon law the image of Jews and Judaism that had been given expression in the anti-Jewish writings of theologians.[1] Beginning at Elvira in Spain, about 305 C.E., a local council of the church legislated against Jews. There the bishops forbade marriage between Jews and Christians, prohibited Christians from eating with Jews, banned adultery between Christian men and Jewish women, and interdicted Christian farmers from having their fields and crops blessed by rabbis.[2]

Traditional Church Statements

Subsequent councils of the church enacted many laws involving Jews and Christians. The early controversy over the date of Easter, whether Easter was to be dated in relation to Passover in the Jewish calendar, was settled at Nicaea by severing Easter from the Jewish liturgical year and

27

dating it in relation to the spring equinox. This argument was called the "quartodeciman controversy," because it focused on the fourteenth of the Hebrew month Nisan. Nicaea's decision helped remove Easter from a Jewish and biblical context and turn it into a rite of spring, thus de-Judaizing Easter. The fourth-century council of Laodicea ordered Christians to work on the Sabbath. Succeeding councils enjoined Christians from eating Passover with Jews, entering synagogues, sharing feasts with Jews, patronizing Jewish doctors or living in Jewish homes, or having Jewish friends. Jews were proscribed from appearing in public during Holy Week, from chatting with nuns, from being judges or tax collectors, from working on Sunday, from holding public office, from owning slaves, and from being plaintiffs or witnesses against Christians in court. Christians were given the right to kidnap Jewish children and raise them as Christians, whereas Jews were required to be baptized and pay tithes to support the church. Ghettos were legislated by the church, new synagogues could not be built, and Jews were prohibited from earning academic degrees. The Fourth Lateran Council in 1215 required all Jews "in every Christian province [to be] marked off in the eyes of the public from other peoples through the character of their dress."

These matters are not medieval history. In 1924, the Provincial Council of the Dutch Roman Catholic Church issued this warning:

> Relations with Jews must be avoided because this people is very estranged from the Cross of Christ, a scandalous thing for them. Parish priests must take care that Christians do not work for Jews who would use them as servants or subordinates. If there is no danger of faith or morals, paid daily work may be undertaken for Jews, either in agriculture or in factories. A grave warning is given, however: such services must not lead to others which would endanger the soul, arising above all for a desire for lucre. Moreover, the faithful must take care—according to the warning of Benedict XIV (Enc. *A quo primum*, 1751)—never to need the help or support of Jews.[3]

Nor does study of liberal Protestants in twentieth-century America find them free of anti-Jewish bias.[4] The contrast between the Fourth Lateran Council of 1215 and *Nostra Aetate* of the Second Vatican Council in 1965 truly justifies calling the latter a "revolution."

However, a considerable transition took place between the earliest post-*Shoah* church statements and those that churches began issuing in the 1960s. The First Assembly of the World Council of Churches (WCC) in 1948, in its statement on anti-Semitism, repeated the Great Commission and argued that "the fulfillment of this commission requires that we include the Jewish people in our evangelistic task." It went on to say:

"We have, therefore, in humble conviction to proclaim to the Jews, 'the Messiah for whom you wait has come.'" The Second Assembly in 1954 made no statement on the relation of the church to the people Israel, but received one which claimed that "to expect Jesus Christ means to hope for the conversion of the Jewish people, and to love Him means to love the people of God's promise." The Assembly did not pass this statement. The 1967 report of the Commission on Faith and Order of the World Council of Churches argued that mission and dialogue are not alternatives to each other, proposing instead that both be pursued. Because this report qualified mission and dialogue by each other, it left things logically in a state of confusion while it also took steps in the direction of moving away from a simple conversionary mission to Jews. The report did contend that after the *Shoah* Christian words had become suspect and that the best and only way in which Christians could testify of their faith to Jews would be by service. The 1982 WCC Guidelines take no clear stand on mission to the Jewish people but instead give voice to various positions, including both those which wholeheartedly affirm a conversionary mission and those which find, to the contrary, that such a mission "is not part of an authentic Christian witness, since the Jewish people finds its fulfillment in faithfulness to God's covenant of old."[5]

Consideration of this possibility—that the covenant between the God of Israel and the Israel of God remains valid and that Jews find fulfillment in faithfulness to that covenant—began to open up a new stage in the churches' understanding of their relationship to Jews and Judaism. Increasingly, the claim is made that the expression "mission to the Jews" places "Jews on a par with heathens and undervalues the specific position of the Jewish people among the nations as well as the fact that Judaism has known the God of the Bible and believed in him long before the birth of the church." Further, the church has a responsibility to ensure "for the Jews, wherever they may be found, conditions for keeping their spiritual distinctiveness," which contradicts any notion of a conversionary mission to the Israel of God.[6]

From here it is but one step to recognize that Jews as Jews witness to the grace of God, as the 1980 Synod of the Evangelical Church of the Rhineland declared when claiming that "in their respective calling[s] Jews and Christians are witnesses of God before the world and before each other. Therefore we are convinced that the church may not express its witness towards the Jewish people as it does its mission to the peoples of the world." The Texas Conference of Churches in 1982 maintained that both Jews and Christians are "witnesses of God in the presence of the world and before each other," and claimed that they "share a common mission to hallow God's name in the world, to stand for human dignity, to pursue peace and justice, and to be signs of hope in God's future."

The 1984 Synod of the Evangelical Church of West Berlin acknowledged Israel's own commission from God to be a light to the nations and declared that Christian witness to Israel means chiefly "to live a Christian life that makes discernible God's Yes to the permanent election of Israel; thus the community of Jesus Christ can prove to be the one that is reconciled with the God who has elected Israel."[7] The radical question posed by this church is not whether Jews are "saved," but whether the church can be reconciled with the God of Israel if it is not reconciled with the Israel of God. An affirmative answer to that question hinges on the church's so living that it makes visible God's Yes to Israel.

This dramatic change in church teaching can best be accounted for by suggesting that it exemplifies the theological method described in the previous chapter, the method that engages in a two-way conversation with the situation in which we find ourselves (here emphasizing that ours is a post-*Shoah* situation) and the tradition (here examined anew for the alternatives to anti-Judaism that can be retrieved from it).

As each topic is discussed in the subsequent chapters in this book, we will first articulate how anti-Judaism has historically shaped it. We do this in order to see anti-Judaism for what it is, as the teaching documents ask us to do. We look at anti-Judaism to *see* it, convinced that there is no magic way in which we can dismiss this or any ideology except by being quite clear about it. We look it squarely in the face because confession is good for the soul, and the soul of theology needs therapy. We will not understand or appreciate any post-*Shoah* way of doing theology unless we see its contrast with the teaching of contempt, nor will we be consumed by the constructive passion of doing theology authentically and appropriately unless we are also bitten by a negative passion to rid ourselves of inauthentic and inappropriate ways of doing it.

New Epistles to the Church[8]

A revolution has taken place in the church's statements about its self-understanding in relationship to Jews and Judaism. Two years after the *Shoah*, a group of Christians meeting at Seelisberg, under the auspices of the International Council of Christians and Jews, issued a statement called "The Ten Points of Seelisberg." Its work marked the first time after the *Shoah* that Christians made an announcement to fellow Christians on Judaism and the Jewish people. It asked Christians to remember that one God speaks to us through both testaments, that Jesus, his disciples, apostles, and the first martyrs were Jews; and that the fundamental commandment of Christianity—love of God and the neighbor—was proclaimed in the scriptures and confirmed by Jesus. It implored Christians not to extol Christianity by demeaning Judaism, to avoid using "Jews" in the exclusive sense of enemies of Jesus, to abstain from presenting the events of Holy Week so as to blame all Jews and Jews alone for his death, to remember Jesus' plea from the cross that his executors be forgiven, and to cease speaking of Jews as if the first members of the church had not been Jews.[9]

Churches were slow to catch up with the spirit of Seelisberg, stumbling haltingly toward a new day in their teachings about Judaism and the Jewish people. Yet, since the Second Vatican Council's 1965 *Nostra Aetate* ("In Our Times"), a veritable revolution in the churches' teaching about Jews and Judaism has occurred.[10] It began small and grew slowly, like a grain of mustard seed, but what was more latent than overt at Rome and Seelisberg has latterly risen to prominence. There is great variety of theological outlook in post-Holocaust church statements, and they would repay study of their diversity and individuality. What concerns us here, however, is the trajectory that can be clearly traced through them from tentative theological first-steps to more recent and forthcoming proposals. Churches recognized the validity of the covenant between God and Israel and later realized that in so doing they had taken a radical stance that called for changing their views on other topics (such as mission). The purpose of this chapter is to describe this trajectory and clarify the direction in which churches are moving in confessing their faith in relation to Judaism and the Jewish people.

The significance of these new statements may be appreciated with the help of J. L. Austin's notion of a "performative utterance."[11] Some statements are best understood as describing a state of affairs ("your glasses are on the desk") or the relations of ideas to each other ("two and two make four"). Such statements can be true or false (one's glasses may be on the kitchen table, and mistakes are possible in arithmetic). Austin wanted to acknowledge the meaningfulness of statements that could not be regarded as simply descriptive or logical. One category of such statements he called performative utterances, in which making a statement is identical with performing an act (as when a couple at a wedding says "I do"). These new statements of the church should be regarded as performative utterances. They are not just so many nice words that may or may not be followed up by actions (although we have to pay attention to the question of changed behavior). They are actions. Changing how we talk about Jews and Judaism is the first step in changing how we act toward Jews. Talk is an important form of behavior.

What kind of act is the church performing in making such statements? Here we may appeal to Whitehead, who argued that "the moralistic preference for true propositions . . . obscured the role of propositions in the actual world." False propositions have fared badly at

the hands of logicians; they are "thrown into the dust-heap, neglected."
Yet if we look carefully at the propositions being set before Christians
by councils (synods, assemblies, commissions) of churches, we would
have to say that most of them are false in the sense that they do not describe the way most Christians understand themselves. Are these new
confessions of the church, then, to be disregarded? No: "In the real
world it is more important that a proposition be interesting than that it
be true." An interesting proposition describes its subject with predicates
not heretofore used of it, inviting us to perceive it in a new way and to
act differently toward it. Whereas we have habitually thought of "the
Jews" only negatively, now we are invited to think and feel differently
about them: "A novelty has emerged into creation."[12] Whereas we have
long-held attitudes toward Jews, now we are challenged to consider
whether these convictions are true, to expose them to criticism and evidence, one sign that we are entertaining a new proposition. Such new
propositions result from our being confronted by the living God of biblical faith who ever calls her children forward into God's future for
them, as she called Abraham to leave Haran and "go . . . to the land
that I will show you" (Gen. 12:1). God ever calls us forward out of the
narrowness, exclusivism, and sinfulness of the past and to reconciliation
with the God of Israel, with the Israel of God, and with all God's creatures, a reconciliation that puts an end to the "dividing wall, the hostility" between Jews and Gentiles (Eph. 2:11–22).[13]

Faith is openness to the future to which God is calling us and to God
the Holy One who calls us forward. God calls us beyond all past attainments to greater life, love, and freedom. God as the One who calls us forward into deeper and wider bonds of relationship is the Holy Spirit.
Hence, as the Texas Conference of Churches declared, these new confessions of faith are the result of these churches' wrestling with the Holy
Spirit. That is the kind of act they are. They invite other Christians to
struggle with the issues involved in relations between Jews and Christians.
They are new epistles to the churches, pastoral and teaching documents.
As teaching documents, they can serve as guides to the reinterpretation of
the tradition, articulating for a post-Holocaust church a new "rule of
faith" (regula fidei) clarifying how the core message of the Christian witness is to be understood at a time when past understandings are seen as
radically defective. This theology will take these documents as such guides.

The post-Holocaust statements from the churches vary widely as to
their authority (sometimes, "clout"). This authority, or "clout," is great
in the case of Nostra Aetate in the Roman Catholic Church, less so in a
statement passed by a general assembly or synod of most Protestant
churches, and in some ways even less in the case of study documents
"received" by ecumenical assemblies. Yet all of them are "teaching docu-

ments" of the churches and share the authority appropriate to such documents, which is the capacity to engender conversation and make a claim on our attention by seriously addressing momentous issues. Let us give them such attention.

Leaving Behind Stereotypes

Christians should drop the habit of thinking in dichotomies when considering Judaism and Christianity. Such dyads as fear/love, works/faith, law/love, deeds/feelings, old/new, flesh/spirit are the workings-out of an ideology of Christian superiority to Judaism. Thinking of ourselves on the "good" side of each dyad was a way to support the works-righteous claim that we good, new, spiritual, loving, faithful, universal, Gentile Christians are in all respects everything new and good that the old, fearful, works-righteous, legalistic, deed-oriented, ethnocentric, fleshly Jews can never be. It was part of the claim that Jews are perverse simply for being Jews; they are works-righteous if they keep the law, hypocritical if they do not, and so in a no-win position. Traditionally, Christians convinced themselves that Jews believe in justification by the works of the law, thus inviting the Jewish response that Christianity stands for a loss of ethics. Typifying Jews as one side of a dichotomy invites them to typify us as the other. In fact, however, cautions against "justification by works" appear frequently in Jewish literature. That God's call places a claim upon a person's whole life, a theological insight accepted by both Judaism and Christianity, does not constitute works-righteousness; those who understand themselves as utterly dependent on God's grace also understand themselves as totally claimed by God. Hence, the recent confessions of the church invite us to a more adequate understanding of Jewish faith.

> The devout Jew delights in the Torah. At the end of the Feast of Tabernacles he celebrates a special festival "rejoicing of the law." "In the way of your decree lies my joy, a joy beyond all wealth" (Ps. 119:14); "I find my delight in your statutes. I do not forget your word" (119:16); "Your decrees are my delight, your statutes are my counsellors" (119:24); "Meditating all day on your law, how I have come to love it" (Ps. 119:97). The Jew is aware of the Torah as a pleasure, not as a burden.[14]

As Christians know and love God through Christ, so Jews know and love God through Torah, the way of life revealed by God. The more Christians understand this about Judaism, the more we understand that God's grace exercises a total claim on our lives.

Confessing the "teaching of contempt"

"We acknowledge in repentance the church's long and deep complicity in the proliferation of anti-Jewish attitudes and actions through its 'teaching of contempt' for the Jews. Such teaching we now repudiate, together with the acts and attitudes which it generates."[15] In this 1987 statement typical of the changing sentiment in the churches, the General Assembly of the Presbyterian Church (U.S.A.) acknowledges the relationship to each other of traditional anti-Judaism (its teaching and practice of contempt for Jews and Judaism), anti-Semitism, and the *Shoah*. The denunciation of anti-Semitism rings throughout the churches' recent confessions, as does the note of the churches' complicity in the *Shoah*, and the awareness that the churches' teaching of contempt was a necessary if not sufficient condition of the Nazi effort to eliminate every last Jew from planet earth.

The Presbyterian statement continues by noting that this anti-Jewish teaching, and its related sentiments and actions, "began in New Testament times," leaving a mark of hostility on "portions of the New Testament." Until today, the teaching, preaching, and worship of the church "often lend themselves, at times unwittingly, to a perpetuation of the 'teaching of contempt.'" Such teaching "was a major ingredient that made possible the monstrous policy of annihilation of Jews by Nazi Germany," in response to which the churches "did little to challenge the policies of their governments." In 1950, the Evangelical Church in Germany expressed its "indignation 'at the outrage which has been perpetrated against the Jews by people of our nation' caused 'by omission and silence before the God of mercy.'" The 1980 Synod of the Evangelical Church of the Rhineland recognized "Christian co-responsibility and guilt for the Holocaust," confessing it with dismay. Following the United Nations' vote that equated Zionism with racism, the 1977 Norwegian Bishops' Conference urged the people of Norway "to show a clear and fearless attitude over against any form of anti-Semitism, including the aggressive anti-Zionism." The bishops argued that to characterize the attitude of the Jewish people toward the Promised Land as racism "reveals both a lack of historical and religious understanding, and intolerance."[16]

The American Lutheran Church in 1974 had admitted that Christians and Lutherans in particular "are the heirs of a long history of prejudicial discrimination against Jews," that Christians regarded Jews "as enemies who were to be eliminated by defamation, extermination, prohibition of their writings, destruction of their synagogues, and exclusion into ghettos and despised occupations." It charged Christians to "become aware of that history in which they have deeply alienated the Jews." This point supports that made by the United Methodist Church in 1972: "The persecution by Christians of Jews throughout centuries calls for clear repentance and resolve to repudiate past injustice and to seek its elimination in the present."[17]

In their statement of 1982, the World Council of Churches put Christians on notice that they cannot enter naively into conversation with Jews without first becoming aware that Christian persecution of Jews has "a long persistent history." The Council observed that historically the church had "assigned to the Jews definite roles in its understanding of God's acts of salvation," roles that were entirely negative. Hence, Christians need to learn how Jews understand their faith in their own terms. All this is in marked contrast to the first two assemblies of the World Council (1948 and 1954), which denounced anti-Semitism as a sign of "man's disorder," but not of the church's disorder.[18] Yet it cannot pass unnoticed that no assembly of the WCC has yet made a *theological* statement on relations between Christians and Jews.

Scores of Roman Catholic documents reject anti-Semitism and theological anti-Judaism and call for Christians to acquire a better knowledge and understanding of Judaism and Jewish self-definition. The United States National Conference of Catholic Bishops in 1967 called for "a frank and honest treatment of the history of Christian anti-Semitism in our history books, courses, and curricula" as well as for an explicit rejection of historically inaccurate images of Jews, such as the view of the Pharisees as hypocritical, decadent, and formalistic.[19]

What is refreshing about the confessions of anti-Judaism or the teaching of contempt in these church documents is the honesty with which they approach the topic. They do not flinch from subjecting the Christian tradition and the New Testament to serious scrutiny and call us to be direct in making very clear what anti-Judaism has been and what has been done because of it. The teaching documents challenge us to face up to the hostility and polemic against Jews found in the New Testament, to admit our lack of understanding of the people Israel, and to recognize that we cannot enter naively into conversation with Jews. They urge us not to objectify anti-Judaism by placing responsibility for it anywhere than upon the church itself: it shows us the *church's* disorder. We are urged with God's help to transform our relationship with the Jewish people from one of name-calling to a dialogue of reciprocal love and understanding, to move from animosity or indifference toward Israel to a relationship of "full solidarity."[20]

Jewish responsibility for the death of Jesus

Two points are particularly pertinent to discussion of this issue. They are distinct yet related to each other. The first has to do with historical and linguistic accuracy. It is inaccurate historically and an improper form of language to blame the crucifixion of Jesus on "the Jews." Most Jews at the time of Jesus, roughly five-sixths of all Jews, lived in the Diaspora. Spread across the length and breadth of the Roman Empire, they never heard of Jesus nor participated in his execution. Nor can we assume that Jesus was widely known within the land of promise. *Some* Jews and *some* Romans (officials and soldiers carrying out orders) colluded in the death of Jesus. What seems to be the most likely story about Jesus' crucifixion will be worked out in Chapter 3 on Jesus.

The second point is that Christians in church today tend to believe what they hear about Jews of long ago. Moreover, they are disposed to project onto Jews of today attitudes that they believe characterize Jews of two thousand years ago. Thus, for Christian preachers and teachers to speak of "the Jews'" having killed Christ is a use of language that reflects and reinforces bias against Jews today. We have a moral obligation to our contemporary neighbors to criticize and revise our historical language.

Some Christians will be surprised to learn that the Council of Trent (1545–63) taught that Christian sinners are more to blame for the death of Christ than the few Jews who were involved in it; the latter certainly "knew not what they did," whereas we know it only too well. Trent stole the march on Vatican II, which declared that "what happened in His passion cannot be charged against all Jews, without distinction, then alive, nor against the Jews of today." Trent's way of rejecting and reinterpreting the deicide charge is present in many Roman Catholic documents. Instead of blaming Jesus' crucifixion on Jews, claimed the 1980 Catholic German Bishops' Conference, "we should think of our own sins." By denying Christ through our works, we daily "lay violent hands on him." The historical burden that holding of Jews responsible for killing Jesus has laid on Jews can only be removed by thorough historical inquiry into the circumstances surrounding the crucifixion and through dialogue with Jews. Rejecting the accusation of collective guilt "pertains as much to the purity of the Catholic faith as it does to the defense of Judaism." The House of Bishops of the Episcopal Church, in 1964, declared that the charge of deicide against Jews "is a tragic misunderstanding of the inner significance of the crucifixion." The involvement of some Jews and some Romans in the crucifixion cannot be the basis of imputing corporate guilt to subsequent generations of Jews (or Romans, should anyone even imagine this option). "Simple justice alone proclaims the charge of a corporate or inherited curse on the Jewish people to be false."[21]

Some church statements contend, as does the statement of the Christian-Jewish Coordinating Committee of Vienna in 1968, that the Roman Imperial System was implicated in the death of Jesus: "We must refer to the concrete legal situation in the Roman province of Judea, according to which the Jews were not empowered to impose the death penalty (Jn 18:31). We do not pray in the Creed, 'suffered under the high priest Caiaphas,' but 'suffered under Pontius Pilate.'"[22] Hence, these pronouncements conclude that Jesus' eschatological message of a new order caused him and his followers to be considered dangerous, with the result that interaction between the Jewish autonomous administration and the Roman occupying power, which are difficult to disentangle, "led to the execution of Jesus by the Romans."[23]

God's thoroughly gracious covenant with Israel

How the churches understand God's election of Israel to be God's people, the covenant between God and Israel today, shapes their understanding of the relationship of the church to the people Israel and raises trenchant questions as to whether there should be a Christian mission to the Jewish people and, if so, what its purpose should be. *Nostra Aetate* started things in motion in 1965 with its profession that all who believe in Christ are children of Abraham according to faith and included in God's call to Abraham to be a light to the nations,[24] that the church of the Gentiles has been grafted onto God's well-cultivated olive tree. To call the church the "new people of God" cannot mean that Jews are no longer the people of God. Here is a sampling of statements from churches rejecting the supersessionist view of Judaism as religiously out of business:

"The singular grace of Jesus Christ does not abrogate the covenantal relationship of God with Israel (Rom. 11:1-2). In Christ the Church shares in Israel's election without superseding it."[25]

"Jesus came not to destroy the Covenant of God with the Jews, but only to affirm it in a manner that would bring the blessing of God's people to non-Jews, also."[26]

"The church's claim to be the sole, new Israel of God can in no way be based on the Bible."[27]

"We reject the position that the covenant between the Jews and God was dissolved with the coming of Christ."[28]

"Judaism cannot be considered a purely social and historical entity or a leftover from a past which no longer exists. . . . St. Paul bears witness that the Jews have a zeal for God (Rom. 10:2); that God has not rejected His people (Rom. 11:1ff)."[29]

"We affirm that the church, elected in Jesus Christ, has been engrafted into the people of God established by the covenant with Abraham, Isaac and Jacob. Therefore, Christians have not replaced Jews."[30]

"Although the church, already in the New Testament, applied to herself several promises made to the Jewish people she does not supersede the covenant people, Israel."[31]

Chapters 9–11 of Paul's Letter to the Romans, dealing with relations between the church and the Jewish people, play a critical role in the teaching documents. Paul's understanding of the faithfulness of God is cited again and again to support the claim that the people Israel has not been rejected by God and that the covenant between God and Israel is still valid, that Jewish faith is a vital, living faith with its own integrity and witness. The new paradigm for interpreting Paul has had a considerable impact on the churches.

As a result, peoplehood is restored to Jews. In the traditional anti-Jewish ideology, Jews were regarded as having been a people until they rejected Christ. In the Enlightenment, Jews could find a place as individuals but not as a people. Since the *Shoah*, churches have seen the moral bankruptcy of denying to Jews the right to be a people. Now churches recognize both as a sociological and a theological reality that the Jewish people exist and have the right to exist. This is a significant reversal of the claim that Jews, as Jews, have no right to exist but should, instead, cease to be Jews by becoming Christians.

With this recognition comes the awareness that Judaism is a living faith with whose representatives we should engage in dialogue. Whereas "dialogue" may at one time have been a smoke screen for "conversion," once churches have affirmed the continuing covenant of the Jewish people, dialogue becomes an encounter with the living faith of the other. The "guidelines" that churches have prepared to assist dialogue repeatedly affirm that "a Jewish-Christian dialogue cannot succeed if the Christian sees in the Judaism of today merely a memorial of his own past—of the time of Jesus and of the Apostles."[32] The World Council of Churches in 1977 counseled Christians to be alert to the "vibrant and continuing development of Judaism in post-Biblical times," of its religious and philosophical literature, its biblical interpretation, its major contributions to contemporary thought.[33]

Anti-Judaism in the New Testament

A hallmark of developments in Christian awareness has been the recognition that portions of the New Testament are marked by anti-Jewish sentiment. The World Council of Churches' "Considerations" of 1982 point out that "some of the controversies reported in the New Testament between Jesus and the 'scribes and Pharisees' find parallels within Pharisaism itself and its heir, Rabbinic Judaism."[34] Such expressions as "the Jews" can lead "to theological anti-Semitism insofar as it refers in an uncritical way to the whole Jewish nation in Jesus' time, whereas in reality the expression 'the Jews' meant, as a rule, the adversaries of Jesus who came from the leading groups of contemporary Jews, particularly the priestly caste."[35] The teaching documents advise us to remember, when dealing with texts that reflect negatively on Jews and Judaism, that Jesus was a Jew, that he lived and taught among Jews, that his teaching reflected the Judaisms of the time, and that controversies must be seen as occurring "within a framework which he not only shared with fellow Jews, but which he and God affirmed."[36] They call to our attention passages that interpret relations between Jews and Christians differently, stressing the inclusion of Gentiles through Christ into the one household of God.[37] Christians are cautioned not to detach Jesus and Paul from their context in Jewish tradition and to avoid the dangerous interpretations to which some passages give rise. Further, we are urged to correct the excessively negative picture of the Pharisees painted by the Gospel writers. Passages dealing with the destiny of the Jewish people must be seen in the light of the prophetic tradition in which the promise of restoration was always joined to threats of rejection.[38] Historical-critical insights relativize Matthew 23 with its seven "woes" against the Pharisees and its charges against them of hypocrisy. It is now seen not as reflecting a situation in the life of Jesus but in the life of the later Matthean church as its messengers met rejection in the synagogue. Matthew, who makes the Pharisees answerable for "all the righteous blood shed on earth, from the blood of righteous Abel to the blood of Zachariah" (Matt. 23:35), presumably knew that Cain, Abel's murderer, was not a Jew.[39]

Not only do the church's teaching documents alert us to the apologetic strains in the Apostolic Writings; they also put us on notice as to a proper way to understand the relation between the two testaments. The term "new" has been used in biblical interpretation "against the Jewish people."[40] "New" has been understood as "brand new," in contrast to and as displacing "old." The "new people of God" were thought to supersede the "old" in God's favor, the "New" Testament to displace the "Old's" authority. "New" has meant that what is "old" has no reason to be, that Jews should no longer exist as Jews but should cease being Jews and become Christians. Some scholars detect the logic of genocide at work here.[41] Hence our documents take pains to emphasize the unbreakable connection between the "Old" and "New" Testaments. They interpret the term "new" in the light of the biblical words *chadash* and *kainos*. These terms connote "renew"; *chadash* is used throughout the Hebrew Bible for the "new moon" and for the "new covenant" promised in Jeremiah 31:31. "'New' means therefore no replacement of the 'old.' Hence we deny that the people Israel has been rejected by God or that it has been superseded by the church."[42] The Apostolic Writers regard the Hebrew Bible as scripture, and it is this of which they speak when they say that the things concerning Jesus Christ took place "in accordance with the scriptures" (1 Cor. 15:3). The two testaments "illumine and explain each other."[43] "In the Old Testament the God of Revelation speaks, the God of Abraham, Isaac and Jacob, who is also the God of Jesus."[44] The Hebrew Bible "is not simply a preparation for the New Testament but possesses religious importance of its own."[45]

Other documents offer a regulatory interpretation of the apostolic writings, claiming that nothing in them warrants denying that the Jewish people are elected by God or that their covenant became invalid. "Far from giving the impression that an *'Old Israel'* had been superseded by a *'New Israel,'* substituted as the new People of God, the picture is that of a (gentile) Christian community being included within the People of God. ('Once you were no people, now you are God's people.' 1 Peter 2:10)."[46] We need to develop more adequate ways of interpreting scripture and more appropriate doctrines of scripture.

The Church Is Rooted in the Life of Israel

Numerous church statements stress the connection between Christianity and Judaism. The Vatican Commission for Religious Relations with the Jews, in its 1975 Guidelines, urged pastors and teachers commenting on biblical texts to emphasize "the continuity of our faith with that of the earlier Covenant, in the perspective of the promises, without minimizing those elements of Christianity which are original." Significantly, the Commission commented on these promises that "we still await their perfect fulfillment in His glorious return at the end of time." The Roman Catholic Church in the Netherlands in 1970 affirmed "the connection which has always existed between the Church and the Jewish people [and] the great spiritual patrimony which they share," asserting that the Jewish people "has been constituted forever as a testimony of God's saving alliance with mankind." It remarked that the liturgy of the church preserves in its essentials the heritage of Jewish worship in the proclamation of the word, celebration of the Passover meal, the ministry of reconciliation in baptism, and the sacrament of penitence. In 1975, the United States National Conference of Catholic Bishops pointed out that "early in Christian history a de-judaizing process dulled our awareness of our Jewish beginnings." The Lutheran World Federation confirmed in 1969 that the solidarity of Lutherans with the Jewish people is "legitimized in God's election and calling into being Abraham's seed a people of promise, of faith, and of obedience peculiar unto him, a people whose unity will one day become manifest when 'all Israel' will be saved" [the committee does not say what it means by this last phrase]. Lutherans are taught not to affirm the church's continuity with Israel "in such a way as to question the fact that present-day Judaism has its own continuity with Old Testament Israel." This solidarity is grounded "in God's unmerited grace, his forgiveness of sin and his justification of the disobedient." Christians can never talk about disobedience and obedience as if the former were characteristic of Jews, the latter of Christians.[47] In 1974, the American Lutheran Church acknowledged that Christians are less aware than they should be "of the common roots and origin of the church and the Jewish tradition of faith and life."[48]

The churches provide sound theological grounding for the claim that the church is rooted in the life of the people Israel. They base this declaration on such fundamental Christian assertions as the grace and promises of God, God's gracious election of both Israel and the church, and the grace of God that justifies without regard to any merit. If the assertion of such grace does not hold true with regard to Israel, neither does it hold true with regard to the church. They also understand Jesus of Nazareth as rooted in the Judaism of his day, as having taken form in the people Israel, and they heed Paul's assertion of the continuing faithfulness of God both to the people Israel and to the church. Equally striking is that the rootedness of the church in the people Israel is an affirmation made in the present tense. The teaching documents of the church do not merely claim that the church in its beginnings *was* germinated in the soil of Jewish faith. Such a statement is true, but says nothing about the relation between the church and the Israel of God today. Instead, the teaching documents affirm that the church *is* rooted in the contemporary Israel of God, with which, therefore, conversation is of critical importance. Through colloquy with the Israel of God, the church's self-understanding and self-knowledge is enhanced.

Christology and the Jewish Jesus

"We confess Jesus Christ the Jew, who as the Messiah from Israel is the Saviour of the world and binds the peoples of the world to the people of God."[49] The Jewishness of Jesus shines through the churches' teaching documents with a clarity previously unachieved in church history. That he was and remained a Jew, that his ministry was restricted "to the lost sheep of the house of Israel," that he was a person of his Palestinian environment, that he submitted himself to the Torah, inculcated respect for and obedience to it, that he taught in synagogues and the Temple, that he was incarnate in the Jewish people, that he shared with the Pharisees many of their teachings—these recognize that whatever Jesus was, he was that Jewishly.[50]

Jesus' reduction of the 613 commandments of the Torah to two, love of God and of the neighbor (Deut. 6:5 and Lev. 19:18), was a typical move within Jewish scriptural interpretation at the time.[51] It is paralleled in Philo of Alexandria, attributed to Hillel, and found in the *Testament of Daniel*, 5:3. Jesus' teaching method was the same as that of the Pharisees of the time, the points on which he disagreed with contemporary Judaism fewer than those on which he agreed, and if he opposed contemporary Judaism, he did so from within it.[52] "Jesus, by His obedience to the Torah and its prayers, accomplished His ministry within the pale of the Covenant people."[53] That Jesus "never severed the bonds with His people" is an important theme in the church's teaching.[54]

A reappraisal of the Pharisees, the chief heavies in the Gospels, is under way. The teaching documents suggest that the words "Pharisee" and "Pharisaism" should be relieved of their largely pejorative meaning.[55] That Pharisaism was "a decadent formalism and hypocrisy, well exemplified by Jesus' enemies" is an idea that should be explicitly rejected.[56] The negative role played by the Pharisees in the Gospels is attributed to conflict not between Jesus and the Pharisees but to conflict between them and the later churches.[57] The pejorative view of them in the apostolic writings "must be corrected by objective information from rabbinic literature."[58] This literature shows that "Pharisaic doctrine is not opposed to that of Christianity," but that the Pharisees and the first Christians were in some ways quite close to one another.[59] Any friction between the two groups probably derived from their closeness.[60] The Pharisees are absent from the Passion narratives. They and Jesus shared certain doctrines (such as resurrection) and forms of piety, and they practiced addressing God as "father." Paul "always considered his membership of the Pharisees as a title of honor (Phil. 3:5)."[61]

Reflection on the historical Jesus elicits consideration on what it means to confess him as "Jesus Christ" or as Lord and Savior. The critically reconstructed Jesus of history corrects Christologies that distort the historical witness in order to make their point. The teaching documents initiate new christological reflection. They are increasingly clear that the term *messiah* (the anointed) had a wide range of meanings and that neither in the Hebrew Scriptures nor in later Judaism does it refer to what Christians have traditionally meant by *savior*. There was a messianic son-of-man, a messianic prophet, a messianic priest, a messianic king, and later a suffering messiah. Their focus is less on the figure of the messiah than on the messianic days, the "Kingdom of God," when hunger, oppression, injustice, suffering, and perhaps even death would be overcome.[62] Because these are still with us, Christians who take seriously the realities of history also take seriously the Jewish "no" to the church's claim that the messiah *has* come. Any church that does not take seriously this "no" does not take seriously its own "yes." Nowhere in the New Testament do we find an undialectical "yes" as an answer to the question whether the messiah has already come.

Rather, we find an "already and a not yet," with the "not yet" acknowledging, if agonizingly, the correctness of the Jewish "no." This is never clearer than in Romans 8:18, where Paul argues "that the sufferings of this present time are not worth comparing to the glory about to be revealed to us," a comment he makes *before* discussing in chapters 9–11 the relationship between Christians and non-Christian Jews.

Whereas some earlier post-*Shoah* statements of the churches asserted that Jesus Christ is the way to God for both Jews and Christians, that if Jews want to find the way to God they must do so through Jesus Christ, more recent ones significantly modify this claim:

> Jesus Christ has a fundamentally different function for the nations [Gentiles] and for Israel. The Jews are called back by him to the God who bound himself to them from the beginning. But the Gentiles are not called back to their origin by Jesus Christ; rather, they are called to something which is radically new in their history. In the proclamation of him as the Messiah of Israel they are confronted with God himself, whom they had not known before. In Christ those who were once far off were given access to him who also was their God.[63]

"Christ is the link (Gal. 3:26–29), enabling the Gentiles to be numbered among Abraham's 'offspring' and therefore fellow-heirs with the Jews according to God's promise."[64] Jesus Christ binds Gentiles to the Israel of God and to the God of Israel.

In the dialogue, Christians discover that Jews can acknowledge that for Christians Jesus "has become the way on which they find Israel's God," but also that the Jewish evaluation of this Christian way hinges less on what Christians say than on whether Christians actively engage in the service of righteousness and peace.[65] When a church confesses that "whoever encounters Jesus Christ encounters Judaism," we are a far cry from the views of those who think that to encounter Jesus Christ is to meet the one who liberates us from Judaism. The Evangelical Church of the Rhineland in 1980 made its acceptance of the permanent election of the Jewish people coherent with its confession of Jesus Christ the Jew, when it avowed "that through Jesus Christ the church is taken into the covenant of God with his people."[66]

God is the God of Israel

God is faithful: "He has chosen his people Israel and he stands by the election."[67] The churches have a new appreciation for the *Shema*, heard in every synagogue service: "Hear, O Israel: The LORD is our

God, the LORD alone" (Deut. 6:4), with which Jesus prefaced his statement of the greatest of the commandments (Mark 12:29f.). "Together
with the Jews, we confess the one God."[68] The Trinitarian understanding of God in Christianity by no means undercuts the oneness of God;
God's becoming enfleshed in the Jew Jesus "presupposes that the one
and unique God of Israel is not an isolated God without relationships,
but a God who turns toward humankind and who is affected by human
destiny."[69] This relational God is known in rabbinic Judaism as well.
God dwells not only in transcendence, but in the midst of God's people, subject to distress and persecution "as Lord, Father, Companion
and Redeemer." The God of Jesus Christ is the God of Israel, of Abraham, Sarah, Jacob, Moses, David.[70] Because the Father of Jesus Christ
is the God of Israel, Israel is connected with our faith in God; the connection with the people Israel is part of the church's proclamation of its
faith in God.[71] The doctrine of the Trinity affirms the identity of the
God of the church with the God of Israel: "The Christian Church
shares Israel's faith in the One God, whom it knows in the Spirit as the
God and Father of the Lord Jesus Christ."[72] The God disclosed in Jesus
Christ to be the Triune Lord "is the same one disclosed in the life and
worship of Israel."[73]

A Mutual Witness

"We affirm that both the church and the Jewish people are elected by
God for witness to the world, and that the relationship of the church to
contemporary Jews is based on that gracious and irrevocable election of
both."[74] What is the mission of the church to the Israel of God? The
first answer is negative: the church must disavow all efforts at proselytism. On hardly any issue, other than the rejection of anti-Semitism,
are the churches more unanimous. Even where uncertainty reigns with
regard to what the church's outreach to Jews should be, proselytism is
repudiated: "We all emphatically reject any form of 'proselytizing,' in the
derogatory sense which the word has come to carry in our time, where it
is used for the corruption of witness in cajolery, undue pressure or intim-
idation, or other improper methods."[75] Proselytism is explicitly dis-
claimed by the Considerations on Jewish-Christian Dialogue of the
World Council of Churches, by the United Methodist Church (U.S.A.),
the Texas Conference of Churches, the Lutheran Council in the U.S.A.,
and the Roman Catholic Church.[76] Other churches implicitly disavow it
by the way they define Christian witness to Jews.

The positive answer is seen in the move away from witness to service.
The General Assembly of the Presbyterian Church (U.S.A.) affirmed in

1987 that both Jews and Christians "are elected to service for the life of the world," and calls on Christians to acknowledge that "Jews are already in a covenantal relationship with God." Dialogue with Jews should try "to heal that which has been broken."[77]

Roman Catholic statements arrive at the same conclusions. The mission to Israel consists "in a Christian life lived in total fidelity to the One God and his revealed Word, so that Jews and Christians emulate each other in their turning to God, and this is the universal salvation of the Jews and all peoples." Christian mission is preeminently "a life lived in fidelity to God and men," in which we remind ourselves that it is faithful Jews "who 'sanctify the divine Name' in the world, living in justice and holiness and causing the divine gifts to bear fruit, who are a true witness to the whole world."[78] Our mission must be one of repentance, taking our share of the responsibility for the break between the church and Israel, "the first schism, the 'prototype of schisms' in the heart of the people of God."[79]

A Common Hope

The Old Testament (Tanach) tells about the life with the God of the patriarchs and bears witness to this God's promise for Israel and the nations. Thus it joins the Christian community and the Jewish people together by the common hope in the victory of God's rule.
            —Synod of the Evangelical Church of Berlin (West)[80]

The continuity between Israel and the church consists in more than memory (the time present of things past) and contemporary encounter (the time present of things present), but is also composed of hope (the time present of things future). Jews and Christians receive from God a common promise of a this-worldly time when God will rule earthly affairs in *shalom*, to which they respond with a common hope (trust in the divine promise). Given the priority of God's grace and initiative in the faiths of the synagogue and the church, our respective theologies are more properly understood as theologies of God's promise than of our hope. That Jews and Christians both await the coming of God's rule is a growing awareness in the churches' teaching.

Christians and Jews are "partners in waiting." Separate from Jewish hope for "the days of the Messiah," Christian hope either collapses (in thinking that redemption has simply been accomplished amid continuing violence and oppression), becomes exclusively otherworldly, or is unintelligible. Christian hope understands itself appropriately only when it remembers that both John the Baptist and Jesus declared the eschatological

vision of Judaism. It is an article of faith for both that, appearances to the
contrary notwithstanding, God is doing everything that it is possible and
appropriate for God to do to bring about peace and justice. "Both Christians and Jews are called to wait and to hope in God."[81] This is not a
sluggish waiting; it is a striving to actualize peace and justice, to em-
bolden the life of the mind, to heed the words of the prophets; to do battle with racism, sexism, militarism, ecocide; to open ourselves to God's
total claim upon us.[82] The mission common to Jews and Christians includes the hallowing of God's name in the world, working for the dignity
of persons as created in God's image, pursuing peace and justice, and
being signs of hope in God's promised future. "Jews and Christians share
a great common hope in a future and final coming of God's reign in the
world, a messianic age."[83]

Implications for Preaching and Teaching

It is chiefly Roman Catholic statements, particularly those written by
diocesan committees, that attempt to translate large theological propositions into specific modes of behavior. To a greater extent than Protestant
statements, Roman Catholic documents spell out the implications of theological statements on relations between Christians and Jews for education (catechesis), preaching, and liturgy. The Roman Catholic contention
is doubtless correct that the actual ways in which prejudice against Jews
was inculcated in generation after generation of Christians were through
the liturgy, education, and preaching. If there is to be change, it will
come not only at the level of theological pronouncement but in attending
to liturgy, education, and preaching in local congregations.

The implications for education (catechesis) are fairly straightforward.
The main points in the new ways in which churches confess their faith
will have to be emphasized in the content of Christian education. How
the Hebrew Scriptures are taught and understood, the relation of the
New Testament to them, the Jewishness of Jesus, the role of some Jews
in the Roman Imperial System's execution of Jesus, Paul's claim that the
promises of God to Israel are irrevocable, the history of Christian persecution of Jews and the teaching of contempt, the introduction of dialog-
ical relationships with Jews in local communities—all are important.[84]

As anybody who attended Sunday school as a youth can remember,
many images of Jews and Judaism illustrated Christian teaching. Often
these images were inaccurate: they served the purposes of claiming
Christian superiority and encouraged disrespect for Jews and Judaism.
Here Protestant churches in particular should follow the Roman
Catholic lead, not only by expurgating anti-Judaism from educational

materials but by preparing new materials that are theologically appropriate and by educating teachers in what should be taught. (How many Sunday schools have been impacted by the new teaching documents issued by the churches?)

The same goes for preaching. Recent studies of anti-Judaism in Christian preaching find that it persists in strength in contemporary Christian preaching, particularly among Protestants.[85] Other studies conclude that anti-Judaism is learned in church, specifically that laity learn it there from clergy and teaching staff.[86] Clergy will not be happy to hear this, and it is hardly true of all of them; nonetheless, these studies make it clear that the advice of several church statements needs to be seriously heeded.

> Care should be taken to see that homilies based on liturgical readings do not distort their meaning, especially when it is a question of passages which seem to show the Jewish people as a whole, or major groups such as the Pharisees, in an unfavorable light. . . . [C]arefulness of expression and historical accuracy should characterize all liturgical and paraliturgical events.[87]

With this last comment, we move from preaching to liturgy, which is equally important with regard to inculcating anti-Jewish attitudes in Christians. Much of traditional Christian anti-Judaism persists in the liturgy, hymns, and services of the church. A particular point of liturgical difficulty surrounds the services held in Holy Week, specifically on Palm Sunday and Good Friday. In planning worship services for Holy Week, pastors should take advantage of all the benefits of recent scholarship pertaining to the events of the last week in the life of Jesus. It is necessary to remember, theologically, that the Christian Passover accomplished in the death and resurrection of Christ would be impossible without the Jewish Passover accomplished in the liberation from bondage in Egypt.[88] Eliminating anti-Judaism from worship is more demanding than these few comments indicate.[89]

Unless education, preaching, and worship in local congregations are appropriate to the good news of God's all-inclusive love and God's command that justice be done to all those whom God loves, none of the church's fine theological pronouncements on relations between Christians and Jews will, in the end, be worth a fig.

3

Jesus of Nazareth

_____

Whoever encounters Jesus Christ encounters Judaism.

—*Roman Catholic German Bishops' Conference, Bonn, 1980*

The study of the historical Jesus in this chapter will not culminate here
in a christological statement. That work will come in a later chapter in
which I will attempt to show that the Jesus of critical-historical reconstruction is not the subject of the christological assertion. Christian faith
always has to do with the testified-to Jesus of the Christian community.
But Christian faith cannot be nonchalant about the historical Jesus or
about the way in which we tell the story of Jesus, which is also a story
about a lot of other first-century Jews. Christians may not ignore the extremely damaging ways, particularly for Jews, in which we have told the
story of Jesus. As feminists have challenged the antiwoman bias in the
telling of the Jesus story, so post-Holocaust theologians challenge the
anti-Jewish bias that infects the way in which the Jesus story is told. Getting the historical Jesus straight, set within the context of Judaism and
the covenant between the God of Israel and the Israel of God, can, at
the least, correct our Christologies. That is what we will let it do here.

We need to remember that a theologian who wanders out into the
field of New Testament studies is like the greenhorn soldier who walked
across the Gettysburg battlefield during a lull in the battle. Soon he was
felled by fire from every direction. But if the alternative to exposing oneself to the criticism of New Testament scholars who come at one from
every conceivable direction is to ignore the New Testament and the important work being done on it, then we will simply soldier naively onto

the battlefield. The "method" of this chapter is to study a number of excellent and recent New Testament scholars writing on Jesus and see what sense a post-Holocaust theologian can make of their work.

The Conflictual Jesus

Before we talk about Jesus of Nazareth, it is advisable to talk about *how* we should talk about Jesus. As a church which is aware that it does its thinking *after* Hitler's attempted "Final Solution of the Jewish question," we should do this because the view of Jesus that we find in the *adversus Judaeos* tradition, although not the only way of giving voice to Christian anti-Judaism, is nonetheless the hinge of anti-Jewish ways of thinking. These ways of thinking are complicit in the "Final Solution." In this tradition, the image and function of Jesus has an intrinsically anti-Jewish character to it. Our oldest "text," the "Sayings Source" (Q), is usually dated about 50 C.E., and strong distancing features already appear in Q's "discourse against the Pharisees" (Luke 11:37–12:1 and Matt. 23).[1] In the Gospels, written from forty to seventy years after the career of Jesus, we have "a self-conscious Christian tradition that deliberately distanced itself from the historical Jewish context in which Jesus had lived and died."[2] In the later *adversus Judaeos* tradition, what the church meant by "Jesus" was understood on the model of conflict with Judaism. His life and death were described as having been played out in conflict with Jews or his teaching as a teaching against Jews and Judaism. The conflict was so acrid that his death on the cross was the logical and necessary outcome of it. The resurrection, by the same token, was viewed as God's rejection of the Jews' rejection of Jesus and, hence, as God's rejection of the Jews.

Thus was Jesus made the one who separates the church and synagogue; he has been the sign of the rejection of Jews and Judaism as well as the sign of the election of the Gentiles at the expense of the Jews. Jesus has been used to warrant the ideological claim of Christianity's superiority to and supersession of Judaism. In pre-Holocaust New Testament scholarship (scholarship can be *after* the Holocaust without being *post-*Holocaust), this classical anti-Jewish use of the figure of Jesus has been founded on historical-critical attempts to reconstruct the life of Jesus (in the nineteenth century) and, more recently, the very words or "voice" of Jesus. Jesus has been described as in conflict with, transcending and overcoming, a degenerate Judaism, a Judaism that never existed.[3] Because such a decadent Judaism was supposed, the quest for the historical Jesus, old or new, sought to oppose Jesus to Judaism.

The Criterion of Dissimilarity

The "criterion of dissimilarity" is used to uncover the historical Jesus behind not only the Gospels and Q but behind the sources and oral traditions that went into their making. One must grant that the use of the criterion of dissimilarity is premised upon correct assumptions: that many teaching materials ascribed to Jesus actually stem from the early church, that critical-historical reminiscence was not a purpose of any Gospel writer, and that no pericope in the Gospels intends to provide a historical reminiscence of Jesus.[4] Given this situation, scholars felt obligated to use the criterion of dissimilarity, which Norman Perrin representatively formulated:

> The earliest form of a saying we can reach may be regarded as authentic if it can be shown to be dissimilar to characteristic emphases both of ancient Judaism and of the early Church.

Perrin is aware that "by definition it [the criterion] will exclude all teaching in which Jesus may have been at one with Judaism or the early Church at one with him." The nature of the Gospels themselves means, he said, that "the brutal fact of the matter is that we have no choice."[5]

One case will show how this criterion is applied. The central feature of Jesus' proclamation of the kingdom, says Perrin, is the forgiveness of sins. Perrin contrasts Jesus' forgiveness of sins with that found in the "best of ancient Judaism." Here he finds that God will quite undeservedly forgive Jews who sin. "When we consider the Gentiles the situation changes somewhat, for a Gentile was a sinner, as it were, 'by definition': he lived apart from the Law and necessarily defiled God with every breath that he drew."[6] Jews can hope for forgiveness; Gentiles cannot. Significantly, "*against* this background" we may "appreciate the startling nature of Jesus' forgiveness of sins, and understand the dispute between himself and those contemporaries who took offence at this proclamation."[7] Jesus "went out of his way to contradict . . . [the] viewpoint" of the best Judaism of his time.[8] Because the criterion of dissimilarity establishes authenticity, Luke's parable of the prodigal son, which Perrin interprets as a story of a Jew who became a swineherd and therefore a Gentile, *must* be authentic. Perrin overlooks the fact that a pro-Gentile attitude would be in the interests of a Gentile-mission gospel.[9] He also seems to be wrong about the view of the "best" Judaism at the time: "'Love' in the sense of 'decent treatment' was also supposed to govern relations with *Gentiles* and even with *enemies*."[10]

In this same vein, Joachim Jeremias comments:

Where is it that Jesus sees the cancer that is not recognized by the pious men of his day? This becomes clearest in his sayings against the Pharisees, with whom he had the most to do.[11]

Similarly, Hans Küng argues that Jesus was involved in a simultaneous quadrilateral conflict with the Sadducees (the ideal type of establishment), the Zealots (the ideal type of revolution), the Essenes (the ideal type of emigration), and the Pharisees (the ideal type of compromise). Jesus' proclamation, behavior, and destiny show this four-cornered antagonism with all the important forms of Judaism, which is why he was tried and executed on a charge of blasphemy, which, Küng claims, was true.[12]

The criterion of dissimilarity is used to show that Jesus was unique, and does so in the only way in which an empirical-historical approach can—by setting him in contrast to his entire Jewish context. If the church is to talk about Jesus of Nazareth differently, in keeping with the way in which it now confesses its faith, we must talk further about *how* we talk about Jesus. We must look again at the "criterion of dissimilarity" and think of another way to reconstruct the figure of the historical Jesus.

Criticism of the criterion of dissimilarity

The criterion of dissimilarity and other criteria associated with it have not gone uncriticized. The basic assumption of historical consciousness involves the relationality of historical events; accounting for what goes into the making of an event sheds light upon it. Every event is internally related to occasions in its causal past. Each moment in a person's life is internally related to events in his or her causal past.[13] This way of making the point was learned from Ernst Troeltsch and Alfred North Whitehead; it is also made by Ludwig Wittgenstein: "To understand a language is to understand a form of life."[14] The first word the church ever heard about Jesus was in the context of the story of the Israel of God with the God of Israel. To remove Jesus methodologically from this context is to fail to understand him.[15] As John P. Meier puts it, the criterion of discontinuity "winds up giving us a caricature by divorcing Jesus from the Judaism that influenced him and from the Church that he influenced."[16] A totally discontinuous Jesus "would have been unintelligible to practically everyone," says Meier. Because the excision of all elements that Jesus had in common with the Judaisms of his time gives us a figure who had no history, no context, and who made no impact, we must challenge the adequacy of the criterion of dissimilarity to the task of reconstructing the historical Jesus.

D. G. A. Calvert finds that eleven criteria for determining the authentic sayings of Jesus are used, five negative and six positive. He further finds that they are all highly unreliable. The negative criteria deny genuineness to a saying; the positive grant it. The first negative criterion, that those sayings are inauthentic which agree with the teaching of the early church, "presupposes that we know all that the later Church taught," that Jesus' teachings were widely different from its, that Jesus did not intend to found a community and did nothing to prepare his followers for such a community. The second rules out those sayings in which Jesus agrees with the Judaism of his time; it "presupposes no connection between Jesus and contemporary Judaism, and indeed no connection between Jesus and the Old Testament."[17] James H. Charlesworth comments that it ensures that any conclusions about Jesus will be "certainly docetic . . . and [are] dangerously susceptible to anti-Semitism or anti-Judaism."[18]

These two criteria eliminate most of the teachings attributed to Jesus. Also, they would make of him a non- or antihistorical person, a visitor from Mars.[19] The criterion of dissimilarity "presupposes a more complete discontinuity between Jesus and Judaism on the one hand and between Jesus and the early church on the other than may actually have been the case."[20] Paula Fredriksen asks: "But if we take seriously the proposition that Jesus of Nazareth was a Jew, would none of his teachings have touched on principles traditionally prominent in his native religion, Judaism (love of God and neighbor, concern for the poor, and so on)? And if the church grew up around the memory of this message, would none of its teachings have related to his?"[21]

The third negative criterion excludes from authenticity sayings that presume a situation unthinkable at the time of Jesus. Its problem is that "it is difficult to assess what would be unthinkable to Jesus." The fourth excludes passages that "contradict other, more genuine sayings." When two texts contradict each other, the question remains as to which is authentic; this test assumes the results of the others. The last negative criterion declares as inauthentic sayings that can be determined to be developments of what is found elsewhere. The assumption that the absence of a statement from Jewish or Hellenistic sources implies its originality with Jesus is clearly fallacious and works only if one has also assumed, theologically, the uniqueness of Jesus' person.

It is difficult on the basis of these criteria to say more than that there is established a probability that some of the recorded teaching of Jesus is less than authentic. We do not find much help in deciding precisely what is unauthentic. The common approach of ruling out the more obviously unauthentic teaching before applying more positive tests is therefore rejected.[22]

The first affirmative criterion is that authentic sayings are positively distinctive from Jewish thought. Yet such elements would often agree with the thought of the later anti-Jewish church, hence violating the first negative criterion. Nor do any statements attributed to Jesus fall outside the range of the Judaisms of his time. The second affirmative criterion, which grants legitimacy to those words that are positively distinctive from the thought of the early church, assumes we can construct that church's thought, and such judgments are often arbitrary. The third admits statements that could *not* be the invention of the early church; it is similar to the prior criterion and turns on how the saying is to be interpreted.[23]

The fourth affirmative criterion accords trustworthiness to sayings that "exhibit Aramaisms . . . and reflect Palestinian conditions." Yet such matters may well have been dropped from authentic sayings as they were translated for a Gentile church. Also, because their absence does not count against authenticity, why should their presence count for it?[24] The fifth grants authenticity to sayings found in more than one tradition, as in both Q and John. This assumes certainty about solution of the synoptic problem, a certainty that does not exist. Also, if the single occurrence of a parable does not count against it, why should its multiple occurrence count for it? Both Mark and Q contain sayings that reflect the situation of the early church rather than facts about Jesus, "so the mere fact of dual attestation proves nothing about the actual course of Jesus' life."[25] The sixth regards as genuine those sayings "which are characteristic of the known teachings of Jesus." This, however, is what the criteria are supposed to establish.

Dissimilarity and "Abba"

In Mark 14:36, Jesus prays: "Abba, Father, for you all things are possible; remove this cup from me; yet, not what I want, but what you want." Here, and nowhere else, Jesus calls God "*abba*" (although Paul twice uses *abba*, in Rom. 8:15 and Gal. 4:6). Gerhard Kittel, an ardent anti-Semite and Nazi, was the first to argue that "Jewish usage shows how this father-child relationship to God far surpasses any possibilities of intimacy assumed in Judaism, introducing indeed something which is entirely new."[26] The term with which children addressed their fathers, *abba* is said to connote intimacy and trust as well as respect.[27] It "was hardly used by Jesus' contemporaries in their prayers if at all."[28] Jeremias popularized Kittel's view, arguing that "not a single instance of God being addressed as Abba in the literature of Jewish prayer" can be found, but "Jesus *always* addressed him in this way (with the exception of the cry from the cross, Mark 15:34 par.)."[29]

How is it concluded, from the single occurrence of one word, that Jesus experienced God with "an immediacy and an intimacy that could find expression only in that cry, 'Abba'"? First, a contrast is made with the formal prayers of Judaism, noticing neither that an agonized utterance from Gethsemane is hardly the occasion for formal prayer nor that we do not know how Jews of the time prayed informally. Second, the stipulation is made that *abba* "presumably lies beneath the Greek *pater* [father]" which the Gospels elsewhere attribute to Jesus. Thus, *abba* is assumed in Matthew 6:9, Luke 11:2, Matthew 11:25, Luke 10:21, 23:34, 46, Matthew 26:42, and nine times in John. Thereby *abba* gains multiple attestation, being found "in all five strata of the Gospel tradition (Mark, Q, Luke, Matthew, John), . . . used in every prayer that is attributed to Jesus except one (Mark 15:34)."[30]

Other, more recent, scholars disagree with Jeremias and his followers on every point of the claim that Jesus called God "*abba.*" They contend (a) that *abba* does not mean "daddy," (b) that there were several different forms for addressing God that were current at the time of Jesus and that refute the assertion that Jesus' putative use of *abba* was exclusive, and that (c) the verses in Matthew and Luke (11:27 and 10:22, respectively) on which Jeremias relies heavily as authentic statements of the historical Jesus are, instead, later community traditions.[31]

Nor is it clear how we know that "abba" underlies *pater* every time the latter occurs. Because the text portrays Jesus as alone when he uttered "*abba,*" who is supposed to have heard his prayer? If *abba* were so important, why did Matthew and Luke drop it (Matt. 26:39; Luke 22:42) the one time Mark used it? Or did they use an earlier version of Mark that did not have it? What seems to be going on here is that a theological understanding of Jesus which originated with Schleiermacher, that Jesus' consciousness of God is the key to understanding his person, is driving some biblical scholars to strain at gnats.[32] We should remember that our language about intimacy with God is borrowed from Judaism, and cease contrasting Jesus' prayers with "Jewish prayer." Other first-century miracle workers "were aware of their special relationship with God: Hanan the rainmaker even prayed that his audience would distinguish between himself and the one who truly granted rain, the *Abba* in heaven."[33] A differentiating characteristic of ancient Hasidic piety was its custom of referring to God as "*Abba*"; "for the charismatic, as for Jesus, God is *Abba.*"[34]

> When the world was in need of rain, the rabbis used to send school-children to him [Hanan], who seized the train of his cloak and said to him, *Abba, Abba,* give us rain! He said to God: Lord of the universe, render a service to those who cannot distinguish between the *Abba* who gives rain and the *Abba* who does not.[35]

In spite of these attestations, John Meier is doubtless correct that "we are not terribly well informed about popular Jewish-Aramaic religious practices and vocabulary in early 1st-century Galilee," and in concluding that "modesty in advancing claims is advisable."[36] For all we know, Jesus, like other miracle workers of his time, *may* have prayed to God as *Abba*. If so, he shared with them the intimacy with God implied by the ability to work miracles; he would not have been unique in calling God *Abba*. The Targums (translations of the Hebrew Bible into Aramaic for purposes of divine worship) give us some indication of how the Bible was read and interpreted at the time of Jesus. Twice the Targumist "has Isaac address his father Abraham with the intimately familiar *abba* (in Gen. 22:7 and 22:10)."[37] This scene may have been the background for the stories of Jesus' baptism ("this is my beloved son") and for the scene in Gethsemane, which appears to be modeled on the supreme trial of Abraham and Isaac, in which Isaac, facing imminent death, appealed to Abraham "My father!" (*'abi*). "The father-son relationship in Genesis 22 may be a far-reaching New Testament model of that between Jesus and God."[38]

We see how the principle of discontinuity tends "to portray Jesus as a non-Jew and as a leader without followers."[39] This predilection flies in the face of Jesus' deep Jewishness and of his effect on those Jews who were his initial followers. No wonder that James H. Charlesworth characterizes as "dangerous and indeed misleading" those "caricatures that tend to emphasize Jesus' *uniqueness* in early Judaism."[40] The unhappy part of this whole discussion is that it is even necessary to engage in it, long after one would think it had been disposed of by earlier writers:

> I have often wondered just how different a man must be to be hanged for it. We are increasingly aware in modern times of the Jewishness of Jesus. He moved within the field of thought current in First Century Judaism.[41]

The Criterion of Embarrassment

Assuming the inappropriateness of the criterion of dissimilarity with its two aspects, and that we can make no operational distinction between the earliest witness to Jesus and would-be "objective" statements from or about Jesus that can be found in the tradition, where are we to turn?[42] As long as we are willing to live with the relativity and corrigibility of all historical-critical statements and accept the fact that Jesus' self-consciousness is beyond our reach, there is the option of "a more precise use to the so-called 'criterion of dissimilarity,'" one that denies authenticity to teachings attributed to Jesus that can be attributed to the concerns of the early "Christian" communities. The attempt to exclude teachings that Jesus had in common with Judaism is dropped; all Jesus' teachings have their roots in Judaism.[43] To avoid confusion, however, we would do better to adopt a name suggested by Paula Fredriksen:

> A modified criterion might speak more appropriately to historical reality. If something stands in the gospels that is clearly *not* in the interests of the late first-century church—disparaging remarks about Gentiles, for example, or explicit pronouncements about the imminent end of the world— then it has a stronger claim to authenticity than otherwise. Stated briefly, anything embarrassing is probably earlier.[44]

Let us call it the "criterion of embarrassment" and use it as Charlesworth and Fredriksen define it. Such a criterion promises to serve us better than E. P. Sanders' attempt to start with certain "almost indisputable facts about Jesus' career and its aftermath," facts that "can be known beyond doubt."[45] The reason why a revised criterion of embarrassment may prove more helpful is that a list of almost indisputable facts does not evade the problems we face with regard to the sayings.

> Quite simply, if Jesus said something, this is a fact (and an event), and as much a fact (and an event), as his supposed entering the temple in Jerusalem on any occasion. And like sayings, "facts," "events," "actions" were always as liable as any saying to be given a different context and a different nuance of meaning, without any sure guarantee that the original "intentional action" would be left in any way discernible.[46]

The vicious circle is this: to distinguish authentic sayings of and information about Jesus in the Gospels from the early church's reinterpretations, "we need to be able to identify the interests of the early church." However, we only know the latter from the Gospels, and we can discern them only if we can already separate the material reflecting the church's interests from that which goes back, if not to Jesus himself, at least to the earliest layer of the tradition.[47] We are reduced to offering hypotheses about the interests of the churches that produced the Gospels and establishing what might prove embarrassing to such communities on the basis of these same hypotheses. Nonetheless, disparaging remarks about Gentiles would seem to be disconcerting to a Gospel that concluded with Jesus' commandment to go and "make disciples of all nations," *panta ta ethne*, "all the ethnics" (Matt. 28:19). Rather than asserting that a fact or saying meets the "criterion of embarrassment," we will give reasons why this might be so. We will start with matters from the beginning and end of Jesus' public career, his relation to John the Baptizer, and his trial and crucifixion, and will then work back from these to his teachings.

Jesus and John the Baptizer

"I tell you, among those born of women no one is greater than John; yet the least in the kingdom of God is greater than he" (Luke 7:28; see also Matt. 11:11).

Why might John the Baptizer have been embarrassing to the early church? We know that the Jesus movement was involved in a strong rivalry with John's community until late in the first century. Disciples of John in Ephesus had to be informed by Paul that John had instructed "the people to believe in the one who was to come after him, that is, in Jesus" (Acts 19:4). If we read the Gospels in the order in which the synoptic hypothesis theorizes that they were written, we see a progressive tendency to make John into a witness to Jesus.[48] Mark portrays John as a harbinger for Jesus and has him declare: "The one who is more powerful than I is coming after me; I am not worthy to stoop down and untie the thong of his sandals. I have baptized you with water; but he will baptize you with the Holy Spirit" (Mark 1:7–8). Of Jesus' baptism, Mark says that Jesus "was baptized by John in the Jordan" (Mark 1:9). Matthew adds that "John would have prevented him, saying, 'I need to be baptized by you, and do you come to me?' But Jesus answered him, 'Let it be so now; for it is proper for us in this way to fulfill all righteousness.' Then he [John] consented" (Matt. 3:14–15). Before the baptism, Luke asserts that Herod "shut up John in prison" (Luke 3:19–20). According to Luke, John could not have baptized Jesus. The Fourth Gospel relates that John "testified to" Jesus (1:15), declared that he himself was "the voice of one crying out in the wilderness, 'Make straight the way of the Lord'" (1:23), and said of Jesus, "Here is the Lamb of God who takes away the sin of the world!" (1:29). It never says that John the Baptizer baptized Jesus. Instead John declares: "I saw the Spirit descending from heaven like a dove, and it remained on him" (1:32). The Fourth Gospel has John deny more than once that he is the Messiah and that he is Elijah or "the prophet."[49] All this, says John Dominic Crossan, is "theological damage control. The tradition is clearly uneasy with the idea of John baptizing Jesus because that seems to make John superior and Jesus sinful."[50]

Who was John the Baptizer? The Gospels' portrait of him is a theological construction on the part of communities embarrassed by Jesus' baptism at his hands; they are not interested in a critical history of John. The document Q has a two-sided picture, where Jesus views John as the eschatological portent of the kingdom of God and the church considers him and his followers as a threat and seeks to limit his role and importance.[51] Mark looks upon John as Elijah with his identity hidden from those around him; he suffers, preparing the way for the fate of Jesus and providing a model for the persecuted church, which also witnesses to Jesus.[52] For Matthew, John is Elijah "christianized," standing on this side of "the law and the prophets." He launches the messianic kingdom of Jesus and was a Christian martyr before Christ; he shows Israel's animosity to God's initiatives.[53] Luke's John is the forerunner of the messiah and not identical with Elijah. Who was John?

The answer begins with the situation at John's time. The Roman Empire denied to Israel control of its life in the Promised Land. Yet God had promised not only the land but instruction (the Torah) about how life in it was to be lived, and the prophets had spoken of God's coming judgment on the wicked and God's promise of hope to the righteous. Some Jews could escape Roman domination and corruption by withdrawing from society, as did the Qumran community. Some could maintain the way of God by applying to their lives the demands of the Torah, as did the Pharisees. Most were compromised by the political, social, legal, economic, and military conditions of Roman occupation. Meanwhile, the Judean wilderness was a refuge from Roman control and a reminder of the hope of Israel, recalling the desert where Jews had lived with Yahweh before they came to the Promised Land. Here the Qumran community waited for the messianic age and the overthrow of Rome. Here John the Baptizer lived and preached his gospel of the coming new age.[54] What was that gospel?

Again, the situation is of help. Roman rule faced Jews with a crisis different from any they had faced before. "The experience of Exile had been well incorporated into their religious consciousness and their theology, but nothing in their tradition prepared them to cope with the crisis of continuing occupation."[55] Earlier, such shocks as that under Antiochus Epiphanes had produced the Maccabean uprising and the hope for the restoration of Israel under the rule of God. Under Roman occupation, a similar development occurred, producing a revival of the prophetic vision or "Jewish restoration theology." John was an apocalyptic preacher, and apocalyptic preaching is political. The message of a coming new order criticizes the present order: "Even now the ax is lying at the root of the trees" (Luke 3:9). Jewish restoration theology recognized no distinction between politics and religion. Whereas preachers like John were probably pacifist, expecting God to bring the new order without military help, they were nonetheless political and nationalist. Hendrikus Boers concludes that John's significance was not limited to "being a forerunner of Jesus." Behind those traditions he finds "another image of John as the final eschatological figure who was preparing the way for God's own coming to the people."[56] Although shaped by the threat of imminent doom, John preached reconciliation. Judah the Galilean was a militarist preacher, advocating revolt against Rome, but equally religious and political. John preached about One [God?] who would come to restore Israel's life under the Torah and without oppression. Such a restoration would occur at Rome's expense. If John had preached about Jesus' coming, why the developing suppression of his baptism of Jesus? However, given the Gospels' tendency to make peace with the Roman Empire, the changing role of John makes sense. In this regard, Josephus' account of the fate of John the Baptizer is illuminating. He is depicted as a "good man" who "exhorted the Jews to lead righteous lives . . . and so doing join in baptism." However, when people responded in large numbers to his preaching,

> Herod became alarmed. Eloquence that had so great an effect on humanity might lead to some form of sedition, for it looked as though they would be guided by John in everything that they did. Herod decided therefore that it would be much better to strike first and be rid of him before his work led to an uprising.[57]

John was a prophet of national restoration under the rule of God, perceived as a threat to Rome. Jesus thought highly of him, declaring that no one born of woman is greater. How highly did he think of John?

> Again they came to Jerusalem. As he was walking in the temple, the chief priests, the scribes, and the elders came to him and said, "By what authority are you doing these things? Who gave you this authority to do them?" Jesus said to them, "I will ask you one question; answer me, and I will tell you by what authority I do these things. Did the baptism of John come from heaven, or was it of human origin? Answer me" (Mark 11:27–30; see also Matt. 21:23–25a; Luke 20:1–4).

Given the Gospels' proclivity to portray John as pointing to Jesus, what is arresting about this story is that in it Jesus points to John as drawing his authority from the same source ("heaven" = God) as did Jesus. Jesus' response to the question about his authority with another question about John's authority is a typical rabbinic exchange, answering a question with a question. "Jesus' counterquestion informs the questioners that they will find the answer to their question by answering the counterquestion: the source of authority for the activity of Jesus and for John's baptism is the same." The statement "among those born of women no one is greater than John; yet the least in the kingdom of God is greater than he" (Luke 7:28; see also Matt. 11:11) bears further comment. The latter part "does not detract from the greatness of John expressed in the first but adds to it by pointing to the benefits that had become available as a result of his presence." John came proclaiming the coming kingdom, and his career "marked the transition between the ages, placing Jesus in the time of the kingdom, which had already arrived."[58] On this reconstruction, Jesus regarded John as initiating the kingdom. Could Jesus have come eating and drinking because he understood himself to live in the time of God's reign, assured that God's liberation of Israel had already taken place? This is possible, but seems to go beyond the evidence. John Dominic Crossan agrees with Boers that Jesus broke with John because he "no longer accepted the former's apocalyptic message." What Jesus called for, instead, is recognition of a kingdom here and now.[59] Yet E. P. Sanders regards this possibility as merely "possible," considerably below "probable."[60] What does emerge is that Jesus, like John, was committed to the restoration of Israel under God and the Torah and apart from Roman domination.

Jesus and Pilate

That Jesus was executed by Roman soldiers acting on orders from Pontius Pilate, on a charge of sedition ("King of the Jews" being the sign placed over the cross), embarrassed the churches that produced the Gospels. The stories of Jesus' execution increasingly downplay Pilate's role. Mark 15:15 and Matthew 27:26 say that Pilate delivered Jesus to be crucified. Luke 23:24 differs: "So Pilate gave his verdict that *their* demand should be granted" (emphasis mine; "their" refers to the crowd). John 19:16 says, "Then he handed him over to them to be crucified." In both Mark and Matthew, the soldiers and the "whole cohort" crucify him (Mark 15:16–20; Matt. 27:27–31). Luke drops the soldiers and the cohort. "They" (the crowd) lead him away to be crucified (Luke 23:26). In John 19:18, "they crucified him."

Pilate's involvement grows ever less. Christians usually think of him as finding no guilt in Jesus and reluctant to execute him. A different picture emerges from other sources. Philo of Alexandria, a contemporary of Jesus, sent a letter to King Agrippa I, who ruled Palestine from 41 to 44 C.E., calling Pilate "unbending and recklessly hard." He accused Pilate's administration of "corruptibility, violence, robberies, ill-treatment of the people, grievances, continuous executions without even the form of a trial, endless and intolerable cruelties."[61] Under Pilate, the country "seethed with unrest. . . . Galilee was a hotbed of rebellion; Jerusalem, especially at festival times, was a cauldron of boiling emotions. Pontius Pilate had only one answer; excite the people to fever pitch, then slaughter them."[62] Pilate's career ended when Tiberius Caesar recalled him to Rome to stand trial in 36 C.E. because Pilate had ordered his soldiers to attack a group of Samaritans. Many were slaughtered. Pilate's "unyielding pro-Roman nationalism brought him into one adventure after another with the Jewish people."[63]

All this comports ill with the Gospels' claim that Pilate desired to release Jesus (Luke 23:20), demanded to be told what evil he had done (Mark 15:14; Matt. 27:23; Luke 23:22), claimed to be "innocent of this man's blood," only to have "the people as a whole" answer: "His blood be on us and on our children!" (Matt. 27:24–25), and did what he did, not out of his own accord but in order "to satisfy the crowd" (Mark 15:15).

Another way in which blame was shifted from Rome to "the Jews" for Jesus' execution was in the "invention" by Mark of a Jewish trial of Jesus.[64] Mark's account violates numerous rules for capital trials spelled out in the tractate *Sanhedrin* of the *Mishnah* (compiled about the year 200 C.E.). These rules were carefully thought out to defend the rights of the accused. The Ninth Commandment, "You shall not bear false witness against your neighbor" (Ex. 20:16), had to do specifically with witness borne in court. Questions have been raised as to whether the rules in the *Mishnah* were known when the Gospels were written. We will return to this question, but for now, let us assume that the Ninth Commandment was known to the Gospel writers. Hendrikus Boers catalogues the Mishnaic rules governing procedures in capital cases. Their point was to assure procedural justice for the accused and provide "the best possible chance of acquittal."[65] Capital cases

1. were to be decided by twenty-three judges.
2. had to begin with reasons for acquittal.
3. required that a verdict of guilty had to be reached by a majority of two.
4. permitted a decision to be reversed only from conviction to acquittal.
5. permitted all to argue for acquittal but not conviction.
6. A judge could change his mind in favor of acquittal, but not vice-versa.
7. could be tried only in the daytime; verdicts could also be reached only in the daytime.
8. A verdict of guilty could not be reached until the next day.
9. Witnesses were answerable for the blood of a person wrongly convicted.
10. Contradictory witnesses were both invalid.
11. The punishment for blasphemy was stoning, not crucifixion.
12. The rules for a conviction of blasphemy were stringent: A person could not be found guilty of blasphemy unless he or she had actually pronounced the divine name, *Yahweh*, itself.
13. Even when a person was being taken away for stoning, everything possible had to be done to make a last-minute stay of execution possible.

According to Mark, the proceeding took place at night, the Sanhedrin sought testimony against Jesus, false witness was borne against Jesus, the witnesses did not agree, Jesus was accused of blasphemy by the high priest and condemned on the spot (Mark 14:53–64; Matthew follows Mark in these regards).

"The trial scene is unlikely on all counts." The Gospels wish to incriminate the Jews and exculpate the Romans in the matter of Jesus' execution. "The elaborate Jewish trial scenes in the synoptic Gospels also tend to shift responsibility to Judaism in an official way and help serve the same purpose." We do not know that there was a Jewish trial of Jesus, that the whole Sanhedrin got together for it, that there was a formal charge, or a formal conviction.[66] Recognizing that we have only one account, Mark's, that it is highly tendentious, and that the Gospel of John contradicts it, scholars are increasingly reluctant to credit Mark's Jewish trial as historically authentic. Fredriksen is willing to "relinquish the effort to see the Sanhedrin trial as history."[67] The Gospels themselves "make clear that none of Jesus' followers were close enough to hear what went on. Therefore, any accounts of these proceedings must represent inferences of later Christians."[68] Perhaps the time has come to regard it as a fiction.

Were the rules or some of the rules governing capital crimes known when the Gospels were written? What might give us reason to think so? First, the Ninth Commandment was presumably known. Because many Mishnaic rules concerned eliminating false witness, we can assume that the idea was known. Second, Luke introduced his Gospel with the remark that, "Since many have undertaken to set down an orderly account of the events that have been fulfilled among us . . . I . . . decided . . . to write an orderly account for you . . . that you may know the truth concerning the things about which you have been instructed" (1:1–4). In his own way, Luke was a critical historian who regarded other accounts as disorderly. On every point where Mark describes the trial as breaking Jewish law, Luke corrects Mark. According to Luke, the trial took place in the daytime, not at night (22:66). Where Mark describes the chief priests and the council as seeking testimony against Jesus (Mark 14:55), Luke does not. Where Mark claims that "many gave false testimony against him, and their testimony did not agree" (Mark 14:56), Luke is silent. Where Mark's witnesses claim to have heard Jesus promise to destroy the Temple (Mark 14:57–58), Luke's do not. When Mark's high priest accuses Jesus (14:60), Luke's does not. When Mark's high priest declaims, "You have heard his blasphemy!" (14:64), Luke's does not. Luke refers to no conviction, nor to a rending of garments. Nor does Luke mention mistreatment of Jesus during the trial. Matthew agreed that contradictory evidence was invalid and so edited out of his account those claims (cf. Mark 14:59 with Matt. 26:61–62). These instances give us a second reason to think that the more important Mishnaic rules were known in the latter part of the first century.

A third reason is John's Gospel, which totally eliminates the Jewish trial from its story. Nor is Jesus in John ever accused of blasphemy. Rather, in John the high priest "questioned Jesus about his disciples and about his teaching" (18:19). Then the high priest sent Jesus to Pilate, who wanted to know whether Jesus was "the King of the Jews" (18:33). In John, this is *the* question. "On balance," states Fredriksen, "John's account seems more credible."[69] John gives a different reason for the role of some Jewish leaders in the execution of Jesus:

> So the chief priests and the Pharisees called a meeting of the council, and said, "What are we to do? This man is performing many signs. If we let him go on like this, every one will believe in him, and the Romans will come and destroy both our holy place and our nation." But one of them, Caiaphas, who was high priest that year, said to them, "You know nothing at all! You do not understand that it is better for you to have one man die for the people than to have the whole nation destroyed" (John 11:47–50).

Fear that Rome would destroy the Temple and the nation was quite realistic. Rome had often taken highly punitive action and would later raze the Temple. The question before Pilate is apparent: insurrection. In all four Gospels he wants to know of Jesus one thing: "Are you the king of the Jews?" (Mark 15:2; Matt. 27:11; Luke 23:3). It was not necessary that Jesus had actually been an insurrectionist for Pilate to have wanted to get rid of him. All that was necessary (and sufficient) was that Pilate, who was very nervous about such matters, *think* that Jesus was inclined to revolution against Rome.[70] E. P. Sanders points out that in the Roman period pilgrimage to Jerusalem "had political implications. The pilgrimage festivals, as times of national remembrance, were prime occasions for social, political and economic protest." Pilate would have been alert to such possibilities and quick to put them down. The Temple was a tax-collection center for Rome; whatever Jesus did in "cleansing" it could well have been viewed as inciting an uprising. Temples in the ancient world had enormous wealth, "both their own and private money deposited there for security."[71] James D. G. Dunn remarks that "the Temple was undoubtedly Jerusalem's main source of revenue."[72] Jesus had a following, talked in terms of a new kingdom and a new order, entered Jerusalem in messianic fashion, and engaged in a demonstration at the Temple (as had Judas Maccabaeus before him). Josephus and Philo point out that Pilate did not waste time on the details of the law. "Were Jesus in this category of perceived troublemakers, his execution would have followed very swiftly upon his arrest."[73] He was crucified for concentrating on what was important to prophets of Jewish national restoration: the people, the land, Jerusalem, the Torah, the Temple.

Jesus and Unrepentant Sinners

At this point, we need to look at the possibility that Jesus "could have been accused of being a friend of people who indefinitely *remained* sinners." E. P. Sanders regards this charge as explaining the offense that Jesus gave to some mainline Jewish groups. Sanders does not think that any body of Jewish leaders would have been offended at a proclamation of God's readiness to forgive repentant sinners. Nonetheless, presuming that at least some Jewish leaders must have been offended at Jesus on grounds other than his proclamation of the reign of God, Sanders postulates that it must have been Jesus' inclusion of unrepentant sinners. "If Jesus, by eating with tax collectors, led them to repent, repay those whom they had robbed, and leave off practicing their profession, he would have been a national hero."[74] Although Sanders does a tremendous job of dismissing silly comment on Jesus and sinners, he is on this point less convincing. He is trying to find grounds that would have led some Jews to cooperate with a Roman execution of Jesus. Not only do we have sufficient grounds for such offense in the realistic Jewish fear of Roman reprisal against the community for not controlling its independent-sounding members, but also we are hard put to find evidence that Jesus associated with unrepentant sinners and tax collectors.

Three points are pertinent here. First, "everybody (*except the Romans*) would have favoured the conversion of tax collectors and other traitors to the God of Israel."[75] The Romans would definitely have disapproved of such activity, and it would have given them one more reason to charge Jesus with insurrection. Second, it is unclear how Jesus himself (or the earliest layer of the tradition) thought of the sinners with whom Jesus supposedly associated. Sometimes he justifies associating with them because they are *not* sinners; his true family are those who do the will of God (Mark 3:35). At others, Jesus justifies his behavior by declaring that it is not the healthy who need a physician but those who are sick (Mark 2:17). And at other times, he justifies his behavior by saying that no one should take offense at him because the kingdom of God has come (Matt. 11:5); the deaf hear, the blind see, and so forth.[76]

Third, there is not a lot of evidence to go on with regard to tax collectors and sinners. John never mentions Jesus' associations with "tax collectors and sinners." In Mark 2:13–17 and its parallels in Matthew 9:9–13 and Luke 5:27–32, there is a story of Jesus sitting at table with "tax collectors and sinners," and in Q (Matt. 11:16-19 and Luke 7:31-35) another story involving Jesus and "tax collectors and sinners." Otherwise, we find that Matthew has three mentions of "tax collectors and sinners," which he has redacted into Q or Mark (Matt. 5:46; 10:3; 18:17) and one in a parable unique to Matthew (21:28-32). In the parable, the "tax collectors and harlots" repent and therefore are not really sinners; otherwise, they serve as negative examples (5:46), or tax collectors become apostles, or (in a formulation of the church) as an example of one to be excluded from the community. In Luke, the first mention of tax collectors in relation to Jesus is redacted into Q and they are said to have "acknowledged the justice of God, because they had been baptized with John's baptism" (7:29). Another says that "the tax collectors and sinners were coming near to listen to him" (15:1), and is followed by an accusation from the Pharisees that he "welcomes sinners and eats with them." Three more references occur in the parable of the Pharisee and the tax collector (18:9-14), which is a good example of Pharisaic self-criticism. The last occurrence is in the story of Zacchaeus, who is pronounced saved by Jesus for his repentance and good works (19:1-10). The reason for Zacchaeus' salvation is that "he too is a son of Abraham" (19:9), an indication of Jesus' mission to the lost sheep of the house of Israel.

We are left with two stories about Jesus' association with tax collectors and sinners (for which the texts attribute three divergent explanations to Jesus). The first is Mark 2:13-17 and its parallels, the story of the call of Levi (Matthew) to be an apostle. In Mark (and Matthew) he is "sitting at the tax booth" (2:14); in Luke, he becomes "a tax collector" (5:27). He responds affirmatively to Jesus' "Follow me." The story says that as Jesus sat at table in Levi's house with tax collectors and sinners, the "scribes of the Pharisees" asked why he ate with them, and he answered: "Those who are well have no need of a physician, but those who are sick; I have come to call not the righteous but sinners" (Mark 2:17). Luke adds that he calls them "to repentance" (5:32), but this is implicit in what it means to be called of God in Israel's story. This story cannot support a claim that Jesus associated with unrepentant sinners; it could support a claim that he thought them sick and in need of restoration to the community of Israel. That Pharisees would have thought that Jesus should not have engaged them strains the historical imagination.

The last account of tax collectors and sinners occurs in Luke 7:31-35 and Matthew 11:16-19. In it, which follows Jesus' claim that "among those born of women no one is greater than John" the Baptist, Jesus says: "For John the Baptist has come eating no bread and drinking no wine, and you say, 'He has a demon'; the Son of Man has come eating and drinking, and you say, 'Look, a glutton and a drunkard, a friend of tax collectors and sinners!' Nevertheless, wisdom is vindicated by all her children" (Luke 7:33–35). Here the claim that Jesus associated with tax collectors and sinners is placed in the mouths of his opponents as part of a threefold accusation. The first is directed at John the Baptizer: "He has a demon." The text does not intend for its readers to regard this explanation of John's activity as true. The second is directed at Jesus: "a glutton and a drunkard." The text does not intend for its readers to regard this accusation as true; no biblical scholar has claimed that Jesus was an alcoholic. The third is also directed at Jesus: "a friend of tax collectors and sinners." Many biblical scholars take this accusation as the gospel-truth, not noticing the inconsistency involved in doing so while discounting the other two. It has no greater claim to truth-status than the claim that John did what he did because he had a demon or the claim that Jesus was a boozer. Sanders may be right that Jesus accepted unrepentant sinners into his community, but it is very difficult to see how we could know this to have been so and easy to see how little evidence there is for it.[77] It is too thin a claim on which to base grounds for Jewish offense at Jesus. Nor is it necessary to account for why some Jews, whether those who collaborated with Rome or leaders who feared for the fate of the whole people, may have concluded that it was best to get Jesus out of the way.[78]

Jesus and the Lost Sheep of Israel

He said to her [the Syrophoenician woman], "Let the children be fed first, for it is not fair to take the children's food and throw it to the dogs" (Mark 7:24–30; parallel in Matt. 15:21–28).

Matthew has Jesus introduce this story with the statement "I was sent only to the lost sheep of the house of Israel" (Matt. 15:24). In the story of the sending out of the Twelve in Matthew, Jesus charged them: "Go nowhere among the Gentiles, and enter no town of the Samaritans, but go rather to the lost sheep of the house of Israel" (10:5–6). Why would these indications that Jesus' mission was "only to the lost sheep of the house of Israel" embarrass the churches that produced the Gospels? Because each Gospel is strongly concerned with the mission to the Gentiles. In Mark, this is clear in his references to the conversion of Gentiles: "The good news must first be proclaimed to all nations" (13:10); the elect are "from the ends of the earth" (13:27); "the good news is proclaimed in the whole world" (14:9). Numerous references to Gentiles occur in the miracle stories of chapters 5 and 7. The Gerasenes are Gentiles, the Decapolis is composed of Greek cities, the woman is a Greek, and the healing of the deaf mute happens in the Decapolis. "Mark is using a cycle of stories developed in the Gentile mission, but that he uses them shows his interest in that mission."[79] At the conclusion of Mark, a Gentile centurion confesses that Jesus is the Son of God (15:39). James D. G. Dunn concludes that the Markan universalistic passage (13:10) "is almost certainly an interpretative addition by Mark (or his source), with a view to the expanding Gentile mission."[80]

Matthew, too, is a Gospel committed to the Gentile mission and ends with the Great Commission in which the risen Jesus commands his followers to "make disciples of all nations" (28:19). Luke is a part of the same mission and, in Acts, ends with Paul declaring to "the Jews" that, because their ears were "hard of hearing," "this salvation of God has been sent to the Gentiles; they will listen" (Acts 28:28).

However, the issue is not easy to resolve. Numerous passages have Jesus including Gentiles in his concern: the banquet parables in Matthew 22:1–10 and Luke 14:16–24 may express an outreach to Gentiles. Jesus is depicted as saying that "many will come from east and west and will eat with Abraham and Isaac and Jacob in the kingdom of heaven, while the heirs of the kingdom will be thrown into the outer darkness" (Matt. 8:11–12; Luke 13:28–29), although this could be a retrojection into Jesus' teaching of the later church's supersessionist views.

Opposed to these are passages that restrict the work of Jesus or the apostles to the people Israel or show Jesus as reluctant to deal with Gentiles. Some scholars find little solid evidence for Jesus' activity among Gentiles.[81] Passages that indicate such activity could have been retrojected into Jesus' career by the later church. On the other hand, the limitation of the disciples' mission to Israel could derive "from a section of the Palestinian church which itself opposed the Gentile mission." E. P. Sanders concludes that we cannot know what Jesus' stance was toward the Gentiles. Jesus' own followers did not participate in a Gentile mission, but the Jesus movement came "*to see the Gentile mission as a logical extension of itself.*"[82]

We may doubt how "logically" this happened. Paul had to go to Jerusalem some twenty years after the career of Jesus and defend his Gentile mission. Although his going to the Gentiles was agreed to by the leaders of the Jerusalem church, they continued to go "to the circumcised" (Gal. 2:9). Paul himself claimed that "Christ has become a servant of the circumcised on behalf of the truth of God in order that he might confirm the promises given to the patriarchs" (Rom. 15:8). Also, Acts reports that "those who were scattered because of the persecution that took place over Stephen traveled as far as Phoenicia, Cyprus, and Antioch, and they spoke the word to no one except Jews" (Acts 11:19).

Other scholars think that Jesus limited his mission to Jews: Jesus' "apparent antipathy toward Gentiles" may be explained by a "Galilean chauvinism" on his part.[83] Jesus "systematically avoids the Greek cities," never going into them but visiting only their neighborhoods.[84] Dunn notices that Jesus "did not go out looking for Gentiles or encourage preaching the good news of the kingdom to Gentiles," although he thinks that Jesus "responded positively to Gentiles who approached him with faith."[85] "Jesus sent those messengers on a mission to houses," argues Crossan, "establishing a rural rather than an urban mission."[86] The towns in which Jesus is reportedly most active (e.g., Capernaum) were "relatively untouched by any deep cultural syncretism with Greek culture."[87] Sepphoris is an important Greek city located just a few miles from Nazareth; it never appears in the Gospels. Nor do the Gospels tell of Jesus visiting Tiberias on the Sea of Galilee, an important Roman outpost named for the emperor who had it built during Jesus' lifetime. Bernard Lee concludes that the Synoptics provide no warrant for the claim "that Jesus has a sense of mission to the Gentiles." He understands the story of the Syrophoenician woman as reflecting the complicated process by which an originally Jewish-Christian movement eventually embraced a mission to the Gentiles.[88]

In stories involving Gentiles in Q the point "is not to exemplify a mission to Gentiles, but to challenge (or embarrass) Jews/Israel into fuller response." Q indicates neither any actual Gentile belief in Jesus nor any evidence that such belief should be understood "as a sign of condemnation for Israel." Rather, the Q people regard themselves as the fulfillment of Israel's hopes, according to which Israel is undergoing restoration, "with the disciples in the role of . . . establishing justice for the people."[89] Yet this restored Israel is not closed to Gentiles; the synagogues were open to Gentile God-fearers, and Jesus may have run into Gentiles there.

Jesus was concerned with his own people, Israel, a point that contradicts the interpretation of his life and teachings as a life lived and teachings taught against Jews and Judaism. The fundamental hope in first-century Jewish restoration theology "was for the restoration of the people."[90] Horsley and Charlesworth regard the directives of Jesus to his disciples to go to the lost sheep of the house of Israel as "extremely early or originally from Jesus himself."[91] The Gentile-mission churches would not have invented them. They are entirely consonant with the understanding of Jesus' relation to John the Baptizer previously articulated. A sign of interest in the restoration of the people was Jesus' appointment of "the twelve" disciples as "symbolic of the restoration of the twelve tribes of Israel."[92] He who would later become a "light to the nations" must first "raise up the tribes of Jacob" (Isa. 49:6).

That the earliest tradition remembers Jesus' mission as directed to all the lost sheep of the tribe of Israel indicates that this was an inclusive mission. That this was so probably accounts for what conflicts there may have been between Jesus and the more well known movements in Judaism at the time, such as the Pharisees. If he was opposed to them, that opposition most likely was to what Dunn calls their "factionalism," drawing boundaries within the people of God. His protest would have been in the prophetic tradition, which criticized "Israel's presumption and tendency to spiritual arrogance . . . , but still all within characteristic Jewish terms."[93] His movement thus reflected Israel's fundamental hermeneutical axiom that the love of God is freely offered to each and all, and that each and all are in turn commanded to love God with all their hearts and their neighbors as themselves. Paul would later press this inclusive logic further, arguing that both Gentiles and Jews are fellow citizens and joint heirs of the kingdom of God.

The Lost Sheep

Blessed are you who are poor,
for yours is the kingdom of God.
Blessed are you who are hungry now,
for you will be filled.
Blessed are you who weep now,
for you will laugh.
(Luke 6:20–21; Matt. 5:3–6)

Who were the lost sheep of the house of Israel, and why is there such emphasis in the Gospels on the poor, hungry, and despairing? Roughly 90 percent of the people in Galilee and Judea in the first century were peasants; the rise of liberation theology and interest in base communities in Latin America spurs us to look at the "Israelite and Jewish peasantry which figures so prominently in biblical history." Roman rule in the first century produced much social turmoil and revolt. Jesus lived among the peasantry in a time of upheaval and cannot be understood apart from this context. His stories reveal two economic classes, the rich man with his steward and the peasantry who owe debts of a hundred measures of oil or wheat, the king and two debtors, the prodigal son in a peasant economy with a few hired servants and a single animal kept for a special feast. In such an economy, the poor produce "surpluses" that are commanded by the rich; conflict between the two is inevitable. The parable of the vineyard (Mark 12:1–9) "only too well exemplifies the tensions in such a society, with its violent confrontation between the resentful tenants and the owner of the vineyard."[94] Yet the peasants have memories and hopes that tell them who they are—members of a society ruled, not unjustly by Caesar and his intermediaries, but justly and by God.

Under imperial rule, the high priests "became the administrators of the government, and the high priest himself emerged as the head of Judean society."[95] They had custody of the Temple treasury, and the Temple served as a tax bank as well as worship center. "The temple tax from Jews all over the empire was coming into Jerusalem at just this time of Passover (turning the Temple area into something like an Internal Revenue Service center on April 15)."[96] The Temple functioned as a tax-collection agency controlled by a foreign, imperial government; the peasants had to pay religiously authorized taxes in its support. Because the high priest was accountable for collecting the taxes, the people came to see its mediator with God "collaborating closely with a foreign, pagan empire."[97] The objection Jews had to Rome's collection of the "head tax," a civil tax, was that it amounted to idolatry. Josephus tells of an open revolt by some Pharisees over the payment of the head ("capitation") tax.[98] Jesus' question to those who asked whether it was "lawful," according to the Torah, to pay it, elicited from him the counterquestion: "'Whose head is this, and whose title?' They answered, 'The emperor's'" (Matt. 22:15–22 and parallels). Each Caesar minted his own coins, including his picture and an inscription. His response that they should render to Caesar what is Caesar's and to God what is God's is construed by Philip Culbertson as a form of "covert civil disobedience," according to which "a coin with neither power nor authority is returned to a government with neither power nor authority."[99] The memory that the people should be governed by God alone meant that Roman rule was totally unacceptable and the tribute paid to Rome was idolatry.

Meanwhile, the peasants were driven into debt, risking a complete loss of land. Landedness in the Bible meant justice, security, and peace; landlessness was the situation of the people in Egypt, in the wilderness, and in exile. There was to be no landlessness in Israel, no homelessness, no destitute poverty.[100] There were provisions in the Torah to prevent loss of land through indebtedness, for the release of debts and debt-slaves every seven years (Ex. 21:2; Deut. 15:1–18; Lev. 25:35–42), and the (at least proposed) Jubilee Year in which everybody could return to the family inheritance (Lev. 25:8–24). Jesus, according to Luke, revived these hopes amid poverty and landlessness in his sermon in Nazareth: "He has anointed me to bring good news to the poor, . . . to proclaim release to the captives and . . . to let the oppressed go free, to proclaim the year of the Lord's favor" (Luke 4: 18b–19).

Wealth piles up among the priestly class in Jerusalem, increasing peasant indebtedness and resentment against an occupying power and its priest/banker intermediaries. Throw into this brew occasional drought and famine, and the religious conviction that things ought to be radically otherwise, and one has a people less than willing to "render unto Caesar," particularly when what Caesar wanted properly belonged to God. E. P. Sanders, who disagrees with the scholars cited in this discussion, nevertheless admits that "the people were hard pressed. . . . The wealthy did not sit down each night and try to devise ways of making the peasantry more comfortable."[101] The burden of taxation and indebtedness meant, among other things, the breakdown of patriarchy. Each family and village was organized by way of generations of the same "house" living and working on the land held by the father. "The social structure was patriarchal." The father was head of the family; the elders were head of the village. One result of the economic exploitation effected by Rome through the high priesthood "would have been a breakdown in the traditional patriarchal authority." The rise in landlessness and in day laborers (present in some parables) is symptomatic of such a breakdown. The Jesus movement was probably a "community without hierarchy," whose members were encouraged to sustain "egalitarian social relations by not reverting to the traditional hierarchies by which the chain of domination had been maintained."[102] At the top of the system stood the Temple, Rome's tax bank. Whatever Jesus intended by his demonstration there, it is not difficult to see it as a "prophetic act symbolizing God's imminent judgmental destruction, not just of the building, but of the Temple system."[103] Had Jesus merely attacked the money-changers, his action would have lacked practical significance, because they were necessary to the Temple sacrifices themselves. "Overturned tables symbolize not purification but destruction."[104] Nor is this direct political rebellion, but an enactment of a future apocalyptic destruction of the Temple by God. Jesus' action in the Temple can be more concretely viewed now that we recognize its role in the politics and economy of the time. His behavior announced to the poor, hungry, and despairing that their liberation was at hand, that God's kingdom approached. No matter how apolitically and nonmilitarily Jesus may have meant it, Pilate was likely to have been upset. Jesus was committed to the restoration of the life of the people Israel under God and the Torah.

Jesus' Parables

To further situate Jesus in the Judaisms of his time, we must look at his parables, which have often been given an anti-Jewish interpretation. Indeed, they may have been redacted by the Gospel writers with a view to doing precisely this. "The evangelists surely added a church vs. nonchurch bite to Jesus' parables."[105] The process of interpreting Jesus' parables in an anti-Jewish way began early. To Mark's parable of the wicked tenants (12:1–12), Matthew added this interpretation: "Therefore I tell you, the kingdom of God will be taken away from you and given to a people that produces the fruits of the kingdom" (Matt. 21:43). Jesus, Christians said, used this parable to lay bare the murderous extremes to which Jews were able to go in resisting God; finally, they murdered God's beloved son. Consequently, God abandoned Israel and transferred the covenant to the church. John Chrysostom, presbyter of Antioch in the fifth century, offered such a reading of the parable of the wicked tenants (Mark 12:1–11 and parallels).

> Many things does he intimate by this parable: (a) that God's providence had been exercised towards them [the Jews] from the first; (b) that their disposition was murderous from the beginning; (c) that nothing had been omitted [by God] relative to a needful care of them; (d) that even when the prophets had been slain, he [YHWH] had not turned away from them, but had sent his very Son; (e) that the God of both the New and Old Testament[s] was one and the same; (f) that his death should effect great blessings; (g) that for the crucifixion, their crime, they were to endure extreme punishment: the calling of the Gentiles and the casting out of the Jews.[106]

We learn how to interpret the parables of Jesus appropriately by locating them in the context of rabbinic parables. Story parables (as distinct from fables with talking animals) appear only in Jewish literature and the Gospels. The story parable "is not fully paralleled elsewhere and seems to be an inner Jewish accomplishment from the Second Temple period." There are some 1,300 rabbinic parables, and scholarly study of them discloses "a remarkable similarity between gospel parables and those of the rabbis."[107] Rabbinic parables and Jesus' parables have a similar form: the body of the story, called the *mashal*, and the interpretation or application, called the *nimshal*.[108] The *nimshal* may vary from context to context or may be revised, dropped, or another may replace it, giving the parable a different interpretation. We saw Matthew add a *nimshal* to Mark's parable of the wicked husbandmen. Such a *nimshal* may serve the purposes of the community for which the *mashal* is retold, but not reflect the point of the earlier telling. "In analyzing the parables of Jesus, then, we are forced to ask in relation to each parable: Who attached the nimshal in the Gospel to the mashal? Did Jesus? The Gospeller? Christian tradition? Or is it accidentally misplaced from a different mashal?" Also, a *mashal* itself may be differently told in order to vary its point. Philip Culbertson finds that each *nimshal* that Matthew adds to his three vineyard parables has an anti-Jewish force to it. If we strip away these *nimshalim* as Matthew's additions, we find (a) that the remaining *meshalim* "have no inherently anti-Jewish content," (b) that the *nimshalim* would have made no sense to

Jesus' Jewish listeners, and (c) that each vineyard parable in Matthew consists of a *mashal* derived from the tradition with a newer *nimshal* attached. Rather than interpreting the parables anti-Jewishly, it is "more consistent with the Jewish identity of Jesus to link the three parables together as a message of comfort to the Jewish people in a time of crisis and upheaval."[109]

Study of rabbinic parables helps us understand the content of Jesus' parables and the way they would have been heard by his listeners. "Jesus' hearers were acquainted with rabbinic parables and easily recognized what Jesus meant."[110] Indeed, Jesus' parables achieve their full range of significance only from their Jewish setting.[111] In Jewish parables that take as their motif human life, the proprietor signifies God, and the consignment of property "means a gracious loan from Him, being entrusted yet never a possession of ours at our discretion."[112] All rabbinic parables are "*'abbatic-'amonic*. In some parables, the *'abba* (the beloved father-king) is in the foreground, in others the *'amon* (the exclusively beloved child); in others both are equally emphasized."[113] Rabbinic parables are always ethically oriented (God's grace should lead to a radically transformed life), and quite a number deal with the salvation history of Israel (God's grace freely offered to Israel).

Jesus—A Servant of the God of Israel

In spite of the complex ways in which the Gospels portray Jesus' relation to Jewish faith, they make it quite clear that he is to be understood as a servant of the God of Israel and hence of the Israel of God. Nowhere is this clearer than in the story of the temptation of Jesus in the wilderness (Matt. 4:1–11; Luke 4:1–13). Here, as Matthew and Luke relate the story, he was "tempted by the devil," who placed before Jesus a threefold enticement. The devil sought to beguile Jesus into commanding a stone to become bread, into accepting from the devil "all the kingdoms of the world," over which the devil promised to give him authority, and into throwing himself off the peak of the Temple, with the promise that God's angels would be sent to bear him up "so that you will not dash your foot against a stone."

To each of these temptations Jesus is said to have responded by quoting scripture: "It is written, 'One shall not live by bread alone.'" "It is written, 'Worship the Lord your God, and serve only him.'" "It is said [Matthew has "written"], 'Do not put the Lord your God to the test.'" Each of Jesus' three responses to temptation is a quotation from Deuteronomy (respectively from Deut. 8:3b, 6:13, and 6:16, following the Lukan order).[114] These citations from Deuteronomy come from a section of that book which opens with the *Shema*: "Hear, O Israel: The LORD is our God, the LORD alone," and the commandment, "You shall love the LORD your God with all your heart, and with all your soul, and with all your might" (6:4–5). The Deuteronomic narrative goes on to remind Israel of the grace of Yahweh in bringing Israel forth out of the bondage of slavery in Egypt and into the land of promise, where Yahweh made to the Israel of God the further gift of the Torah "for our lasting good" (6:24). And the reason why Yahweh did this was "not because you were more numerous than any other people," but "because the LORD loved you and kept the oath that he swore to your ancestors, that the LORD has brought you out with a mighty hand, and redeemed you from the house of slavery" (7:7–8).

Jesus' victory over the temptation of the devil is achieved by recalling the covenant between the God of Israel and the Israel of God and by observing the terms of it: He will live by the word of the God of Israel, worship only the God of Israel, and will not tempt the God of Israel. Jesus will not place himself above the commandments, the Torah, of the God of Israel. He came, as Paul contended, as "a servant of the circumcised on behalf of the truth of God in order that he might confirm the promises given to the patriarchs" (Rom. 15:8), to which Paul added "and in order that the Gentiles might glorify God for his mercy" (15:9).

Jesus—A Galilean Jew

"Teacher" (*didaskalos*) is how Jesus is addressed in the Gospels, over sixty times; sometimes this is explicitly stated as "rabbi," which at the time of Jesus expressed esteem but did not have its later, technical meaning. *Yeshua* is his name in Aramaic (*Joshua* in Hebrew), a name that means "Yahweh is salvation." That we no longer use the name *Yeshua* "tends to cut Christians off from the taproot of their religion, the Hebrew-Jewish tradition."[115] *Ha Notsri* is where he came from, Nazareth. *Yeshua ha Notsri:* this is how we speak of Jesus in context. Many Christians fail to note that his name is a theological claim that puts us on notice as to the One with whom we have to do when we have to do with Jesus.

What is not the case with regard to *Yeshua ha Notsri,* a teacher in Israel, is important. It is not the case that he disagreed in any significant way with the Torah in Second Temple Judaism and certainly not in any way that would lead to his death (those who know the least about Second Temple Judaism find a lot of conflict between Jesus and "the Law"; those who know the most do not).[116] On this subject a Jewish scholar, speaking cautiously, commented: "Jesus ben Joseph, the teacher from

Nazareth, was not an antinomian. He cherished the Jewish tradition and taught his disciples to follow it. Although in certain respects his teachings may have been distinctive, in their form and for the most part in their content they were in line with the Pharisaic/proto-rabbinic understanding of the law, as far as we can reconstruct it."[117] If Jesus had any major conflicts with the Torah, he failed to communicate them to his disciples. Nor did Jesus have any conflicts with the Pharisees over *whether* to keep the Torah. With regard to *how* to keep it, he and they may have disagreed over what he regarded as their factionalism. (They, of course, would have looked at it differently, perhaps wondering why they should play into the hands of Antiochus and Caligula by yielding on the point of Jewish identity.) Yet many of the conflict-stories in the Gospels are retrojections into the life of Jesus of debates between late first-century Christians and the Pharisees in the synagogue across the street.[118]

Jesus was a Galilean (that is, non-Judean) Jew, committed to the "lost sheep of the house of Israel," a wandering teacher committed to the renewal of Jewish life under the Torah. Many of his teachings took a form quite close to that of the contemporary liberal Pharisaic school of Hillel. "The sabbath was made for humankind, and not humankind for the sabbath" (Mark 2:27) has a familar ring in Jewish ears: "Scripture says: 'The Sabbath is holy for *you*' (Exodus 31:14). This means that it is given to you, not you to the Sabbath."[119] Jesus was a Galilean *hasid* who healed and exorcised and commanded the weather. Like the Pharisees but unlike the Sadducees, he believed strongly in the age to come, the new era in which the God of Israel, not Caesar, would reign; Jesus apparently thought that the new age would come "soon," but in eschatological talk "soon" does not mean "real quick." It means that history is in a deep crisis.

Jesus did not proclaim himself, but the good news of the coming reign of God. The Synoptics never have Jesus make any declarations about himself. His statements about the "Son of man" are in the third person. After his death and resurrection, the disciples began to proclaim him: "The Jesus who *has* a message changes into the Christ who *is* the message."[120] It needs to be emphasized that in the Judaisms of his time and later there never was *one* coherent understanding of "the messiah." John P. Meier notes that "the designation 'Messiah' in 1st-century Judaism was vague, ill-defined, and open to many interpretations."[121] In the first century, messianic expectation took several forms: that of the priest-messiah, who would restore the priesthood itself to its proper status; that of the prophet-messiah, a final prophet similar to Moses (the greatest prophet), who would lead his people out of bondage; that of the hidden-and-revealed-messiah, who would be unaware of his future dignity until his actual anointing; and that of the slain-messiah, who would die on the eschatological battlefield.[122] Nor did Judaism ever develop one doctrine of the messiah; rabbinic literature "presents no well-crafted doctrine of the Messiah."[123] There never was a single Judaism, hence, no single view of the messiah: "'The Messiah' is an all but blank screen onto which a given community would project its concerns." The messiah was pictured as "whatever people most wanted—king, savior, wonder-worker, perfect priest, invincible general, or teacher."[124] "The messiah" is a construct that can be found in no one place in rabbinic literature. "The messiah" means "the anointed." When we ask "the anointed what?" no clear answer is forthcoming. To claim that Jesus radically transformed *the* Jewish notion of the messiah is unwarranted.

4

The Triumph of Grace
in Paul's Theology

God's covenant with the Jewish People has not been
rescinded or abrogated, but remains in full force, inasmuch as "the gifts and the call of God are irrevocable"
(Rom. 11:29).

—*The United Church of Christ Sixteenth General Synod, 1987*

A new paradigm for reading and interpreting Paul is emerging at the
hands of biblical scholars. Although scholarly literature on Paul is so ex-
tensive as to make dealing with it a virtual impossibility for anyone other
than a specialist, we will consider five of these alternative interpretations
of Paul in recent scholarship. Of them, the first appears the least probable
and the last the most probable, although it is not argued that the three
middle types carry with them increasing degrees of probability. Rather,
they cumulatively contribute to a new paradigm for interpreting Paul.

Perspectives on Paul

The first of these five ways of interpreting Paul's relation to the Torah
and to the covenant of God with the Jewish people is familiar and traditional. This approach holds that Paul rejects Judaism as such. This view
is characteristic of much Protestant, particularly Lutheran, scholarship
and tends to read Luther's conflict with the medieval church back into
Paul as Paul's conflict with Judaism. The other four are revisionist. The
first revisionist approach contends that Paul affirms Judaism and rejects
Judaizing, that he is concerned with the inclusion of Gentiles on equal
terms in his congregations, not with the exclusion of Judaism.[1] A second
revisionist approach argues that Paul rejects Judaism, not because he
finds anything wrong with it, but simply because it is not Christianity.[2]

The third maintains that contradiction and inconsistency are constant features of Paul's thought about these matters and that Paul did not realize that scripture was not on his side of the argument.[3] The fourth nontraditional way of understanding Paul resurrects the distinction between moral and ritual law; it regards Paul's conflict as with the ritual law (understood as the "identity markers" of Israel), which Paul regarded as limiting God's grace.[4] The first and fourth of these revisionist positions agree that God's continuing faithfulness to the people of Israel is a central rather than peripheral element of Paul's understanding of the gospel.

The four revisionist positions reject the traditional interpretation of Paul because they refuse the description of first-century Judaism on which it is based. Together they constitute a new perspective on Paul, although the significant disagreement among them indicates that just what this new perspective is has not yet been made clear and convincing. The purpose of this chapter is to discuss and assess the relative strengths and weaknesses of these perspectives on Paul, to see if one of these newer interpretations might be more adequate, and to try to articulate Paul's theological stance toward the Torah and God's covenant with the people Israel. We do this aware that the oldest comment on Paul's letters remains valid: "There are some things in them hard to understand" (2 Peter 3:16).

Paul the rejector of Judaism

We may take Ernst Käsemann, a highly reputed contemporary biblical scholar, as representative of the customary approach, concentrating on one essay in which the characteristic themes of his treatment of Paul and the Jews all come to expression.[5] He argues that Paul "sharpened" the anti-Semitism of the ancient world when he wrote of the Jews that they "killed both the Lord Jesus and the prophets, and drove us out; they displease God and oppose everyone by hindering us from speaking to the Gentiles so that they may be saved. Thus they have constantly been filling up the measure of their sins, but God's wrath has overtaken them at last" (1 Thess. 2:15–16).[6] Against this, Käsemann plays off as an antithesis what he regards as Paul's concern in Romans 11, "the winning of Israel for Christ." What unites these two concerns in Paul's theology is his commitment to and "experience of the justification of the ungodly." Käsemann interprets Paul in Philippians 3:4–9 as erecting "a boundary between himself and his own past—as the past of a devout Jew." It is precisely Paul's own life *as a devout Jew* that Paul now counts "as refuse." As a devout Jew, not as a Jew who misunderstood Jewish faith,

Paul "had been pursuing a righteousness of his own, only to find the pursuit rendered pointless when Christ revealed to him quite another righteousness as being God's will and salvation." Käsemann is claiming much more than that some Jews misunderstood their faith, or even that all Jews some of the time misunderstood their faith. Such statements, if they were what he means, are unobjectionable and apply with equal force to Christians. Käsemann is claiming that *devout* Jews necessarily misunderstand their faith as long as that faith remains devoutly Jewish. The lesson that only the godless are ever justified cannot be learned in Judaism: "So long as this lesson has not been learned at the foot of the Cross of Jesus, the godhead of God is not truly acknowledged and honoured: and in consequence man has not yet become human."[7]

Hence, Paul's real opponent "is the devout Jew, not only as the mirror-image of his own past—though that, too—but as the reality of the religious man." By "religion," Käsemann means "confusing an illusion with God." Paul sees precisely this confusion actualized in the devout Jew, because the devout Jew misunderstands the announcement of God's will "as a summons to human achievement and therefore as a means to a righteousness of one's own." This is the "root of sin"; Käsemann identifies the attitude of "the devout Jew" with "religion" and "religion" with "sin." "The devout Jew" confuses an illusion with God because the question "who is God?" can "*only* be answered from the Cross of the risen Jesus." Here and *not* from the literature of Israel (except as read in the light of the cross), we learn that God is the "enemy and judge of every human illusion—especially every pious illusion—which professes to exhibit to God saving works, to make claims, to glory in one's own achievement and to take comfort in one's own righteousness." This is why Paul comes into conflict with Israel. Instead, Israel (particularly devout Israel), connects righteousness with religious achievements and demonstrable possessions, such as circumcision and the patriarchs. Paul understands as Israel does not that righteousness can be ours only because we receive it daily from God as a gift.[8]

Käsemann sees the relationship between the covenants in a supersessionist fashion; Paul does not speak of a "*renewed*, but of a *new* covenant." Moses is the antitype of faith; Paul's hope for Israel is *not* built on the idea of a remnant. The relationship is discontinuous: "God's righteousness appears as creation out of nothing and as the resurrection of the dead." Devout Jews can become truly human only by accepting the fact that faith in the true God can be learned nowhere else than at the cross of the risen Christ, and that this faith contradicts the religion and illusion to which they are committed. Indeed, says Käsemann, Israel plays a representative role for Paul: "In and with Israel he strikes at the hidden Jew in all of us, at the man who validates rights and demands over against God on the basis of God's past dealings with him and to this extent is serving not God but an illusion." Yet, Jews will be saved precisely because the gospel is a gospel of the justification of the ungodly, which is "the only hope both of the world in general and also of Israel."[9]

Käsemann's argument has a long prehistory in Protestant biblical interpretation and is found in numerous other contemporary scholars as well. One is Matthew Black, who makes essentially the same claim as Käsemann. Quoting Romans 1:17 ("For in it the righteousness of God is revealed through faith for faith; as it is written, 'The one who is righteous will live by faith.'"), Black argues:

> The key to an understanding of Paul's essential thesis is his conviction of the total bankruptcy of contemporary Pharisaic "scholasticism," which seemed to base the whole range of active right relationships within the Covenant ("righteousness") on the meticulous observation of the injunctions of the torah as expanded in the "tradition of the elders." This was "legalistic righteousness," a form of ethics based entirely on a code, external and "written," losing sight entirely of the gracious personal will of a holy and good God, of which it was originally intended to be the divine vehicle of expression.[10]

Black regards Romans 3:21–26 as the *locus classicus* for Paul's "great thesis." The passage begins as follows: "But now, apart from law, the righteousness of God has been disclosed, and is attested by the law and the prophets, the righteousness of God through faith in Jesus Christ for all who believe." As Black reads Paul, this "thesis is developed against its antithesis, viz., the rabbinical doctrine of 'justification by works.' A basic assumption of contemporary rabbinical Judaism was that a man could be 'justified,' i.e., acquitted before the Judgment Seat of God, on the grounds of his performance of works of the Law."[11]

This traditional interpretation of Paul is only as good as the view of Judaism at Paul's time on which it rests. This view of Judaism as works-righteous, legalistic, confusing the illusion of a righteousness of one's own with the grace of God, is contradicted by Jewish scholars and Christian scholars of Judaism. Lester Dean writes: "When we Jews hear about Paul's description of Judaism as legalistic and based upon self-works, we are astounded. This is neither what we believe today, nor what is found in the Hebrew scriptures, nor what is found from any of the sources at the time of Paul."[12] George Foot Moore long ago analyzed a basic reorientation that had taken place in works produced by Christian writers on Judaism in the nineteenth century. He noted that through the eighteenth century, "Christian interest in Jewish literature had always been apologetic or polemic rather than historical." These writers intended to demonstrate from the "Old" Testament that Jesus was the fulfiller of its hopes, promises, and "predictions," veritably the Messiah and Son of God. Other significant motifs in their writings embraced

> the emancipation of Christians from the Mosaic law, or the annulment of the dispensation of the law altogether, or the substitution of the new law of Christ; the repudiation of the Jewish people by God for their rejection of Christ, and the succession of the church, the true Israel, the people of God, to all the prerogatives and promises once given to the Jews.[13]

The goal and means of Christian writers on Judaism shifted in the nineteenth century. These "later authors would have described their aim as historical—to exhibit the beliefs and teachings of Judaism in the New Testament times or in the early centuries of the Christian era." In spite of their new purpose, they utilized primarily the views of Judaism that they had inherited from their predecessors, "without giving sufficient consideration to the fact that it [these views] had been gathered for every conceivable purpose except to serve as material for the historian." About this way of doing history he notes that "a delectus of quotations made for a polemic purpose is the last kind of a source to which a historian would go to get a just notion of what a religion really was to its adherents."[14] Moore excoriated modern scholars for their biased interpretations of Judaism, for their one-sided use of Jewish sources, for their inadequacy, for an a priori attitude toward the Jewish sources, which attitude sought only to use them as a foil for its own self-validation, and for using a method that belittled everything Jewish and aggrandized everything Christian.

Charlotte Klein argues that a whole raft of contemporary Christian biblical scholars badly misunderstand matters of "law" and piety in early Judaism.[15] Fifty-six years after Moore's classic essay, E. P. Sanders published his *Paul and Palestinian Judaism*, in which he delineates the historical course of the "Weber/Schürer/Bousset description of Judaism." Here he shows that, among others, Conzelmann, Fuller, Bultmann, Billerbeck, Käsemann, and R. H. Charles continue to use the Weber model for interpreting Judaism. Sanders' description of Judaism presents a much-needed and unhackneyed approach, which moves him to conclude that "the Judaism of before 70 kept grace and works in the right perspective, did not trivialize the commandments of God, and was not especially marked by hypocrisy." He proceeds to note:

> The frequent Christian charge against Judaism . . . is not that some individual Jews misunderstood, misapplied and abused their religion, but that Judaism necessarily tends towards petty legalism, self-serving and

self-deceiving casuistry, and a mixture of arrogance and lack of confidence in God. But the surviving Jewish literature is as free of these characteristics as any I have ever read.

Rather, "the gift and demand of God were kept in a healthy relationship with each other . . . and humility before the God who chose and who would ultimately redeem Israel was encouraged."[16]

The work of such people as Moore and Sanders, however, has not yet altogether managed to relieve us of the standard description of Paul. The "Weber/Schürer/Bousset-model" of interpreting the Judaism that Paul opposed often results in the fact that Jews and Christians view Paul in identical terms, although obviously their respective evaluations of him radically diverge. As early as 1914, the Jewish scholar C. G. Montefiore pointed out three major differences between rabbinic Judaism and the religion that Paul was said to have rejected. Rabbinic Judaism understood the law as God's gracious gift to God's people, intended to teach them to live according to the "way of life," not the "way of death." Consequently, "the core and essence of the Rabbinic religion are contained in that one familiar phrase, 'the joy of the commandments.'" Second, repentance and God's forgiveness were readily available in rabbinic Judaism: "Let a man repent but a very little, and God will forgive very much. For He delights in the exercise of forgiveness far more than in the exercise of punishment." Third, Paul's theology was incredibly more gloomy than that of rabbinic Judaism, which would never have claimed that one lone transgression could account for bringing all people under the wrath of God.[17] Montefiore concluded that whatever Judaism Paul knew, it was not rabbinic.

Montefiore's successor, H. J. Schoeps, produced a study of Paul that is one of the more important contributions to scholarship on Paul in this century. Schoeps viewed Paul's understanding of Torah as law (*nomos*)—as a "sum of prescriptions to be kept," the doing of which would earn God's grace—as the most radical difference between Paul and the rabbis. This understanding of the Torah constitutes Paul's "fundamental misapprehension" of what Jews mean by "law," which they regard as "integral to the covenant."[18] Lester Dean labels this interpretation "Paul's 'Erroneous' Description of Judaism."[19] Israel's relation to God is essentially determined by the covenant of divine grace, of which Torah is the affirmation.

No wonder that "for the Jew, Paul is the apostate; for the Christian, he is the first great apostle of the gospel of the Son of God to the Gentiles." According to J. Christiaan Beker, the model of Paul as the originator of catholic Christianity was the model of Paul as having liberated Christianity "from its so-called Jewish limitations. Paul the catholic theologian was the 'universalist,' and the key to his achievement was his antipathy to everything Jewish." Says Beker: "Paul's catholicity was bought at the expense of his anti-Judaism: the more catholic, the more anti-Jewish." Beker also refers to and rejects the Weber/Schürer/Bousset "line of scholarship" that has "perverted many generations of Christian scholarship on Judaism." Toward the end of his magnificent study of Paul, he comments that "this popular picture of Paul as the originator of catholic dogma and the enemy of Judaism is completely erroneous."[20]

The old paradigm for reading Paul, which claims that Paul rejected Judaism as such, that the incident on the Damascus Road was his "conversion" from it, must be rejected for the following reasons. First, "there is no evidence for the existence of the Judaism that Paul, according to this theory, describes."[21] Jewish literature of the time views Israel's election and the giving of the Torah as God's gracious gift. Further, obedience to Torah "is the proper response to the gift of Torah, but it does not *earn* salvation as such."[22] When sin does occur, means of grace are provided whereby one can return to God. Nothing in historical Judaism matches the description given of it by the traditional perspective on Paul. Second, the traditional perspective fails to deal adequately with all of Paul's affirmative comments about the law. The law "is one of Israel's great privileges (Rom. 9:4), the key to decent community life (Gal. 5:14) and the standard for community behavior *even for Gentile Christians* (I Cor. 14:34). One *can*—and Paul did—attain righteousness under the Law (Phil. 3:6); and the Christian, too, though 'in the Spirit' and 'under grace,' must nevertheless follow it (e.g., Rom. 13:8ff.)." Nor does the traditional view take into account the seldom quoted statement of Paul: "Circumcision is nothing, and uncircumcision is nothing; but obeying the commandments of God is everything" (1 Cor. 7:19). Last, as Fredriksen comments, the traditional reading of Paul makes him morally incoherent, because "it holds that Paul believed in a God who gave a Law that he knew no one could possibly fulfill, or who condemned men for their zeal in fulfilling his own commandments."[23]

Paul the rejector of Judaizing

The first revisionist approach argues that Paul rejects not Judaism but Judaizing, that he was concerned with the inclusion of his Gentile converts in the church on equal terms with Jewish believers. Paul denied neither the legitimacy of Judaism nor the continuation of the covenant between God and the Jewish people.[24]

All revisionist approaches insist that Paul is to be interpreted solely on the basis of his own writings and that views attributed to Paul by Acts and the Pastoral Epistles, particularly when they contradict what Paul himself says in his authentic letters, must be discounted.[25] The "Paul rejects

Judaizing" paradigm insists on interpreting Paul in the light of his commitment to be an "apostle to the Gentiles." Paul's concern was not with salvation from his Jewish past, nor with justification by faith in the sense of an answer to the tortured wrestlings of a Luther with the "impossible" demands of the law.[26] Concomitant with this, the incident on the Damascus Road is not regarded as Paul's "conversion" from a now-intolerable Jewish past, but as his "call" to "proclaim him among the Gentiles" (Gal. 1:16). Those who deny that Paul was "converted" use the word in the sense of conversion from one religion to another: "The usual conversion model of Paul the Jew who gives up his former faith to become a Christian is not the model of Paul but of ours."[27] Krister Stendahl has pointed out the literary similarities between Paul's account of his call and those of several biblical prophets—for example, Jonah—who were commissioned to take the "way of life" to Gentiles. Interestingly, these prophets were given no word for Israel. A demurrer must be entered here. "Conversion" need not mean "transfer from one religion to another." All Methodists have heard the story of John Wesley's conversion, yet none thinks of him as having switched religions. What they think is that Wesley came into a deeper appropriation of the Christian faith. In this sense, we may speak of Paul's conversion.[28] Meanwhile, we are well advised to remember that at Paul's time the church and the synagogue were not yet separate. Followers of the Way were still a movement within the Judaisms of the first century. "Christians" did not yet call themselves "Christians" nor their religion "Christianity," a term missing from Paul and, but for one instance, from the New Testament.

Lloyd Gaston and others who articulate this revisionist approach insist that Paul's account of the meeting in Jerusalem is absolutely crucial to understanding him: "When James and Cephas and John, who were acknowledged pillars, recognized the grace that had been given to me, they gave to Barnabas and me the right hand of fellowship, agreeing that we should go to the Gentiles and they to the circumcised" (Gal. 2:9). Gaston contends that Paul "kept this agreement throughout his career, confining his preaching strictly to gentile God-fearers, and never encouraging Jews to abandon the Torah."[29] This is of a piece with what Paul says of his commissioning: "But when God, who had set me apart before I was born and called me through his grace, was pleased to reveal his Son to me, so that I might proclaim him among the Gentiles . . ." (Gal. 1:15–16). Paul was not authorized to preach among Jews and did not. His gospel was "for the uncircumcised" (Gal. 2:7). His letters bear this out, mentioning, as they do, Gentiles: "how you turned to God from idols, to serve a living and true God" (1 Thess. 1:9); "You know that when you were pagans, you were enticed and led astray to idols that could not speak" (1 Cor. 12:2); "beware of those who mutilate the flesh!" (Phil. 3:2); "Formerly, when you did not know God, you were enslaved to beings that by nature are not gods" (Gal. 4:8); "among all the Gentiles . . . including yourselves" (Rom. 1:5). Concludes Gaston: "Paul writes to gentile Christians, dealing with gentile-Christian problems, foremost among which was the right of gentiles *qua* gentiles, without adopting the Torah of Israel, to full citizenship in the people of God."[30]

Gaston argues that the concept of Torah had two meanings in early Judaism. Within the covenant it was understood under the rubric of grace. All Israel has a share in the world to come, and to be in the covenant is considered salvation. Outside the covenant, Torah functioned differently: *"For gentiles, who do not have the torah as covenant, Torah as law functions in an exclusively negative way, to condemn."*[31] Paul can speak of "law" in this second sense "as a power which oppresses Gentiles and from which they need to be redeemed."[32] Followers of Shammai would have been zealous for the law in this sense, and, on the basis of several passages where Paul speaks of his earlier life as one of being "zealous" for the law, Gaston identifies the early Paul as a Shammaite. Consequently, Gaston uses "Torah" to refer to the first sense of "law," and "law" to designate the second. He interprets passages in Paul that are negative on the law as having to do with the second sense of law, because in these passages (e.g., Gal. 3:21–4:11), the past of Gentiles is being discussed, not that of Jews. In this sense, Paul's Gentile followers are said to be no longer "under the law," but are now "under grace." It would make no sense to say of Gentiles who follow Jesus that they are no longer "under the Torah," because they never were under the Torah. Nor is the phrase "under the Torah" found in any Jewish writings of the time "to express relationship to Torah, but seems to have been used by Paul to designate the gentile situation." When Paul is most disapproving of "the law," "he opposes it to—the law, i.e., the Torah! Opposed to 'the other law, the law of sin' is 'the Torah of God'" (Rom. 7:22f.).[33]

Paul's argument with his fellow Jews "is never about Judaism as such but rather about a Jewish understanding of Gentiles."[34] Paul's contention was not with Judaism per se, but with forcing Judaism upon Gentiles, specifically forcing certain ritual requirements upon them, in order to allow them to be included in the people of God. Gaston makes much of Markus Barth's argument that the Pauline phrase "works of the law" alludes to the Gentile adoption of Jewish practices, not to the situation of Jews within the covenant.[35] John Gager has helpfully organized Gaston's position, which he calls "a new synthesis," into a series of propositions about Paul.[36]

First, Paul had no interest in disparaging the Torah for Israel but was committed to a "positive justification of the status of Gentile Christians." Second, Paul did not encourage Jews to abandon Torah for belief in Christ, and he was wrongly resisted by Jews if this is, indeed, why some Jews did resist him. Third, for Paul Jesus was not the messiah, nor a new Moses, but the one who confirmed God's promises to Abraham regarding the Gentiles. Fourth, Paul disagreed with his fellow Jews because they did not recognize his claim that "in Christ God had established the righteousness of Gentiles apart from the Torah," not because they were legalistic or lacked zeal for the Torah. Fifth, before his commissioning, Paul denied "that Gentiles could attain righteousness without assuming full responsibility for the Torah"; afterwards, he denied that Gentiles had to "assume any responsibility for the Torah *in order to establish their righteousness.*"[37] Sixth, given Paul's expectation of the imminent return of Jesus (see Rom. 8:18), both he and Jewish Christianity must be seen as a "bridge generation" before the end. Paul was not trying to establish a separate, ongoing religion.

A variation on the Gaston/Gager hypothesis has been offered by Francis H. Agnew, who argues that Paul's concerns were practical and pastoral in nature. He wanted to free his Gentile converts from the necessity of practicing the rite of circumcision or of abiding "by the dietary, purificatory, and liturgical aspects of the Hebrew law." In order to achieve this goal, Paul "devised a 'straw' adversary who represented not only the judaizing tendencies of his actual Jewish-Christian opponents but also the position of works-righteousness pushed to its logical humanizing extreme, thus allowing for the full explanation of the gratuity of salvation."[38] Agnew's argument has the merit of taking into account the nature of ancient rhetoric.

Jeffrey S. Siker's study of Paul's use of the figure of Abraham is a persuasive contribution to the Gaston/Gager paradigm. Siker argues that in Romans Paul invokes Abraham "to argue for Gentile inclusion on the one hand (4:16–18; 15:9), and to assert God's continued election of non-Christian Jews for the sake of God's promises to faithful Abraham, on the other hand (11:25–36; 15:8)." The significance of Romans lies in the fact that only in Romans does Paul deal with the issue of non-Christian Judaism. On Siker's analysis of Romans, Paul is concerned to rebut Gentile Christians in Rome "who appear to suggest that Jewish rejection of the Christ means Jewish exclusion from God's promises (11:13, 25)." Paul's response to them is to reassert "the place of non-Christian Jews within God's people (11:11–12, 28–32)." Paul's employment of Abraham in Romans is not to be confused with that in Galatians, where he avails himself of the figure of Abraham "to combat Jewish-*Christian* opponents who are preaching a rival gospel."[39]

This first version of the new paradigm for reading Paul, articulated by Gaston and others, has many strengths that make it attractive, and it doubtless moves the discussion ahead of the stalemate in which the traditional paradigm leaves things. It situates Paul and his letters in context, and whenever we are closer to the setting of texts, we find more reliable guidance in their interpretation. "The immediate context of the Pauline letters points irresistibly to an overwhelming preoccupation on Paul's part with the religious status of Gentiles in relation to the Torah." John Gager correctly understands Gaston to take seriously Paul's presentation of himself as an apostle to the Gentiles, that his Torah-free gospel was targeted at Gentiles, and that his gospel "was principally *about* Gentiles: 'Scripture foresaw that God would justify the Gentiles . . .'" (Gal. 3:8). There was also a wider context: Paul's concern with the relation of the Torah to Gentiles was "shared by Jews and Gentiles even before the advent of Christianity."[40] Gaston's interpretation frees scholars from the need to invent a caricature of Judaism in order to make sense of Paul's antagonistic statements about the law; "they are directed against Judaizers, not Judaism per se."[41] Paul's apparently contradictory remarks about the law/Torah can now be made sense of and are not, after all, contradictory. Neither Jews nor Gentiles have to have recourse to the Torah "in order to establish their righteousness." Nonetheless, like Jews, Gentiles are to keep the commandments, summarized in the love principle, not to establish their righteousness but as an appropriate response to the divine grace. And, as Gaston points out, this perspective on Paul explains the absence in his letters of the concept of repentance, *tshuvah*, return to God. "Paul never speaks of repentance, a concept central not only to prophets and rabbis but also to the teaching of Jesus. Not only that, he also never speaks of forgiveness." The reason is that Paul is not speaking to Jews but to Gentiles; Jews, in the covenant, could always "return" (*tshuvah*) to God. Gentiles, outside the covenant, were being asked to turn to God for the first time; what they need "is not guilt but liberation, not repentance but life from the dead, not a turning back (*tshb*) but a 'turning *to* God from idols'" (1 Thess. 1:9).[42] Nonetheless, this new paradigm also has some problems, and it is to them that we now turn.

First, perhaps the greatest problem with Gaston's perspective on Paul is precisely its attractiveness to Christians who are committed to work at improving relations with Jews. Gaston gives us exactly what we need, a new "ecumenical" Paul. It is alluring, perhaps too much so. Because it is so attractive to people committed to overcoming millennia of Christian anti-Judaism, we should probably suspect that, however much is gained in Gaston's perspective, something is overlooked. Also, as John Gager has pointed out, Gaston's concern is motivated by "a profound theological urgency"; that is: "No longer is it a case of the legitimacy of Judaism. Unless they succeed in finding within the New Testament some area which is substantially free of anti-Judaism, the issue becomes the illegitimacy of Christianity."[43] We know that when historical inquiry is motivated by theological urgency it can, though it need not, go awry, which is why so many views of the historical Jesus tell us more about their authors than their subject. Gaston's Paul *may* tell us as much about Gaston as it does about Paul. Even so, Gaston moves the discussion considerably ahead of where it would otherwise be. But we need to exercise some suspicion on those options that we find most attractive. Gaston's view eliminates many difficulties in Paul, yet proves too lacking in nuance.

Second, some texts in Paul indicate that the views set forth by Gaston and Stendahl need to be considered further. Interpreting the incident on the Damascus Road as Paul's call to be an apostle to the Gentiles rather than as a conversion downplays the decisive significance that this incident had in Paul's life, plus the fact that Paul did disclaim *something* from his past, his "earlier life in Judaism" (Gal. 1:13). Gaston's view that Paul was a Shammaite, and that it was this that he rejected, receives little support even from those who more generally support Gaston.[44]

Third, taking Paul's account of the Jerusalem conference as absolutely crucial and contending that Paul consistently abided by it, taking his Torah-free gospel only to Gentiles, may be a mistake. Paul's account of the conference is likely no less tendentious than that of Luke-Acts, and there is evidence that Paul's congregations were mixed congregations of Jews and Gentiles. Says Paul:

> To the Jews I became as a Jew, in order to win Jews. To those under the law I became as one under the law (though I myself am not under the law) so that I might win those under the law. To those outside the law I became as one outside the law (though I am not free from God's law but am under Christ's law) so that I might win those outside the law. . . . I have become all things to all people, that I might by all means save some (1 Cor. 9:20–22).

In the heart of his classic discussion of Jews and Gentiles (Rom. 9–11), Paul refers to Jews who do not believe in Christ as "branches [that] were broken off" (11:17). And, although Gaston says that Paul never refers to Jesus as "the Christ," is it insignificant that one time that he does so is in Romans 9:5? Also, however one interprets Romans 11:26 ("and so all Israel will be saved"), clearly it places Israel's salvation in the future, thus indicating that all is not well, according to Paul, with Israel here and now.

In what other way, then, can we understand Paul?

Judaism is not Christianity

The second revisionist approach to Paul is that of E. P. Sanders, who is to be credited with the monumental achievement of having undermined the view of first-century Judaism that undergirded the traditional anti-Jewish reading of Paul. Nonetheless, Sanders thinks that Paul finally opposed Judaism simply because "it is not Christianity."[45]

The significant achievement of E. P. Sanders is to have discredited the understanding of the Judaism of Paul's time as a works-righteous, legalistic religion that led to the "boasting" for which Paul supposedly criticized it. Setting out "to compare Judaism, understood on its own terms, with Paul, understood in his own terms," Sanders argued for what he calls a position of "covenantal nomism" in Judaism.[46] What Sanders sought was the "pattern of religion" manifest in each, which he defined as "the description of how a religion is perceived by its adherents to *function*. 'Perceived to function' has the sense not of what an adherent does on a day-to-day basis, but of *how getting in and staying in are understood*: the way in which a religion is understood to admit and retain members is considered to be the way it 'functions.'"[47]

Sanders found a pattern of "covenantal nomism," according to which, as Francis H. Agnew puts it, "the good deeds of the law are viewed as the wholehearted response of the believer to the offer of salvation constituted in its very possibility by the gift, and only by the gift, of the gracious God."[48] Sanders finds this pattern at work in the Tannaim, the sectaries at Qumran, and in the apocrypha-pseudepigrapha. *Getting in* is a matter of grace; *staying in* has to do with obedience and using the means of atonement graciously provided by the covenant for transgression. A Jew's undertaking to obey the law is requisite to preserving the relationship with God, but this does not imply that salvation is "earned" or granted as a "reward" for a purely human achievement. Nor did Judaism regard "keeping" the law as difficult: "Surely, this commandment that I am commanding you today is not too hard for you, nor is it too far away. . . . No, the word is very near to you; it is in your mouth and in your heart for you to observe" (Deut. 30: 11–14).

Several points are pertinent to Sanders' analysis of rabbinic Judaism. First, much of its literature is "halakhic" in character. Its business is to take the generalities of biblical understandings of what we are to do, such as "love your neighbor as yourself," and spell them out in precise ways. Outside readers, which most Christian students of rabbinic literature have been, encountering the many distinctions and definitions found there, come away thinking of rabbinic religion as a petty legalism. Sanders' point accords with Stephen Westerholm's remarks that behind the legal effort lay the conviction "that obedience to the commands marks the privilege and obligation imposed on Israel by the covenant with her God."[49] Second, all this was in the context of the covenant of Israel with God, a covenant established and maintained by God's gracious initiative and a covenant to which God was unqualifiedly committed. Third, much

Jewish literature, like much Christian literature, is homiletical/rhetorical in nature and to be understood as such; in such literature it is often the need of the moment that explains where the stress is placed in the message. It will not do to read such thinkers as "systematic theologians." Fourth, much is made in rabbinic literature of God's rewarding obedience and punishing disobedience. Before concluding, however, that Judaism had a reward-and-punishment attitude, several alternative considerations need to be taken into account. God's justice was understood within the context of the covenant, not outside of it. Many statements in rabbinic literature stress the importance of motive and intention over actual accomplishment; others are incomparable exclamations of the grace of God:

> There are ten words for prayer. One of them is appeal for grace. Of all the ten, Moses used only this one, as it is said, "And I appealed for grace with the Lord at that time" (Deut.3:23). R. Johanan said: Hence you may learn that man has no claim upon God; for Moses, the greatest of the prophets, came before God only with an appeal for grace. R. Levi said: Why did Moses do so? The proverb says, "Be careful lest you be caught by your words." God said to Moses, "I will be gracious to whom I will be gracious. To him who has anything to his account with me, I show mercy, that is, I deal with him through the attribute of mercy; but to him who has nothing I am gracious, that is, I deal with him by gift and gratis."[50]

One's standing before God in the covenant was not based on perfectly keeping the law, but membership in the people Israel, God's covenant community. Fifth, rabbinic literature abounds in protestations about the efficacy of atonement and repentance. The following is a good example:

> R. Helbo said to R. Samuel b. Nahmani: "Since I have heard that you are a good Haggadist, tell me the meaning of Lam. 3:44, 'Thou hast covered thyself with a cloud that our prayers should not pass through.' He replied, "Prayer is likened to a bath, repentance to the sea. As the bath is sometimes open and sometimes shut, so the gates of prayer are sometimes shut and sometimes open, but as the sea is always open, so the gates of repentance are always open. When a man wishes to bathe in the sea, he can bathe in it any hour he likes. So with repentance, whenever a man wishes to repent, God will receive him." But R. Anan said: "The gates of prayer, too, are never shut."[51]

Sanders finds it "universally held" in the Judaisms of Paul's time that "God has appointed means of atonement for every transgression, except the intention to reject God and his covenant."[52]

Sanders concludes that there is massive consensus between Paul and Palestinian Judaism as to the relationship between grace and works. On his analysis, grace is the way for both Paul and Palestinian Judaism whereby one "gets in" the religious system; works are the way one "stays in" it. Both Paul and Judaism hold that works are necessary to maintain one's standing in the community of salvation. Paul's contemporaries in Judaism would have agreed that righteousness is by faith, not works.

Nonetheless, according to Sanders, Paul does find something wrong with Judaism. The trouble with Judaism is simply that "it is not Christianity."[53] Only Christ saves; the law cannot save. Sanders' position has many advantages. It makes Christians more aware than many have wanted to be of the extent to which Paul holds the law in high regard ("Circumcision is nothing, and uncircumcision is nothing, but obeying the commandments of God is everything" [1 Cor. 7:19]), of the utterly Jewish content of Paul's ethics as well as of the way in which he functioned as a rabbi for his congregations, providing for them "rulings" on matters of practice. Also, to Sanders goes the credit for providing the impressive scholarship that has undone the traditional Christian consensus about first-century Judaism.

Nonetheless, there are also weaknesses in Sanders' position. For all its dissimilarity to the traditional view of Paul, it replicates some cardinal points of that interpretation. Fredriksen points out that the inexplicable nature of Paul's rejection of Judaism (on Sanders' interpretation) makes Paul's "historical and cultural context essentially irrelevant to his theology." Sanders' Paul is no less morally incoherent than the traditional Paul: "Why would God have presented his Law as his will and the path of righteousness and life, in order only to reveal, at the eleventh hour, that its real purpose was to condemn?"[54] Gaston and Gager point out that Sanders often takes Paul to be talking about Judaism when the context in Paul's letters would indicate that he is talking about Gentiles and Gentile problems.[55]

There are two things to note about Sanders' Paul before leaving him. The first is pointed out by Sanders himself: Paul "does not provide an adequate basis for a Jewish-Christian dialogue." Yet Paul cannot simply be cited against that dialogue as though we could know what Paul would think of it. Paul thought that "the fullness of the Gentiles" would soon come in and that "all Israel will be saved." Paul's apocalyptic stance did not disappear from his latest letter, but is reaffirmed in it. Nothing that Paul expected to happen soon has happened yet. Whether Paul would still think that there was no other way to be saved than through Jesus Christ "is simply imponderable."[56] Second, Sanders reminds us of 2 Peter's remark that Paul's letters are "hard to understand" (3:16). For Sanders, there is no explaining *why* Paul rejected Judaism. The utterly arbitrary character of Paul's thought, according to Sanders, helps us understand how the next alternative could be proposed.

Paul was utterly incoherent

The third revisionist approach to Paul, that of Heikki Räisänen, holds that Paul was thoroughgoingly incoherent. If so, we should expect no help from Paul in thinking our way through Jewish-Christian relations today. Räisänen's argument is that Paul's view of the law "can only be understood if the tensions and self-contradictions in it are taken seriously." What it would mean to "understand" a self-contradictory Paul raises difficulties of its own. Paul's contradictions are that he regards the law as a thing of the past, to which Christians have died, and under which they no longer live. "Christ is the end, that is the termination, of the law." Nonetheless, Paul urges his readers to reflect Christian love in their lives by telling them "that love is the fulfillment of that very law." Also, Paul can back up his practical suggestions "by appealing to words of the law." Nor does Paul admit that he invalidates the law; instead he upholds it. "Paul thus wants to have his cake and eat it."[57] Paul sometimes wants to abolish, sometimes to fulfill, the law.

With regard to whether the law can be fulfilled, Räisänen interprets Paul's position to entail that those outside the Christian community must not be able to fulfill the law, or "Christ would have died in vain." Inside it, however, Christians must be able to fulfill the law, or "Christ would be as weak as the law was (Rom. 8:3)." Paul uses "denigrating generalizations" to show that neither Jews nor Gentiles fulfill the law and absurdly radicalizes the law's demands to show that only 100 percent fulfillment of them, which is impossible, will count. Yet Paul also thinks that "God's will in the law can be fulfilled even by non-Christian Gentiles," and some Gentiles actually do what the law requires. As for himself, he is "blameless" with regard to the law (Phil. 3:6). Nor does he have radicalized standards in mind when he speaks of Christians' ability to fulfill the law. When Paul differentiates Christian ability from Jewish inability to fulfill the law, he "compare[s] Christian life at its best with Jewish life at its worst."[58]

Paul usually held that the law was of divine origin, except that on one occasion he held that it was given by angels and therefore is inferior. Its purpose was negative: "to increase and even bring about sin." When Paul gives this explanation of the law, he contradicts his other explanation, that the origin of sin goes back to Adam's fall. Nor does he explain why an apostle's commandment does not lead to sin, whereas a commandment of the law does. Sometimes, Paul argues that the law also had a constructive function: "it was designed to lead men to life." Paul's implied view of God in these arguments is odd. The positive function of the law reduces it to God's initial, failed effort "to save humanity; the negative one logically leads to a somewhat cynical picture of God's strategy."[59]

Further, Räisänen agrees with such scholars as Schoeps and Sanders that Paul "misconstrues" Jewish understandings of faith and salvation. As he sees it, Paul regards Christ and the law as representing opposing systems of salvation and erects a contradiction between the works of the law, on the one hand, and Christ, grace, Spirit, faith, and promise on the other. Among apostolic writers, only Paul "sees such a sharp contrast between law and grace or faith. Apparently Paul misconstrues Jewish 'soteriology,' ignoring the pattern of gratuity on which it was based as well as the role accorded to man's repentance."

> The starting point of Paul's thinking about the Torah is the Christ event, not the law. This structure of thought he fully shares with other early Christian writers. No other writer, however, is led to such radical and negative conclusions with respect to the law as Paul: the law incites man to sin and increases transgressions; the law ought to be fulfilled 100 percent; Jews do not fulfill the law whereas the Christians do; the law was given through angels, not by God. All these negative statements are made problematic because other *Pauline* statements contradict them. *Paul's most radical conclusions about the law are thus strangely ambiguous.* There is something strained and artificial in his negativity—artificial from his *own* point of view.

One result of Paul's strained negativity toward Judaism and the law is that his distorted portrayal of Judaism "has, contrary to Paul's intentions to be sure, had a share in the tragic history of Jews at the mercy of Christians."[60]

Räisänen makes a forceful argument. According to him, it is Paul who "tears apart, not without violence, what belonged together in 'genuine' Judaism. It is he who drives a wedge between law and grace, limiting 'grace' to the Christ event." Räisänen correctly argues that Paul's position is often a *petitio principii*, making of the law a source of justification and moral power, something it never was in Judaism.[61] But what are we to make of Räisänen's interpretation of Paul? Is Paul as thoroughgoingly incoherent as he is depicted? Does "law" always mean the same thing in every context in which Paul uses it? Is there some relative distinction that can be made between moral and ritual law, which might shed light on Paul? Although this distinction cannot be pressed too far (idolatry being both a ritual and ethical affair), it is clear that the major points of contention between Paul and his opponents were over matters of ritual law (circumcision and the dietary laws). Do Paul's discussions of law deal with Jewish or Gentile problems? For that matter, were those whom Paul was opposing always the same groups? Some Pauline scholars contend not only that Paul's opponents differed from place to place but that there even "are different types of opponents at the same place at different periods."[62] Paul's opponents at Galatia, for example, have been variously identified as Jewish Christian "Judaizers," as superheated Gentile converts, and as Jewish Gnostic Christians. But they are also tentatively identified as Jewish Christian missionaries grounded in a form of syncretistic Judaism stemming from Asia Minor.[63] Although deciding the opponents' precise identity is not something about which scholars can reach consensus, the possibility of a variegated set of opponents (and therefore of issues between them and Paul) should make us hesitate before concluding that Paul was radically inconsistent.

Paul and Jewish "identity markers"

The fourth revisionist approach to Paul builds on the work of Sanders and others in destroying the pejorative image of Judaism at the time of Paul, yet contends that the emerging new perspective on Paul can make better sense of him than has so far been realized.

Arguing that E. P. Sanders has given us an unparalleled "opportunity to look at Paul afresh, . . . to let Paul be himself," James D. G. Dunn nonetheless argues that Sanders himself missed the larger significance of his own discovery.[64] Dunn wants a view of Paul that does not make him as arbitrary as Sanders' Paul, nor as incoherent as Räisänen's Paul, and that does not remove from Paul all argument with Judaism (as Gaston does). Dunn begins his treatment of the new perspective on Paul with a look at Galatians 2:15–16 and its context: "We ourselves are Jews by birth and not Gentile sinners; yet we know that a person is justified not by works of the law but through faith in Jesus Christ." The form of Paul's words shows that he is appealing to a view held by Jewish Christians, to Jewish sensibilities: We Jews know that we are not justified by works of the law. This, says Dunn, "is covenant language, the language of those conscious that they have been chosen as a people by God."[65] Paul here addresses Jews whose faith in Jesus Christ is not in contradiction to but is "an extension of their Jewish faith in a graciously electing and sustaining God." The contrast with "Gentile sinners" reflects Paul's awareness that Jews are God's covenant people. Underlying this is Paul's sense of God's covenant righteousness, found also in the Psalms and Second Isaiah, "where God's righteousness is precisely God's covenant faithfulness, his saving power and love for his people Israel." Dunn disagrees with Sanders' claim that justification has to do simply with "getting in," works with "staying in." God's justification is the divine recognition that one is in the covenant, "whether that is in *initial* acknowledgment, or a *repeated* action of God, or his *final* vindication of his people."[66] Here, the first time in Paul's letters that "justification" is discussed, we do not have an attack on a supposedly Jewish idea that God's justification can be earned.

Yet, what did Paul mean when he denied (three times) in this passage that justification comes "by works of the law"? The context of the passage makes clear that the concerns were circumcision (at Jerusalem) and the dietary laws (at Antioch); it is these that Paul has in mind. Dunn and Alan Segal make it clear that when we find negative statements about the law in Paul, the context is always one in which "membership requirements" are under discussion. Paul's positive statements about the law, on the other hand, reflect contexts where questions of behavior are raised.[67] Circumcision and the dietary laws were widely looked upon as peculiar to Jews. To Gentile outsiders they functioned as "identity markers," identifying their practitioners as Jews; to Jews they worked in the same way, functioning as "badges of covenant membership."[68] Their role was similar to that of Baptism and the Eucharist in the church today; it is almost impossible to think of the church without them ("almost" because there is The Society of Friends). In any case, *this* is what Paul attacks: "the idea that God's acknowledgment of covenant status is bound up with, even dependent upon, observing of these particular regulations."[69]

Alan Segal, discussing the same passage, agrees that Paul intended "that gentiles should enter the Christian community without having to perform the ceremonial law, as Jews did." When Paul is arguing about "works of the law," "he is talking about the ceremonial laws of Judaism." Paul was trying to create a new, united community, a church composed of Jews and Gentiles, which called for the "destruction of the *ritual* distinction between Jew and gentile within the Christian sect." Traditional Jesus followers were confronted by Paul with the concept of one community in which there was "no longer Jew or Greek" (Gal. 3:28), and where Jewish ritual in the form of "identity badges" was rendered insignificant. At the same time, Paul is not proposing jettisoning the moral Torah; "he is in favor of changing and, in fact, dispensing with many ceremonial rules."[70]

Two clarifications are issued by Dunn with respect to this point. First, neither Paul nor those whom he criticizes regard "works of the law" as earning God's favor; they are "given by God . . . , they serve to demonstrate covenant status." They are part of the proper response of God's covenant people to God's grace. What Paul denies is that "God's grace extends only to those who wear the badge of the covenant." Nor, second, do "works of the law" mean "'good works' in general." Rather, the phrase refers to identity markers. Nor is the point at issue justification by faith; "it is much less obvious than once appeared that the typical first-century Jew would have denied justification by faith." Rather, Paul's point is that justification by works of law (understood as identity badges) and by faith in Jesus Christ "are *antithetical opposites.*" Paul's opponents in Galatians 2:11–21 (Peter, the men who came from James and even Barnabas, Paul's missionary partner) proceeded on the assumption that faith in Jesus Christ did not necessitate giving up their identity badges. Paul's logic of justification by faith held that "what is of grace through faith cannot depend in any sense, in any degree, on a particular ritual response." Paul, holding that the gospel had already been proclaimed when God promised Abraham, "All the Gentiles shall be blessed in you" (Gal. 3:8; see Gen. 12:3 and 18:18), further held that Christ was the "yes" to God's promise and that therefore "the covenant should no longer be conceived in nationalistic . . . terms."[71] Works of the law (covenant works) had become too closely identified with Jewish works, an identification inappropriate both to the way things began with Abraham and to the purpose that the covenant had been intended to fulfill— to be a blessing to the Gentiles.

Dunn's further clarifications are important. What Paul denies is not "works" in some general sense; faith is not to be passive but "working through love" (Gal. 5:6). Paul denies the requirement of a *particular* work as a condition on the grace of God. Nor is Paul denying the need for any ritual expression of faith (whether circumcision or baptism); what he denies is a *"nationalism"* that limits the grace of God to those with the proper identity badges.[72] Presumably, Paul would have resisted later Christian efforts to make baptism and the Lord's Supper into the same kind of grace-limiting "identity badges." "What Jesus has done by his death and resurrection, in Paul's understanding, is to free the grace of God in justifying from its nationalistically restrictive clamps for a broader experience (beyond the circumcised Jew) and a fuller expression (beyond concern for ritual purity)."[73]

Three further points need to be made to round out Dunn's analysis of Paul. First, this understanding is taken to be at issue in the Letter to the Romans as well; the "boasting" that Paul there has in mind is a "boasting in Israel's special relationship with God through election, the boasting in the law as the mark of God's favour, in circumcision as the badge of belonging to God."[74] Dunn follows up this interpretation of Romans with his subsequent commentary on it.[75] Second, the standard Christian misreading of Paul as having broken with Judaism as a whole and with the law as such is as rigorously set aside here as in either Sanders or Gaston. Also, because the usual reading of Paul offered by Jewish scholars takes for granted this misreading, it too is set aside. What is often regarded as Paul's misunderstanding of Judaism turns out to be a misunderstanding of Paul. The merit of the Dunn/Segal paradigm for reading Paul is that it not only refuses (with Stendahl, Gaston, Sanders, et al.) to interpret Paul as an early Luther, but it further refuses to interpret Paul in a way that would have made no sense to Paul's Jewish contemporaries. A further merit is that the Dunn/Segal view does provide some reason to suppose that Paul had an argument to make with his Jewish contemporaries, although that argument was not over the legitimacy of Judaism. Third, on this interpretation Paul does not belittle good works in general, nor does he have in mind the (supposedly Jewish) view that good works earn merit with God. Hence, the Dunn/Segal Paul neither disparages law as such nor breaks with Judaism as a whole. Also, he is a more "coherent" Paul than Räisänen knows, one who can elsewhere provide quite a positive view of the law. "Paul's solution does not require him to deny the covenant, or indeed the law as God's law, but only the covenant and the law as 'taken over' by Israel."[76]

Paul never wrote of himself as having left Judaism or the Jewish people; nor, given his imminent expectation of the *parousia*, did he regard the church as a long-lasting historical phenomenon that "superseded" the Jewish people. *After* writing Romans 9–11 on relations between Gentile Christians and non-Christian Jews, Paul comments: "Salvation is nearer to us now than when we became believers" (13:11). He was not anticipating a long future for the church, nor one in which it would become completely Gentile and generate a tradition of "teaching contempt" for Jews and Judaism. It is doubtful that Paul ever thought of himself as anything other than a Jew whose life was transformed by seeing in Jesus Christ God's "Yes" to the promise made to Abraham.[77] It is critical to note that what eventually came about was precisely that against which Paul fought so hard: "The church became a new, third entity."[78] As others have pointed out, Paul does not even have a word with which he can refer to Christianity.[79] The reason for this, as Segal understands Paul, is that Paul had not the slightest wish to portray Christianity "as a completely different phenomenon from Judaism, for, as he clarifies in Romans, he saw it as the fulfillment of Judaism and as part of it." Given the ambiguities of the word "fulfillment," Segal should follow Paul and call Christianity the "confirmation" of Judaism; Christ "confirms" the promises made to the patriarchs (Rom. 15:8). He is God's "Yes!" to God's promises (2 Cor. 1:20), which is why "we say the 'Amen' [so be it!], to the glory of God" (2 Cor. 1:20). Paul's warning to the Gentile Christians in Rome not to "boast over the [broken-off] branches" (11:18) has gone unheeded. What Paul warned against happening is precisely what did happen: "Gentile Christianity has boasted of its special knowledge at the expense of Israel."[80]

Paul's Situation

Crucial to understanding what Paul said and why he said it is an attempt to reconstruct his situation, tentative as any reconstruction must be. Apparently there were developments, late in Paul's career, that prompted his arguments with his fellow Jews within the Christian community. We observe that the early church did not begin with clear, well-thought-out, and uniform practices that were observed in the same way everywhere. Its practices developed at different speeds in different places, and centuries elapsed before uniformity in practice and orthodoxy in thought were decided (if they ever were). The issue of whether a particular practice should be continued would arise only as developments caused it to be challenged.

Something like this seems to have been the case with regard to Paul and his preaching of the gospel to Gentiles. Although Gentiles did not have to observe ritual practices prescribed by the Torah (circumcision and the dietary laws) in order to enter or stay in the Pauline community, the inclusion of Gentiles without requiring them to be circumcised does *not* seem to have been Paul's unique contribution to the early church. Prior to the rise of the church, the synagogue allowed Gentile "God-fearers" to participate in its services without making any ritual demands on them, allowed them to study and discuss the Torah, to participate in conducting the synagogue's charitable works, all while these same Gentiles, if they were members of the city council, performed "the public sacrifices required of their office."[81] Early Christianity was deeply influenced by the synagogue and Hellenistic Judaism, Paul particularly so, and with it and the later rabbis "stood within the 'liberal' stream of Deutero-Isaiah. The Kingdom of God would include two peoples: Gentiles, redeemed from idolatry, and Israel, redeemed finally from exile."[82] The Christian movement seems from the very onset to have admitted Gentiles to enter it without requiring them to "convert" to Judaism. From its inauguration in Jerusalem, the church counted among its participants those whom the Book of Acts calls "Hellenists." They were the vanguard of the church's movement into the vast Hellenistic world; "they were missionary-minded and theologically venturesome."[83] Paul's introduction to the Christian faith took place in a Hellenistic context, during which time he participated in the Damascus and Antioch churches, living with and learning from these Christians. "Paul lived in a gentile community during his formative years as a convert."[84] Paul's gospel did not require Gentiles to submit to Jewish ritual for admission to or retention in the community, but that was not Paul's doing. Rather, "James, Peter, and John endorsed Paul's Gospel, despite the importuning of the 'false brethren,' because that had always been the basis on which Gentiles had been admitted."[85] Paul had preached his understanding of the gospel to Gentiles for sixteen or seventeen years (Gal. 1:18; 2:1), before having to go to Jerusalem and give an account of himself to the "pillars" of the church. Paul's companion, Titus, a Greek, was not required to be circumcised (Gal. 2:3), and, according to Paul, the Jerusalem authorities agreed "that we should go to the Gentiles and they to the circumcised" (Gal. 2:9). The way in which Wayne Meeks puts the matter is instructive: "The dispute was about circumcision, that is, whether the gentiles who *had* joined the followers of Jesus at Antioch must *now* undergo the normal rite of incorporation into the Jewish community."[86] As Fredriksen concludes: "Clearly, by the late 40s, consensus on this issue was breaking down."[87] Why was this?

To this question, two sets of answers are posed, one having to do with matters internal to the early church, the other pertaining to Jews and Judaism. With regard to the early church, initially and for some time those who heard the message of Jesus Christ, whether Jews or Gentile God-fearers, "joined an ekklesia within the synagogue."After some time, the movement became increasingly, then predominantly, composed of Gentiles, while, at the same time, two other things happened: the lengthening delay of the *parousia*, coupled with the failure of the gospel to attract Jews, constituted a crisis for the community. All these factors taken together, plus the positive response the church had received from Gentiles, subverted the movement's prospects among Jews. "When the church was still predominantly Jewish, Gentile participation was a welcome affirmation of the Gospel; as it became more and more Gentile, it compromised its identity as a renewal movement *within* Judaism, and hence its chances for success among Jews."[88] Hence "the circumcision party," as Paul calls it, urged that Gentiles in the church go beyond being *included* and become *converts* to Judaism. So they pressed upon the Antioch congregation, which, according to Acts, had been the first to have Gentiles in its midst, to have all members of the community observe the ritual laws of Judaism pertaining both to circumcision and to table-fellowship.

Meanwhile, Jews in and out of Palestine were feeling Roman heat, to the extent that many regarded their very existence and identity as being at stake. Caligula instigated a long crisis over his insistence that a statue of himself be erected in the Temple (40 C.E.). A series of inept and brutal Roman governors, each worse than the one before, inflicted indignity and suffering upon the people. Fadus required that the high priest's vestments be returned to Roman custody and put down the rebellion of Theudas; Tiberius Iulius Alexander crucified the sons of Judas the Galilean, James and Simon, on charges that they agitated the people against Rome. Josephus calculates that twenty- to thirty-thousand people were killed in a Jerusalem riot against Cumanus. There was a series of disorders involving Zealots in Samaria, and Josephus claims that Judea was infested with Zealots.[89] Jewish heritage, identity, national and religious rights and prerogatives were under siege. The threat would grow more severe, culminating in war with Rome. Nor were only Jews in Palestine in difficulty; Jews in major cities throughout the empire, including Antioch and Alexandria, suffered from mob violence and local governmental misrule. Philo of Alexandria petitioned Caligula in defense of Jews and Judaism.[90] Claudius expelled all Jews from Rome in 49 C.E., apparently over the furor raised in the synagogues over the success of the Jesus movement in Rome.[91]

Hence, this movement's practice of including Gentiles without the halakhic requirements of circumcision and the dietary laws, which themselves were "identity badges" for Jews, "was perceived to be a threat to Jewish institutions and traditions."[92] These "identity badges," which Segal refers to as "markers," were far from unimportant to Jews. Not only did circumcision carry transcendent significance as "the first and most obvious sign of the covenant of Judaism, the mark of belonging to the Jewish people." Also in the background were memories of the Maccabean revolution, which had been fought to throw off the yoke of the oppressor Antiochus IV Epiphanes, "who had forbidden circumcision."[93] Ritual practices like circumcision and the dietary laws were tied up with questions of survival and identity: Could Jews survive as Jews? Roman threats to Judaism and the memory of past threats would have put greater "pressure on those involved in the new movement to show themselves as faithful and loyal Jews."[94]

Also, Paul is trying to create one new community of Jews and Gentiles. Are they to become one in the sense of being able to marry one another and to eat together? For Jews, that would have been possible only on the condition that Gentiles reach a level of ritual purity that would enable both groups "to engage freely in these intimate social activities."[95]

However one reconstructs the complexities of the situation among such churches as the one in Antioch, it is clear that the conservative Jesus followers ("the certain people [who] came from James," the "false believers"; Gal. 2:12; 2:4) upped the ante on the kinds of practices in which Paul was engaged. Paul's response was to denationalize Jewish restoration theology and present an interpretation of salvation aimed at bringing in "the full number of the Gentiles" (Rom. 11:25), and when *that* happens "all Israel will be saved" (Rom. 11:26).

The Triumph of Grace in Paul

In Romans 9–11, Paul discusses the relation between Gentile Christians and the broken-off branches, Jews who have not believed in Jesus Christ. Here we witness the "triumph of grace" characteristic of Paul's theology: if the gospel of the unmerited and unfathomable grace of God does not continue to Jews in spite of their unfaithfulness, then that very same gospel which Paul proclaims to Gentiles is shown to be false.

The first paragraph of Romans 9–11 (9:1–5) lays down the parameters within which everything that follows must be understood:

> I am speaking the truth in Christ—I am not lying; my conscience confirms it by the Holy Spirit—I have great sorrow and unceasing anguish in my heart. For I could wish that I myself were accursed and cut off from Christ for the sake of my own people, my kindred according to the flesh. They are Israelites, and to them belong the adoption, the glory, the covenants, the giving of the law, the worship, and the promises; to them belong the patriarchs, and from them, according to the flesh, comes the Messiah, who is over all, God blessed forever. Amen.

Paul begins by confessing the "great sorrow and unceasing anguish" of his heart, a confession he introduces with a highly emphatic, triple assertion that he is telling the truth, not lying, and that his conscience bears him witness. "Paul wants his audience to be in no doubt of the depth of his identity with and concern for his own people."[96] Reminiscent of the scene between Moses and God in Exodus 32:32, Paul could wish that he were "cut off from Christ for the sake of my own people." Here Paul deliberately evokes the connection with Moses. After the incident of the golden calf, God was angry with the people Israel and said to Moses, "Now let me alone, so that my wrath may burn hot against them and I may consume them; and of you I will make a great nation" (Ex. 32:10). God offered to cut a deal with Moses: to wipe out the people Israel because of their sin and start afresh with Moses, from whom God would "make a great nation." Moses' response was to confess to God that "this people has sinned a great sin; they have made for themselves gods of gold. But now, if you will only forgive their sin—but if not, blot me out of the book that you have written" (Ex. 32:31–32). Moses would rather be cut off from God than that God cut off the people Israel. Paul wishes that he were "cut off from Christ for the sake of my own people, my kindred according to the flesh." Thus Paul affirms his solidarity with the people Israel.

Paul is talking here about Jews who do not believe in Jesus Christ. What prompted him to write about them is a question to which we may never have a definitive answer. His text gives us one clue: Gentile Christians in Rome have to be cautioned by Paul not to "boast over the branches" that have been broken off God's olive tree so that the Gentiles might be grafted into it (Rom. 11:18). Pagan Rome had long been characterized by anti-Jewish sentiment, and Claudius had recently expelled all Jews from Rome.[97] Paul may well have been the first Christian writer to identify the rise of Gentile Christian anti-Judaism and try to counter it.[98] We would do well to heed what Paul says about Jews apart from Christ in Romans 9–11.

They are Israelites. Paul does not say that they are the "old" Israel, simply that they are Israel. Nor does he ever call the church the "new Israel," a phrase altogether absent from the apostolic writings. That Paul calls them "Israelites" instead of "Jews" indicates that he is not thinking of them primarily as his "kindred according to the flesh," but as the people of the covenant. Peter von der Osten Sacken points out that Paul does not say that they "were" Israelites, nor that they "will be" Israelites. They simply are what they have been since the election at Sinai, *bene Yisrael*, the people of God.[99] These nonbelieving Jews are the people of God, by God's electing grace, by God's decision, by God's naming of them (Gen. 32:28). To know Israel is to know that it is the Israel of God.[100] But to know who the Israel of God is requires knowing something of the God of Israel. Israel belongs to God, not vice versa; Israel is God's people (Rom. 11:1). The God of Israel is the God of steadfast love (*hesed*), undeviating faithfulness, amazing grace, a God whose love is all-inclusive and who set the covenant with Israel within the context of larger covenants with all humanity (Abraham) and indeed with "every living creature . . . on the earth" (Gen. 9:16). The loyalty of God to God's covenant promise to Israel was unimpeachable for the Jew and remained so for Paul. As any viewer of *Fiddler on the Roof* knows, Jews have been arguing with, railing at, praying to, sinning against, ignoring, and dying for the sanctification of this God's name for a very long time. Who is Israel? A people that "lives from its reception of the divine word of promise and that has its foundation and continuing existence in that word."[101]

To them belong[s] the sonship. The Hebrew Bible understood the election of Israel as God's adoption of Israel as God's specially beloved child, for example: "When Israel was a child, I loved him, and out of Egypt I called my son" (Hos. 11:1). "Adoption" connotes "chosen, selected, picked, handpicked." Paul is not referring to a natural process of having a child, but to an act of deliberate choosing, the better to underscore the sense of election.[102] Israel's gracious adoption by God's original election is the foundation of Israel's hope and the reason why "all Israel will be saved." Paul here argues that the gospel of God's love graciously offered to all the Gentiles is coherent with God's initial act of grace toward Israel. Gentiles and Jews should see each others' adoption by God as confirming their own.

To them belong[s] the glory, the *doxa,* the manifest presence of God, the *shekhinah.*[103] The word for "glory," *doxa,* refers to "the glory of the Lord," recalling the many disclosures of God to the Israel of God throughout their history with God. Paul deals with the assurance of faith that tells Israel that God is *with* them, in the wilderness, in the Promised Land, in exile, in suffering, that God is Immanuel, God with us. God is present to, with, and for Israel; God is the One whose self-naming declares, "I will be there as the One I shall be there as" (Ex. 3:14). God is present with Israel.[104]

To them belong the covenants. Biblically, covenant making is a primary form of the grace of God. As von der Osten-Sacken comments, "The essential mark of these personal divine self-imposed obligations is their unbreachable binding force."[105] The covenants with Noah, with Abraham, with Israel at Sinai, with David are the gracious gifts of the God of a singular promise and a singular command; they represent both *gift* and *call*, and "the gifts and the calling of God are irrevocable" (Rom. 11:29). The certitude that all Israel will be saved is grounded in God's gracious gift and calling to Israel.

To them belong[s] the giving of the law (*torah*: way, path, instruction). The "law" involved here is the Mosaic law, which Paul understands as a gracious gift from God and one of Israel's greatest blessings. Paul clearly implies a positive attitude toward the law, the teaching that makes it possible for Israel to live in accordance with the way of life. "I have set before you life and death. . . . Choose life. . . ." (Deut. 30:19). Paul knows that the Torah "promised life" (Rom. 7:10). As we have seen, Paul had argued in Galatians that "we Jews" know that we are not justified by "works of the law," that is, the ceremonial law; earlier in Romans this principle of justification by faith apart from questions of identity badges means that God is not the God of Jews only, but of Gentiles also, the God who "will justify the circumcised on the ground of faith and the uncircumcised through that same faith" (3:29–30). Hence, Dunn can claim that the law "was one of the blessings given to Israel in which Gentile believers can now share—the law understood as the law of the mind, the law of the Spirit of life, of course (7:23, 8:2), but no less the law of God given to Israel at Sinai."[106] Another way to put this would be to contend that Paul's claim is that through Jesus Gentiles come into relationship with the God of Israel, that indeed it was this God who was in Christ "reconciling the world to himself" (2 Cor. 5:19), and that this God is the God of both promise and command.

To them belong[s] the worship. With this expression, "the worship," Paul has now listed the most important defining characteristics of the Judaism of his time. They were (1) the "glory," the One God of the *Shema* ("Hear, O Israel: The LORD is our God, the LORD alone") present to Israel, (2) the covenant with Israel as the people of God, (3) the Mosaic law as the constitutive document of the covenant people, spelling out the appropriate way for the people of God to live in response to God's grace, and (4) the worship of God with its means of grace making possible atonement and forgiveness. But it is no longer only Jews who worship the One God; wherever Gentiles gather in the name of Jesus Christ, they worship the maker of heaven and earth and redeemer of Israel.

To them belong the promises. These promises, later said by Paul to be irrevocable, included the dual promise to Abraham that his seed would be a light to the nations and the promise of a land. The promises include the covenants and God's many pledges to be "with" the people Israel. These promises are now accessible also to Gentiles. The tradition of Christian anti-Judaism systematically expropriated all the promises of the Bible for the church and assigned all its prophetic criticisms and condemnations to the Jewish people. Also, it assigned the law, regarded as superseded, exclusively to the Jewish people. But Paul here argues a dual case: the promises *belong* (present tense) to the Israel of God, although not exclusively, and the law belongs (present tense) to the Jewish people, but not exclusively; Gentiles now participate in the blessings of both promise and command. Gentiles are constrained to love their neighbors as themselves, which Paul understood as a summary of the law and the prophets, and both Gentiles and Jews live by the grace of God.

To them belong the patriarchs. Paul's language says, in the Greek, simply "to them belong the *fathers (pateres)*." Paul, who is accustomed to argue that Abraham is the "father" of Gentile Christians, indeed of "all who believe," here argues that Abraham and the other forebears in faith are not the exclusive possession of Gentile Christians but belong as well to the Israel of God. At the same time, neither is this relationship of faith going back to Abraham the sole proprietorship of the Jewish people. The promise to Abraham was never for the exclusive benefit of Israel, but was intended for all the peoples. Nonetheless, in Romans Paul has to argue against a growing Gentile tendency to look down upon the Israel of God as if from a superior position: "Do not boast over the branches [that have been broken off] . . . ; remember that it is not you that support the root, but the root that supports you" (11:18).

And from them, according to the flesh, comes the Messiah. Here Paul refers to the Messiah, "*ho Christos.*" He has not forgotten that "Christ" is a title, although for the most part in his writings it appears with "Jesus" as a title that has become a name. When he says that the Christ is from the people Israel "according to the flesh (*kata sarka*)," he again reminds his readers that, like Abraham and all the other items on his list, the Christ also stands in another relationship, this one to the Gentiles. Gentiles, who are "brothers and sisters" neither of the people Israel nor of Jesus as Paul is ("my own people, my kindred according to the flesh" [9:3]), nonetheless are reconciled to the God of Israel and the Israel of God through the agency of the Christ. The all-inclusive love of God for each and all is revealed to Gentiles through Christ.

The heart of Romans 9–11 is Paul's metaphor/parable of the olive tree (11:17–24). We will resist taking it as an allegory and stick to the central point. The function of the metaphor, which Paul develops in order to refute Gentile boasting vis-à-vis Jews (11:18), is to remind Gentiles that the people Israel is the tree, and the broken-off branches will be grafted back into *"their own* olive tree" with less difficulty than it took to engraft the Gentiles into what Karl Barth called *"their* [the Jews'] old tree."[107] Presumably, the God of the Bible could have made a brand-new start with the Gentiles. But God chose not to do so. Hence, the Gentiles, like it or not (and most have not), were given and called by God to enter into the long-standing relationship of the God of Israel with the Israel of God. *"Some"* branches were broken off, so that Gentiles could be grafted into the root stock. Not all the branches were broken off, nor was the tree cut down and a new one planted. The proper response to grace is gratitude. Instead of boasting over the Jews, Gentiles should "stand in awe."

Paul closes his discussion by calling the whole question a "mystery" (11:25). "A hardening has come upon part of Israel, until the full number of the Gentiles has come in. And so all Israel will be saved" (11:25–26). Here Paul repeats a theme he stated earlier: "Through their stumbling salvation has come to the Gentiles, so as to make Israel jealous" (11:11). Somehow, and just "how" may be the part that Paul designates as a "mystery," the "no" of "part of Israel" to the gospel of Jesus Christ is the means by which "salvation has come to the Gentiles." So part of Israel is hardened, but this "hardening" is far from being God's *last* word on the subject; it is a strictly temporary hardening—until the full number of the Gentiles has come in, when "all Israel will be saved." Somehow, "their rejection is the reconciliation of the world" (11:15). Paul's use of "hardening" recalls the liberation of the people Israel from slavery in Egypt, in which story God hardened the heart of Pharaoh (Ex. 7:3; 14:4). Perhaps there is involved here no more than a characteristic biblical realism with regard to how the purposes of God are accomplished in history: in, through, and by means of ordinary, messy, and ambiguous realities. Had Pharaoh been deeply concerned with the plight of the Hebrew people, had he seen to it that they were well fed, well housed, well clothed, given fair and equal treatment in the Egyptian society and economy, would they have followed Moses and Aaron through the desert to a land of promise? Would they have been interested in the Torah? Israel's redemption was in part thanks to the hardening of Pharaoh's heart. Paul seems here to be drawing a loose analogy between Israel's own salvation and that of the Gentiles. Had Christian missionaries been able to spend all their time on a surprisingly fertile Jewish mission field, they would have had little opportunity to turn their attention to Gentiles. Perhaps something as simple as that is what Paul is saying here, with the obvious proviso that he regards all this as God's doing. It was God who hardened Pharaoh's heart in order to accomplish God's purposes with Israel, and it was God who hardened the hearts of part of Israel in order that Christ could "confirm the promises given to the patriarchs" (Rom. 15:8).

In any case, no more than did Gentile disobedience disqualify them from God's grace, did Jewish disobedience place Jews outside the pale of God's grace. All are justified by grace. God's ways are indeed "unsearchable" (11:33). Meanwhile, Israel's salvation is predicated on God's original, gracious election of Israel as a people, and Israel as a whole will be saved. Interestingly, Paul does not say that this will happen when they "believe in Christ," but when "the full number of the Gentiles has come in . . . so all Israel will be saved" (11:25–26). Several scholars argue convincingly that Paul understands Israel's being "saved" *not* by the missionary activity of the church, *but* by the eschatological return of Christ.[108] It is no accident that Paul's words here closely resemble those of Isaiah: "Your people shall *all* be righteous; they shall possess the land forever" (60:21; emphasis mine). David Satran points out that this verse is the support for the famous opening line of the *Mishnah* in the tractate *Sanhedrin*: "All Israel has a share in the world to come."[109]

5

Covenant

—·—·—·—·—·—·—·—·—·—

We affirm that the church, elected in Jesus Christ, has been engrafted into the people of God established by the covenant with Abraham, Isaac and Jacob. Therefore, Christians have not replaced Jews.

—*General Assembly of the Presbyterian Church (U.S.A.)*

The thesis of this chapter is that the proposition stated above constitutes a properly Christian understanding of the covenant, and that this proposition coheres with the doctrine of the utterly unconditional and free grace of God made known to the church in Jesus Christ. The anti-Jewish antithesis to this proposition, that the "new" covenant renders the "old" null and void, is, in the strictest possible sense, a heresy—"that falsehood" which Barth claimed "is the specifically Christian form of sin."[1] In this new confession, the church is not "being nice" to Jews but, finally, is telling the truth. This thesis shall be argued in two steps. First, the supersessionist understanding of covenant dominant throughout most of church history will be described, laying bare the works-righteousness at its heart (to describe the anti-Jewish option is to criticize it). Second, an alternative doctrine of covenant will be articulated. This doctrine is shaped by the norm of the gospel itself, the promise of the love of God *freely* offered to each and all and the command of God that justice be done to each and all. In between the two steps, we will consider some Jewish understandings of covenant.

Shadow and Reality

In the traditional doctrine of the covenant, the church's claim that it displaced Judaism in the economy of salvation and in God's affection took clear form. In what it said about the Jewish people, the church defined itself as the community that benefited from their displacement. The supersessionist interpretation of the covenant took form in the Letter to the Hebrews. Apart from Hebrews, New Testament references to "covenant" number fourteen. Hebrews, with nineteen references to covenant, is concerned to show that Jesus' priesthood is superior to the Levitical priesthood. This new priesthood is older than that of Levi and was established as superior (Heb. 7:1–10). Had perfection been attainable through the Levitical priesthood, there would have been no need for "another priest arising according to the order of Melchizedek" (7:11). Christ has become the new high priest not by birth but by virtue of a life that overcame death (7:16). The weak, useless law has been set aside and a better hope introduced, "through which we approach God" (7:18–19). "Jesus has also become the guarantee of a better covenant" (7:22).

Whereas all the priests of the former covenant died, Christ, the priest of the new covenant, "continues forever" (7:24). Whereas they had to offer sacrifices daily, he offered his "once for all" (7:27). Whereas they were priests subject to weakness, the new high priest is "a Son who has been made perfect forever" (7:28). Jesus serves as high priest "in the heavens" in the "true tent"; earthbound Jewish priests serve only "a sketch and shadow of the heavenly [sanctuary]" (8:1–5). Hebrews affirms the shadowy character of earthly realities and the forward movement of God's purposes to fulfillment.

> But Jesus has now obtained a more excellent ministry, and to that degree he is the mediator of a better covenant, which has been enacted through better promises. For if that first covenant had been faultless, there would have been no need to look for a second one (8:6–7).

Hebrews says of Jeremiah's promise of a new covenant written not on tablets of stone but on the heart: "In speaking of 'a new covenant,' he has made the first one obsolete. And what is obsolete and growing old will soon disappear" (8:13).

Hebrews contrasts the old and the new sacrifices. The earthly priests went continually into only the first, outer, tent, but into the inner one "but once a year" (9:6–7); this indicates the difficulty of access to God under the old covenant and that "the way into the sanctuary has not yet been disclosed as long as the first tent is still standing" (9:8). Jews have no access to God without a priest, and no efficacious priest without Jesus Christ. He "came as a high priest of the good things that have come, then through the greater and perfect tent (not made with hands, that is, not of this creation), he entered once for all into the Holy Place" (9:11–12a). Hebrews contrasts heavenly with earthly, and present with past realities, differentiating the old sacrifices, which had to be repeated, from those of Christ, which are "once for all." The old were efficacious only for purifying the flesh (9:13); the new purify "our conscience from dead works to worship the living God!" (9:14).

Christ "is the mediator of a new covenant" (9:15); his death redeems "those who are called" from "the transgressions under the first covenant" (9:15). The first covenant and sanctuary were copies of the heavenly things, and purified with rites involving blood, which are foreshadows of Christ's own blood. "For Christ did not enter a sanctuary made by human hands, a mere copy of the true one, but he entered into heaven itself, now to appear in the presence of God on our behalf" (9:24). Nor does he offer himself repeatedly, but "has appeared once for all at the end of the age to remove sin by the sacrifice of himself" (9:26). The argument culminates in 10:1–18, recapitulating what has gone before with different emphases. Its thesis is that the worship of the old covenant is a copy of the heavenly pattern, a shadow of the eternal reality, whereas that of the new is an entry into this eternal reality itself. The worship of the former covenant "can never . . . make perfect those who approach" (10:1). The reasons for this conclusion are that the sacrifices had to be repeated and that it is impossible for the blood of bulls and goats to take away sin (10:2–4). For Hebrews, Christ "abolishes the first [covenant] in order to establish the second" (10:9).[2] Hebrews makes it clear that those who received the imperfect revelation mediated through Moses were unable to enter into the promise of rest because of unbelief (3:19). The new covenant having been established, God no longer remembers our sins and misdeeds, and there is no longer any need for "any offering for sin" (10:18). The ineffectual work of the old priests has been rendered otiose by the complete and perfect sacrifice of Christ.

Hebrews drastically overstates matters. That Temple sacrifices were ineffectual because they were repeated is a bizarre argument, particularly from a church that repeats its worship services weekly and, in some cases, daily. The claim that they were ineffectual at all is strange: they were means of grace that granted assurance of forgiveness to sinners. Hebrews also inflates the significance of Christ's complete and perfect triumph over sin, else why should he be "waiting 'until his enemies would be made a footstool for his feet'" (10:13)? Why does he still have enemies?

Scholars debate the purpose of the Letter to the Hebrews and the audience to which it was addressed. It was traditionally thought to have been addressed to "Jewish Christians" who were considering abandoning their new faith and returning to the synagogue. The book, however, addresses no real issues between the church and the synagogue, and its attack upon the Temple priesthood assaults an institution that the Roman army had already destroyed. Whatever its purpose, Hebrews put forth a

supersessionist argument against Judaism, claiming that the covenant between God and the Israel of God had been abolished. The author's positive purpose was commendable, to contend that the grace of God
through Jesus Christ is freely and utterly available to all sinners, and that
the word of this grace is a sure and certain word on which we can rely.
But we see two things clearly: the author's constructive thesis calls for the
dismantling of the negative, supersessionist framework in which it was
cast lest the very grace it proclaims as radically free be conditional after
all; and its displacement theology was to have a long and tragic history.

Standard reference works reflect anti-Jewish views of the covenant. Gerhard Kittel's *Theological Dictionary of the New Testament* ends its article on
covenant in the "Old Testament" with the remark: "The old covenant is
forgotten, and should remain so."[3] Alan Richardson's *Theological Dictionary of the Bible* regards the prophets' view of the Hebrew people as one
that led them to look forward "to the day in which God shall fashion a
new instrument, more adequate to his purpose." To which the author
adds that "all the NT writers regard the church . . . as this new instrument,
and see the fulfillment of Israel's destiny in the new covenant." This Bible
dictionary then asserts: "The Christian Church is, in fact, the New Israel,"
without taking into account the fact that the expression "new Israel" never
occurs in the New Testament.[4] Anti-Jewish views are passed along under
the guise of scholarship with no criticism of their ideological bent.

The Covenant Is Not Both Theirs and Ours

What Hebrews initiated, the Epistle of Barnabas continued. Written
around the end of the first century C.E., probably in Alexandria, the
Epistle of Barnabas enjoyed broad appeal in the ancient church and for a
while was regarded as scripture. What exercised the writer was that some
in his community argued that "the covenant is both theirs [the Jews']
and ours." He found it quite intolerable that people who know "the way
of righteousness" should "rush off into the way of darkness." This erroneous view of the covenant had to be corrected by the view which holds
that they "lost it, after Moses had already received it." Barnabas argues
that after Moses received the tablets of the Law, he broke them upon
discovering the Hebrews worshiping idols. With that act, says Barnabas,
"their covenant was broken, in order that the covenant of the beloved
Jesus might be sealed upon our heart, in the hope which flows from believing in Him."[5] According to this view, the Jews *never* had a covenant
with God.

Barnabas introduces another argument, that their covenant has *now*
been abolished by God. Of Jewish sacrifices, he affirms that God has

"abolished these things, that the law of our Lord Jesus Christ, which is without the yoke of necessity, might have a human oblation." Barnabas appropriates the prophets' criticism of fasting to argue that God rejects *Jewish* forms of worship; meanwhile, God has been patiently working to prepare a people, the Gentiles, who would "with guilelessness believe in His Beloved." Therefore, "we should not rush forward as rash acceptors of their laws." As it was the work of Christ to "fulfill the promise made to the fathers," and to do so by "preparing a new people for Himself," so the Anti-Christ leads some to destruction by tempting them to say that "the covenant is both theirs and ours." The truth is, however, that they have been "rejected" as part of the work of Christ who "came in the flesh with this view, that He might bring to a head the sum of their sins who had persecuted His prophets to the death." Barnabas interprets references to Christ as the new Adam (Adam = land) to mean that Christ fulfills the promise to Abraham of a land: "We, then, are they whom He has led into the good land." Barnabas' reason was that since "land" in Hebrew is *adama*, and since "Adam" was so named because he was made from the earth, and since Christ is the "second Adam," Christ fulfills the promise of land. The promise is not made to Jews, but to us: *We* are the ones led into the good land. The land was to flow with milk and honey, which Barnabas interprets by arguing that "as the infant is kept alive first by honey, and then by milk, so also we, being quickened and kept alive by the promise of faith and by the word, shall live ruling over the earth."[6] Here is Barnabas' exegesis: land = Christ; milk and honey = faith and the word. Here we see the truth of W. D. Davies' remark that "for the holiness of place, Christianity has fundamentally substituted the holiness of Person: it has Christified holy space."[7]

Barnabas' method of interpreting scripture, applying all prophetic criticism to the Jews and appropriating all gracious promises for the church, yields to a typological mode which tries to show that events, laws, and stories in the Bible point to Christ as their intended meaning. The point is to demonstrate that Christians and not Jews are the heirs of the covenant. Barnabas takes the two peoples in Rebecca's womb as types of the Jews and the Gentiles; "the one people shall surpass the other, and the elder shall serve the younger." The younger people are the Gentile Christians, the elder the Jews. Jacob's blessing of Ephraim rather than Manasseh was in order that "the elder shall serve the younger." The Lord did give to the Jews the covenant promised to them, "but they were not worthy to receive it, on account of their sins." "Moses, as a servant, received it; but the Lord himself, having suffered in our behalf, hath given it to us, that we should be the people of inheritance."[8]

Barnabas draws two further conclusions. First, the Jewish Sabbath is false. Isaiah's criticism of inauthentic worship shows God's rejection of the Sabbath of the Jews. For Barnabas, God says to the Jews, "I shall make a beginning of the eighth day, that is, a beginning of another world." Second, Jews falsely persist in placing their trust in the Temple rather than in God. Yet their Temple, as predicted, has been destroyed through war. In its place there now exists an "incorruptible Temple," into which we (not they) have been introduced.[9] The church is the true Israel, Israel the false Israel. Those who think that they share the good things of God with Jews do the work of the Anti-Christ. Barnabas' alternative was to claim the scriptures for the church with a method that denied it to Jews, and to antedate the Jews' rejection and the church's election to the very beginning of revelatory history. He repeats an older theme: the scriptures are ours, not yours, because you do not understand them.[10]

Tertullian also argued that Jews are a rejected and subjugated people, rejected *by* God and subjected *to* the church. He uses the two peoples allegory to contend that the "prior and 'greater' people—that is, the Jewish—must necessarily serve the 'less'; and the 'less' people—that is, the Christian—overcome the 'greater.'" Jews have forsaken God and begun to serve images, whereas Gentiles quit the idols whom they used to serve and "have been converted to the same God from whom Israel . . . had departed." Thus has the lesser people attained to "the grace of divine favour, from which Israel has been divorced." Tertullian interprets Jeremiah's promise of a new covenant as arguing that circumcision was "temporary, inwrought for 'a sign' in a contumacious people, so the spiritual has been given for salvation to an obedient people." "Old Testament" promises of a new covenant mean that "*our* people" will replace the Jews: "Therefore, as we have shown above that the coming cessation of the old law and of the carnal circumcision was declared, so, too, the observance of the new law and the spiritual circumcision has shone out into the voluntary obediences of peace." The "temporal sabbath" has been displaced by an "eternal sabbath," observed by Christians; of the Jewish Sabbath Isaiah declared, "*Your* sabbaths my soul hateth." So were "earthly oblations" replaced by "spiritual sacrifices," with the latter being acceptable to God and the former not.[11]

Anti-Judaism defines the church

Throughout the early and medieval period of church history, the *adversus Judaeos* literature continued to reiterate these same points.[12] In Christian anti-Judaism, not only Jews were defined; Christian anti-Judaism also defined the church. The doctrine of the church formulated by the church's teachers was the other side of the anti-Jewish coin.

Cyril of Jerusalem in his catechetical lectures on the doctrine of the church, given around the middle of the fourth century, delineates what makes the church "catholic." He summarizes Christian understanding of the church in his time: that the church is catholic means that it (1) is spread through the whole world, (2) teaches the whole faith, (3) is throughout all the classes of society, and (4) brings a universal remedy to every kind of sin. This said, Cyril contrasts the church with the "assembly" (*ekklesia*) called together by God in Leviticus and Deuteronomy. Once there was an *ekklesia* of the Jewish people, but "since then the Jews have fallen out of divine favour because of their conspiring against the Lord, and the Saviour has built up from among the Gentiles a second assembly or church," built "upon a rock." Cyril justified his views biblically, interpreting criticisms of the "assembly" of God as rejecting the Jews, and biblical promises as applying exclusively to the church. In Cyril's anti-Jewish reading, when Psalm 26 says "I have hated the church of the evildoers," this pertains to "the first church" of the Jews. When the psalm declares "Lord, I have loved the beauty of thine house," it talks of the second church of the Gentiles. The former has been "cast off," the latter abounds in the world. Malachi's "I have no pleasure in you, says the LORD of hosts," applies literally to Jews, and his promise that "my name is great among the nations" (Mal. 1:10–11) applies literally to the Gentile church. The new, second church is universal (catholic), unlike the old, ethnocentric "church," which it replaces. It "alone bears sway in all the world."[13]

Anti-Judaism shapes the church's understanding of its sacraments. Irenaeus interprets Malachi as indicating "that the first people would cease to make offerings to God, but that in every place a sacrifice would be offered to him, and that a pure one; and that his name would be glorified among the nations." Consequently, it is "the Church's offering . . . which is counted as a pure sacrifice before God and which is acceptable to him," not that of the synagogue. "The people of God *had* sacrifices and his Church *has* sacrifices. The only thing that has changed is the particular form of the offering; this is no longer made by slaves but by free men." Irenaeus explains the invalidity of contemporary Jewish offerings by the deicide charge: "From the outside they seemed to be making their offerings rightly, but just like Cain, they were envious within. And so they murdered the righteous one, and rejected the advice of the Word, just as Cain had done." Whereas the church makes its offering to God "in simplicity of heart," "the Jews do this no longer. Their hands are full of blood, for they would not receive the Word through whom offering is made to God."[14]

These assertions are one and all inappropriate to the Christian faith. The claim that Jews lost the covenant because they were not worthy of it is simply works-righteousness. Works-righteousness takes a gift provided by the free and unconditional grace of God and turns it into a condition apart from which God is not free to be gracious. Works-right-eousness has nothing to do with an entirely different matter, the question of whether we are to do works of love toward the neighbor. With regard to the covenant, works-righteousness contends that God is not free to covenant with whomever God pleases but only with those who *deserve* to receive it. It claims that we deserve it, Jews do not. Christian anti-Judaism reflects a reward and punishment mind-set. Jews are punished by losing the covenant; we are rewarded with receiving it because we deserve it. Because the church defines itself in what it says about God's covenant with the Jews, we must note the result: the church defined itself as anti-Jewish, other than Jewish, and better than Jewish, forgetting that all our theologizing is to be done to the greater glory of God, not to our glory. Supersessionist understandings of covenant are shot through with ideology; they justify injustice perpetrated on Jews and the "victory" of Christians over Jews in the Roman Empire after Constantine. On all counts, displacement understandings of the covenant are totally inappropriate because they contradict the good news of God's unconditional love. Because they helped make possible the Holocaust (by implying that Jews should cease to exist *as* Jews), these claims could not be made in the presence of the burning Jewish children. When churches today confess a new understanding, that Christians have been *engrafted into the people of God established by the covenant and have not replaced Jews,* they rectify an old theological error and articulate their faith in a way coherent with the gospel of God's thoroughly gracious love.

The strange witness of unbelief

In its displacement interpretation of the covenant between the God of Israel and the Israel of God, the church traditionally claimed that God's promise to Israel of a land had been abrogated, that promise having been "fulfilled" in Jesus Christ. The role of the Jews in history is to wander and suffer in homelessness, thereby attesting to the truth of God disclosed in Jesus Christ.

Rome was victorious in the two wars of rebellion in Roman Palestine (66–70 and 132–135 C.E.). At the end of the first the Temple was destroyed, and at the end of the second the Emperor Hadrian barred Jews from the city of Jerusalem (Jews were never barred from the land). Jerusalem was converted into a pagan city and a sanctuary to Jupiter placed on the spot where the Temple had stood.[15] Christian apologists seized the opportunities afforded by these events. Historical contingencies were interpreted as God's will: "Those who slandered Him [Christ]," declared Justin, "should be miserable." Jews suffer today because they are guilty of not recognizing the One with whom they had to do in their history, and because when he appeared among them, they killed him.

> For the circumcision according to the flesh, which is from Abraham, was given for a sign; that you may be separated from other nations, and from us; and that you alone may suffer that which you now justly suffer; and that your land may be desolate, and your cities burned with fire; and that strangers may eat your fruit in your presence, and not one of you may go up to Jerusalem.

"Accordingly," claims Justin, "these things have happened to you in fairness and justice, for you have slain the Just One."[16]

Irenaeus, bishop of Lyons from about 178 C.E. to the end of his life, about 200 C.E., fought against gnostic anti-Judaism with its rejection of the "Old Testament" and against Judaism itself. In performing this tightrope act, he countered the Marcionite objection to Christianity—that Jerusalem was destroyed because it was the city of Yahweh, the God who created this world and revealed the Law to the Jews—by contending that Jerusalem was "rightly forsaken" because the Jews "are no longer useful for bringing forth fruit."[17] Here we see the patristic strategy for countering Marcion's objections to the God of the Bible: the defenders of the God of the Bible "'salvaged' that God for Christians precisely by means of the anti-Judaic myth."[18]

Tertullian argued as well that because Jews have forsaken God in rejecting Christ, it is "in accordance with their deserts" that they "should be prohibited from entering the holy city."[19] Origen (c. 185–c. 254 C.E.) repeated the theme of Jewish suffering and homelessness, both now and hereafter, "on account of their unbelief and other insults which they heaped upon Jesus," transcendentalizing military conquests, and declaring that "these calamities they have suffered, because they were a most wicked nation, which although guilty of many other sins, yet has been punished so severely for none, as for those that were committed against our Jesus."[20]

We find in Augustine (c. 354–c. 430 C.E.) a "systematic" treatment of Jewish homelessness, bearing in mind that his views would prove influential in the church throughout the Middle Ages. In his *Reply to Faustus*, Augustine treats the story of Cain and Abel as a nine-point allegory on the relation of the Jews (Cain) to Christ (Abel).[21] Cain and the Jews find their offering to God rejected, for God prefers the faith of the "new covenant" to the "earthly" observance of the old. Cain and the Jews offered well, but did not divide well, missing the coming of Christ. They do not confess their sin and receive grace; instead, they kill the innocent brother. Neither can answer the question, Where is your brother? Cain is cursed to be a mourner and abject; the Jews are cursed from the church and under the law. They till the ground that yields no fruit—the ground of Jewish worship.

Yet Christians are not to *make* Jews suffer for their crime. Rather, Jews will groan and tremble on the earth, witnessing to the fate of those who reject Christ. They will wander. "So to the end of the seven days of time, the continued preservation of the Jews will be a proof to believing Christians of the subjection merited by those who . . . put the Lord to death."[22] The "wandering Jew" makes "the strange witness of unbelief" in dispersion from the land of promise. Augustine built his myth of the wandering Jew into the theology of history that he wrote after Alaric sacked Rome in 410. In *The City of God*, Augustine explains that God founded "the kingdom of the Jews" and preserved it, "as long as they remained in the true religion." His problem was to explain why the fall of Jerusalem was the fault of the Jews and the fall of Rome not the fault of the Christians. After articulating how the Jewish people and kingdom were brought into existence by God, Augustine argues that "if they had not sinned against Him with impious curiosity, which seduced them like magic arts, and drew them to strange gods and idols, and at last led them to kill Christ, their kingdom would have remained to them, and would have been, if not more spacious, yet more happy, than that of Rome." Now, however, "it is through the providence of that one true God" that they "are dispersed through almost all lands and nations." They lost their land and kingdom, initially "instituted by divine authority, and afterwards, in due time, by the same authority taken away from the people of God." The Jews lost also their capacity to see the truth. Augustine interprets Psalm 69:23 ("Let their eyes be darkened so that they cannot see") as having been read out in God's judgment on the Jews: "What wonder, then, if those whose eyes are dimmed that they see not do not see these manifest things?"[23]

Augustine explains that, before Christ, God afflicted the Jews "with continual adversity, to prove that the building of another temple had been promised by prophetic voices." Then he takes up the birth of Christ "whereby the Word was made flesh; and of the dispersion of the Jews among all nations, as had been prophesied." The Jews who slew Christ and would not believe in him "were yet more miserably wasted by the Romans, and utterly rooted out from their kingdom, . . . and were dispersed through the land so that indeed there is no place where they are not." By their own scriptures they are "a testimony to us that we have not forged the prophecies about Christ." Some Jews believed in Christ and are the "saved" remnant of Israel. The rest do not believe their own scriptures, "which they blindly read." What God did with the Jews was to see to it that they should serve the church "everywhere . . .

as witnesses among all nations to the prophecies which were sent before concerning Christ." God manifested to the church "in her enemies the Jews the grace of His compassion, since, as saith the apostle, 'their offence is the salvation of the Gentiles.'"[24] God said: "Slay them not," and "Disperse them." Until the middle of the sixteenth century and Pope Paul IV (1555–1559), papal policy toward Jews, set as a norm by Gregory the Great (540–604), reflected Augustine's teaching.[25]

Modern, liberal displacement views

Anti-Judaism did not disappear with the arrival of modernity. What happened in liberal and neo-orthodox theology was that classical anti-Judaism reappeared in new form. Now we have more contemporary scholarly and/or theological reasons for viewing Judaism as a dead faith, a fossilized remain that nonetheless lives on, a faith that continues obdurately to miss its election. This modern/contemporary anti-Judaism exists in two forms: a higher-critical and a dialectical theology form.

In Protestant, predominantly Lutheran, historical-critical approaches to biblical study, we find a picture of Judaism from the time of the Exile as a religion in decay, a picture significantly at odds with that drawn by such recent scholars as E. P. Sanders. The portrayal of Second Temple Judaism as a putrefying religion owes much to Julius Wellhausen.[26] He developed a three-stage view of biblical history, which arose from (1) simple Mosaic piety to (2) the heights of prophetic monotheism, but after the return from exile declined (3) into a legalistic and rabbinic form of faith. In its degradation, Judaism became a mixture of an ethical and nationalist worldview that can no longer be regarded as genuine faith. This period is characterized by several "mistakes," of which the very return from exile to the land of promise was not the least. We see here a preference for "wandering" Jews; they should not have returned home. The deterioration of Judaism was caused by an excessive focus on the Temple cult, law, legalistic piety, and the Pharisees as the scholarly interpreters of the law. No longer led by prophets, Judaism became a religion run by priests and scholars; the wellsprings of inspiration ran dry. Such leadership "transformed their spiritual point of view into a legalistic preoccupation with the ritual laws of worship."[27] Critics in this tradition renamed postexilic Judaism "late Judaism" (*Spätjudentum*), to make clear that the "shift to a nation in the late sixth century B.C.E. marked the overall degradation of biblical Israel from the heights of prophecy to mere law, and from a free, spontaneously religious people to a Temple-bound cult."[28]

"Late Judaism" was in decline and on the way to its death. In relation to it, Jesus and Paul could be understood only in terms of the starkest contrast. Overwhelmingly, German scholars characterized "late Judaism" as inauthentic, as having turned its back on faith in the God of Israel and the prophetic message. Henceforth, Judaism is on the wrong track. Georg Fohrer said that it had failed in its "divine task by constantly falling away from the way of life imposed on [it] . . . and wanting to use God merely as metaphysical security for their own life."[29] "Late Judaism" is an absurd result of decadent, "blind" rabbinic scholarship obsessed with the letter of the law. It mistakenly sought to reestablish the political security of the people in a state of their own, failing to realize that Jews are a "religious community" rather than a nation and that ideally they should live under nomadic conditions, wandering among the nations, to ensure the purity of the central Jewish message of freedom. It misinterpreted the sufferings with which Jews were inflicted:

> For it certainly cannot be overlooked that all this was provoked largely by the misuse of powers lying in Jewish hands—a misuse which again has its cause in the ancient abandonment of Israel's task and in its typically human quest for enjoyment and security of life.[30]

Such biblical scholars move with ease between ancient Israel and the contemporary state of Israel, as does Hans Werner Bartsch with his thesis that the essential thing for Israel since biblical times was never the settled condition of the people in a particular country but the fulfillment of a special ideal for which a country of their own is not necessary. Israel's task is to realize an ethical idea: "Jerusalem acquired a kind of symbolic value for a social order which, in contrast to the existing slave-owning society, provided freedom for everyone." Bartsch contends that reestablishing the state of Israel contradicts the appropriate task of Jews, which is to proclaim freedom. This can best be done by repudiating all claims to the city of Jerusalem.[31] Jews can most purely express their longing for freedom when they are in a nomadic or ghettoized condition. Augustine's ideology of the wandering Jew lives on after him.

"Late Judaism" is preparatory for and inferior to Christianity. Jesus is interpreted as having rejected this "old" Judaism and, with his words and work, no longer forms a part of the history of Israel. In his crucifixion by the Jews, *Jewish history comes to an end*. On this model, "late Judaism" was in a state of decadence, orthodoxy, and legalism—its faith externalized and rigid. God had become distant and the prophetic message forgotten. Law and legalistic piety typify "late Judaism"; Joachim Jeremias goes so far as to call legalistic piety the "cancer" of Judaism.[32] Such piety "separates us from God." Consequently, legalistic exegesis of the "Old Testament" is "blind," and Jews are "deaf to the gospel."

The third theme in the anti-Jewish interpretive model is the Pharisees, *the* enemies of Jesus' teaching. Jon Sobrino discusses Jesus' approach to prayer under the rubric of "Jesus' criticism of contemporary prayer," interpreting the parable of the Pharisee and the publican to mean that "Jesus condemns the prayer of the Pharisees [note the plural] because it is the self-assertion of an egotistical 'I' and hence vitiated at its very core." The Pharisee's "pole of reference" is not to God but to himself. The Pharisee is "even less oriented toward other human beings. He holds them in contempt . . . and he thanks God that he is not like them."[33] Jesus contradicts the Pharisees on every point, which brings him to his death; the religious leaders of Judaism have him killed because of his teaching.

The claim that the Jews had Jesus executed on a religious charge of blasphemy is the fourth major theme of modern anti-Judaism. Jesus "is eventually condemned because of his conception of God."[34] With this, "late Judaism" passes off the scene, its history over, to be replaced by the "new Israel." What else was possible when "the whole battle between Jesus and Judaism would come down to the question of God," when Jesus' "understanding of and relation to God . . . brought [him] into direct opposition to Judaism," when the stage was set "for the final struggle between Jesus and Judaism"?[35] Judaism passes away and the promise to the people Israel of a land in which to live according to God's *torah* becomes empty. The historical role that Christian theology, exercising hegemony over history and God's purposes, assigns to Israel is to wander and suffer in exile and provide the strange witness of unbelief.

The strange case of Karl Barth

In Karl Barth we face an enigma. He resisted Hitler, helped form the 1934 Barmen Declaration of the Confessing Churches, denounced Nazism, was suspended from his teaching post at Bonn and in 1935 forced out of Germany. Shortly after the close of the Second Vatican Council, Barth visited Pope Paul VI in Rome and remarked to the Secretariat for Christian Unity:

> Today there are very good relations between the Roman Catholic Church and many of the Protestant churches, between the Secretariat for Christian Unity and the World Council of Churches. The number of ecumenical study—and work—groups is growing very fast. The ecumenical movement is clearly being impelled by the Spirit of the Lord. But we should not forget that there is ultimately only one truly great ecumenical question: our relation to Judaism.[36]

Barth made other extraordinary statements on relations between Jews and Christians. He held that an anti-Semitic or a-Semitic church loses both its faith and the object of its faith.[37] He affirmed of the people Israel that we Christians are "guests in their house, . . . new wood grafted onto *their* old tree."[38]

Nevertheless, Barth's attitude toward Judaism and the Jewish people was mixed. I say "and the Jewish people" because we may not forget that when theologians legitimize Jewish suffering we are talking about Jewish women, Jewish children, Jewish men, whose suffering is being theologically justified. Although Nazism taught Barth that anti-Judaism is also anti-Christian, he continued the tradition of Christian anti-Judaism. Writing in 1940, Barth saw the misfortunes of the Jewish people as a witness to Christian truth, precisely as had the *adversus Judaeos* theological tradition.

Barth made a series of points to this effect, declaring that God determines that Israel will serve the elected people of God, the church, of which Israel is a part, by reflecting the judgment from which God has rescued human beings in Jesus Christ. Israel "is not an obedient but an obdurate people," by whom the Messiah is delivered up and for whom he is crucified. Israel should become obedient to its election; it should "enter the Church and perform this special service in the Church." Why Israel should want to enter the church to reflect there the judgment from which God has rescued human beings is a question Barth does not address. Israel is disobedient to and resists its election. It forms the synagogue, seeking to "realise its true determination beside and outwith the Church," and so "creates schism, a gulf, in the minds of the community of God." Outside the church, all that Israel can set forth is "the sheer, stark judgment of God," an "outmoded and superseded" revolt against God's grace. In their unbelief, the Jews create "the spectral form of the synagogue." In the sense that Jews provide the strange witness of unbelief, Barth affirms that "the existence of the Jews . . . is an adequate proof of the existence of God."

> The Jews of the ghetto give this demonstration involuntarily, joylessly and ingloriously, but they do give it. They have nothing to attest to the world but the shadow of the cross of Christ that falls upon them. But they, too, do actually and necessarily attest Jesus Christ Himself.[39]

This claim is not an aberrant appearance in Barth's theology but part of his argument that in Christ God "takes the lost cause of humanity, who have denied him as Creator and in so doing ruined themselves as creatures, and makes it his own."[40] The theological question is, How could Barth regard the cause of the Israel of God as lost apart from God's act in Jesus Christ? Is the whole of the history of the Israel of God prior to and since the time of Jesus nothing more than a denial of God? Does the Hebrew Bible give voice to nothing more than Israel's rejection of God? Are the covenants that God graciously made with Israel null and void, so that Israel's election is to be found only within the church? Does the new covenant rescind all prior ones, including the utterly gratuitous covenants? In calling Israel a disobedient people and saying that the shadow that falls across the Jewish ghettos of Nazi-occupied Europe is the shadow of the cross, Barth made an improper use of words. One cannot say these things in the presence of the burning children, not without identifying the shadow of the cross with the shadow of the swastika, which *did* fall across the ghetto.

Although Barth properly contends that "Jesus Christ would not be Jesus Christ apart from Israel," he shows an innocence of Jewish faith in remarking that "Israel is nothing apart from Jesus Christ." Yet Barth is a strange case. On one hand he can contend that "in this Jewish nation [people] there really lives to this day the extraordinariness of the revelation of God." Those who are ashamed of Israel are ashamed of Jesus Christ and their own existence. The attack on Israel in Nazi Germany was "the attack on the rock of the work and revelation of God, beside which work and which revelation there is no other." Anti-Judaism and anti-Semitism are forms "of godlessness beside which, what is usually called atheism (as confessed say in Russia) is quite innocuous." Anti-Semitism brings one into conflict with Christ, "for the mission, the prophetic, priestly and kingly mission of the nation Israel is identical with God's will and work, as surely as it has been set forth and revealed in Jesus Christ." Israel's election was not for its own glory, but so that it could carry out the prophetic mission of being a light to the Gentiles, which mission has been "fulfilled, revealed and accomplished in Jesus Christ." Yet the picture of Israel given in the scriptures is of a people who oppose their own election and prove unworthy of it and are broken by the judgment that afflicts them because they defy grace.[41]

Barth so thinks because he reads Romans 9–11 as arguing for "one community of those who come to faith out of Israel, together with those who are called out of the heathen to the Church." There is not supposed to be "a Church of the Jews and a Church of the heathen." Disobediently, the Jews maintain "a Synagogue, existing upon the denial of Jesus Christ and on a powerless continuation of Israelite history, which entered upon God's fullness long ago."[42] The synagogue is "the shadow-picture of the Church." Barth reiterates a long-standing ideology, which the Christian Roman Empire and later medieval states enacted into laws prohibiting the building or repairing of synagogues.[43] That Barth can speak so assuredly of Jewish sinfulness and failure, as if there were no Jewish faithfulness, no prophetic self-criticism, is astounding. Whether he was influenced by the evaluation of *Spätjudentum* emanating from the Wellhausen school is debatable; that he shares its assessment is not. That after the Holocaust he can blame the suffering and death of a million and a quarter Jewish children on Jewish sinfulness raises immense questions of theological appropriateness and credibility. Rather than sinfulness and failure, the persistence of the Jewish witness of faith through two millennia of Christian persecution is one of the most profound witnesses of faith ever made. If the discussion is over whether a religion is unworthy of its election, Christianity is as good a candidate for the honor as any.

Whatever Paul's arguments with his fellow Jews, they did not entail regarding the cause of the Jews as "lost" apart from Jesus Christ. Here we heed a modified form of Lloyd Gaston's insight, that apart from contrary evidence we should read Paul as commenting on Gentile problems.[44] Paul's second-generation interpreter, the author of Ephesians, is more on target than Barth:

> So then, remember that at one time you Gentiles by birth, called "the uncircumcision" by those who are called "the circumcision"—a physical circumcision made in the flesh by human hands—remember that you were at that time without Christ, being aliens from the commonwealth of Israel, and strangers to the covenants of promise, having no hope and without God in the world. But now in Christ Jesus you who once were far off have been brought near by the blood of Christ. (2:11–13)

We may imagine Ephesians addressing Barth's Teutonic ancestors, members of those Germanic tribes who busied themselves religiously by worshiping Wotan and Thor and baying at the moon. They were "dead through the trespasses and sins in which [they] . . . once lived," but have been "made alive" through Christ (2:1–2, 5). It is they whose cause was lost, who were "without God *[atheoi]* in the world," strangers to the covenants of promise, having no hope. God took up Israel's cause in the Exodus and at Sinai and ever and again throughout Israel's history, perhaps even in the darkest night of the *Shoah*. In Jesus Christ, God took up the lost cause of Gentiles, part of God's promise to Abraham, so that they might be "no longer strangers and aliens, but . . . citizens with the saints and also members of the household of God" (2:19). Later, Barth's position seems to have shifted. Of Jews he said: "They have the promise of God; and if we Christians from among the Gentiles have it too, then it is only as those chosen with them, as guests in their house, as new wood grafted onto their old tree."[45]

Going Up to Jerusalem

In thinking anew about how to frame its understanding of covenant, the church must go up to Jerusalem to listen to the Jewish tradition. Here covenant making is a form of God's grace to which walking in God's way (Torah, *halakah*) is Israel's proper response; its purpose is to teach Israel to order its life so that it may live justly and be a light to the Gentiles to whom God and God's name are to be made known. God's making a covenant with Israel at Sinai and giving to Israel the Ten Commandments (the ten "words," as they are called in Judaism) is prefaced with these words: "I am the LORD your God, who brought you out of the land of Egypt, out of the house of slavery" (Ex. 20:2). This statement summarizes the first nineteen chapters of Exodus, the prologue to God's giving of the Torah. This preamble states in the indicative mode what God has done for Israel. In a manner parallel to Paul's writings, the indicative of God's grace precedes the imperative. The structure of thought in both cases is the same: promise and command, call and claim, proclamation and paranesis, divine initiative and human response. "The God who speaks here," declared Gerhard von Rad, "is the God of grace."[46] The prologue bases Israel's obligations to God on God's gracious deeds on behalf of Israel.[47] By honoring the commands of God, Israel affirms God's gracious gift to and rule over Israel. "God ruling" is what Jesus meant by the "kingdom of God." Israel narrates the history of God's gracious acts on its behalf before it tells of the giving of the Torah to ensure that keeping the commandments will be understood as Israel's response to God's unmerited good pleasure. Complying with the Torah is the means of an intimate and loving relationship with God, of "communion with a loving and personal God."[48]

As Israel understood itself, its existence as a people depended not on its merits or other noteworthy qualities, but on an affair of the heart. "Although heaven and the heaven of heavens belong to the LORD your God, the earth with all that is in it," declared the Deuteronomist, "yet the LORD set his heart in love on your ancestors alone and chose you, their descendants after them, out of all the peoples, as it is today" (Deut. 10:14–15). Israel is therefore to love God, to walk in God's ways and keep God's commandments (Deut. 10:12–13). At the heart of Israel's covenant with God is a mutual love, God's unmerited love for Israel and Israel's love for God.[49] By walking in God's way, Israel expresses its gratitude for God's grace. God's "teaching" (*torah*) is born in love and given voice in law.

In the prophets, we find the same relation between the gracious love of God and the dual commandment of the love of God and the neighbor. The religion of biblical Israel was patriarchal (although hardly more so than that of the church), yet seldom uses "father" to refer to God, doubtless because of its connections with fertility cults. The scriptures of Israel employ the language of intimate, tender, parental love of God for Israel and speak of Israel as God's beloved child or son (Ex. 4:22–23). Images of Israel as God's child, of God and Israel as bride and groom, and motherly images of God's tenderness all express God's love for Israel. The analogy of marital love between God and Israel is present in the Torah where following other gods is threatened by the statement: "For I the LORD your God am a jealous God" (Ex. 20:5; Deut. 5:9). The root word for "jealous" is used in the technical sense of a husband who is jealous for his wife. The legal formula expressing the covenantal relation between God and Israel, "I will walk among you, and will be your God, and you shall be my people" (Lev. 26:12; Deut. 29:13), is drawn from the sphere of marriage. Hosea writes of God as having loved Israel as a child, having taught Ephraim to walk, having bent down and suckled Israel (11:3–4). The rudimentary experience of the prophets was an awareness of the pathos of God with Israel, a feeling of the heart of God and a hearing of God's voice.[50] Because the prophets experienced the heart of God, they taught *torah* to the people, "the instruction of the LORD" (Isa. 30:9).

Because the range and profundity of God's compassion is so great, God is a God of forgiveness. God's steadfast love or grace (*hesed*) made evident in mercy is an essential of Israelite faith. God's "righteousness" refers to the reliability, the long-suffering quality, of God's love.[51] "Have mercy on me, O God, according to your steadfast love; according to your abundant mercy blot out my transgressions" (Ps. 51:1). While Israel was yet a sinner, God redeemed it from Egypt (Psalm 106). God's righteousness is what the Reformers called God's "active righteousness," by which God justifies sinners. It signals God's readiness to forgive, God's dependable love. The sacrificial rituals were means of grace by which God's forgiveness was made available to the people.[52]

The essential structure of biblical faith is not a circle with one center but an ellipse with two foci: the love of God freely offered to each and all, and the dual command of God that we love God and do justice to each and all of those others whom God loves. The commandments are not external, arbitrary impositions, but a form for expressing gratitude and a means of grace. *Torah* is inadequately translated by "law," particularly in the light of the Christian tradition's predominantly pejorative treatment of "law." *Torah* means teaching or instruction, the guidelines by which Israel is to walk in the way of God. Judaism refers to the Ten Commandments as the "ten words" or "utterances." They are "the ten quintessential statements of God to the Israelite nation."[53] It is more than merely interesting that they are stated in the indicative, with no hint of reward or punishment connected with them. "You shall not kill." God's people are to be a witness people, testifying by the way they live to the love and justice of God. The broadest meaning of *torah* is instruction in God's gracious will for a people who accept God's gift of grace. In the whole range of meanings that *torah* has in the Scriptures of Israel, it is comparable to what Christians mean by "gospel."[54]

Throughout the story preceding and following God's covenant making with Israel at Sinai is the conviction that Israel is a people chosen of God: "The LORD your God has chosen you out of all the peoples on earth to be his people, his treasured possession" (Deut. 7:6). All the strata of tradition in the Pentateuch are cognizant that "chosenness" has to do with God's freely offered love and the appropriate response of Israel to that love, which is Israel's service to God and the peoples of the earth. God chooses Israel to serve God's all-inclusive purposes. This understanding of chosenness is communicated by the "Yahwist" account of God's call to Abraham: "In you all the families of the earth shall be blessed" (Gen. 12:3). The "Elohist" story makes the same point with the figure of Joseph, stressing that it was not only Joseph and his brothers and his father's house and Egypt that were saved by God's choosing of Joseph, but *"all the world* came to Joseph in Egypt to buy grain, because the famine became severe throughout the world" (Gen. 41:57, emphasis added). Second Isaiah provided the most forceful interpretation of chosenness in the various servant songs:

> It is too light a thing that you should be my servant
> > to raise up the tribes of Jacob
> > and to restore the survivors of Israel;
> I will give you as a light to the nations [Gentiles],
> > that my salvation may reach to the end of the earth.
> > > (Isa. 49:6)

God's seeking love and searching presence were no special privilege, nor a guarantee of superiority.[55] Chosenness did not entail an exclusive privilege:

> You only have I known
> > of all the families of the earth;
> therefore I will punish you
> > for all your iniquities.
> > > (Amos 3:2)

Israel was to be a priestly people, serving others, not itself. God's covenant was not merely for Israel's good but for the good of all human beings, Gentiles and Jews. God chose Israel as an instrument so that all peoples may come to know God and God's purposes for them. Not only did God promise Abraham that "in you all the families of the earth shall be blessed," but Isaiah taught Israel that this promise would be confirmed when Israel would teach Assyria and Egypt to worship God (19:23–25).

Second Isaiah, in Babylonian exile, interpreted God's purpose in sending Israel into exile as a missionary one: "I have given you as a . . . light to the nations, to open the eyes that are blind" (Isa. 42:6–7). Israel's Babylonian neighbors will begin to say, "'I am the LORD's,' another will be called by the name of Jacob" (44:5). The story of Jonah reminds Israel of her responsibility to Nineveh, a center of Gentile culture. The postbiblical Jewish tradition would further develop its understanding of the vocation of the Jewish people to serve as a source of light for all the world.[56]

Christians often view the covenant as easily degenerating into a mere legal relationship contracted for the mutual benefit of both parties. This overlooks two matters. First is that of the two types of covenant found in the Bible, some are completely promissory and gratuitous. The covenants with Abraham (Genesis 15 and 17) and with David (2 Samuel 7; Psalm 89) are respectively concerned with the gift of land and kingship and impose no obligations on Abraham or David. The covenant with Abraham and his descendants is valid eternally. "Even when Israel sins and is to be severely punished, God intervenes to help because He 'will not break his covenant' (Lev. 26:43)."[57] Paul refers to this covenant when he claims that "the gifts and the calling of God are irrevocable" (Rom. 11:29). Second, the Torah, the visible seal of the Sinai covenant, is not a set of legal obligations that, once obeyed, becomes the basis for a reward claim. It is a gracious disclosure of the conditions of a truly authentic life that entails justice in and beyond the community. Elements of legalism or works-righteousness can appear in Judaism, but this is equally true of Christianity. The covenant forms the background for understanding the prophets' denunciation of Israel's apostasy as well as for their choice of such images as marriage and adultery to illustrate the meaning of covenant. Their message was never that Israel had broken a legal contract, or that it is now to be punished rather than rewarded, but that Israel had forsaken the gracious God who originally liberated and would ultimately redeem Israel and who remains faithful to the covenant in spite of Israel's sinfulness and limitations.

The covenant between the God of Israel and the Israel of God at Sinai is the fundamental covenant of the scriptures. But this covenant is read back into history; so the J-document tells of the covenant between the Lord and Abram (Gen. 15:17–18) and P carries it further back to Noah (Gen. 9:8–17). This story stands as witness that God's covenant, historically made with Israel, applies to the whole human race and to all the animal kingdom; "and with every living creature that is with you, the birds, the domestic animals, and every animal of the earth with you, as many as came out of the ark" (Gen. 9:10). As an extension of the same principle, Ecclesiasticus 17:12 carries the covenant back to Adam: "He established with them an eternal covenant, and showed them his judgments."

Adonai is a covenant-making God, and the covenants are God's ordinances. Covenant making is an attribute of God expressed as *hesed*, grace, steadfast love. So within the covenant with Israel we find subsequent covenants. The promise to David (2 Sam. 7:11–13:16) is interpreted as a covenant (2 Sam. 23:5). The later covenants reaffirm in new situations the original covenant, as does the "new" covenant promised in Jeremiah 31:31–34. Now the Torah is to be written on tablets of human hearts, not of stone; God always intended that the Torah be taken to heart.

Of the covenantal themes in the Hebrew Bible, two are particularly worthy of mention as they developed in Judaism. These are the grace of God in electing and establishing a covenant with Israel and the relation between particularity and universality in the covenant. Christian commentary has paid insufficient attention to both. We begin with some rabbinic comments on grace. An interpretation (*midrash*) on Psalm 119:124 reads as follows:

> "Deal with thy servant according to thy *hesed* (grace)" (Ps. 119:124). Perhaps thou has pleasure in our good works? Merit and good works we have not; act towards us in *hesed*. The men of old whom thou didst redeem, thou didst not redeem through their works: but thou didst act towards them in *hesed* and didst redeem them. So do thou with us.[58]

A rabbinic commentary on Deuteronomy 3:23, where Moses tells of having prayed to God, makes the same point:

> There are ten words for prayer. One of them is appeal for grace. Of all the ten, Moses used only this one, as it is said, "And I appealed for grace with the Lord at that time" (Deut. 3:23). Rabbi Johanan said: Hence you may learn that man has no claim upon God; for Moses, the greatest of the prophets, came before God only with an appeal for grace. . . . God said to Moses, "I will be gracious to whom I will be gracious. To him who has anything to his account with me, I show mercy, that is, I deal with him through the attribute of mercy; but to him who has nothing I am gracious, that is, I deal with him by gift and gratis."[59]

The next comment emphasizes a verse describing the exodus from Egypt, prior to the giving of the covenant at Sinai.

> "Thou didst lead them in thy mercy *(hesed)*" (Exodus 15:13). Thou hast wrought grace *(hesed)* for us, for we had no works, as it is said, "I will mention the lovingkindnesses of the Lord" (Isaiah 63:7), and again, "I will sing of the mercies of the Lord forever" (Ps. 89:1). And, from the beginning, the world was built only upon grace *(hesed)*, as it is said, "I declare the world is built upon grace" (Ps. 89:2).[60]

Deuteronomy 7:7 states: "It was not because you were more numerous than any other people that the LORD set his heart on you and chose you—for you were the fewest of all peoples." On this a rabbinic commentator remarks:

> Not because you are greater than other nations did I choose you, not because you obey my injunctions more than the nations (Gentiles); for they follow my commandments, even though they were not bidden to do it, and also magnify my name more than you, as it is said, "From the rising of the sun, even to the going down of the same, my name is great among the Gentiles" (Malachi 1:11).[61]

God's covenanting grace is all-inclusive in scope. The prophets had articulated this theme: "Blessed be Egypt my people, and Assyria the work of my hands, and Israel my heritage" (Isa. 19:25). "Are you not like the Ethiopians to me, O people of Israel? says the LORD. Did I not bring Israel up from the land of Egypt, and the Philistines from Caphtor and the Arameans from Kir?" (Amos 9:7). The rabbinic interpretation of Malachi 1:11 differs from the works-righteous interpretation of it in the Christian *adversus Judaeos* tradition.

The logic of grace is a universalizing, inclusive logic. Being overwhelmed with the sense of being loved by God is only adequately articulated in the language of inclusion—I, too, am included, even me! Knowing oneself to be loved by God brings with it an amazement at being included. So the rabbis' claim for Israel was that although Israel was indeed the first to be included in God's covenant, Israel was not to consider itself as exclusively embraced. The reading of the covenant back into the stories of Adam, Noah, and Abraham is a working out of the logic of grace. The covenant becomes an eternal, all-inclusive covenant. This is not to say that Israel's faith was never parochial, that it never regarded the covenant as a private affair of the people Israel, but to affirm that such a "stance does not really represent the authentic expression of Judaism."[62]

Increasingly, it was realized that God's all-inclusive love extended concretely to Gentiles:

> Turn to me and be saved,
>   all the ends of the earth!
>   For I am God, and there is no other.
> By myself I have sworn,
>   from my mouth has gone forth in righteousness
>   a word that shall not return:
> "To me every knee shall bow,
>   every tongue shall swear."
>
> (Isa. 45:22–23)

The rabbis said: "Though his goodness, loving-kindness, and mercy are with Israel, his right hand is always stretched forward to receive *all* those who come into the world, . . . as it is said, 'Unto me every knee shall bow, every tongue shall swear.'"[63]

The theme of God's all-inclusive love was implemented by emphasizing the covenant with Noah and the Noachide laws, seven laws regarded by rabbinic tradition as the minimal duties enjoined by the Torah on all people. Every non-Jew is a "child of the covenant of Noah," a technical term including all human beings except Jews. Everyone who accepts the minimal obligations of this covenant is to be regarded as a "resident alien" and comes under the Levitical commandment toward aliens:

> When an alien resides with you in your land, you shall not oppress the alien. The alien who resides with you shall be to you as the citizen among you; you shall love the alien as yourself, for you were aliens in the land of Egypt; I am the LORD your God (Lev. 19:33–34).

Any righteous Gentile has a share in the world to come. Gentiles are justified in whatever faith they have. They need not become Jews, but need only keep the seven Noachide commandments. The six negative Noachide laws prohibit idolatry, blasphemy, bloodshed, sexual sins, theft, and eating from a living animal. The positive commandment is the injunction to establish a legal system. Muslims have long been regarded as Noachides in view of their strict monotheism, and Christians have been so regarded since the late Middle Ages in spite of what rabbinic Jews regard as *shituf* ("strange admixture") in our doctrines of the Trinity and the incarnation.

The judgment that Christianity is to be regarded as a kind of monotheism and its corollary that Christians are not idolaters is found in the *Schulchan Aruch* (*Yoreh Deah*, 151).[64] This development continued in the seventeenth and eighteenth centuries, particularly in the work of Rabbi Jacob Emden, who argued that Jesus never meant "to abrogate the Torah so far as Jews were concerned, but had wished merely to spread Jewish tenets and the seven Noachide commandments among non-Jews."[65] It was left to Franz Rosenzweig to attempt to see Judaism and Christianity as equally valid and complementary. Judaism is the Life—the faith that was with God at the beginning—whereas Christianity is the way toward God of those not yet with God. Judaism is the fire, Christianity the rays. Judaism is the star of redemption turned in upon itself, Christianity the cross with its arms branched outward. Nonetheless, for Rosenzweig, Christianity was in a subordinate position: "Christianity cleaves to Jesus because it knows that the Father can be reached only through him. Precisely the good Christian forgets God Himself in the face of the Lord Jesus."[66]

Jewish inclusiveness with regard to the covenant, qualified as this inclusiveness may be, is more theologically generous and aware that covenant making is a form of God's grace than has been the Christian tradition. It is clear that a view of Christians as Noachides with a little *shituf* tossed in for good measure is unacceptable from a Christian point of view. A Noachide does not even have to know God, simply to refrain from serving false gods. If the understanding of the Christian claim that having Jesus Christ as Lord is theologically the same as having the God of Israel as God, then the Noachide-*shituf* interpretation of Christianity will not suffice.

The logic of grace means that as Judaism reinterprets its tradition it tends to monotheize and universalize its understanding of covenant again and again. Had it not been for centuries of Christian belligerence toward Jews, manifest in attempts at forced conversion, population expulsion, child stealing, lynch-mob actions, and suppressive legislation, this logic of grace would probably have worked out a more forthcoming and assertive proclamation of the radically free and universally available grace of God. The Christian tradition bears a lot of responsibility for the Jewish view of it as second-rate. Christians cannot expect to keep Jews on the defensive and to hear from them more adequate views of the covenantal reality of Christianity.

Yet the Jewish tradition contains within itself insights that Christians can develop into a more adequate understanding of covenant. In addition to seeing God's covenantal grace as eternal, universal, and inclusive of the whole created order, there is the claim that the covenant itself is a gracious gift, not founded on any works-righteousness. God gives the covenant without regard to merit, out of *hesed*, and remains steadfastly faithful to the covenant, even when the other party is not faithful. As the *Exodus Rabbah* (XLI.4) puts it:

> It is usual for an earthly king to bestow gifts on his subjects and furnish supplies for them, as long as they are loyal to him, being then obliged to support them; but as soon as they rebel against him, God forbid, he has no obligation whatsoever towards them, and he immediately cuts off their supplies as a penalty for denying his royal authority. With God, however, it is not so; for while they were busy provoking Him to anger on earth, He was occupied in heaven with bestowing upon them a Torah that is instinct with life.[67]

The Promises of God Are Irrevocable

Christian understandings of covenant must be corrected and shaped by Jesus' commitment to his people and Paul's claim that the word of God to Israel could not fail, nor God's promises be revoked. The

Calvinist tradition made a partial departure from the predominant *adversus Judaeos* view of covenant, a departure that we propose to develop.

Mary Potter Engel's excellent study of John Calvin's attitudes toward Jews and Judaism concludes that on this point Calvin is "maddeningly complex."[68] Any one who has studied chapters seven through eleven of Book Two of Calvin's *Institutes of the Christian Religion* would be reluctant to disagree with this judgment. On the one hand, Calvin strongly insisted that God's promise to and covenant with the people Israel was unconditional, unbreakable, and gracious. Calvin employed what Engel calls an "'extension model' of salvation," resisted separating the people of God into us "good Christians" and those "bad Jews," and did not have a displacement model of the church.[69]

On the other hand, Calvin often makes statements exactly opposing the above.

> His perpetuation of many traditional negative stereotypes of and traditional abusive rhetoric toward Jews; his failure to say virtually anything positive above circa- and post-gospel era Jews; his grounding of the one covenant of the one God with the one people in a preexistent Christ; his use of the displacement model of salvation—these all argue against an unequivocally positive assessment of his role in the history of Christianity's relationship to the Jews and Judaism. In fact, much of his strong language contrasting adopted Christians and rejected Jews easily supports traditional Christian supersessionism.[70]

At one point in the *Institutes*, Calvin asks: "Does this still seem a little unclear?"[71] The answer can only be "yes." We will attempt to clarify it by arguing that Calvin theologically broke through the anti-Judaism of the Christian tradition, then failed to see the implications of his own breakthrough. Like Columbus, he missed the full sweep of his own discovery.

In discussing the "similarity of the Old and New Testaments [Covenants]," Calvin claims that "all men adopted by God into the company of his people since the beginning of the world were covenanted to him by the same law and by the same bond of doctrine as obtains among us." He condemns "certain madmen of the Anabaptist sect, who regard the Israelites as nothing but a herd of swine," and sets forth a radical claim: "The covenant made with all the patriarchs is so much like ours in substance and reality, that the two are actually one and the same. Yet they differ in the mode of dispensation." Calvin insists that (1) the Jews "were adopted into the hope of immortality," not merely to a hope for carnal prosperity and happiness; (2) God's covenant with them "was supported, not by their own merits, but solely by the mercy of the God who called them"; and (3) they "knew Christ as Mediator, through whom they were joined to God and were to share in his promises."[72]

Calvin meant that Christians may not expropriate for themselves promises made to the people Israel: "Let no one perversely say here that the promises concerning the gospel, sealed in the Law and the Prophets, were intended for the new people." Not only was "the Old Testament . . . established upon the free mercy of God," but the Israelites are "equal to us not only in the grace of the covenant, but also in the signification of the sacraments." Calvin denies supersessionism: the same benefits that are available to Christians through the sacraments were available to Israel; the Lord "manifested his grace among them by the same symbols." Christians are to disabuse themselves of thinking that they are superior to Jews "through the privilege of baptism." The very formula of the covenant "I . . . will be your God, and you shall be my people" (Lev. 26:12) meant that God graciously gave God's people communion with God and all the benefits of grace. We who are children of God "must be reckoned as members of his [Abraham's] tribe (Gen. 12:3). Now what could be more absurd than for Abraham to be the father of all believers (cf. Gen. 17:5) and yet not to possess even the remotest corner among them?"[73]

So far, Calvin breaks with the entire *adversus Judaeos* tradition at its works-righteous theological heart. What the *adversus Judaeos* tradition does with Jesus Christ is to turn him into a condition apart from which God is not free to be gracious; to receive God's grace one must do the "good work" of Christian believing. No, says Calvin: the covenant that bound the Jews was founded on God's grace.

Yet Calvin immediately reverts to anti-Jewish ways of understanding the "old covenant." That covenant, he says, differs in five ways from the new covenant. Although all five "pertain to the manner of dispensation rather than to the substance," they turn out to be substantive differences. The hopes of Israel were nourished in their covenant by God's decision to display the promise to them in ways that they could (1) "see and . . . taste, under earthly benefits." These earthly promises "corresponded to the childhood of the church" and were "types" of the real thing; hence God "gave his covenant to the people of Israel in a veiled form." The old covenant (2) "in the absence of the reality, . . . showed but an image and shadow in place of the substance; the New Testament reveals the very substance of truth as present." It was not only shadowy and ineffectual but "temporary because it remained . . . in suspense until it might rest upon a firm and substantial confirmation." With this shadow/reality metaphor, stressing the ephemeral nature of the covenant with Israel, Calvin in his next assertions lapses into displacement rhetoric. These (3) argue the letter/spirit, old/new dichotomies:

the former covenant was "literal, the latter spiritual doctrine; the former he speaks of as carved on tablets of stone, the latter as written upon men's hearts." "The former is the preaching of death, the latter of life; the former of condemnation, the latter of righteousness; the former to be made void, the latter to abide." Calvin next articulates (4) the bondage/freedom, fear/joy; law/gospel bifurcations, and uses the two peoples allegory, dear to the heart of Christian anti-Judaism, to argue that Hagar the bondswoman "is the type of Mt. Sinai where the Israelites received the law; Sarah, the free woman, is the figure of the heavenly Jerusalem whence flows the gospel." The last (5) difference is that "the Old Testament has reference to one nation, the New to all nations." Here the calling of the Gentiles "is a notable mark of the excellence of the New Testament over the Old." Aware that several prophets had confirmed this calling, Calvin explains that "its fulfillment was postponed until the Kingdom of the Messiah."[74]

Calvin's differences raise critical theological questions. Why would God disclose the covenant to Israel in a "veiled form" and mislead Israel as to the nature of God's promises? Why would God reveal a "shadowy" covenant that would need to be replaced? What are we to say of the morality of such a God? Why would God reveal a covenant that preached death and condemnation? Why would God saddle Israel with bondage and fear? Has the promise that the Gentiles would see the light been *fulfilled*? Do all Gentiles see the light? Has this promise instead been *confirmed*, as Paul put it (Rom. 15:8)? If the covenant with Israel preaches death, condemnation, bondage, and fear, what sense does it make to say that the same grace is available through it as through the church? These things are not clear.

Nor do they become as clear in the Calvinist tradition as is sometimes asserted. In his article "Covenant," R. E. Clements fails to mention the entire history of the discussion of covenant in the *adversus Judaeos* tradition, moving from the New Testament to the Genevan tradition. The Westminster Confession of 1647, says Clements, in "its emphasis upon 'one covenant under different administrations,' has lent to this aspect of the Reformed tradition a strong regard for the gracious elements of the OT administration and a rejection of the notion that it presents a 'covenant of works.'"[75] The Westminster Confession refers to a covenant of grace "differently administered in the time of the law and in the time of the gospel," but says of the ways of administering this covenant "in the time of the law" that they were "types and ordinances delivered to the people of the Jews, all foresignifying Christ to come, which were *for that time* sufficient and efficacious."[76] The orientation of this covenant was to the coming of Jesus Christ. In the time of the gospel, "Christ the substance was exhibited," and the covenant was "held forth in more fullness, evidence, and spiritual efficacy, to all nations, both Jews and Gentiles; and is called the New Testament."[77] There are not two substantially differing covenants, but one covenant of grace "under various dispensations." Yet the earlier mode of dispensation was efficacious *for its time* and no longer. The later dispensation more fully manifests the grace of God and is spiritually efficacious to all, Jews and Gentiles. Because what is more full is less empty, and because the earlier covenant was efficacious only for its time, Calvin's ambiguities remain.

Similarly, the Puritan theologian William Ames stresses that "the free, saving covenant of God has been one and the same from the beginning," varying only in its "manner of application of Christ" or in its administration. Yet as Ames progresses through the succeeding administrations, important matters become ever more clear, and what is given in one era prefigures what is to come. Nor were the synagogues "complete churches," any more than "the church of the Jews" was genuinely catholic, being a "national church." The administration of the covenant since the time of Christ is "altogether new" and "perfect," nor is any other "to be expected to which it would give place as to the more perfect." The doctrine of grace is "expressed not in types and shadows, but in a most manifest fashion." Moses was "veiled," the church not. Grace is freer now, because "government by law, or the intermixture of the covenant of works, which held the ancient people in a certain bondage," has been done away with.[78] Ames's view that prior administrations give place to later, more perfect ones remains supersessionist. It has the merit, shared with the Calvinist tradition generally, of drawing the Old and New Testaments closer together and seeing the moral law as belonging to God's gracious promise of salvation. But it says nothing about the validity of the covenant of the Israel of God with the God of Israel *after* the time of Christ.

The Faithfulness of God

Christian understanding of the covenant can be freed of its inherent anti-Judaism and works-righteousness only by being brought under the criterion of the gospel: the good news of the love of God graciously offered to each and all and the dual command of God that in turn we love God with all our selves and our neighbors as ourselves. We can cut the Gordian knot with which even the best Christian interpretations of covenant have tied themselves up into works-righteousness and *self*-justifying ideology only by taking with utter seriousness the radical implications of the claim that justification is by grace. Calvin's incoherence on the doctrine of covenant, after an otherwise good beginning, results from his failure to see the implications of his central insight, that nobody is justified by any merit or work and that God's gracious covenant making with God's covenant partner is therefore incapable of being made conditional upon the behavior of that covenant partner. As long as any Christian theologian continues to say that Jews prove themselves "unworthy" of their covenant, that theologian continues not only to pledge allegiance to works-righteousness, but to raise the question of how worthy Christians have been. To that extent, grace has not yet triumphed in Christian theology. Surely the Christian claim to partnership in the covenant and access to God's grace can never appropriately be formulated in terms of Christian worthiness and Jewish unworthiness.

The Love who is God, whom we come to know in the biblical witness, requires us to deliteralize the understanding of God that we find in the *adversus Judaeos* tradition. That tradition pictured God as the heavenly projection of an "earthly king," a petulant, irritable, impatient God who snatches the covenant away from one partner and transfers it to another. Such a God is not long-suffering, faithful, dependable. Christians are admonished to love their neighbors and are reminded that love "bears all things, believes all things, hopes all things, endures all things" (1 Cor. 13:7). Yet the *adversus Judaeos* tradition has also taught us to believe in a God who decidedly does not bear and endure all things, but who is fickle, unstable, untrustworthy, a God who might any day find us "unworthy" of God's grace. This is not the same God who, while we were yet sinners, justified us, set us right with the God of Israel and the Israel of God.

What is at stake in the struggle against Christian anti-Judaism is nothing less than what Christians are willing to affirm about God. The only proper Christian understanding of God, that is appropriate to the good news made known to us in Jesus Christ, affirms God's "pure, unbounded love."[79] The ultimate circumambient reality and mystery in which we live, move, and have our being, the ground and end of our lives, is an inexhaustible love. God's love is not contingent, provisional, or partial, but unqualifiedly all-inclusive and unconditional. This is the truth given to Christians and in the witness and theology required of them. If we have not this to say, we have nothing to say and would be better off saying just that. God is the unreserved, unlimited faithfulness who alone endows our fleeting days with abiding worth.

These things we avow because we confess that all that is given to us to know of this ultimate and circumambient mystery in which we live is disclosed to us in the history of the Israel of God with the God of Israel, which history includes Jesus and Paul who are, as Barth rightly said, nothing without Israel. What is there disclosed to us is that the boundless love at the ground and end of all our being and becoming is the

Holy One of Israel, the God whose command that we love God and do justice to the neighbor is grounded in having graciously made a covenant with us, a covenant contingent upon and only upon God's freely offering it to us. God freely elected Israel, freely chose Abraham and Moses, freely liberated Israel from oppression, and it is not the place of the church to put God on notice that we require this decision to be changed. This God also freely acted in Jesus Christ, self-revealing the heart of the Love who is God, "a light for revelation to the Gentiles and for glory to your [God's] people Israel" (Luke 2:32).

Israel's covenant with God hinges on nothing but God's free grace, and the Torah (teaching, way, command) of God likewise hinges upon nothing but God's free grace. Both covenant and command, call and claim, depend on and give voice to God's all-inclusive love, freely offered. The command of God that we do justice to the neighbor and the stranger, that we love them as ourselves, itself declares God's all-inclusive and free love. It appertains to the nature of God's grace that God ever remains steadfastly loyal to God's people, whatever their sin and disobedience may be. Christians, whose sins are by our own admission quite dreadful, need particularly to hear and heed this word: that as with the Jews so with us, God always stands ready to forgive our sin; even the judgment of God, however we might articulate that, stands in the service of God's mercy and God's purpose of reconciliation, putting things right between and among God's creatures and between them and God.

"God," says Paul, "is faithful" (1 Cor. 1:9; 10:13; 2 Cor. 1:18). It is essential to, of the very being (esse) of, the faith in God at the heart of both the Jewish and Christian traditions to affirm that God is faithful and that it is precisely God's faithfulness to all God's creatures that requires our faithfulness, in turn, both to God and to all those to whom God is faithful. By the same token, in both Judaism and Christianity sin is construed in its most elemental sense as disobedience to God and to the history of God's gracious acts, as disloyalty to God and to those to whom God is loyal (those being all the recipients of God's all-inclusive love). Sin is infidelity to the faithful God, and infidelity to those to whom God is faithful. Anti-Judaism is the paradigm case of sin; it is nothing less than a lack of allegiance to the faithfulness of the God of Israel and the Israel of God. The claim to have displaced Jews in God's favor is the supreme instance of *hubris*, matched, if at all, only by its implicate that Christianity alone, among all the faiths of the world, finds itself blessed by God.

Barth, in a different place in his *Church Dogmatics*, emboldens us to refer to anti-Judaism as "sin," and to name it a "lie," specifying the specific form of sin that it is.[80] Barth argues that it is precisely as we are confronted with the gospel of God's radically unconditional love in Jesus

Christ that we seek to evade the truth here made known to us: "Evasion means trying to find another place where the truth can no longer reach or affect [us], where [we are] secure from the invading hand of its knowledge, and from its implications." Barth's insight is that it is necessary to know the truth in order to lie; "untruth can do its work only in the face of the truth."[81]

Hence, "anti-Jewishness is the Christian sin," as Robert T. Osborn argues, "the sin of which Christians alone are so singularly capable." Osborn's point is that the God of Israel has made Godself known to Gentile Christians only through the Jew Jesus, a member of the Israel of God. Through Jesus, Christians have had disclosed to them the truth about God and Israel, and Christians are the "only Gentiles . . . to find themselves in a position sinfully to deny it."[82] The most fundamental lie involved here is the one that seeks to evade the implications of the utterly unconditional grace of God by taking the gift of God in Jesus Christ and turning that gift into a condition apart from which God is not free to be gracious. By this evasion, Christians manage to deny that the truth made known to us in Jesus Christ is essentially a Jewish truth, a truth previously shared only by the God of Israel with the Israel of God, and by the same token refuse to admit that the Israel of God is any longer included in the love of the God of Israel. This is a lie.

Christians need to set aside the prideful, sinful, and works-righteous anti-Judaism so persistent in the Christian tradition, and come to a new humility, one that recognizes and accepts the fact that Christians are Johnny-come-latelies in the history of salvation. Salvation is authentic self-understanding; to be saved is to understand oneself in any ultimate sense in terms of and only in terms of the love of God graciously offered to us and in terms of the command of God that we love God and the neighbor-in-God. The God of Israel is the God of a singular promise and a singular command: the utterly unqualified and free (gracious) offer of God's love as the only appropriate basis for our self-understanding and the utterly demanding and costly command that we both understand ourselves only in terms of this gracious love and that we act in ways appropriate to it, loving God and the neighbor in turn. As with Israel, so with the church, the love of God graciously offered enables and empowers us, when and if we understand ourselves in terms of it, to love God with all our selves and our neighbor as ourselves, the summary of all the commandments. No more than Christians do Jews find it easy to avoid idolatry, to refrain from rendering ultimate and absolute the good but finite and relative things of this world. Sex and money, symbolized in the golden calf, tempt all of us to devote ourselves ultimately to what is less than ultimate and to what is ultimately destructive. But Jews have wrestled with the God of Israel for a long time, and so have been the Israel of

God. And they have come away blessed. We Gentiles, as Ephesians is there to remind us, have only recently been brought in from the cold to reside with Israel in the household of God; there we are fellow citizens, not the only citizens, and certainly not the first citizens. Rather than being grateful at having been included, we have spent our history trying to kick the Israel of God out of the house of God. Here we need to remember Karl Barth's remark that we are guests in the house of Israel, and be thankful for the hospitality shown to us.

6

The Authority of Scripture

---·--·--·--·--·--·--

Anti-Jewish sentiment and actions began in New Testament times. The struggle between Christians and Jews
in the first century of the Christian movement was
often bitter and marked by mutual violence. The depth
of hostility left its mark on early Christian and Jewish
literature, including portions of the New Testament.

—*General Assembly of the Presbyterian Church (U.S.A.)*

Not only biblical scholars and theologians but churches as well, in their
teaching documents, are coming to recognize that parts of the New Testament bear on them the scars left over from first-century conflicts. The
animosities felt by small, beleaguered, and alienated communities of two
thousand years ago became part of Holy Scripture and are read and proclaimed throughout Christian history until today as the "word of God."
Historical critics offer various explanations of these expressions of enmity, explanations that situate these outbursts in their contexts and help
us to understand how they arose. A post-*Shoah* theology, however, must
be attentive not only to the first-century explanatory contexts of hostility
against Jews and Judaism that occur in the New Testament, but also to
the roles that negative statements about Jews and Judaism have played
and continue to play in subsequent church history. Whatever explanation a biblical scholar may give of the association of Jews with the devil
in John 8:44 ("You are from your father the devil, and you choose to
do your father's desires. He was a murderer from the beginning and
does not stand in the truth, because there is no truth in him"), a post-
Holocaust theology is mindful that such a text was used in church history to torment Jews and create an image of them as children of the
devil, an image that found expression in art and in the minds of Christians. Jews were dehumanized with the help of such a text, placed outside the universe of moral obligation of Christians; Christians found
their mistreatment of Jews justified, and went on record to say so.

139

The church has come to face, after the *Shoah*, a profound crisis of scriptural authority. How can texts that could be used to warrant the teaching and practice of contempt for Jews possibly be authoritative in the church today? What is the authority of the New Testament today? Does the church's repentance of its anti-Judaism not also require it to repent of having accorded authority to scriptures that are themselves either anti-Jewish or capable of being so construed?

Several issues are involved in this discussion. First, there is a question as to how we should best understand and name these expressions of hostility in the New Testament. Sometimes they are referred to as "anti-Jewish." Are they "anti-Jewish"? Or are they, rather, the result of sharp, internal disagreements between various kinds of Jews in the first century as to what constitutes authentic Judaism? Were Christianity and Judaism sufficiently separate from one another in the late first century to allow us to speak of Christianity as "anti-Jewish"? Sometimes they are more strongly labeled "anti-Semitic." Is this a proper name for them, or is it anachronistic to read a later racism back into the New Testament? Or, alternatively, is this a reasonable designation for what some scholars see as a "national" rejection of the Jews in the New Testament and hence as close to the way in which racial hatred is thought of today?[1] Should we drop both expressions in exchange for regarding these marks of hostility as instances of "polemic" or "slander"?[2]

A second issue is how the authority of the Christian canon is to be articulated. Since the church fixed the canon in the late fourth century, it has been regarded as the normative apostolic witness to the "once for all" event of Jesus Christ. Historically, the canon has been understood to voice a unified witness of faith in spite of the fact that it has long been recognized as containing a wide variety of literatures and perspectives. The decisive question Christians face today is whether in our theological reflections on relations between Christians and Jews we will continue to grant normative canonical status to those expressions of hostility against Jews that appear in a large body of New Testament writings. If not, what will be the rule that governs our interpretation of the New Testament, and from where will we derive it? Can we locate in the New Testament a normative understanding of the gospel, a deeper witness, that requires us to criticize and reject its more superficial and accidental locutions?

A third issue is how the authority of the New Testament is to be understood in relation to that of the Old Testament. Everything the church in its *adversus Judaeos* tradition said negatively about the "old covenant," it also said about the "Old Testament." It contrasted to the "New Testament," as law to gospel, as inferior to superior religion, as outdated and superseded to that which displaces it, as absolutely or relatively empty to that which "fulfills" it, as shadow to reality, and so forth. All of these models provided justification for a Christian expropriation of the Hebrew Scriptures from Judaism while denying their integral meaning. The church sought to swallow and strangle the testimony of the *Tanakh*. No real conversation with Jews and Judaism will be possible apart from a recognition of the authority and integrity of the Hebrew Bible. Nor will a real conversation of Christians with Jews be possible without recognizing the authority of the New Testament.

The issue of the relation of the two testaments to each other has to do not only with how that relation is to be understood, but with the role of Christian hostility against Judaism and the Jewish people in the very formation of the canon itself, particularly in the separation of the scriptures into two testaments, old and new. Given the claim that the new covenant succeeds and displaces the old, as Christianity usurps the place of Judaism in God's favor, it is not surprising that someone would make an effort simply to rid the church of the Hebrew Bible or "Old" Testament. Precisely this seems to have happened in the middle of the second century. Marcion appeared on the scene and put together a list of books that he claimed should constitute Christian scripture. It consisted of Paul's letters and the Gospel of Luke. Marcion believed the God known to the Hebrews to be inferior to the God disclosed in and to Jesus: the former created this evil, material world, but the latter is a spiritual being who redeems us from it. Marcion's theology was dualistic in a sense similar to that of Gnosticism. Law and justice prevail in this physical world. Opposite to this is the Christian gospel, which finds its center in the good news of the love of God who forgives even the worst of sinners; this god who is the "other," or "foreign," god is drastically different from the god who rules this world. The latter is the god whom Jews worship. The "other" god is far above this god of the earth and justice and is loving, peaceful, and good.[3]

Although finally defeated, Marcion successfully found followers; numerous congregations became Marcionite. He also led the church to adopt a new policy. Before Marcion, Christians apparently formed their scriptures simply by adding books to the Bible of Judaism. The letters of Paul are added to the "other scriptures" in 2 Peter 3:15–16.[4] Marcion radically altered this arrangement. By rejecting the Jewish Scriptures altogether and proposing a new set of authoritative writings for this new people of God participating in a new covenant with a different and better God, Marcion forced the church to respond. The church repudiated his suggestion of rejecting the "Old" Testament, but henceforth the scriptures were divided into an Old and a New Testament, changing forever the way Christians would perceive their scriptures. "The very concept of a New Testament as distinct from the Old may well go back to

Marcion's repudiation of the Jewish scriptures."[5] As an esteemed patristic scholar points out, Marcion was no isolated case in the early church:

> All Gnostic systems depend upon a principle that is at variance with Christianity—the dualism of matter and spirit. That the body was basically evil, and in no sense the creation of a good God, was a central tenet. It led Gnostics to dispute the underlying message of the Old Testament, and to contrast the creator-God with the God revealed in Jesus Christ. In consequence, . . . the Old Testament was rejected, and new Christian books were substituted in its place. It is interesting that not only the first New Testament canon comes from Gnostic sources, but Gnostics were the first to give New Testament passages the authority once enjoyed by the Old Testament (Basilides), to write a New Testament commentary (Heracleon), and to make a Gospel harmony (Tatian). This peculiar interest in a *New* Testament stems from the rejection of the old.[6]

A fourth issue is quite practical: after all the exegetical, historical, and theological work has been done on the expressions of hostility against Jews found in the New Testament, so what? Ordinary Christians and most pastors are not avid readers of biblical and theological scholarship, and the New Testament, which they do read (or at least hear in church), remains unaffected. Should Christians develop a "non anti-Jewish lectionary," or non anti-Jewish translations of the New Testament, similiar to lectionaries and translations that seek to reduce or eliminate sexism? Alternatively, what message is conveyed when sexist language is removed from a translation, but expressions of anti-Jewish animosity are left intact?[7] Because this is the one issue not to be addressed later in this chapter, let me here state my view of it. I think that all distortions of the biblical text that have been introduced through the processes of transmission and translation should be corrected; some of its exclusivism and anti-Judaism are traceable to the assumptions of translators. But attempts to provide a "totally cleaned-up" version of the Bible will always fail because those who would do the cleaning up are neither omniscient nor sinless, and because if everything that anybody finds objectionable in the text is removed, little would be left. What is left would be relatively uninteresting, because texts would no longer require us to wrestle with them; they would so fully reflect our views as in no way to call us into question. It is better to have an imperfect text than one that we think is perfect but which in fact is not and in which the remaining distortions are tacitly approved. What we need in the church are better study Bibles than we now have, critically annotated, and much better teaching of the Bible in the churches than we now have.[8]

Late First-Century Polemic

Severe as the hostility against Jews and Judaism in certain parts of the New Testament is (and it is sometimes relentless), post-Holocaust theology needs to recognize this material as the contingent polemic of late first-century churches rather than regard it as "anti-Jewish" or "anti-Semitic." As contingent polemic, we may dispense with it. This proposal entails no lessening of the intensity of the polemic against Jews in the New Testament; the Synoptic Gospels, for example, all contain and conclude with a caustic attack on Jews. Nor does it in any way justify an ideological appropriation of New Testament polemic to create and reinforce injustice against Jews and Judaism, a purpose to which the church frequently put its handling of the New Testament's language of invective. The proposition seeks to accomplish two things: to come up with an understanding of the strong distancing elements in the New Testament adequate to the context in which they were produced and to see them as the contingent polemic of the late first-century church, thus relativizing them of any authority over the faith and life of the church. Nor does this proposition deny that *some* of the apparently "anti-Jewish" remarks placed in the mouth of Jesus in the Gospels actually stem from the historical Jesus. Such remarks, however, would constitute inner-Jewish self-criticism of a prophetic sort—like the prophets Jesus identified with the people he criticized. A post-Holocaust theology is most concerned with how a later Gentile church ideologically misuses Jewish self-criticism, directing it exclusively against the Jews and exempting the church from prophetic self-criticism.

When I say that post-Holocaust theology needs to see this material as contingent polemic rather than as anti-Jewish or anti-Semitic, I speak critically as much of my own prior attempts to interpret this material as of any other post-Holocaust theologian.[9] Theologians who have been morally anguished by the history of the church's teaching of contempt have a difficult time not seeing the polemics of the New Testament through the lens of the *adversus Judaeos* tradition and concluding that they are of a piece with one another. Thus, ironically, they agree with a fundamental premise of the *adversus Judaeos* tradition itself, that the New Testament is anti-Jewish. It now strikes me as helpful to argue instead that, like many original scriptures of religious movements and in ways very similar both to Jewish and Gentile literature of the Hellenistic era, the New Testament contains polemic against precisely those religious groups to which it was most closely related and by which its writers felt most directly threatened. The strong similarities that New Testament polemic shares with other religious slander show that this polemic in itself does not express the distinctive Christian witness.

Polemic against surrounding religious groups is not unique to the New Testament. The Hebrew Bible itself, as Yehezkel Kaufmann and Jon Levenson have shown, depicts other religions as "fetishism, the worship of mindless matter," in which gods and goddesses are equated with their icons. Levenson has argued that the misrepresentations of Pharisaism and Judaism in the New Testament correspond to the Hebrew Bible's misrepresentation of "pagan" religion, that "no one with an acquaintance with Mesopotamian or Canaanite religion can accept that we have in this identification a sensitive or even perceptive understanding of the role of iconography in those traditions."[10] Levenson makes a comment about polemic that we would do well to remember: "Polemic is by nature reductionistic. Its goal is to present the opposition as ridiculous."[11] Norman Beck notes that the Hebrew Bible reserved its sharpest polemic for its nearer neighbors, the Canaanites and their cultic practices, by rendering one of its symbols, the serpent, into the agent of Eve's seduction.[12] When such polemic is accepted as literal truth, historical-critical scholarship can undo the misrepresentation.

The Koran has protracted slices of polemic against Jews in which it argues, parallel to the Christian *adversus Judaeos* tradition, that "humiliation and wretchedness were stamped upon the Jews and that they were visited with wrath from Allah because they disbelieved in Allah's revelations and killed their prophets wrongfully." It also contains, to a lesser extent, anti-Christian polemic, asserting that Christians have never properly understood the gospel of Jesus, that they and Jews each accuse the other of believing nothing true although both read the scriptures, and that they have forgotten part of their covenant, causing enmity and hatred to arise among Christians. To portray the Koran as containing only polemic against Jews and Christians would be quite unfair. It does contain a polemic with which Christians should by now be familiar. The Book of Mormon engages in invective against Jews and Christians, referring to the latter as "the church of the devil," borrowing a New Testament image ("synagogue of Satan," Rev. 2:9). The Book of Mormon copies Paul's metaphor of the olive tree with its broken-off and grafted-in branches, with a predictable change in who the grafted-in branches are. The Mormon church is the "church of the Lamb of God," distinguished from "the church of the devil" (Christianity). Christianity stripped the most precious parts away from the gospel, including many covenants of the Lord, perverting the ways of the Lord and blinding the eyes and hardening the hearts of people. It is the "whore of all the earth." The *Divine Principle* of the Unification Church makes a doubly supersessionist argument that as Christianity has displaced Judaism so it in turn is superseded by the followers of the "Lord of the Second Advent." The Unification Church "is attempting to do to Christianity and to the specifically Christian sacred writings the same things that the early Christians did to their satisfaction to Judaism and to the Jewish Scriptures."[13]

These religious literatures also have a capacity for self-criticism, learned from the Hebrew Bible, and passages that express respect for other religions. Polemic against other, particularly closely related, religious groups is a standard feature of literatures regarded as "scripture." This is not to argue that any religious truth claim necessarily involves hostility to other truth claims or malice toward the people who hold them. Our task is to learn how to frame Christian truth claims in a way that does not entail rejection of authentic Jewish truth claims or hostility toward Jews.

New Testament polemic against Jews and Judaism is further relativized by placing it in the context of the ancient conventions of polemic in the Hellenistic world, as Luke T. Johnson has done.[14] Arguing that the derogatory language used of Jews and Judaism in the New Testament "is a source of shame (finally) to Christians, and a well-grounded source of fear to Jews," Johnson contextualizes the New Testament's polemic in "the conventional rhetoric of slander in the Hellenistic world." Socially, the church was small in comparison to Judaism, "new" in a culture where "old" was prized and novelty viewed as "belated"; it met in house churches rather than elegant temples or synagogues: "in the beginning, the messianists were David to the non-messianists' Goliath."[15] The church was sporadically persecuted, testimony to which fact is provided by Paul's statements about his own activities, and the Gospels contain memories of being kicked out of synagogues and punished by synagogue authorities (Mark 13:9; Matt. 10:17; Luke 21:12; John 16:2). Acts also has Paul regularly in conflict with his deepest enemies, "the Jews," but this goes considerably beyond Paul's accounts, according to which he found his deepest opposition among his fellow missionaries.[16] A small and persecuted group will often effect a rhetorical leap across the power gap that separates it from stronger groups. In this context, and with internal problems of its own, the early church voiced a rhetoric of excess laden with the potential of being dangerously appropriated by a later, powerful church.

The language to which it had recourse was the typical polemic of the time and was "found as widely among Jews as among other Hellenists." Johnson discovers among Hellenists, whether philosophical schools or religions ("philosophies" functioned as philosophico-religious cults in the ancient world), a stereotyped rhetoric for heaping abuse on those movements that were closest and most dangerous to one's own group. Plutarch defended his Platonist school against the Stoics by calling them "buffoons, charlatans, assassins, prostitutes, nincompoops." He finds such language everywhere, among Stoics, used by Apollonius of Tyana and Euphrates of each other, and it was nowhere "affected by facts." Its purpose was not to refute another group, but to build up one's own; it was "primarily for internal consumption." Jews such as Josephus and Philo employ abusive language to talk about Gentiles, and some of their epithets are close to what we find in the Gospels. Gentiles are described as blasphemers, blind, a seed bed of evil, liars, foolish by nature, idolaters.[17]

Jews could be quite vituperative with one another. Josephus heaps endless abuse on the heads of his opponents, dropping his greatest scorn on the Zealots and Sicarii, but saving some good bits for the Samaritans as well. The Essenes harbored an animosity to all non-Essenes, dividing humanity between "the sons of light" (the insiders) and the "sons of darkness" (everybody else). "The Qumran rule of thumb," claims Johnson, "is that you cannot say enough bad things about outsiders."[18] The Essenes ritually scream maledictions against "men of the lot of Satan":

> Be cursed of all your guilty wickedness! May he deliver you up to torture at the hands of all the wreakers of revenge! Be cursed without mercy because of the darkness of your deeds! Be damned in all the shadowy place of everlasting fire! May God not heed you when you call upon him, nor pardon you by blotting out your sin! May he raise his angry face toward you for vengeance! May there be no peace for you in the mouths of those who hold fast to the fathers! (1QS 2:4–10)[19]

The payoff of this analysis is that by showing that the New Testament's slander of Jews is customary and pedestrian, it is unmasked, stripped of the pretense to truthfulness that we place upon it. It no more accurately characterizes Jews than do the Book of Mormon's references to the church as the church "of Satan" adequately characterize it. Second, this inquiry helps us see that the New Testament's slander against Jews was aimed at reassuring "Christians," not converting Jews. Third, realizing that this kind of slander was common parlance, that everybody did it, relativizes our version of slander. The "curse" on the Jews in Matthew 27:25 was "common coinage"; "there were not many Jews or Gentiles who did not have at least one curse to deal with."[20] The problem with the New Testament is that it is too much like other literature from its time and place. Yet in one respect it was and remains utterly unlike all the other vituperation amid which it arose: the New Testament became Holy Scripture of a church that, eventually, became established and, from its position of privilege, read and interpreted its intra-Jewish slander from a Gentile, anti-Jewish perspective. This text was also read as absolute, not relative, out of rather than in context, as the *ipsissima verba* of Jesus rather than as the conventional mode of insult common to Hellenistic argument. We cannot make the New Testament responsible for its later misinterpretation and misuse.

Another reason for regarding the defamation of Jews and Judaism in the New Testament as part of the polemic of the times rather than as "anti-Judaism" or "anti-Semitism" is that neither Judaism nor Christianity had, as of the late first century, achieved anything like the definition and separation that they would later obtain. Samuel Sandmel taught us that there were "Judaisms" in the first century, but no one "Judaism," and that early Christianity was "a Judaism."[21] Exactly when Judaism and Christianity became two clearly separate religions remains unclear. What is striking is that, beginning in the fourth century at Elvira, Spain, the church began passing canon laws, the intent of which was to break the close relations that pertained between Jews and Christians. Equally noticeable is that many anti-Jewish tracts produced throughout the next several centuries sought to sever relations between Jews and Christians; in the fourth century, Chrysostom berated his Antioch congregation for "frequenting synagogues and Jewish homes."[22] Most New Testament authors were not Gentiles, but Jewish members of the Jesus movement. They were, says one scholar, "Jewish-Christians of an indeterminate type."[23] Norman Perrin and Dennis C. Duling regard the Synoptic Gospels as all documents of "Hellenistic Jewish Mission Christianity."[24] On the one hand, it is precisely in these Gospels that some of the harshest polemic occurs, yet on the other we cannot simply read this polemic anachronistically as of a piece with later Gentile Christian anti-Judaism or anti-Semitism, however much the latter could seize upon it, and however much we may regret the venomous nature of the polemic.

There is considerable evidence that churches represented by Luke were composed of Hellenistic Jews committed to the Gentile mission. These churches had as their major polemical targets the more traditional Jesus followers, the "Jewish Christians" who opposed Gentile Christianity. Both Luke-Acts and Mark seem primarily exercised by this antagonism. In Acts the "Jewish Pharisees," such as Gamaliel, are friendly to the church, but the "Christian Pharisees," the ones in the church, unfriendly; these are those whom Luke does not like, the traditional Jewish Christians.[25] Werner Kelber interprets Mark's Gospel as in conflict with the oral tradition and authorities of the conservative Jerusalem church; the deep alienation that commands Mark's Gospel reflects not only its commitment to the new revelation it is disclosing to its Gentile Jesus followers but also its novelty vis-à-vis the conservative Jerusalemite Jesus followers.[26] Raymond E. Brown finds that the community of John's Gospel had numerous enemies: the world (Gentile unbelievers), "the Jews" (with whom the Gospel depicts numerous arguments), followers of John the Baptist, crypto-Christians unwilling to leave the synagogue, Jewish Christians of inadequate faith, and traditional Christians, represented by Peter, who is unfavorably contrasted with "the beloved Disciple."[27] Jesus' prayer "that they may all be one" (17:20–21) was an intercession that the Johannine community needed to make. John's community had many "enemies," and it did *not* have Jesus' commandment to "love your enemies" (Matt. 5:44; Luke 6:27). The members of the Johannine community are instructed, instead, to "love one another" (13:34–35), a commandment that at least raises the question whether John's Gospel is sectarian. John's community began in and was kicked out of the synagogue; the anger in the Gospel represents John's anguish over this forced separation.[28]

Without denying the intensity of the slander against the Jews that is found in parts of the New Testament, we should regard this calumny as typical of what passed for "interreligious" discourse at the time and as reflecting animosities that occurred in the late first century, when all sorts of Jewish and Christian groups were under severe pressure from one another, from Rome, and from their "pagan" neighbors. If we call this polemic the "anti-Judaism" or "anti-Semitism" of the New Testament, we invite the conclusion that Christianity is essentially anti-Jewish and anti-Semitic. That conclusion is a word of despair to all Christians who seek to liberate their tradition from its ideological bondage. But if we regard the slander against Jews found in the New Testament as a contingent expression, we can then dismiss it as incompatible with the gospel as also normatively articulated in the New Testament. This is what David Tracy proposes when he argues that these "anti-Judaic statements of the New Testament bear *no* authoritative status for Christianity. . . . The heart of the New Testament message—the love who is God—should release the demythologizing power of its own prophetic meaning to rid the New Testament and Christianity once and for all of these statements."[29]

The Authority of the New Testament

If the church is to come to terms with the question of the authority of the New Testament in a post-Holocaust age, it can neither simply affirm that authority in terms of the classic doctrine of inerrancy nor abandon the authority of the New Testament in favor of according all authority to the Hebrew Bible or Old Testament upon which the New Testament is turned into mere commentary. How these two diametrically opposite views of scriptural authority make impossible an appropriate Christian affirmation of the authority of the New Testament can be seen in two, diametrically opposite, responses to the theological work of Paul M. van Buren. In an appreciative response to van Buren's work,

Lloyd Gaston comments on what he calls van Buren's "most radical proposal." Recognizing that pejorative statements about Jews are in the New Testament, Gaston interprets van Buren as freeing Christians today from "an almost impossible bind." He asks how van Buren can do this, that is: "By what criterion can one designate significant parts of the New Testament as no longer authoritative for the Christian Church?" The answer is ingenious: "By restricting the term 'Holy Scriptures' to *Tanakh*, and by consistently referring to the 'Apostolic Writings,'" says Gaston, "van Buren solves many problems with a single stroke. Holy Scripture in the sense of the Hebrew Bible now becomes the criterion for determining what is authoritative in the Apostolic Writings."[30] The *Tanakh* becomes the criterion for determining which parts of the Apostolic Writings are authoritative. The question here is not whether Gaston's interpretation of van Buren is adequate.[31] It is whether Gaston's view of the authority of the New Testament is adequate.[32]

The benefits of Gaston's view are that the New Testament is seen in continuity with Holy Scripture, that it is not set in antithesis to Holy Scripture, and that it speaks directly to the situation of Christians in our post-*Shoah* era. These advantages are not to be gainsaid. Yet the weakness is glaring: it is that the New Testament is no longer Holy Scripture and no longer authoritative. Authority is analytic in the name "Holy Scripture." If we decide no longer so to designate the New Testament, we decide it is no longer authoritative for us. If the problem for the post-Marcionite church was whether the Old Testament was biblical, for Gaston it is whether the New Testament is biblical.

The issue is nuanced. If scripture is authoritative but not authoritarian, its authority must be a rule-conferred authority. The scriptures are a *norma normata*, a norm or criterion that is standardized by reference to a higher norm. Interpreters are not at the mercy of authoritarian scriptures; they can appeal to a higher norm, a *norma normans*, a norming norm that is not in turn normed. We turn to this *norma normans* for what is authoritative, and it determines what is definitively authoritative in the scriptures. This Gaston locates in the *Tanakh*, and not in the New Testament (whereas van Buren finds the rule that we must interpret the New Testament in the light of the Hebrew Bible in the New Testament itself). Whatever in the latter might be authoritative is determined to be so by reference to the *norma normans*, the *Tanakh*.

Appealing as this may seem to Christians concerned to reenvision Christianity in the light of the reality of Judaism and the Jewish people, it is not adequate. I do not disagree with Gaston that the New Testament is a normed norm. But his version of the norming norm can no longer be called Christian. In his view the New Testament is postscriptural tradition and not authoritative except insofar as it can be shown to be appropriate to scripture. This looks like a Protestant view of scripture as preceding tradition and authoritative over against it, pushed back one historical step.

Alternatively, it is a view of the authority of the New Testament to which Jews might respond warmly, but which they would not accept as applicable either to the *Mishnah* and *Talmud* or to the subsequent tradition of rabbinic decision making down to today. The right of rabbis to interpret and change the Torah is not authorized by the Torah, yet their tradition of doing so has its authoritative moments for different groupings within Judaism. The Pharisees as a scholarly class interpreting and deciding the requirements of *torah*, the oral as distinct from the written Torah, the synagogue as a house of *torah* study, are all absent from the *Tanakh*. Pharisaic Judaism and later rabbinic Judaism constitute a revolution in relation to the Hebrew Bible.[33] How can we expect Christians to accept a view of the authority of the New Testament that Jews would not accept of the *Mishnah*? If we grant that the New Testament as it stands constitutes a rule-conferred authority, we must find its rule within it.

Another response to van Buren's work, also one that claims to appreciate his perception of "the need to reiterate the organic-covenantal linkage between Jews and Israel and to remind the church of the essential Jewishness of Christianity," shows the problem of the authority of the New Testament from a radically different perspective. Arthur F. Glasser claims that "the underlying issue" presented by van Buren's work is that of "truth as revealed in scripture." That the truth is revealed in the New Testament is a point on which Glasser is not prepared to yield. He categorically rejects van Buren's reconstructed view of Jesus Christ in the context of Israel and claims that Jesus is truthfully presented in the Gospels, even when spewing forth slander against Jews: "Fortunately, the church has continued to believe that the mind of Jesus Christ is accurately portrayed in the Gospels. Indeed, there is no *a priori* reason why this portrayal of Him may not be accurate nor why it may not correspond with His own self-understanding." The crucifixion and resurrection account for the "data" of the New Testament, not some latter-day reconstruction. For Glasser the truth about Jesus is found in the New Testament, a book "written by Jews within two brief generations of Jesus' death and when its details could be confirmed by Jewish eyewitnesses still living."[34]

If Gaston is willing to relocate authority outside of the New Testament because of the slander against Jews that it contains, Glasser is unwilling to admit that there is anti-Jewish slander in the New Testament: "Down through church history some Jews and Gentiles, in their reading of the Scriptures, all too often poured into certain texts the accumulated prejudice and hostility of centuries to the neglect of their plain meaning." Glasser cannot see how the "plain meaning" of certain highly charged New Testament texts could be utilized by people prejudiced against and hostile toward Jews. Although he does not use the word, the New Testament is clearly "inerrant" for Glasser, an inerrancy he accounts for by reference to the crucifixion and resurrection and seeks to justify by appeal to such historical-critical results as comport with his views.[35] The result incoherently blends the traditional scripture principle with a conservative use of historical-critical method, unmindful that such a method, regardless of its results, cannot get beyond probabilities on historical matters and relativizes its subject matter.[36] Using a probabilistic method to support an absolutist position is an odd way of doing one's theological business.

The theological payoff of Glasser's approach to the authority of the New Testament reaffirms supersessionism:

> If there had been no resurrection, there would never have been a Christian Church, a gospel of life-transforming power through the resurrected Christ, a conversion-to-Christ experience untold millions have subsequently experienced, the subsequent *replacement* of the Jewish Sabbath by the Lord's Day and the existence of the New Testament.[37]

The Lord's Day displaces the Sabbath. It is probably fair to take these two observances as standing for two religious systems and peoples, one of which replaces the other. Not only is this supersessionist, implying that the replaced religious system should no longer exist because God has dismissed it, but it questions Glasser's affirmation of the "organic-covenantal linkage" between Israel and the church. Is it intelligible to speak of an organic-covenantal linkage between the church and a *replaced* Israel? There we have the problem posed between two positions, one of which affirms continuity between Israel and the church but denies the authority of the New Testament and the other of which affirms the authority of the New Testament without qualification, but denies the continuity between the church and Israel. Neither is capable of articulating an interpretation of the authority of the New Testament in the context of a new relation between the church of God and the Israel of God.

The "Scripture Principle" Is Supersessionist

The "scripture principle," in terms of which the church has traditionally expressed its understanding of the authority of the New Testament, not only entails the doctrine of scriptural inerrancy that makes a critical reappropriation of the authority of the New Testament impossible after the Holocaust, but necessitates as well a supersessionist understanding of the church's relation to the people Israel. The oldest and most enduring model of scriptural authority in Christianity is called "the scripture principle." Peter C. Hodgson and Edward Farley have ably described and analyzed it, providing us with an account upon which it would be difficult to improve.[38] The principle was created by Jews in the Diaspora subsequent to the Babylonian Exile. No longer having the land, Temple, or priesthood as focal points of their religious practice, they created in their place the synagogue and the written Torah. Although representing a tremendous advance in Israelite religion, this development was not lacking in ambiguity. The idea of scripture came to entail a written deposit of complete, definitive regulation that authorized cultic and moral regulations. The scripture principle exhaustively locates revelation in the past and claims that the written text is "totally and equally valid in all its parts and details." It periodizes history into discrete stages with revelation fixed in the past. This past epoch is normative, and there can be no new revelation. Although Christianity claimed that there had been a new revelation of God in Jesus Christ, it nonetheless adopted the scripture principle but, in doing so, had to reperiodize salvation history.[39]

The scripture principle presupposes an *identity* between what God intends to communicate and what comes to expression in scripture; it entails inerrancy. The text and its content are regarded as possessing the "qualities of inerrancy, infallibility, and absolute truthfulness." Consequently, the contents of the text are *leveled*, the inerrant truth being distributed equally throughout it. Further, this truth is *immutable*, universally valid for all future generations.[40] Let us note for future discussion that Farley and Hodgson do not mention that the Pharisees and, later, the rabbis broke the power of the scripture principle in Judaism by developing the idea of the "oral *torah*," which they laid alongside of the written Torah and by developing an exegetical method by which they claimed to derive their revolutionary interpretations from the immutable meanings deposited in the past.[41]

The church adopted the scripture principle, with its associated idea of a written canon, in spite of some misgivings (Tertullian complained that "the Holy Spirit was chased into a book") and in spite of modifications the principle had to undergo at Christian hands.[42] These alterations included the reperiodizing of salvation history, relocating the age of revelation in a less distant past; a shift from *torah* to gospel as the genre of scripture; and a hyphenated scripture composed of an Old and a New Testament, with the former having only provisional validity. Such shifts contradict the fundamental ideas of the scripture principle, its claims to immutability and the fixing of revelation in the past, but the church adopted it and its associated apparatus: "a canon of officially recognized authoritative writings, atomistic exegesis and proof-texting, and the establishment of revelation as the foundation of theology contained in human-historical deposits regarded as inspired and infallible."[43] The work of theologians, on the terms of the scripture principle, is to translate the truth of scripture for the present epoch; there is no room, in principle, to inquire into the scriptures, although theologians often did just that.

Not surprisingly, the scripture principle is at work in Glasser's response to van Buren. Glasser rejects critical efforts to get behind the texts of scripture and defends the supersessionism that is built into the reperiodization of salvation history presupposed by the Christian development of the scripture principle and the provisional authority of the Hebrew Bible presupposed by the scripture principle. We cannot fail to note as well the triumphalism built into the scripture principle's way of thinking of God as an in-the-world-being who intervenes in the world process with infallible communications.

Theologians who formally defend the scripture principle, no matter how much they transcend it in their exegetical or hermeneutical work, cannot avoid addressing the task of Christian theology after the *Shoah*, because the scripture principle itself is too large a theological claim on behalf of the church's supersession of Judaism and the covenant of the Jewish people with God to be overcome. A more direct approach to the problem, advocated here, would be to overthrow the scripture principle in favor of an appropriate formulation of the authority of scripture. The great theologians in the history of the church manifest a considerable tension between their ways of interpreting scripture and their insistence on retaining the scripture principle, a tension no less evident in Luther and Calvin than in Augustine. Luther implicitly challenged the scripture principle but would not do so explicitly, and Calvin disallowed any challenge to the scripture principle, in spite of the fact that he went some way toward undermining it. Consequently, the principle was hardened in the era of Protestant scholasticism and remains so in contemporary representatives of that movement, for whom the scriptures remain the *norma absoluta* of theological reflection.

A More Liberating Jewish Approach

Rabbinic Judaism broke the back of the scripture principle with its institution of the "oral *torah*" and a variety of exegetical methods that justified novel interpretations of Judaism as legitimate results of the reading of scripture; here we listen to the Jewish tradition in order to learn from it a more liberating approach to the issue of scriptural authority. There is a Jewish story according to which Moses came back to earth and visited the academy of Rabbi Akiba ben Joseph (c. 50–c. 135 C.E.), a compiler of the oral *torah* on which the *Mishnah* is based. Sitting in Akiba's classroom, Moses was impressed with Akiba's ability to interpret parts of the Torah that he himself found difficult to understand. What was remarkable, however, was that when asked for the source of his teachings, Akiba explained that they were the "law which Moses received at Sinai."[44]

The most penetrating analyses of the role of scripture and its authority in Judaism with which I am familiar come from Jacob Neusner and Michael Fishbane. We will let their work guide us through the Jewish understanding of scriptural authority. Neusner points out that each variety of Judaism confesses the supremacy of scripture's authority yet "also says pretty much whatever it wants about Scripture." These varieties of Judaism will impute to one passage of scripture a wide range of meanings, with the result that "the role of Scripture in the communities of Judaism is to validate what people want to say anyway." Scripture is all-important as an authority, yet subordinate to the needs of the communities interpreting it, authoritative but subsidiary, equally a source "of proof texts and pretexts."[45] An equally candid analysis of Christianity would probably come to the same conclusions.

Another factor operative in Jewish appropriations of scripture is the question, after scriptural authority has been affirmed, of which parts of scripture will be selected by a community for interpretation. Neusner points out that when the evangelists of the New Testament were writing the Gospels, they took apocalyptic prophecy as the scriptures on which they would focus their attention, seeking to show that these scriptures pointed to Jesus Christ. But the scriptures that were conclusively important for rabbinic Judaism were "the laws of the Priestly Code," of which they gave an account that "fulfilled" scripture. Both the evangelists and the later rabbis claimed that their accounts "fulfilled" scripture, but they worked with different slices of scripture. The evangelists did not argue that Christ "fulfilled" the laws of the Priestly Code, nor did the sages and rabbis argue that their account "fulfilled" apocalyptic prophecy; without denying apocalyptic, they downplayed it. Scripture was authoritative for both, given their respective choices about which scriptures would be considered. One important conclusion that Neusner draws from these observations is that Judaism highlights "the potential of Scripture to generate and precipitate fresh and remarkably profound and original thought about Scripture itself, and about its authority."[46]

A curious fact about the *Mishnah*, the foundational document of rabbinic Judaism and the first source to codify authoritatively the practices that today are referred to as Judaism, is how infrequently it claims to develop or clarify what scripture said, how seldom it quotes scripture, how rarely it associates its positions with those of scripture. It seems utterly detached from scripture. "So, superficially," says Neusner, "the *Mishnah* is tradition, totally indifferent to Scripture." Any claim of scriptural authority for its positions and decisions "is difficult to locate within the internal evidence of the *Mishnah* itself." This situation generated a question after the *Mishnah* had been composed: people wanted to know why they should heed this work. If God had given the Torah to Moses, why was that not sufficient? Who are these newcomers with their statements and decisions that we should listen to them? What authority does the *Mishnah* have? To this question, two widely different answers were given. The first was the answer of "oral *torah*," which means that the *Mishnah* itself constitutes *torah*, a *torah* which was given orally to Moses on Sinai and had been handed down orally "until given the written formulation now before us in the *Mishnah*." On this line of reasoning, the *Mishnah* does not quote scripture because it has no need to do so; it *is* scripture or "enjoys the same authority as scripture." It claims that its authority is "co-equal with that of scripture."[47] When God uttered " '*all* these words' (Exodus 20:1 [italics added]) at Sinai, said R. Elazar ben Azariah, he spoke the exoteric Torah *and* the various—even contradictory—words of human exegesis. . . . The revolution of Rabbinic Judaism was established. The one-time event of Sinai became an ever-recurring moment when the human words or exegetical tradition actualized the words of God at Sinai."[48]

The other answer, found in the two Talmuds, is that everything that is valid in the *Mishnah* can be demonstrably derived from scripture. Once the Talmuds quote a passage from the *Mishnah* and ask after the source of these words, the answer always is "As it is said in Scripture." The rabbis developed various methods for penetrating (*darash*) scripture, coming up with new interpretations (*midrashim*) of it. But the point of this answer, contrary to that of the first, is that the *Mishnah* is secondary to and derivative from scripture, whereas the first contended that the *Mishnah* was self-sufficient in relation to scripture and equal to it in authority.[49]

What was going on here, and this is where Neusner's analysis proves most helpful, was that the drafters of the *Mishnah* had their own world with which they had to come to terms and their own questions, generated by the task of coming to terms with that world, which they brought to the scriptures. These questions directed them both to the set of scriptures to which they paid attention and to pay attention to certain aspects of those scriptures. The question with which the framers of the *Mishnah* were faced was that with which the editors of the Priestly Code had been faced, which was why they turned to it. The experiences of exile and return to Zion left Israel with a bifurcated sense of dislocation and identity. Having a sense of themselves as God's chosen people, an elect nation, Israel found itself, in the midst of the economic, cultural, political, and military life of the region, "anything but distinctive and special." Its life governed by the standard patterns of the Near East, Israel suffered a striking disharmony between its sense of identity and "the sense of dislocation and disruption engendered by the equally confusing experience of the breaking down of barriers and boundaries among cultures." The Priestly Code answered this question; in a time of hellenization it stressed "the exclusivist character of the Israelite God and cult."[50] Israel's identity was liturgically celebrated in the Temple, and all life in the land of Israel was oriented to the Temple. The question for the framers of the *Mishnah* was the same, one of identity: dispersed among Gentiles in the land of promise, living in communities separated from one another, constantly encountering other cultures and religions, dominated by Rome in a land in which God was supposed to rule, the question "who are we?" arose with a new urgency and poignancy. Hence they turned to the Priestly Code from which they derived the rules of holiness for the sanctification of daily life, rules that provided a way to serve God and a set of identity markers for the people.

What Neusner describes, although he does not so term it, can be called a "conversational" approach to the question of scriptural authority and interpretation. Conversation follows the back and forth of question and answer. Passages of scripture have their own questions, to which they pose answers; later passages of scriptures face different questions, to which they pose different answers. We take to scripture the new and different questions of our own situation and, reading it with them in mind, find new answers. Scripture has "the potential . . . to generate and precipitate fresh and . . . original thought about Scripture itself, and about its authority."[51]

We learn several things about scriptural authority from listening to this discussion of Jewish uses of scripture. First, when it functions properly, scripture "authors" our creativity; it sets us free to come up with fresh interpretations of scripture that are adequate to the pressing demands of our own time. Second, the best model for scriptural interpretation is conversation, in which we bring to scripture our questions to which we seek answers appropriate to the tradition of biblical and, in our case, Christian faith. Such a question and answer model was operative in the formation and writing of scripture itself. Neusner gave a prime example of precisely such a model in his account of the question that the Priestly Code sought to answer. Another is obvious in Paul's response to the attempt in his congregations to make certain ritual laws into limitations on the grace of God. When later Christians took Paul to mean something very different, that we are obligated to do no *moral* works of love to the neighbor, the Epistle of James responded by arguing that "faith by itself, if it has no works, is dead" (2:17). James is not contradicting Paul; it is answering a different question. If scripture interprets and reinterprets itself in a conversational manner in which past formulations exercise no heteronomy over the present, then it is appropriate for scripture itself to be interpreted in a similar way.

Third, we learn to work with a more creative understanding of the relation to each other of scripture and tradition. Protestants have long operated on the assumption that scripture precedes tradition and that tradition plays a predominantly negative role in the church. We now know that the Bible itself is the result of a long process of the formation and re-formation of traditions. As the meaning of the Latin word *traditio* (to pass on) implies, these memories were passed on in several authoritative channels: groups of story tellers, prophets, priests, sages, apostles, those who had been with Jesus. Paul refers to his own activity as handing on what he had received (1 Cor. 11:23). These were the traditions of the people of God, in the two forms of that people as Israel and as the church. The written documents constitute the precipitate from this fluid process of tradition, and the form in which we have them reflects the processes of editing, compiling, and redaction to which they were subjected. "Traditions came before scriptures, and scriptures came before the Bible: for 'the Bible' implies a fixed and closed collection, and this was not reached until a very late stage when a so-called 'canon' of scripture was drawn up."[52] The formation and closing of the canon did not conclude the creative and critical process of tradition (creative because tradition created the canon, critical because it had to decide what to exclude). But it changed the character of postscriptural tradition. It caused other traditions from the biblical period to vanish, with the result that Christians for all practical purposes have no traditions about Jesus other than those contained in the canon. For another, the closing of the canon meant that postcanonical tradition would differ from precanonical tradition, the difference being that it now became exegetical, adopting a hermeneutical function in relation to that part of the tradition now represented by the canon. Protestants are developing a greater appreciation of the role of tradition in creating and interpreting the canon, and are learning that tradition can be both a creative and a self-correcting process. They are coming to understand that the notion of *ecclesia semper reformanda* (the church must always reform itself) is itself a tradition, and a good one. The problem with simplistic understandings of the Reformation's formula *sola scriptura* (the Bible alone) is that the Bible is never alone. The only real option to tradition that is self-critical is tradition that is not.[53] Roman Catholics are learning that the tradition defined itself canonically and in doing so gave scripture a critical role in reforming all tradition, including itself. Tradition, also, is never alone; it always carries the Bible with it.

Fourth, although Neusner does not discuss it, we learn also that we need a norm that will both stand on the side of freedom, releasing rather than inhibiting the power of the gospel, and that will rule out of bounds any and all ideological distortions of the gospel (the promise of the love

of God graciously offered to each and all and the dual command of God
that we in turn love God and our neighbors).

A Norm in the Service of Freedom

The task of developing an understanding of scriptural authority appropriate to the Christian faith and adequate to our understanding of
how such proposals have been ideologically distorted requires that we
formulate a norm of scriptural interpretation (a norm of appropriateness
or what the Reformers called the "material norm") that stands in the
service of freedom—the freedom of God to be gracious—and the freedom of theological interpretation to reform the church.

The Word of God was Martin Luther's canon of biblical interpretation;
much of what he had to say on the question of scriptural authority and interpretation, in a revised form, remains pertinent to post-Holocaust theology. By the expression "Word of God" Luther meant several things: the
second person of the Trinity, the incarnate Lord, the scriptures that witness to the Word of God, and the active preaching of the church through
which the Word is heard and believed. The Word of God, for Luther, that
our lives can be transformed solely by trusting that God justifies us, comes
only through scripture actively used in preaching.[54] He was not arguing
for the primacy of the scriptures, but for the primacy of the gospel to
which they witness.[55] The scriptures "were the 'Word of God' in a derivative sense for Luther—derivative from the historical sense of Word as deed
and from the basic sense of the Word as proclamation."[56]

The Word of God was for Luther the *material norm*, by which he established what was authoritative in books that occupied a *formal* position in the canon of scripture. Luther's christological canon of
interpretation was his "canon within the canon," found at the heart of
the scriptures themselves. With this he tested various biblical books and
found several of them wanting. Two that he was willing to drop from
the canon were the Letter of James and the Book of Revelation. He rejected James because it did not, in his judgment, "drive Christ into the
heart." Whether Luther was correct in his judgment of James is not the
issue; the point is that he had a norm of interpretation that freed him to
criticize the canon. A biblical book is not authoritative if it fails to preach
the doctrine of God's radically free grace; on the other hand, whatever
does preach Christ "would be apostolic, even if Judas, Annas, Pilate, and
Herod were doing it."[57] The *formal norm* of the scriptures was always to
be tested by the *material norm* of the Word of God understood as the
good news of God's justifying grace made known to us through Jesus
Christ. Thus we are free to criticize scripture. Luther's partial divergence

from the scripture principle and inerrancy came about because he demanded that the authority of scripture be derived from the evangelical substance that lay at its heart.

Some aspects of Luther's understanding of scriptural authority cannot be appropriated by a post-Holocaust theology, and others stand in need of some revision. Even when we note all the relevant qualifications on Luther's law/gospel distinction (that the Hebrew Bible is not to be equated with law nor the New Testament with gospel, that the gospel is heard in the Old Testament and law in the New, that the difference between the two has to do with two functions that the same word of God plays in the heart of the believer, and that the same word may therefore be law or gospel, depending on the way in which it addresses the believer), still we have to say that Luther failed to understand law as expressing the grace and command, the call and claim, of God, seeing law in essentially negative ways as restraining the wicked (civil law) or as driving us to despair over our sin ("theological law"). He saw the entire body of commandments given to Israel as the civil law of the Jews and hence as not binding on Christians: "I dismiss the commandments given to the people of Israel. They neither urge nor compel me."[58]

Luther predominantly formulated his understanding of the gospel in terms of grace alone (*sola gratia*), which was a one-sided formulation. A post-Holocaust theology must insist that the gospel be understood as an ellipse with two foci, not a circle with one center. The two foci are promise *and* command, call *and* claim, the proclamation *and* paranesis of the biblical witness. Luther had adequate grounds in his own theology for framing his understanding of the gospel in a similar way.[59] Because he so stressed "grace alone," he could fail to appreciate the Letter of James' emphasis on the works of faith. James does not articulate the whole gospel, any more than do some of Luther's favorite passages, but it articulates the claim the gospel lays upon us. Luther did not see that James was not answering the same question to which Paul responded; thinking that he was, Luther could only reject James. This was a mistake, although his freedom to criticize scripture remains critical.

Third, what caused Luther's "canon within the canon" to fall into disfavor was that although Luther allowed it to test the scriptures, he did not allow the scriptures to test it. He proclaimed it as if it were invulnerable to criticism and reformulation. In contrast, we must insist that any proposed canon of interpretation drawn from the scriptures, which is what is meant by a "canon within the canon," is a theological construction from the scriptures to be brought in turn into conversation with the scriptures for the purpose of testing them, but is itself open to testing and reformulation. A conversational approach to formulating a norm of interpretation cannot clutch at dogmatic finality.

Fourth, Luther's canon of interpretation functioned within a generally supersessionist outlook and tended to drive apart the two testaments, in spite of his qualifications on the law/gospel dichotomy. Although he rightly insisted that justification is by grace, through the active response of faith, this is hardly a new idea in the New Testament, nor does it appear in the Hebrew Bible merely as a harbinger of things to come. It is the ground of the existence of the Jewish people as such, who are called into being by the grace of God. So, however much one appreciates Luther's canon of interpretation, we must resituate that canon within the larger body of scripture and use it to interpret the New Testament in the light of, not against, the Hebrew Bible.

A Re-presentative Understanding of the New Testament

A norm of appropriateness that affirms the singular promise and singular command of God and understands the relation of the testaments in a nonsupersessionist way can best be articulated by a re-presentative understanding of the New Testament and a canonical situating of its witness within the orbit of the hermeneutical axioms of biblical Israel. Schubert M. Ogden's proposal for construing scriptural authority promises to be of great help to Christian theologians attempting to rethink the Christian witness in the light of the reality of Judaism and the Jewish people. Scripture, as Ogden approaches the matter, can be authoritative only with respect to the appropriateness of Christian theological assertions, "with respect to the end of bearing the distinctively Christian witness of faith."[60] Ogden does not regard scripture as authoritative with respect to determining the intelligibility of Christian theological assertions.

Scripture is the norm of appropriateness for all theological proposals, yet even its normative character is rule-conferred. Although it is normative with regard to all other theological norms, "it itself ultimately stands on the same level as those who are subject to its authority *vis-à-vis* Jesus the Christ."[61] We who are subject to its authority are not thereby deprived of our theological freedom. As with any authorized authority, we can appeal over the head of scripture to the One who authorizes it. Its authority is not authoritarian, but governed by that to which it is the authoritative witness. It is a norm in the service of God's freedom to be gracious, of the freedom of Jesus Christ to overrule our misuse of freedom, and of the freedom of the interpretative tradition to be self-critical.

Ogden tries to get at scripture as *norma normans* by reconsidering the issue of canon. In one sense, canon refers to a collection of writings recognized by the early church. In this sense it is an invention of the post-Marcionite church, although its contents were previously available. In the proper sense of the term, canon is "whatever of or in those writings is in fact authorized by Christ through the church's continuing experience under the guidance of the Holy Spirit."[62] The test is whether these writings are genuinely apostolic, which is the criterion to which the tradition appealed in establishing the canon. In validating the canon, however, the early church applied ambivalently the criterion of apostolicity (whether a writing was authored by someone in turn authorized by Christ himself). It decided questions of apostolicity by reference to the content of books. Orthodox content implied apostolic authorship.

If one insists on using the early church's own criterion, then it must be the apostolic witness to Jesus Christ itself that is the canon within the canon or the canon of interpretation to which the materials holding formal position within the canon as a list of books must be subjected. One task of theology is to criticize the Christian witness of the New Testament in the light of the norm of appropriateness, the "canon" in the sense of the apostolic or earliest witness itself. The New Testament as a set of books is criticizable Christian witness. The canon, accessible only through historical reconstruction from the New Testament, is the apostolic testimony to Jesus.[63] Therefore, merely to show that an assertion is found in the scriptures fails to authorize it as theologically appropriate. One must further establish that this scriptural source "is itself authorized by the apostolic witness of faith."[64] The earliest stratum of witness that can be reconstructed "is itself the norm of appropriateness."[65]

The content of this apostolic witness lies behind the New Testament in what Ogden calls the "Jesus-kerygma," but is found in the New Testament, for example, in Paul, who succinctly formulates the Christian witness: "Yet for us there is one God, the Father, from whom are all things and for whom we exist, and one Lord, Jesus Christ, through whom are all things and through whom we exist" (1 Cor. 8:6). Ogden interprets Paul to say here that "what it means to have God as our Father is existentially the same as having Jesus Christ as our Lord." God the Father is "the covenant God of Israel who has disclosed himself in Israel's history, and thence through the law and the prophets, to be the God of a unique promise and demand." Paul intends to affirm that the revelation of God in Jesus Christ "is the decisive revelation to all mankind of the same promise and demand re-presented by the Old Testament revelation (cf. Romans 3:21)." The word spoken in Jesus Christ is "precisely the *same* word" that was earlier "re-presented through 'the law and the prophets.'"[66]

The strength of Ogden's proposal, in relation to the task of constructing an appropriate post-*Shoah* Christian theology, lies in its total avoidance of the works-righteousness inherent in supersessionism. The "new" knowledge of God of which Christians can lay hold is exactly identical with the primordial revelation of God previously re-presented in the faith of Israel. Our salvation does not "become possible" in Christ—a statement that the New Testament nowhere affirms—but in him what was previously possible and actual in the history of Israel now "becomes manifest." This coheres with a thoroughgoing acceptance of the radical implications of the principles *sola gratia—sola fide*: When "the event of Jesus becomes a condition apart from which God is not free to be a gracious God, the heretical doctrine of works-righteousness achieves its final and most dangerous triumph." By accepting the radical implications of these notions central to the Reformers, Ogden moves beyond the Reformers' own positions. In other words, Paul rightly affirmed that Abraham is "the father of all of us" (Rom. 4:16) not because Abraham believed in Jesus Christ, but because he "believed God, and it was reckoned to him as righteousness" (Rom. 4:3).[67]

Ogden's understanding of scriptural authority renders explicit the monotheizing basis of the Christian witness—that "we are Christ's," but that "Christ is God's" (1 Cor. 3:23; 11:3)—and makes the only condition of salvation one that can be formulated without reference to Jesus Christ as stated in the parable of the Last Judgment (Matt. 25:31–46). The only demand we must meet to receive salvation is that we accept God's love for ourselves and thereby become freed to respond to the concrete needs of the neighbor.[68] Christian triumphalism and exclusivism in relation to Judaism and the Jewish people are rejected.

There are two reasons for questioning, however, whether Ogden's representative view of scriptural authority, helpful as it is, is adequate to the needs and insights of post-Holocaust theology. One is that the earliest witness of the Christian faith, the "Jesus-kerygma," must be reconstructed from behind the writings of the early church by historical-critical method. What we determine this earliest witness to be will be subject to all the variableness to which historical-critical reconstruction, even when tightly controlled, is prone. As our chapter on Jesus in context showed, the methodological approach using the criterion of dissimilarity to reconstruct the historical Jesus, which approach reigned supreme for so long, is being widely abandoned, and no new approach has arisen to take its place, other than the concern to relocate Jesus in context. How to do that remains a difficult question. The problem for reconstructing the earliest Christian witness is that the method that would allow us to get at it is, perforce, the same with which we might be able to reconstruct the historical Jesus; this is so even if one accepts, as I do, Ogden's point that there is no operational distinction between the earliest witness and the empirical-historical Jesus nor any way to move from the latter to the former. Further, historical-critical method can never claim to reach results that are more than probable and that are not subject to further correction. We are left peering over the edge of an archeological dig, hoping that what is dug up will not be itself somehow inappropriate. What if the earliest community was hideously sectarian and exclusivistic? Do we then take our medicine and admit that exclusivism is inherently Christian?

The other difficulty is that the authority of the Hebrew Bible is not adequately stated in this proposal. Obviously, Ogden does not subject it to the New Testament. It is subject to the Jesus-kerygma, as is the Hebrew Bible. Ogden's view of the authority of the Hebrew Bible is that it "document[s] the particular linguistic form of the question of human existence . . . to which the Jesus-kerygma presents itself as the answer." The meaning of the Jesus-kerygma is that it is a development of the understanding of existence "variously expressed in the writings of the Old Testament." The Hebrew Bible, therefore, stands in relation to the Jesus-kerygma as question to answer or presupposition to assertion. This does not deprive it of authority, because "the authoritative answer to a question must endow the question itself with an equivalent authority."[69]

Here Ogden seems to have fallen into an inconsistency.[70] If the Christian witness is a re-presentation of precisely the same word that was earlier re-presented through the law and the prophets, as Ogden has said it is, how then can this witness stand in relation to its earlier and identical re-presentation as an answer to a preceding question? Certainly Ogden does not here mean that the Hebrew Bible is a rhetorical question, but a genuine question, and a genuine question is one to which the questioner does not know the answer. Were Ogden's proposal adequate, I take it that the Hebrew Bible would ask on behalf of the people Israel such questions as "who are we?" and "what are we to do?" And the Jesus-kerygma would answer, "you are people who can understand yourselves authentically in any ultimate sense in terms of and only in terms of the gracious covenantal love offered to you by the God of Israel, and what you should do is to love the God of Israel with all your selves and your neighbors as your selves." Seen in this clear a light, we must respond by saying that the Hebrew Bible is no mere question. It is also an answer, an answer which, as Ogden rightly claims, has lately been re-presented to us. On these two points, then, the locus of the *norma normans* of distinctively Christian scripture and the affirmation of the authority of this scripture without regarding it as the answer to the Old Testament's question, we have to make one more consideration.

We turn to canonical criticism because of its obvious relevance to our discussion: "Christianity has become so systemically Marcionite and anti-Semitic," says James Sanders, "that only a truly radical revival of the concept of canon as applied to the Bible will, I think, counter it." The suggestion offered by canonical criticism is that we look at the scriptures as distillates from a living tradition, something on the following order. At any point on their historical trajectory, we find the people Israel confronted with a hermeneutical task. They have a tradition and the new experience of the contemporary generation. They must interpret the new experience in the light of the tradition in order to understand it and to incorporate it in the living tradition. To do this, they must also reinterpret the tradition if it is to incorporate this new experience and be credible in the face of it. They must do both in order to pass on their faith to the next generation. Hermeneutics is generational joining. "Process," as Sanders says, "was there from the start and continues unabated through and after the periods of intense canonical process of stabilization." The community of faith regularly "contemporized earlier value-traditions to their own situation." In each new historical situation and over major cultural shifts, the people "needed to know ever anew *who they were and what they should do.*" They developed an "amazingly theocentric" canon; "it is basically God's story."[71]

Every time Israel interprets its faith, it reinterprets it. We never find it luxuriating in uninterpreted experience. There is no need for Israel always to say the same thing that it said before, although its foundational commitments remain constant, and sometimes the reinterpretation will have to deny what was earlier claimed: "As I live, says the Lord GOD, this proverb shall no more be used by you in Israel" (Ezek. 18:3). Our attention, therefore, must be given to what canonical criticism regards as Israel's hermeneutical principles or axioms in terms of which it interpreted and reinterpreted its tradition. This turn will provide us with the norm of appropriateness that the Bible's redactors used to reinterpret the biblical tradition and will enable us to locate Ogden's formulation of the norm within the hermeneutical process discernible in scripture and in both testaments, rather than "behind" the New Testament.

The hermeneutical axioms used in the canonical process are essentially three: (1) the Bible is a monotheizing literature that regularly struggles "within and against polytheistic contexts to affirm God's oneness," and this monotheizing axiom of interpretation is expressed in two further hermeneutical axioms, the (2) prophetic and the (3) constitutive. The prophetic axiom stresses that God is the God of *all*, the constitutive that God is the particular Redeemer of Israel or the church. The prophetic axiom proclaims challenge; the constitutive assures promise.[72] Each gives voice to the grace of the one God. In situations that require the community to be challenged, the prophetic mode is stressed, and Israel is reminded of God's love for Egypt and Assyria (Isa. 19:25). In situations where Israel is oppressed and beleaguered and needs to be reminded of God's love for it, the constitutive mode is emphasized, and God recalls to Israel's attention that Israel is God's first love.

These same hermeneutic modes should be used to read a passage of scripture today. "No one comes to the Father except through me" (John 14:7) can be read in an exclusivist way. "In fact," states Sanders, "reading the Bible exclusively in the constitutive mode can issue in a totally denominational, if not tribal, reading of the whole Bible." Read in an exclusivist way, John 14:7 denies to God the freedom to be gracious apart from Jesus Christ, thereby turning God's gift into a condition apart from which God is not free to be gracious. The same passage could be read prophetically in the light of John 10:16: "I have other sheep that do not belong to this fold," to show that an exclusivist reading is self-serving and "canonically false."[73]

A totally constitutive reading of the Bible is idolatrous. It proclaims that God loves us and only us, and that all of the prophetic criticisms found in the Bible are directed at others. This is precisely how the *adversus Judaeos* tradition interpreted the Bible, appropriating for the church all the promises of God to the people Israel and applying all the prophetic criticisms to "the Jews," thus turning prophetic self-criticism into an ideology of opprobrium against an alienated other. An entirely prophetic reading of the Bible would be empty, depriving the reading and hearing community of any reassurance as to God's love graciously offered to it. The only appropriate reading, therefore, is one in which the prophetic and constitutive axioms are held together in the larger context of the theocentric or monotheizing faith of Israel and the church.

The New Testament is authoritative where it struggles to monotheize the Christian witness and articulates the all-inclusive, free grace of God, proclaiming the constancy of God's faithfulness to God's particularly beloved people (whether Israel or the church). However much the New Testament reinterprets Israel's faith, and in it we find many attempts to interpret this new event of Jesus Christ in the light of the traditions of Israel ("according to the scriptures") and to reinterpret that tradition in the light of this new event, it does so appropriately where it monotheizes its new interpretation, thinks theocentrically of Jesus Christ as presenting to us the promise and command, call and claim, of the God of Israel, and balances a constitutive and prophetic hermeneutic.

Paul the apostle shows us all these moves in several places, of which we cite one: "For we hold that a person is justified by faith apart from [ritual] works prescribed by the law. Or is God the God of Jews only? Is he not the God of Gentiles also? Yes, of Gentiles also, since God is one; and he will justify the circumcised on the ground of faith and the uncircumcised through that same faith" (Rom. 3:28–30; bracketed term mine in the light of Chapter 4). As Sanders understands him, Paul "monotheized constantly in his reading of Scripture for his churches and pursued a theocentric hermeneutic in working out his understandings of Christology

and ecclesiology."[74] Where the New Testament uses biblical hermeneutics to interpret its witness, authentically proclaiming the theocentric
gospel of God's love graciously offered to each and all and God's dual
command of love for God and the neighbor, or where it can fairly be interpreted as doing so, it is fully authoritative and biblical. Where it or its
interpreters fail to teach its normative message of the singular call and
claim of the singular God of Israel, it is not. But the emphasis must be on
the responsibility of the interpreters of scripture; whatever scripture or a
scriptural passage may or may not have meant once upon a time, the
Bible is not responsible for how it is later interpreted and applied.

Canonical criticism enables us to locate within the scriptures a revised
version of what the Reformers wanted to find, a norm that stands in the
service of freedom, and to ground there as well Ogden's formulation of
the norm of appropriateness, and it helps us see this norm well displayed
in both testaments. Here neither testament stands as the norm by which
the other is to be assessed; each must be measured in the light of a norm
of interpretation that each affirms. Also, canonical criticism liberates us
to interpret scripture as it interpreted itself, certainly not a move inappropriate to scripture.

The situation that faced the people Israel and the early church also
confronts us: we must interpret the new events of our time, including
the attempt in the most historically Christian part of the world to see to
it that not another Jew lived on planet earth, in the light of the Christian
tradition, and we must reinterpret that tradition if it is to be credible,
morally plausible, and appropriate to itself after that event. Doing so is
painful, if only because one discovers how deeply the Christian tradition
was complicit in that crime. Radical change necessitates radical reinterpretation.[75] But the *adversus Judaeos* tradition itself was a radical reinterpretation, showing us that we need norms to govern and criticize our
new interpretations, norms that will speak for rather than against the
freedom, grace, and all-inclusive love of God, and that will support all
new and free interpretations which themselves, in turn, affirm the freedom of God.

7

Christology

—·—·—·—·—·—·—

We confess Jesus Christ the Jew, who as the Messiah
from Israel is the Saviour of the world and binds the
peoples of the world to the people of God.

—*Synod of the Evangelical Church of the Rhineland*

Although hardly the only issue needing to be rethought by a post-Holocaust theology, Christology is, as Rosemary Ruether designates it, the
"key issue" in any such rethinking. Her pointed way of putting the question can hardly be improved upon: "Is it possible to say 'Jesus is Messiah' without, implicitly or explicitly, saying at the same time 'and the
Jews be damned'?"[1] Clearly, Ruether thinks that it *is* possible to confess
Jesus Christ without saying "and the Jews be damned." Her development in *Faith and Fratricide* of a new covenantal theology and a proleptic Christology that places the eschatological hope ahead of both Jews
and Christians who in common wait for it takes a considerable step in
the direction of a revised Christology. This chapter will analyze the basic
christological models of the ancient and modern church with regard to
their relation to anti-Judaism and ask what would constitute an appropriate model for construing Christology after the Holocaust.

Classical Christology, in spite of its concern to refute those who argued that the One who was incarnate in Jesus Christ was not the God of
Israel as well as those who argued that God could not have been incarnate in a genuine human being, nevertheless did not free itself from saying that "Jesus is the Christ and the Jews be damned."

In the numerous anti-Jewish tracts produced by early and medieval theologians, the figure of Jesus Christ plays a strong and central role. In our
survey of supersessionist understandings of the covenant, we saw the crucial significance of Jesus Christ as the one by virtue of whom the covenant

167

is removed from the Jews and given to the church, the "old" covenant destroyed and a "new" one made with the church. Jesus Christ is the focal point of traditional anti-Judaism and the "hinge" upon which the replacement of Jews with Gentile Christians turns. The "work" of Christ in making salvation possible for Gentiles makes salvation impossible for Jews as Jews; it is possible for them if they become Christian but not if they obdurately insist on being Jews. This is not the only anti-Jewish theme in traditional Christology. Classical Christology affirms Jesus Christ as a *divine* (as well as human) object of faith and pillories Jews for not recognizing the divinity of Jesus Christ; were they to recognize it, they would have to convert. It speaks of the *teachings* of Jesus as teachings against Jews and Judaism. It talks of the *life of Jesus* as a life lived against Jews and Judaism, and of his *crucifixion and death* as at the hands of Jews and Judaism. It presents the *resurrection* of Jesus by God as a victory over Jews and Judaism. Jews and Judaism are used as a foil in opposition to whom and to which the church sets forth its understanding of who Jesus is (the person of Christ) and what he does (the work of Christ). In the modern and contemporary periods of church history, this tendency to view Jesus and Judaism as antithetical grows more rather than less pronounced. The clash between the Christ of the church and the people and faith of Israel is potent, acrid, and consequential. Jesus Christ is the means by which the church displaces Israel in the love and grace of God. He sides with us, against Israel, in making it possible for Christianity to be everything new, creative, spiritual, and universal, which the old, stubborn, carnal, and ethnocentric Jews by definition cannot possibly be.[2]

Athanasian Christology

Because there can hardly be a more authoritative representative of classical Christology than Athanasius, its staunch and resolute defender, we review his christological reflection for an example of this Christology. Our purpose is not to rehearse the development of the church's Christology up to the Council of Nicaea and beyond; that has been well and often done and can be found in many sources.[3] The burden of Athanasius' Christology in *On the Incarnation* is to show that the Word (Logos), who as the Redeemer reclaims us for God, is the Word through whom we were created. The Logos reclaims us through a triple action: the life-bestowing, death-overcoming power of the Word heals our illness of body and soul, our being-toward-death; the Word's teaching restores to us the true knowledge of God, which we had lost; and the Word's sacrifice on our behalf pays the debt that all owe to God but none can pay. Athanasius agreed with what Irenaeus had earlier proclaimed, that Christ "became what we are that He might bring us to be even what He is Himself."[4] Athanasius' work is also an apology, defending a claim "which Jews traduce and Greeks laugh to scorn" and reassuring Christians who are aware that Jews and Greeks have other views.[5]

Athanasius' first reason for the incarnation is that by departing from the Logos who created us, humanity lost the principle of life and was wasting away: "Transgression of the commandment was turning them back to their natural state, so that just as they have had their being out of nothing, so also, as might be expected, they might look for corruption into nothing in the course of time." People began to sin and to die; death "gained . . . a legal hold over us." God now has a problem: Having said "the soul that sinneth, it shall die," it would violate God's majesty to indicate that God did not really mean it; but the destruction of God's creature, made in God's image, would violate God's majesty and goodness. Redemption is possible, but not by mere repentance. Having descended into a state of corruption, human beings need to be re-created, which can only be accomplished by the Word's becoming flesh: "He took pity on our race, had mercy on our infirmity, and condescended to our corruption, and, unable to bear that death should have the mastery—lest the creature should perish, and his Father's handiwork in men be spent for nought—he takes unto himself a body, and that of no different sort from ours." The Word, being immortal and incapable of dying, took a body capable of death so that he could satisfy "the debt by his death" and clothe "all with incorruption, by the promise of the resurrection."[6]

Whereas Athanasius' first argument for the incarnation articulates the theme that Jesus Christ is the *life* of the world, the second claims that he is the *light* of the world. In departing in sin from the Word, humans lost the principle of reason by which they knew God. In spite of all God's witnesses, they sank into mental degradation and superstition. Whereas humanity was created in the image of God, enabling them to know God, they turned from the knowledge of God to that of earthly things. Thus human beings "darkened their soul, as not merely to forget their idea of God, but also to fashion for themselves one invention after another." So committed did they become to idolatry that even God's gift of the law and the prophets did not lead them to raise their heads toward the truth. God's only possibility was to renew "that which was in God's image, so that by it men might once more be able to know him."[7]

The Logos incarnate in Jesus, however, had all the characteristics of a Hellenic deity: it was impassible, immutable, incapable of change in any respect or of being affected. Hence, "not even when the Virgin bore him did he suffer any change, not by being in the body was [his glory] dulled: but, on the contrary, he sanctified the body also. For not even by being in the universe does he share in its nature, but all things . . . are quickened by him."[8] The Logos effects others, but is in no way affected by them. Against the Docetists (who argued that the Logos did not really take on a human body but merely seemed *[dokeo]* to do so), Athanasius argues that "the actual body which ate, was born, and suffered, belonged to none other but to the Lord."[9] The body of Jesus carried out human functions, the Logos constituted him as a person. The Logos cannot suffer, but participates in suffering in this buffered way, protected by the body of Jesus. Unlike the Arians, who drew a line between the immutable God and the lesser being who was incarnate in Christ, Athanasius drew a line between the Logos and the body of Christ. Thereby God is protected from interacting with the world.

Athanasius added a "Reply to Objections: Jewish," in order "to rebuke . . . the disbelief of the Jews, . . . from the Scriptures, which even themselves read."[10] His "Reply" is a digest of the church's abundant *adversus Judaeos* literature. Whether it was directed to Jews to convince them or to Christians to shore up their identity vis-à-vis the well-established Jewish tradition is not clear.[11] He argues from the Septuagint that the promises predicting Christ have been and could only have been fulfilled in Jesus.

Jesus' birth from a virgin foretold by Isaiah 7:14 is shown to be fulfilled in Matthew 1:23. Other prophecies relate yet more details surrounding Jesus' birth, such as his coming out of Egypt. Jesus' suffering and death are predicted in the suffering servant passage of Isaiah 53, his manner of death on a cross by Deuteronomy 28:66 and Jeremiah 11:19 (which at least mentions a tree). None other than a death on a cross could fill the bill of items prophesied in the scriptures. Hence, "all Scripture teems with refutations of the disbelief of the Jews."[12] Athanasius recites a biblical genealogy to show that none of them was born of a virgin. Nor did any king of Israel triumph over all his enemies while still a child, nor was there one in whom "all the nations have placed their hopes and had peace, instead of being at enmity with them on every side." No prophet or patriarch died on the cross for the salvation of all or went into Egypt and destroyed their idols. Nor was any great one of Israel pierced in hands and feet or hung upon a tree; to none of them does the prophecy apply, "ye shall see your Life hanging before your eyes" (Deut. 28:66). "Who, then, is he of whom the divine Scriptures say this? Or who is so great that even the prophets predict of him such great things? None else, now, is found in the Scriptures but the common Saviour of all, the Word of God, our Lord Jesus Christ." Only he was born of a virgin, died on a cross for our salvation, and brought to an end the idolatry of the Egyptians. Only the miracles of Christ fulfill the predictions of what Christ would do; prior miracles are impressive, but "not like the wonder wrought by the Saviour."[13]

Jews persist in denying "plain facts" and insist that they look for the fulfillment of the eschatological promises of scripture but that "the Word of God is not yet come." On this point they are "forever harping, not blushing to brazen it out in the face of plain facts." They are not convinced by Daniel's prophecy, that Christ will come, be anointed, be declared not simply a human being but Holy of Holies, and that Jerusalem is to stand *until* he comes. Hence "the Jews are trifling, and the time in question, which they refer to the future, is actually come. For when did prophet and vision cease from Israel, save when Christ came, the Holy of Holies? For it is a sign, and an important proof, of the coming of the Word of God, that Jerusalem no longer stands."[14] The truth has come; we no longer need the shadow. Nothing is unfulfilled; the Jews are fairly refuted.

Athanasius pursues a difficult line of exegesis, arguing that the prophecies in scripture are clear enough to see that Christ fulfills them, but that it is necessary that Christ further clarify them. If they are indistinct, Christ cannot be clearly seen to fulfill them nor Jews faulted for failing to see that he has done so; if he has not further clarified them, they could refer to someone other than Jesus, particularly the Messiah whom Jews still await. Therefore, Athanasius employs a double-sided hermeneutical strategy, interpreting prophecies typologically and fulfillments literally. When the prophecies hope for a king to shoulder the government, they cannot be taken literally, because Jesus ran no government. Thus, "king" does not mean "king"; it means "Christ." Fulfillments, however, are interpreted literally (not allegorically), lest another fulfill the promises. The exegesis that makes one testament orthodox makes the other heretical and vice-versa.

Classical Christology was systematically related to soteriology; who Christ was and what he did were construed so as to make salvation possible. Salvation meant immortalization of the mortal, divinization of human beings: Christ "became what we are that He might bring us to be what He is Himself." The grace of salvation was made available to believers *through* the sacramental system; it was channeled grace. Gregory of Nyssa explains that sin is like a "poison" that we had eaten and that is "disintegrating our nature. It follows that we were in need of something to restore what had been disintegrated; we needed an antidote that would enter into us and by its counteraction undo the harm already introduced into the body by the poison." When Christ's immortal body enters ours as the eucharistic bread, "it transforms it entirely and makes it like itself." As food and drink are transformed into flesh and blood, Christ's human body by virtue of "the indwelling of the divine Word . . . was transmuted to the dignity of divinity." The bread on the altar is transformed into the body of the divine Word, "as the Word himself declared: 'This is my body.'" By partaking of the theanthropic body of Christ our bodies are immortalized: "Now the reason why God, in his self-revelation, joined himself with our perishable nature was to divinize humanity, by union with deity."[15]

What are we to make, post-Holocaust, of this traditional Christology? We cannot ignore the trenchant criticisms offered in the history of theology. Part of the task of traditional Christology was to ascertain how Christ reestablishes humanity's relationship with God. By contrast, the intent of the Reformers' doctrine of justification by grace through faith was less to respond to this question than to depose it. In the tradition, salvation is a two-step affair: the situation of human beings must be changed radically in order to make them acceptable to God, and as a result, reconciliation with God eventuates. "For Luther, by contrast, there is no such preparation. Christ is given to us as free gift, and he *is* our fellowship with God."[16] Transformation of life is the result of God's gracious gift, not its condition. Post-Holocaust theology's hermeneutic of suspicion thinks there is a works-righteousness at the heart of the tradition; the grace of God is not radically free to each and all. Adam's sin is universally efficacious, its results freely distributed and inescapable. Adam is freer with his sin than Christ with his benefits, which are available only to *some* and then only on condition that they do something to get them. Because Jews do not meet the condition of salvation by becoming Christians and participating in the sacraments, they are not saved.

The metaphysics in terms of which classical Christology was framed has not only broken down, but is now widely seen to be inappropriate in its impact on Christology. The impassible, immutable Logos incarnate in Jesus but unaffected by the joys and sufferings of the body it assumed is more like Aristotle's "unmoved mover" than the God of the Bible, who is consistently described as interacting with the sufferings of the people of God.[17] The tradition's insistence on God's immutability undercut the point it was trying to make with the doctrine of incarnation and weakened it as a symbol. The immutable Logos is no more "with" us for being in a body than not.

The tradition never gave a coherent account of its claim that Jesus is both divine and human, one person in two natures. The most it managed, with Chalcedon's four negations, was to establish parameters within which the discussion could take place; Chalcedon did not explain the meaning of its own formulation. One way of putting the problem is to say that every time the tradition emphasized the fullness of human nature in Jesus Christ (in obedience to the claim that whatever Christ did not assume he did not save), it tended in a Nestorian direction; whenever it countered its Nestorian impulses, it moved in a monophysite direction. Every time the docetic-monophysite thrust was beaten back on one point, it returned on another. Athanasius himself is an example, for he committed what later came to be the Apollinarian heresy when he asserted that the Logos took the place in Christ of the human spirit. Athanasius' Jesus was not fully human. But the "fully human" Jesus has two minds, two wills, two spirits, one divine and the other human. How are all these one person? That was the problem of Nestorius, whose Jesus resembled a two-horse team. Nestorius was condemned, only to have a later ecumenical council react against a newer form of the docetic-monophysite thrust—the monothelite heresy that Jesus had only one will and that divine—by declaring that Jesus had two wills (which had been Nestorius' claim). The two wills and minds are in perfect harmony, with the divine always in control (being omnipotent and omniscient) and the human "nature" of Christ doing the suffering. Is that a recognizable human being?

To these a post-Holocaust theology would add that another reason why the tradition could never give a coherent account of the humanity of Jesus was that, although it talked about incarnation, its language remained incredibly abstract. The Logos assumed "human nature" (*humanum*) or "a human being" (*hominem*) of the generic sort. What must be firmly said is that God was incarnate in the Jew Jesus, *Yeshua ha Notsri*, neither in abstract human nature nor in a generic human being. God was and in Israel's story could only have been incarnate in a Jew; Athanasius and other Gentiles could have encountered the God of Israel in the first instance only in, through, and by means of at least one Jew. Although there were many "incarnations" in the Greco-Roman world, none was the incarnation of the God who liberated and would ultimately redeem Israel.

Athanasius and the tradition no longer understand the significance of Israel's "no" to Jesus Christ as did the apostle Paul, for whom it was a mystery of God but for whom also it was a "no" for which God was ultimately responsible and which God used for God's own purposes. Paul, grieved as he was over Israel's "no," argued that it came about because God hardened the hearts of Israel so that the Gentiles could be saved. For Paul, Israel's "no" was not a willful no, much less what Athanasius called it—"trifling." It was more God's doing than Israel's, and the church benefited from the "no." "For your sake," Paul said, they have become "enemies" (Rom. 11:28; the usual translation reads "enemies of God," except that the NRSV notes that the Greek lacks *of God*; why then supply it?).

The doctrine of the incarnation is critical to the church's faith after Auschwitz, as is the doctrine of the Trinity. Each helps the church see that as it encounters Jesus Christ it encounters the maker of heaven and earth, the God who brought Israel out of Egypt, who revealed God's self to Israel in history and through the law and the prophets and who will ultimately redeem Israel and all humanity, and who is made known to the church in Jesus Christ through the preaching and teaching of the Christian faith. When we have to do with Jesus Christ, we do not merely have to do with "the man from Nazareth," although we most assuredly have to do with the man from Nazareth. The incarnation and the doctrine of the Trinity save the church from that unitarianism of the second person which is inherently anti-Jewish.

Anti-Judaism in Modern Christologies

In modern theology, classical Christology was less argued against than assumed to have collapsed of its own weight and a new beginning made in Christology, one based on the "historical Jesus." In this development, anti-Judaism was reestablished on a new footing and became more strident than it had been in the ancient church. Modern Christology redefined everything. Jesus becomes increasingly, and by the nineteenth century predominantly, the "historical Jesus" as reconstructed by critical historians, the "empirical-historical Jesus" who serves as the ground and warrant for the christological confession. His "person" becomes that of a historical human being who knows God perfectly, the perfect believer. Whereas in classical Christology the Logos was subjectively incarnate in Jesus Christ (the Logos was a divine subject united with Jesus as a human subject), now God is objectively incarnate in Jesus, present to the consciousness of Jesus as the object of his faith. In a stroke, Jesus Christ shifts from being the one *in* whom Christians believe to being himself the "perfect believer," the "first of the believers," *with* whom we believe, the pioneer of our faith. Perhaps no contention is dearer to the heart of modern Christologies than this one, and we find it from Schleiermacher's insistence on Jesus' perfect "God consciousness" to recent affirmations of the uniqueness and constancy of Jesus' "abba experience." In Christology, it is important to get the prepositions straight, and the "modern" prepositions are all wrong.[18]

The uniqueness of Christ in classical Christology was that his *person* was comprised of two natures, one human and one divine; only he was consubstantial with us as to humanity and with God as to divinity. In modern critical-historical Christologies, the only way to establish the uniqueness of Jesus is to contrast him with his context; he is unique precisely to the extent that he is differentiated from and opposed to Jews and Judaism. This we find as early as Kant and Hegel's opposition of Jesus to Judaism and as recently as Jeremias' setting him in antagonism to the "cancer" of the Pharisees.[19] The *work* of Christ is redefined. In classical Christology, Christ's work was to deliver humanity (or believing humanity) from death, sin, and ignorance; now the work of Christ is to liberate humanity from bad religion. Bad religion is authoritarian religion that heteronomously imposes alien laws on human beings; Judaism is its definitive expression. Christ becomes the one who "saves" us from Judaism. "Salvation" in classical Christology was from sin, death, the devil, and the wrath of God, with salvation from death articulated in terms of the "medicine of immortality" available in the Eucharist.[20] It also meant living a new and transformed life in love and service to the neighbor. In modern Christologies, salvation becomes a this-worldly process according to which we are emancipated from oppressive structures, initially authoritarian religion and later a wide variety of forms of cultural repression, bureaucratic manipulation, economic exploitation, and sexual and racial oppression. We can hardly discuss all of these concerns, but the pattern is clear.

Anti-Judaism in Kant and Hegel

The two philosophers most influential on modern liberal Christologies were Kant and Hegel, whose understandings of Judaism led each to set Jesus and Christianity in the sharpest antithesis to it. Kant and Hegel are the preeminent philosophers of modern Protestantism. Each stood for freedom in philosophy, religion, ethics, and history. Hegel developed a philosophy of history in which freedom was the central category. Both were firmly committed to the emancipation of human beings from authoritarianism, with Kant defining the meaning of Enlightenment as "man's release from his self-incurred tutelage."[21] The point of enlightenment was to have the "courage to think" and free ourselves from authoritarianism, which itself always asks us to turn our minds over to someone else. Kant had his deepest influence on Hegel, who in turn profoundly influenced the quest for the historical Jesus.

Kant regarded Judaism as the antithesis of freedom. Religion for Kant consists in the fact "that in all our duties we look upon God as the lawgiver universally to be honored," and the way religion is determined "hinges upon knowing *how God wishes* to be honored and obeyed." A divine will may command "either through laws in themselves *merely statutory* or through *purely moral* laws." Judaism is Kant's premier example of a "merely statutory" religion, Christianity of a "purely moral" one. A statutory religion is authoritarian because knowledge of its laws can be gained "not through our own reason alone but only through revelation," whereas "pure moral revelation, through which the will of God is primordially engraved in our hearts, is not only the ineluctable condition of all true religion whatsoever but is also that which really constitutes such religion." A statutory religion is "an historical faith . . . in contradistinction to pure religious faith."[22]

Because they are radically divergent types of faith, "the Jewish faith stands in no essential connection whatever, i.e., in no unity of concepts, with this ecclesiastical faith . . . , though the Jewish immediately preceded this [the Christian] church and provided the physical occasion for its establishment." Christianity derives no spiritual patrimony from Judaism, which was "a collection of mere statutory laws upon which was established a political organization; for whatever moral additions were then or later *appended* to it in no way whatever belong to Judaism as such." Genuine moral values cannot be Jewish, because morality requires freedom, which merely statutory Judaism rejects. It intended to be "merely an earthly state," with morals of the sort "which a political organization can insist upon and lay down as coercive laws, since they relate merely to external acts"; even the Ten Commandments "are directed to absolutely nothing but outer observance." Therefore and because it "involves no belief in a future life," Judaism "is not a religious faith at all."[23]

Yet among this people and in the midst of their "theocracy," "there suddenly appeared a person whose wisdom was purer even than that of previous philosophers, as pure as though it had descended from heaven." They were "ripe for a revolution," because they had suffered so long from "all the ills of an hierarchical constitution" and because the ethical doctrines of freedom of Greek thinkers, "doctrines staggering to the slavish mind," had gradually begun to inspire them. Christianity utterly forsook "the Judaism from which it sprang, and grounded [itself] upon a wholly new principle," bringing about "a thoroughgoing revolution in doctrines of faith."

> The subsequent dispensing with the corporal sign which served wholly to separate this people from others warrants the judgment that the new faith, not bound to the statutes of the old, nor, indeed, to any statutes whatever, was to comprise a religion valid for the world and not for one single people.[24]

Jesus Christ, the teacher of the gospel and self-announced "ambassador from heaven" (a phrase Kant uses to point up the discontinuity between Jesus and Judaism), "declared that servile belief is essentially vain" and that the only saving faith is moral faith. Christianity's advantage over Judaism is that it comes "*from the mouth of the first Teacher* not as a statutory but as a moral religion."[25] Kant restates supersessionist understandings of Christianity's relation to Judaism, affirming that "the corporal sign" of the covenant between God and Israel was "dispensed with," that Jesus appeared among Jews as a complete novelty, teaching a freedom in relation to God unknown to "slavish" Jews and effecting a thoroughgoing revolution in matters of faith, his only connection with Judaism being "physical."

The young Hegel was either anti-Christian or antiecclesiastical and motivated by a love for ancient Greek "folk religion" and Kant's doctrine of ethical autonomy.[26] By the time he wrote *The Spirit of Christianity*, Hegel had discovered Christianity's moral principle as love and love as the heart's beauty, which he took as synthesizing the beauty of Greek religion and Kant's emphasis on freedom. To this the antithesis became Judaism; contrasted with Greek and Christian beauty, Judaism is ugly, stressing disunion rather than union, hostility rather than friendship to nature.[27] Jews at the time of Jesus were a people "whose spirit was now overwhelmed by a burden of statutory commands which pedantically prescribed a rule for every casual action of daily life and gave the whole people the look of a monastic order." Worship and morality were "ordered and compressed in dead formulas, and nothing save pride in this slavish obedience to laws not laid down by themselves was left to the Jewish spirit," additionally embittered by Roman occupation.[28]

Enslaved to authoritarianism, Jews "were incapable of forging a faith by their own exertions or of grounding one in their own nature." Their exclusivism was why they "utterly abhorred and despised all surrounding peoples," regarding union with them as "a horrible abomination." The Roman presence made them cling adamantly "to the statutory commands of their religion; they derived their legislation from a jealous God." This legislation consisted of a "countless mass of senseless and meaningless actions, and the pedantically slavish spirit of the people had prescribed a rule for the most trivial actions of daily life." Abraham's initial act, leaving Ur of the Chaldees, was "a disseverance which snaps the bonds of communal life and love." Spurning the beautiful relationships of his youth, he "wanted *not* to love, wanted to be free by not loving." His spirit of uncompromising antagonism led him to be "a stranger to the soil and to men alike," and he made this separation of himself from others evident "by a physical peculiarity imposed on himself and his posterity." The only thing beyond Abraham's power was love; "even the one love he had, his love for his son . . . was not so strong as to render him unable to slay his beloved son with his own hand." And in his jealous God "lay the horrible claim that He alone was God and that this nation was the only one to have a god." The liberator of this nation, Moses, was in turn its lawgiver, who "freed it from one yoke [and] laid on it another. A passive people giving laws to itself would be a contradiction." The antithesis of Judaism was "the world and all the rest of the human race." Even the much-vaunted Sabbath of the Jews would be a "vacuity" to free people.[29]

Jesus' relation to the Jews is predictable. He who was one with God was utterly rejected by them: "How were *they* to recognize divinity in a man, poor things that they were, possessing only a consciousness of their misery, of the depth of their servitude, of their opposition to the divine, of an impassable gulf between the being of God and the being of men? Spirit alone recognizes spirit." "Faith in something divine," says Hegel, "cannot make its home in a dunghill. The lion has no room in a nest, the infinite spirit none in the prison of a Jewish soul."[30]

Given the "impurity" of Jewish life, the only relation Jesus could have to his compatriots was to "train them, to develop in them the good spirit which he believed was in them, and thereby to create men whose world would be his world." He came not to bring peace, but a sword that would cut himself and his disciples off from Judaism. Although Jesus appeared among Jews, he was "possessed of a new spirit entirely his own." There was in Jews no spark of life that he could kindle into flame. His self-disclosing comments, "I am the truth," show the "separation of his personality from the Jewish character." Jesus opposed the Jews on every question, chiefly on the concept of God whom Jews regarded as "their Lord and Governor," but who to Jesus was related to "men" as "a father to his children." The "loveless nature" of the Jews caused them to be shocked by Jesus' message of love and to respond to it with "hatred"; they could not see that in contrast with their "reversion to obedience, reconciliation in love is a liberation." The sermon on the mount directly attacks the laws of Judaism, exhibiting "that which fulfills the law but annuls it as law and so is something higher than obedience to law and makes law superfluous." Jesus struggled not merely against one aspect of Judaism but "set himself against the whole. Thus he was himself raised above it and tried to raise his people above it too." He censured the life of his people "at its roots" and sought to lead them to another God, "the God of all mankind," and "to the renunciation of their lifeless, spiritless, and mechanical worship."[31] Unfortunately, he failed to expect the resistance he would receive from a people who had submitted to "an obstinate mania for servility" and who would obdurately oppose the bearer of freedom and love.

These emphases reappear in Hegel's later works. Commenting in *The Phenomenology of Mind* that it is only when something is "entirely bad that there is an inherent and immediate necessity in it to wheel round completely into its opposite," Hegel remarks of the Jews "that it is precisely because they stand directly before the door of salvation, that they are and have been the most reprobate and abandoned."[32] Exactly what the Jewish people should be, they renounce and put beyond themselves; only by taking back into themselves what they have renounced can they reach a higher level of existence. In his *Lectures on the Philosophy of Religion*,

Hegel continues to understand Jews and Judaism as he did in his early essays. Jews assert an exclusiveness "in complete contradiction with the idea that God is to be conceived of only in universal thought, and not in one particular characterisation." There is in Judaism "not the slightest trace of the thought that God . . . has acted in an affirmative way amongst other peoples too." It is a religion of the wrong sort and Jews "a people adopted by covenant and contract on the conditions of fear and service." Judaism is oriented to "what is external, and not to what is inward and moral."[33]

It is an old saw in historical theology classrooms that nineteenth-century theology did "what Kant said it could and Schleiermacher said it should." Although quintessentially modern thinkers who did not continue the thought forms of the medieval church, Kant and Hegel reinterpreted traditional anti-Judaism and reaffirm it in relation to their respective philosophical outlooks. Both were immensely influential on modern theology. In spite of his disdain for efforts to write a life of Jesus, Hegel provided the intellectual underpinning to all "christologies from below" with his insistence on the unity of the divine and the human or the incipient divinity of humanity. This is reflected in the assumption of Christologies from below that Jesus is divine precisely to the extent that his humanity was perfect. They then attempt to show this by a historical-critical reconstruction.[34] To be divine or "unique" in the way in which Jesus is supposed to have been is identical with being *completely* human, *the* human being. The emphases of Kant and Hegel on Jesus and Judaism recur throughout the era of "historical Jesus" Christologies.

The pattern of modern Christologies

Modern, historical-Jesus Christologies "from below" reflect the christological logic outlined above and the emphases of Kant and Hegel. Let us look at some representative examples of this Christology. Although Schleiermacher preceded the strictly historical-Jesus Christologies of the nineteenth century, the germ of this way of doing Christology is present in his work. Piety or faith for Schleiermacher is "the consciousness of being absolutely dependent, or, which is the same thing, of being in relation with God." The various religions manifest this God-consciousness organized as different stages of development and into different kinds. In relation to this variety of religions, Christianity possesses an "exclusive superiority." Christianity, Judaism, and Islam occupy the highest plane of religious development, although Judaism is "almost in process of extinction," and "by its limitation of the love of Jehovah to the race of Abraham betrays a lingering affinity with Fetichism." Judaism and Christianity are monotheistic religions of the teleological type, but although Christianity succeeds Judaism, so "far as concerns its historical existence and its aim, its relations to Judaism and Heathenism are the same." Earliest Christianity "cannot be explained by means of the Jewish piety of that or of an earlier time, and so Christianity cannot in any wise be regarded as a remodelling or a renewal and continuation of Judaism." The new covenant is in direct antithesis to the Old, and "almost everything else in the Old Testament is, for our Christian usage, but the husk or wrapping of its prophecy, and whatever is most definitely Jewish has least value."

Sin for Schleiermacher means that one has an imperfect God-consciousness; to the extent to which one's God-consciousness is not united with one's awareness of other objects of consciousness, one is in need of redemption. Obviously the redeemer cannot be in this same situation; he "is like all men in virtue of the identity of human nature, but distinguished from them all by the constant potency of His God-consciousness, which was a veritable existence of God in Him." Jesus is perfectly aware of God, and this is what it means to speak of God as incarnate in Jesus. God is objectively incarnate in Jesus as the object of his God-consciousness. Thus, Jesus cannot be "explained simply by what was historically given Him," that is, Judaism. He stands in but does not stem from the corporate life of Israel: "If the man Jesus was really ideal, or if the ideal became historical and actual in Him . . . in order to establish a new corporate life within the old and out of it, then certainly He must have entered into the corporate life of sinfulness, but He cannot have come out of it, but must be recognized in it as a miraculous fact (*eine wunderbare Erscheinung*)." Jesus' perfect God-consciousness entails that his personal development "must be thought of as wholly free from everything which we have to conceive as conflict," and that "at every moment even of His period of development He must have been free from everything by which the rise of sin in the individual is conditioned." So construed, Jesus is the norm that authorizes all Christian teaching: "All doctrines and precepts developed in the Christian Church have universal authority only through their being traced back to Christ," which idea of authority is grounded in "His perfect ideality in everything connected with the power of the God-consciousness." Christ's work is what only a person with a perfect God-consciousness can do, and that is to assume "believers into the power of His God-consciousness, and this is His redemptive activity."[35]

In Schleiermacher we see all the ingredients of the modern historical-Jesus Christology from below: the human being, Jesus, was perfectly conscious of God, is the norm of all Christian doctrine, is our redeemer in the sense of drawing us into the power of his faith in God, is the one in whom God was incarnate as the object of Jesus' piety. Anti-Judaism in Schleiermacher is not strident, nor does it reflect personal animosity toward Jews.[36] In his lectures on the life of Jesus, Schleiermacher often does not take the Gospels at face value in their negative views of various kinds of Jews and frequently explains that some piece of apparently anti-Jewish invective put into the mouth of Jesus is not to be regarded as Christian teaching. This is notably the case in his treatment of John 8:39–59, where Jesus accuses the Jews of having the devil for their father. Here, said Schleiermacher, Christ was not presenting a doctrine, something to be taught in the church, although he assumes the historicity of the account.[37] Schleiermacher is confident that Jesus' religious development took place with no serious influence from the Judaisms in his vicinity; he was relatively uninfluenced in essential matters by the Essenes and Pharisees because otherwise he would have been shaped by their errors, and error in religion is inseparable from sin. Christ's moral, intellectual, and religious development took place without error; otherwise he would not have been perfectly God-conscious.[38] His awareness of God owes little or nothing to Judaism.

We turn to Adolf Harnack to find the quintessential Christology of modern contemporary Protestantism. His influence on the way of doing Christology has outlived the career of theological liberalism and in its fundamental logic is in basic agreement with many contemporary revisionist and liberation theologies. This is particularly so with respect to Harnack's appeal to the empirical-historical Jesus as the ground and warrant of his christological claims. The conviction that made Harnack a liberal was his belief that the exercise of historical responsibility required the present liberation of Christian faith from an infallible authoritarianism, which he knew in the theology of Protestant orthodoxy. Modern people should not be expected to live in the house that authority built. Harnack summoned Christians to appropriate their religious heritage critically and make it their own.

In *The Mission and Expansion of Christianity*, Harnack deals with the figure of Jesus to account for the rise of the universal mission of the church. He observed that Jesus addressed "his fellow countrymen. He preached only to Jews." His message arose from the heart of Judaism. "Not a syllable shows that he detached this message from its national soil, or set aside the traditional religion as of no value. Upon the contrary, his preaching could be taken as the most powerful corroboration of that religion." Jesus "took his stand upon the soil of Jewish rights, i.e., of the piety maintained by Pharisaism." Yet the Pharisees, who preserved the best in Judaism, also debased it. Against their "selfish, self-righteous temper," Jesus "waged war." In battling the "loveless and godless" Pharisees, he broke "with the national religion, for the Pharisaic position passed for that of the nation; indeed, it represented the national religion." Harnack argues that the church's universalism was based on the universalism of Jesus' message, evident in his prediction of "the rejection of the nation and the overthrow of the temple." Jesus "shattered Judaism, and brought out the kernel of the religion of Israel. Thereby—i.e., by his preaching of God as the Father, *and by his own death*—he founded the universal religion, which at the same time was the religion of the Son."[39]

Harnack knew well the anti-Judaism of the Apostolic Fathers. He saw that Paul's view that the "church did not abrogate the special promise made to the Jews" was nothing more than "a Pauline idiosyncrasy" in the ancient church. He characterized theological anti-Judaism as insisting that the Jews never were the chosen people, that the Old Testament has nothing to do with the Jews but belonged from the outset to the church, and that the Jews are punished by the burning of the Temple and the destruction of Jerusalem for having crucified Christ. Then he wrote a paragraph that is difficult to believe:

> Such an injustice as that done by the Gentile church to Judaism is almost unprecedented in the annals of history. The Gentile church stripped it of everything; she took away its sacred book; herself but a transformation of Judaism, she cut off all connection with the parent religion. The daughter first robbed her mother, and then repudiated her! But, one may ask, is this view really correct? Undoubtedly it is, to some extent, and it is perhaps impossible to force anyone to give it up. But viewed from a higher standpoint, the facts acquire a different complexion. By their rejection of Jesus, the Jewish people disowned their calling and dealt the deathblow to their existence; their place was taken by Christians as the new People, who appropriated the whole tradition of Judaism, giving a fresh interpretation to any unserviceable materials in it, or else allowing them to drop. . . . All that Gentile Christianity did was to complete a process which had in fact commenced long ago within Judaism itself, viz., the process by which the Jewish religion was being emancipated and transformed into a religion for the world.[40]

This displacement of the Jewish people and their replacement by the church is legitimated by the work of Jesus in shattering and overcoming Judaism. Jesus' significance lies in the payoff statement of theological anti-Judaism, that the Jews' place "was taken by Christians as the new People." A critical-historical approach to Jesus is used to restate this ancient ideological claim.

In Harnack's *What Is Christianity?* he claimed to employ "only the methods of historical science" and to avoid apologetics entirely. Mixing them would bring historical research "into complete discredit." He tried to get at both the "main features" of Jesus' message and his "character" or "person" by way of the Synoptic Gospels. Aware of the difficulties in using the Synoptics as sources of historical knowledge, Harnack knew that "we are unable to write any life of Jesus," that "our materials are insufficient for a 'biography.'" Nor, with all his writing, did he produce a life of Jesus. Yet he was convinced that the tradition in the Synoptics had been fixed early and that we could discern the main features of Jesus' teaching, how his life issued in the service of his vocation, and the impression he made on his disciples. He was also persuaded that Jesus "himself was what he taught."[41]

In spite of admitting that we cannot write a life of Jesus, Harnack insisted that Jesus "lived in religion, and it was breath to him in the fear of God; his *whole* life, *all* his thoughts and feelings, were absorbed in the relation to God." He did not explain how we know that Jesus never had a feeling not absorbed in the relation to God or could warrant the claim that Jesus "lived in the continual consciousness of God's presence." Yet this claim was important to Harnack because he recognized that there was nothing in Jesus' teachings not already present in Judaism. What counts is not novelty of teaching: "Words affect nothing; it is the power of the personality that stands behind them."[42] Teaching does not constitute the gospel; "the personal life which awakens life around it as the fire of one torch kindles another" is the heart of the matter.[43]

Harnack acknowledges that the Pharisees were in possession of everything that Jesus proclaimed.[44] Unfortunately, they were also in possession of much else: "As regards piety, the spring of holiness had, indeed, long been opened; but it was choked with sand and dirt, and its water was polluted. For rabbis and theologians to come afterwards and distill this water, even if they were successful, makes no difference. But now the spring broke forth afresh, and broke a new way for itself through the rubbish." Jesus compares favorably to the rubbish as to Hegel's "dunghill." His preaching of the acceptable year of the Lord to the poor, the brokenhearted, and the captives was "a definite signal for contradiction" of the prevailing religious system. It brought him into "immediate opposition with the official leaders of the people," who were aware of God's presence only in the law, whereas Jesus "saw and felt Him everywhere."[45]

Jesus sifted the elements of the Jewish tradition, discarding everything particularistic and Jewish and keeping everything genuinely religious and universal. He kept all the ideas of the kingdom of God in which there was a spark of moral force and "accepted none which encouraged the selfish expectations of his nation." The gospel, declares Harnack, "is in nowise a positive religion like the rest; it contains no statutory or particularistic elements; . . . *it is, therefore, religion itself.*" It is superior to both Judaism and Hellenism. An unrelentingly pejorative characterization of Jews and Judaism at Jesus' time runs through Harnack's text. He claims that the Pharisees and priests "had little feeling for the needs of the people." As religiopolitical leaders, they "held the nation in bondage and murdered its soul." His setting Jesus in total contravention to everything Jewish allows him to say; "After all, then, the truth was something new."[46] Never before had it been expressed so consistently and with such "claims to supremacy." Jesus' ethic embodies a higher righteousness and a new commandment; his overcoming of Judaism is Harnack's revisionist doctrine of the work of Christ. Christ saves us from bad religion, Judaism.

The other aspect of Harnack's Christology is his revised doctrine of the person of Christ. For Harnack this is the person of the historical Jesus "who himself was what he taught," all of whose life and feelings were absorbed in the relation to God, who lived in the continual consciousness of God's presence. We have commented on the impossibility of establishing these comments as the empirical-historical propositions Harnack claims them to be. What is important about them is that they indicate why, for Harnack, it is true to say that Jesus is the Christ—because he was the perfect believer. "No one had ever yet known the Father in the way in which Jesus knew him." Matthew 11:27 attributes to Jesus the statement that "no one knows the Father except the Son," which Harnack takes to mean that "it is 'knowledge of God' that makes the sphere of Divine Sonship" and that Jesus became aware of having the consciousness of a unique relation to God as a Son. In classical Christology, the Logos was subjectively incarnate in Jesus; Jesus had two natures and two wills, one of each human and divine. For Harnack, God is objectively incarnate in Jesus' consciousness as an object of knowledge. Jesus' knowledge of God, so superior to anyone else's as to be categorically different, constituted his person. Jesus' self-knowledge warrants his teaching that freed religion from Judaism. In both his teaching and person, Harnack's approach to Jesus "from below" sets Jesus in opposition to Judaism. Harnack's Christ supplants the synagogue with the church and the Jews with the Gentile Christians. The payoff of Harnack's theological anti-Judaism shows up in his interpretation of Paul: "Someone had to stand up and say, 'The old is done away with'; he had to brand any further pursuit of it as a *sin*; he had to show that all things were become new."[47]

By way of summary and critique of the liberal-revisionist christological model, the following observations are made: (1) the work of Christ was to overcome inauthentic, authoritarian religion (identified with Judaism); (2) the person of Christ was the empirical-historical Jesus construed as the perfect believer who was what he taught and serves as the warrant for what he did; (3) so construed, Jesus is inappropriately made over into the first of the believers, the one *with* whom we believe instead of the one *in* whom we believe *with* the apostles; (4) this empirical-historical Jesus was the norm of Christology and Christian theology, thus necessitating reading back into that figure what must be read out of him, which was the rejection of authoritarian religion; (5) the putative empirical-historical claims made for the empirical-historical Jesus (for example, that his every thought concentrated on his relation to God) are impossible of verification; (6) insisting on regarding the empirical-historical Jesus as the subject of Christology and hence unique inevitably results in setting him in opposition to the Judaism(s) of his time; (7) this kind of Christology assumes a pejorative view of Judaism and founders when that view is falsified by subsequent scholarship.

Harnack's emphasis on Jesus as the perfect believer finds popular form more recently in the argument initiated by Gerhard Kittel and developed and popularized by Joachim Jeremias that Jesus called God *"abba,"* that Jesus *always* called God *abba,* and that his doing so shows the unique relationship that Jesus *felt* with God. The case for this view was analyzed and criticized in Chapter 3, on Jesus. That this model remains effective in Christology cannot be exhaustively shown here, but a look at some liberation theologians of Latin America, who are a group of thinkers radically different from those of the liberal era, provides evidence that the modern revisionist Christology based on the empirical-historical Jesus is alive and well.

Liberation theologians begin their christological work by analyzing the concrete religious praxis of the church and popular religion, finding the Christology practiced there inauthentic and corrupt. Joao Dias de Araujo classifies the images of Jesus in the culture of the Brazilian people into five types: the dead Christ (defeated by the forces of evil), the distant Christ (far away while personal piety is directed to a more available saint), the powerless Christ (who is less important than others, particularly than Mary), the Christ who inspires no respect (the crucifix displayed in the bordello), and the disincarnate Christ (a pallid, waxy figure, estranged from daily life).[48]

Saul Trinidad and Juan Stam characterize the Christs of Latin American Protestant preaching differently: the Santa Claus Christ (dispensing cheap grace), the magic-potion Christ (the automatic solution to every problem), the beggar Christ (pleading for acceptance), the passport Christ (one's ticket to heaven), the asocial Christ (separating the convert from the world), the cosmic Christ of glory (above the battles of history), the Christ of Calvary alone (the Protestant answer to the defeated Christ), the guerrilla Christ (a Latin American zealot), and the middle-class Christ (who converts people from socialist labor unions).[49]

The socioeconomic function of this defeated Christ is to form the people of Latin America "by a pedagogy of submission and passivity." In the dolorous Christ, Latin American peasants see their condition reflected back to them and worship it. "Indeed this Abject Jesus is nothing but the image of the conquered Amerindian, the poorest of the poor, for whom nothing has changed since Cortes, the miserable denizen of the immense barrios that fringe the great cities."[50] This religious praxis celebrates passivity as the response to oppression. The defeated Christ is the Christ of "established impotence."[51] The role of Christology in Latin America is to sacralize the *conquista* and the oppression it produced, making a virtue of resignation and suffering. The helpless and harmless "baby" Christ and the humiliated, defeated Christ reflect "eight centuries of struggle, agony, and suffering under the oppressor."[52] The thrust of Latin American liberation Christologies is to attack the Christ who moves from infancy through death to heavenly glory without ever having lived.

The move that most liberation theologians make is back to what was Harnack's starting point. Ignacio Ellacuria asserts: "Today more than ever before it is simply absurd to pretend to construct a Christology in which the actual, historical course of the life of Jesus is not the decisive element."[53] Jose Miranda deals "with the historical Jesus and not the Jesus of some heavenly world nor the Christ of the ecclesiastical Eucharist," reasoning that datable time "does not allow of manipulation." Only the historical Jesus "can judge our differences and be measure of our theologies." Furthermore, claims Miranda, "New Testament 'truths' are historical facts." The content of faith is "*a fact,* namely, that Jesus of Nazareth, man among men, is the very same Messiah anxiously awaited for generations."[54] The claim to base christological assertions on an empirical-historical foundation, indeed that christological propositions *are* empirical-historical "facts," is evident. Jon Sobrino claims of his Christology that its "fundamental goal . . . is to reevaluate the historical Jesus, specifically his status as Son of God, that is, as the one who is historically related to the Father and dependent on his own historical situation." His aim is to reevaluate "Jesus' own faith: to let Jesus become not only the primary content of our faith, but also a structural model for that faith, that is, to let him emerge 'as extraordinary believer,' the one who first lived the fullness of faith."[55] Sobrino makes the same move that Harnack made, back to the historical Jesus, and makes for this Jesus the same claim—that he was the "extraordinary believer." How we are to know this in a critical-historical way, Sobrino does not explain. Nor does he argue his assumption that Jesus' having been such a believer constitutes his significance. Yet Jesus Christ here is the first of the believers *with* whom we believe. In Ellacuria, Miranda, and Sobrino we find the same model and warrant-structures articulated by Harnack.

That these work out in a demonstrably anti-Jewish way is clear from the work of Severino Croatto, whose Jesus regularly offends "the Jews," attacks "the Jews," and is attacked by "the Jews." He offends them by opposing the "work of liberation" to the "'repose' of a false conscience": Hegel's "vacuity" is Croatto's interpretation of the Jewish Sabbath. Jesus' claim to be God's equal "offends the Jews even more."

> In striking fashion, Jesus seeks out the sick, the lowly, sinners, children, foreigners. What is special about these categories of persons, or common to them? They all "lack" something: health, opportunities in life, prestige before the "just" and the judges, capabilities, acceptance among *the Jews*. They are all marginalized.

Except for the foreigners on his list, he might have said that Jesus went to sick Jews, lowly Jews, sinning Jews, Jewish children, marginalized Jews, and Jews without prestige in society. One might claim that he went to all the "lost sheep of the house of Israel" (Matt. 15:24). But Croatto pictures Jesus as going to non-Jews whom "the Jews" did not accept: "The Jews marginalized the sick." "Even today," claims Croatto, "religious circles in Israel oppose granting residence visas to non-Jews. The 'Holy Land' is for a particular, chosen race." Like those to whom he went, Jesus was marginalized by "the Jews" and "the Pharisees," who plotted to kill him.[56]

Croatto's Jesus directs his "conscientizing word" against the Pharisees and "the Jews" on behalf of *human beings*. He "empties the very meaning of the legalistic Pharisees' concerns." He repeats the theme of Pharisaic blindness: "The Pharisees understood the truth but failed to 'see' it. Therefore they plotted against Jesus in order to destroy him." Jesus was concerned to liberate the oppressed, but not the oppressors: "As a matter of principle, Jesus *is not about* to conscientize Israel's leaders, but denounces their sin against the light on the occasion of a deed performed among the marginalized."[57] (Croatto overlooks the risen Jesus' "conscientizing" of Saul, who persecuted the church.) His conscientizing word and liberating praxis led necessarily to his death at the hands of "the Jews." "There is no doubt, based on the convergence of all four evangelists on this point, that it is the *Jews* who proceed against Jesus." Jesus "aroused the fury of the power groups—high priests, elders, scribes, Pharisees—and motivated their decision to eliminate him" because his praxis unmasked "the superstructural and ideological universe that the leaders of Israel controlled, and whose axis of viability was the law understood as 'tradition.'"[58] Jesus was condemned to die as a "religious subversive."

Croatto's liberating Jesus is not new. He is the Jesus of the *adversus Judaeos* ideology in slightly new garb—old wine in a new skin. He contradicts "a law that oppresses" (Croatto knows no other kind of law) and seeks to liberate "a people oppressed by Jewish structures and tradition." Thus, Jesus "brought down on his head all the wrath of the Jewish authorities, rather than that of the Romans."[59] Jesus needs to be liberated from the oppressive ideology of anti-Judaism.

Jesus Christ and the God of Israel

A post-Holocaust Christology will make it clear that to encounter Jesus Christ is to encounter the God of Israel, maker and redeemer of heaven and earth. Jesus is the one through whom by the witness of the church Gentiles are called to understand themselves in relation to the God of Israel and to the Israel of God; that when they proclaim that Jesus is the Christ they can do so only to the greater glory of the God of Israel. Christology may be corrected by the historical Jesus' commitment to the Israel of God and to the God of Israel. As Jesus Christ is a gift to the church of the God of Israel, so is he also a gift from the Israel of God.

Christology is not "Jesusology." Christology cannot be coherently based on and warranted by putative empirical-historical statements about Jesus without being anti-Jewish. To inquire historically as to what was the case with this Jesus whom the church calls Christ and Lord is one thing; to claim to warrant christological conclusions by appeal to the results of historical-critical inquiry is quite another. The former is a legitimate enterprise, the latter not. Christologies warranted by appeal to the historical Jesus are anti-Jewish because such Christologies tacitly assume the uniqueness of Jesus and seek to establish that uniqueness in the only way they can, by setting Jesus apart from and against his entire Jewish context. To come to his conclusion that "Jesus is different," Hans Küng must first contend that Jesus was situated at the heart of a simultaneous quadrilateral conflict with four ideal types of Jews (Pharisees, Sadducees, Essenes, and Zealots representing respectively the types of compromise, establishment, withdrawal, and revolution).[60]

That Christology cannot be warranted by appeal to the empirical-historical Jesus without being anti-Jewish raises the question whether Christology should be so grounded. Assuming that the historical Jesus was a relative and finite human being, we must ask, Is it theologically appropriate to absolutize the relative in this case any more than in any other? Or is doing so merely another way of committing idolatry, with all the horrible price that idolatry exacts, which in the case of the anti-Jewish Jesus is all too clear? H. Richard Niebuhr argues that "the great source of evil in life is the absolutizing of the relative, which in Christianity takes the form of substituting religion, revelation, church or

Christian morality for God."[61] Nor may Jesus be substituted for God.

Paul Tillich was well acquainted with the difficulties of gaining warranted empirical knowledge of the historical Jesus. We cannot be confident, he claimed, that his name was "Jesus." "No special trait of this picture [of Jesus] can be verified with certainty."[62] Tillich wrestled inconsistently with this awareness, insisting also that there had to be at least one personal life in which existential estrangement had been overcome.[63] Yet Tillich had earlier and better grounds for arguing against basing Christology on the empirical-historical Jesus. He defined final (normative) revelation in this way: "A revelation is final if it has the power of negating itself without losing itself." Final revelation sacrifices its own finite conditions. The bearer of it surrenders his or her finitude (including all finite perfections, such as being the "perfect believer") and "becomes completely transparent to the mystery" revealed. As Tillich sees it, had Jesus claimed for himself the kind of ultimacy claimed for him by modern Christologies, he would have been heteronomous and demonic. The stories of the temptations and of Peter's urging him to avoid the cross symbolize attempts "to make him an object of idolatry, [which] . . . is the elevation of the medium of revelation to the dignity of the revelation itself."[64] One cannot help but notice the parallel between Tillich's refusal to absolutize Jesus and John Dominic Crossan's argument that Jesus espoused a "brokerless kingdom," of which not even he was the middleman.[65]

Tillich's version of Luther's *theologia crucis* is at work here; the cross stands as the sign that all genuinely revelatory events point beyond themselves to the ultimate and do not claim ultimacy in themselves; all heteronomies and absolutisms are crucified, broken. This understanding of the revelatory power of Jesus Christ and his cross "condemns a Jesus-centered religion and theology."[66] Jesus alone, apart from God, cannot possibly be Christ and Lord. Jesus is the Christ because he sacrifices what is merely finite in himself; he is revelatory without being heteronomous. Authentic revelation theonomously points beyond itself to God. In Christology properly understood, no finite being imposes itself on other finite beings in the name of God, nor is Christianity's universality based on a claim to its superiority over other religions, and therefore not over Judaism.

Tillich did not work out this Christology consistently. He wavered between affirming these things to be true of the "biblical picture of Jesus as the Christ," the receptive pole of the revelatory event, and a desire to make untenable empirical-historical statements about Jesus, such as: "In all his utterances, words, deeds, and sufferings, he is transparent to that which he represents."[67] The other limitation in Tillich's Christology is that the empirical-historical Jesus plays *no* role in it. Although this Jesus should not be the *norm* of Christology or theology generally, he can *correct* or *negate* Christology, and we have seen that such recent reconstructions as that of Crossan can come to the aid of Tillich's interpretation of the biblical picture of Jesus as the Christ. Nonetheless, Tillich did begin to stake out an alternative christological model that is theologically useful post-Holocaust, and in his Christology he avoided all traces of anti-Judaism, an accomplishment seldom reached in Christian history.

Jesus Christ is our savior, not just a norm

Jesus Christ is more than any mere norm. We begin to construct an alternative, post-Holocaust christological model by abandoning the claim made or assumed by virtually all revisionist Christologies that the empirical-historical Jesus is the "measure of our theologies." As long as Jesus is regarded as the norm of appropriateness of our theologies, he will have to function in such a way as to provide what we need. Feminist theology's treatment of the historical Jesus serves as an example. The problem with feminist theology is that in its constitutive assertions it is right. Women are fully human, clearly the equal of men, and need liberation from sexist oppression. But if the only way to warrant being a Christian feminist is by appeal to the empirical-historical Jesus as a norm, then Jesus will turn out to have been a feminist. We will then have, as we do, significant studies showing that Jesus gathered about himself an inclusive egalitarian community.[68] Here we face several problems: Was Jesus' community really inclusive, or can it be argued that it included only Jews? Is it not anachronistic to retroject late twentieth-century concerns into the early first-century figure of Jesus only to read them out again? If Jesus was not a feminist, am I still not free to be one? Is it the role of Jesus (or whatever we take to be the norm of appropriateness) to authorize our conformity to him or to author our freedom and creativity, our right to reform the church? Dare we allow the historical Jesus to be himself, a first-century Jew, different from us, or must he reflect our concerns and ideals back to us? If so, how can he ever correct us?

Second, instead of the empirical-historical Jesus as the norm of appropriateness—we would do better with the gospel itself as a norm of appropriateness: the promise of the love of God graciously offered to each and all and the dual command of God that we love God with all our selves and our neighbors as ourselves. If we interpret Jesus Christ in the light of this norm, we will understand his significance not in relation to himself alone but in relation to the God of Israel whose promise and command he discloses to us, and in relation to ourselves whom he brings face to face with the promise and command of the God of Israel.

In bringing us to face the decision whether we will understand ourselves in any ultimate sense in terms of and only in terms of the love of God graciously offered to us and in terms of the command of God that we love God and the neighbor, Jesus Christ offers us salvation and is properly spoken of as our savior. Jesus Christ is more than any mere norm. The gospel taken as our norm of appropriateness helps us see both that when we "confess that Jesus Christ is Lord," we will do so, as did Paul, "to the glory of God the Father" (Phil. 2:11) and that so to confess Jesus Christ is to be saved by him. If Christ does not point us beyond himself to the gracious God of Israel, he inevitably becomes an idolatrous and exclusivist Christ. The claim that the gospel is the promise of God's grace lovingly offered to each and all and the command of God that we love each and all reminds us that we must ever monotheize our understanding of Jesus Christ, which is exactly what the church has sought to do in its doctrine of the Trinity. We do well to remember that the seeds of the doctrine of the Trinity lay in the church's efforts to resist the extreme anti-Jewish claim of the Gnostics that the God whom Christians know in Jesus Christ is not the God of Israel but a better, superior God. When the church responded with the claim that no, indeed, it was the God of Israel who was in Christ reconciling the world to Godself (2 Cor. 5:19), it insisted that the God of Israel, the God of Jesus, was the God effective in and through Christ for the redemption of the world. Thereby it also insisted that it is the God of Israel who is our ultimate savior and who gives us Christ Jesus as a free gift. It is not that Christ gives God to us, much less that Christ saves us from God, but God who gives Christ to us, thereby saving us from sin and error and from alienation from God, from Christ, from the Israel of God, and from the covenants.

When we developed this account of the norm of appropriateness, we argued that what is needed is a norm that stands in the service of freedom, specifically the freedom to reform the church and theology in the direction of greater appropriateness and authenticity. Taking the gospel as the norm of appropriateness frees us as it frees Jesus. Jesus is freed to be a Jew of first-century Galilee, one who is stubbornly himself and free to correct our Christologies when we formulate them in ways that forget or oppose the God of Israel and the Israel of God. We are freed to develop Christologies that address problems of which Jesus never dreamt, such as how to articulate a properly feminist Christology in the service of the freedom of women from oppression, or how to explicate a post-Holocaust Christology that repudiates and overcomes the church's long resentment against the Jewishness of Jesus. We are freed from having to show that Jesus supports our Christologies; we do not even have to show that Jesus supports the doing of Christology per se (those who feel constrained to argue that the historical Jesus had a "tacit Christology" can now relax).

Toward a Constructive Theology

Let us consider the following proposition: *We believe in Jesus Christ, to the glory of the God of Israel, with the apostles.* We believe *in*, not with, Jesus Christ. Although theologians since the time of Schleiermacher have argued that Jesus' God-consciousness was perfect (that he was the "perfect believer"), Christians are not asked at baptism or confirmation whether they believe *that* Jesus' faith was perfect but whether they believe *in* Jesus Christ. Here the practice of the church improves on most Christologies. To believe in Jesus Christ is to confess that it is through Jesus Christ as witnessed to in the church that we are brought to understand ourselves in terms of the love of God freely offered to us, as accepted and justified, and in terms of the command of God that we love God and our neighbors in turn, called to a new and radically transformed life. To realize that we do not live that new and radically transformed life is to confess that we are at one and the same time justified and sinful (*simul iustus et peccator*). It is in, through, and by means of the church's preaching of Jesus Christ that we are forced to deal with the questions "who are we?," "who is God?," and "what are we to do?" And it is through being confronted with the church's proclamation of Jesus Christ that we learn that we are those who can only understand themselves authentically in any ultimate sense as the objects of God's unfathomable affection. Through the church's proclamation of Jesus Christ we learn that God is the steadfastly faithful God of Israel who keeps promises and on whom we may unfailingly rely to be faithful and trustworthy. It is through the church's proclamation that we learn that we are to love all our neighbors as ourselves and in whose behalf we are to work for justice and liberation. Through this proclamation we learn to define our neighbors as those whom God has given us to love. Through the church's proclamation of Jesus Christ we learn that he is the one who brings us to this self-understanding of who God is, who we are, who the neighbor is, and what we are to do. And so it is he in whom we believe.

We believe in *Jesus* Christ, to the glory of the God of Israel, with the apostles. If we said only that we believe "in Christ," we might misleadingly give ourselves the impression that whatever Christ is—the Logos, the wisdom of God, the power of creative transformation—is some free-floating divine principle in *which* we believe. But Christians know *whom* they have believed. To confess faith in *Jesus* Christ is to acknowledge the stubborn facticity, the unbudgeable particularity, of the Jew Jesus *in* whom we believe. To confess *Jesus* Christ is to confess faith in the one who takes form in the history of the people Israel and in the scripture of Israel.[69] Paul argues (Rom. 10:5–13) that this Jew Jesus was the content of the Torah, which always was and is near to Israel. The promise and command, call and claim, of the God of Israel were disclosed to Jews and witnessed to by Jews for over a millennium before any Gentile heard the name Jesus of Nazareth. The Jew Jesus participated in and was shaped by a community and tradition going back to Abraham and Sarah. He was connected to, interrelated with, and constituted by a Jewish tradition of faith in the God of a singular promise and a singular command. To abstract the Jew Jesus from his context, tradition, and people and set him apart from and over against them as a lonely hero of faith is to commit the "fallacy of misplaced concreteness."[70] To commit this fallacy is to regard a part as the whole. With regard to Jesus Christ, the fallacy of misplaced concreteness presumes to have Christ apart from the Jew Jesus and all that the Jew Jesus brings with him: the God of Israel, the Israel of God, the community of faith around Jesus then and now, and Jesus' commitment to all these. It alienates what we mean by Christ from this stubbornly Jewish Jesus and refuses to allow him to correct our abstractive and anti-Jewish Christologies. The "dangerous memory" of this stubbornly Jewish Jesus remedies vacuous Christologies.

We believe in Jesus *Christ*, to the glory of the God of Israel, with the apostles. To confess our faith in Jesus *Christ* is to take note of the equally irreducible fact that the christological confession is and can be made only in the present tense. It is true that people *have* confessed faith in Christ in the past, and prayerfully to be hoped that they *will* do so in the future. But every time this confession is made, it is made in the present tense. Jesus Christ is *now* the living lord of the church, the one through whom by the witness of the church we are now laid bare before the maker and redeemer of heaven and earth. One difficulty with Christologies that seek their warrant in the empirical-historical Jesus is that they make their statements about Jesus in the past tense. They cannot do otherwise, for the events they seek to describe lie in the past. It seems possible to read whole books that repeatedly stress who and what Jesus *was* without ever entertaining the thought that this misses the point. Christian faith is contemporary faith, not a remembrance at second hand of a figure receding into the ever more remote past. The christological confession that Jesus Christ is lord is an assertion about the meaning of Jesus Christ to us now and about who we are called and claimed to be by the re-presentation to us in the church of the church's witness to Jesus Christ. The encounter with the new being in Jesus Christ, to use Tillich's language, is contemporary every time it happens.

To assert that Christian faith is contemporary faith in a living lord propounds the truth of the risen Christ. For Christologies that base themselves on the empirical-historical Jesus, the "resurrection" (the reason for the quotation marks will be made clear later) is unnecessary, an addendum that might or might not be appended to a Christology. The reason is clear: if we answer the question, What does it mean to say that "Jesus is the Christ"? by claiming that in his lifetime Jesus of Nazareth was the perfect believer and perfect practitioner of his beliefs, we have no need of the resurrection. Jesus is the Christ because in his life he believed in God in every moment and never failed to entertain God's highest aims for him. To such a Christology, as David Griffin rightly says, the resurrection is optional.[71] But we have rejected such a Christology and so reject that Christology's rejection of the resurrection of the Jew Jesus.

The "object" of our present faith is Christ present to the church through its witness and sacraments, as well as through "the least of these" through whom the needs of Christ are presented to those who live under the command to love the least of these as they love themselves. Christian faith is faith in Jesus Christ as the *living* lord of the church. This is both the point of talk of "the resurrection" and the point that is obscured by talk of "the resurrection." Because the Gospels got placed first in the canon when the New Testament was put together, and because they are always read, especially on the central days of the Christian year, their stories dominate the Christian imagination in ways that hide most of the New Testament witness from us. The story of the ascension in Acts, for example, gives the impression of Jesus going "away," leaving. A youth group for which I was responsible in the 1960s talked of the ascension as the "lift-off." The space age was upon us. But the appearance stories in the New Testament are also ascension stories, stories of the presence of the living *lord*, and they stress that Christ is present and *ruling over* the powers and principalities of the world, from which we are now freed and so responsible for how we act toward the neighbor. This is the point of "ascension talk" in the New Testament, and it is a very different point from the one that tends to emerge from the "picture" of the ascension in Acts.

So it is with the resurrection. When we look to the earlier witnesses to the living Christ in the New Testament, we find that the present faith of the church is encouraged by "the power of his resurrection" (Phil. 3:10), that when Christians made "their testimony to the resurrection of the Lord Jesus" (Acts 4:33), they pointed to signs of the living Christ, to "this that you both see and hear" (Acts 2:33), see in the sacraments and hear in the preaching of the word. The risen Christ speaks to the church through prophets and, later, in the Gospels themselves speaks over the heads of those with whom he is discoursing in the story to the readers and hearers of the Gospels. The contemporaneity of faith in Christ typifies the entire life of Christian faith and worship. From the beginning, Christians have affirmed the presence of the living Christ. With Luther, the church has claimed that "in faith itself Christ is present."[72] The New Testament places great stress on this assertion. Christ is the head, we the members (Paul). Christ is the vine, we the branches (John). Ours is a life in Christ: "It is no longer I who live, but it is Christ who lives in me" (Gal. 2:20).

Whereas the term "the resurrection" draws attention to a past event, the burden of the New Testament witness is to point up various ways in which Jesus is present to and ahead of his followers. The "young man" whom the women in Mark's Gospel encounter instructs them to "go, tell his disciples and Peter that he is going ahead of you to Galilee" (16:7). To say this is neither to deny that in the event of the resurrection something happened to the man Jesus, nor to affirm that in the resurrection something happened merely to the disciples. It is to deny that trying to figure out what happened is worthwhile or productive of anything more than speculation. Nowhere does the New Testament describe the resurrection, nor does any witness claim to have seen it. The stories of the empty tomb are late explanations of the disciples' experiences of the living Christ. Yet the reality is quite the opposite: it is the living Christ who explains the New Testament, not the New Testament that explains the living Christ. In themselves the stories of the empty tomb do not produce faith, but despair and anxiety. Only the appearance of Christ produces faith as its response. Nor do attempts to tell us with what kind of body Christ was raised get us anywhere. For Paul, it was a "spiritual body" (1 Cor. 15:44) and for John one that could come into a room without opening the door and yet invite Thomas to "reach out your hand and put it in my side" (John 20:27).

Marc Chagall's painting *White Crucifixion*, which hangs in the Art Institute of Chicago, depicts Jesus on the cross wearing around his waist the prayer shawl of an observant Jew, reminding us that the one who died for us is a member of the people Israel, *Yeshua ha Notsri*. This Jesus of Nazareth is the one whom God raised from the dead and is now the living Lord of the church. When the church affirms that the Christ who was raised still bears the marks of the crucified Jew who died on a Roman cross, it puts us on notice that the risen Christ will not now do anything different from what the Jew Jesus did in relation to his disciples. As Jesus then confronted his disciples with the promise and command of the God of Israel, so Jesus now in the church confronts his followers, increasingly and later almost exclusively Gentiles, with the same promise and command. The church's confession is that the Christ through whom God calls the church forward into God's new future for it, a post-Holocaust future that we hope will be different from what it was in the past, that this Christ lives and beckons the church to respond to the call forward, to move out of the wilderness of anti-Judaism in which it has so long wandered and into the promise of God's reconciliation among all the peoples of the earth but foremost between Christians and the Israel of God in whom was formed the Jew Jesus, our living lord.

The resurrection and the cross belong together. Without the resurrection, the cross would be blind; without the cross, the resurrection would be empty. The resurrection interprets the cross as God's victory over sin and death. Christ's continuing activity in the church as its living Lord derives its content from the ministry of Jesus and the love of God shown forth on the cross. These together with the ascension constitute the exaltation of Christ, which is God's answer to Christ's act of self-emptying. Because he became "obedient to the point of death . . . on a cross . . . God also highly exalted him and gave him the name that is above every name," that "every tongue should confess that Jesus Christ is Lord, to the glory of God the father" (Phil. 2:8–11). *Yahweh* is the name that is above every name, and this is the name that was bestowed on Jesus, whose name (*Yeshua*) means "Yahweh is salvation." Consequently, we can only properly confess that Jesus Christ is Lord "to the glory of God the father" of Jesus Christ, the God of Israel.

Jesus has been raised to "the right hand of God," a statement that can only rightly be understood in the light of the saying *Dextra Dei ubique est* ("the right hand of God is everywhere"). Talk of the ascension does not mean that Jesus is gone, away, but that he is everywhere, hence near: "Do not say in your heart, 'Who will ascend into heaven?' (that is, to bring Christ down) or 'Who will descend into the abyss?' (that is, to bring Christ up from the dead). But what does it say? 'The word is near you, on your lips and in your heart'" (Rom. 10:6–8).

As we study the stories of the appearances of the risen Jesus, it is important to attend to what Jesus *says*. Our one firsthand account is from Paul, who comments that God "was pleased to reveal his Son to me, . . . that I might proclaim him *among the Gentiles*" (Gal. 1:15–16; emphasis added). That Jesus commanded Paul to proclaim him among the Gentiles is a theme reiterated in all three Acts accounts of Paul's encounter with the living Jesus. In Romans, Paul refers to Jesus Christ, who "was declared to be Son of God with power according to the spirit of holiness by resurrection from the dead, Jesus Christ our Lord, through whom we have received grace and apostleship to bring about the obedience of faith *among all the Gentiles* for the sake of his name" (1:4–6; emphasis added). In Luke, Jesus' last appearance to the disciples has him saying to them "that repentance and forgiveness of sins is to be proclaimed in his [the messiah's] name *to all nations* [*panta ta ethne*, "all the Gentiles"] (24:47; emphasis added). So in Matthew, the risen Christ closes the Gospel commissioning the apostles to go "and make disciples of all nations [*panta ta ethne*, "all the Gentiles"], baptizing them in the name of the Father and of the Son and of the Holy Spirit, and teaching them to obey everything that I have commanded you" (Matt. 28:19–20). The risen Jesus continues to do what he did in his lifetime—confront his followers with the promise and command of the God of Israel—and the mission to the Gentiles results from the ministry of the risen Jesus.

We believe in Jesus Christ, *to the glory of God*, with the apostles. An implicate of the good news of the grace of God lovingly offered to each and all and of the command of God that we love God with all we are and our neighbors as ourselves is that we do all our theologizing "to the greater glory of God" (*ad maiorem dei gloriam*). In our devotion to Jesus Christ, we Christians sometimes forget this rule. Although we know better, we remain strongly Marcionite in our self-understanding. Forgetting to do all our witnessing to and thinking about Jesus Christ to the greater glory of God was not a fault of that apostolic church which all Christians claim to emulate: "For us," said the apostle Paul, "there is one God, the Father, from whom are all things and for whom we exist, and one Lord, Jesus Christ, through whom are all things and through whom we exist" (1 Cor. 8:6). Of the eschaton, Paul proclaimed:

Then comes the end, when he [Christ] hands over the kingdom to God the Father, after he has destroyed every ruler and every authority and power. For he must reign until he has put all his enemies under his feet. The last enemy to be destroyed is death. For "God has put all things in subjection under his feet." But when it says, "All things are put in subjection," it is plain that this does not include the one who put all things in subjection under him. When all things are subjected to him, then the Son himself will also be subjected to the one who put all things in subjection under him, so that God may be all in all (1 Cor. 15:24–28).

At the close of the hymn that Paul quotes in Philippians come these lines: "so that at the name of Jesus every knee should bend, in heaven and on earth and under the earth, and every tongue should confess that Jesus Christ is Lord, to the glory of God the Father" (2:10–11). "You belong to Christ," says Paul, but "Christ belongs to God" (1 Cor. 3:23). Every proper Christian theological statement is about God; every proper christological statement, whether of witness to Jesus Christ or of critical reflection upon the meaning of that witness, is about God. "God is the subject of all the verbs of the Torah-Christ story."[73] Paul M. van Buren makes the point:

One hears frequently today in certain circles of "knowing Jesus Christ as your personal lord and Savior." Without questioning the validity and importance of that to which this phrase refers, I would suggest that it is a misleading abbreviation of what is at stake in meeting Jesus Christ. According to the early witness, a relationship with Jesus Christ that stopped with him would not be authentic and so could be neither with a Lord nor a Savior. The relationship with him that is salvific is the one that brings a person before the God of Israel whom he called Father, and who is, as Israel's, also the world's Lord and Savior.[74]

Although every proper theological statement may be about other matters, such as how we are given and called to understand ourselves in relation to God, or what the meaning of Jesus Christ is to us as the one through whom we are again and again confronted with the God of a singular promise and a singular command, or how we are to understand the situation of the neighbor in need of liberation, nonetheless we are again confronted with this God of a radically free promise and total claim upon us, who is ultimately the subject of every proper theological and christological statement. If we fail to remember that all christological and soteriological statements have God as their subject—God is the author of our salvation—we will render Christ into a limit on the grace of God and claim that apart from Christ there is no saving knowledge of God. Our rule reminds us that God is the limit of christocentrism, not vice versa.

Textually, let us look at the canonical context of the claim in Philippians 2 that "at the name of Jesus every knee should bend, . . . and every tongue should confess that Jesus Christ is Lord, to the glory of God the Father." This Philippians hymn paraphrases Isaiah 45:22–23: "Turn to me and be saved, all the ends of the earth! For I am God, and there is no other. By myself I have sworn, from my mouth has gone forth in righteousness a word that shall not return: 'To me every knee shall bow, every tongue shall swear.'" This prophet helped the people Israel to understand in exile who they were and what they were to do: they were missionaries of God among the Gentiles. Egyptians, Ethiopians, and Sabeans will come to Israel and say: "God is with you alone, and there is no other; there is no god besides him" (45:14). The prophet looked back to the Abrahamic promise and discerned not only the promise of land (from which Israel was now banished) but the promise that Abraham's descendants would be a light to the Gentiles. In the light of this aspect of the promise, the prophet interprets to exiled Israel God's purpose with Israel's situation. Paul, in turn, saw the promise of God to Abraham that through Israel the Gentiles would be blessed as confirmed (Rom. 15:8) in Jesus Christ in whom "every one of God's promises is a 'Yes.' For this reason it is through him that we say the 'Amen,' [so be it]

to the glory of God" (2 Cor. 1:20). When every tongue confesses Jesus
Christ is Lord, we have to remind ourselves what is being confessed. Because the name "Jesus" (*Joshua, Yeshua*) means "Yahweh is salvation,"
every tongue confesses that "Yahweh is salvation [Jesus] Messiah
[Christ] is Lord, to the glory of God the Father." This confession can be
properly made in no other way. God the Father is the God of Israel,
who continues to love Israel; hence this confession is also made by those
who know that the salvation of the Gentiles was "prepared in the presence of all peoples, a light for revelation to the Gentiles and for glory to
your people Israel" (Luke 2:31–32).

We believe in Jesus Christ, to the glory of God, *with* the apostles.
Without the apostles we would not believe; no apostles, no subsequent
Christian tradition. When the women in Mark are asked to go and tell
the apostles of the resurrection, they carry the first apostolic word of the
risen Jesus. Without the apostles (messengers) of every subsequent generation, no contemporary Christian community would exist. Affirmatively, this means that the context in which Jesus Christ is confessed and
lives as Lord is the church. The church, in responding to the grace of
God in Jesus Christ by confessing its faith in him, is constituted as
church through the Holy Spirit. In confessing its faith in Jesus Christ,
the church declares not only who it understands God to be, nor only
who it understands Jesus Christ to be and his meaning to the church,
but it also declares who it understands itself to be as church. Christology
is not merely an answer to the single question, Who is Jesus? but to the
triple question: Who is God, Who are we, and What is the meaning of
Jesus Christ to us? To confess Jesus Christ is to be brought face to face
with God, the maker and redeemer of heaven and earth and the God of
Israel. To confess Jesus Christ as Lord is to declare who God is (the God
of utterly free grace and total claim), who Jesus Christ is (the one
through whom, by the grace of God, we have been brought to understand ourselves in relation to God), and who the church is (those who
confess that they can understand themselves in any ultimate sense in
terms of and only in terms of the all-inclusive love of God).

In saying who Jesus Christ is, the church defines itself. Every christological statement says something about those making it as well as about
God and Christ; how we understand Christology discloses how we understand ourselves. Every christological title we give to Jesus Christ, as
van Buren points out, allots a parallel term to the church. "If Jesus is
master, then the Church is made up of his servants. If he is called
Teacher, then Christians are his disciples. If Jesus is Lord, then the
Church is his possession. If he is the Word of God, then the Church
consists of hearers of the word."[75] If the word we hear is a word of
grace, we are its grateful hearers.

The implication is clear: if we make exclusivistic statements about Jesus Christ, claiming that apart from him there is no salvation, we say the same of the church: outside it there is no salvation (*extra ecclesiam nulla salus*). Cyprian of Carthage, whose view of the church forced him to ask, "How can those who are not in the church be . . . loved by Christ?" also had to declare as "enemies" all those not with Christ.[76] If we call Christ the "only" savior of the world and mean that only those who do the good work of believing in Jesus Christ can be saved, we define the church as the only community that is saved. This way of naming Christ and the church is inappropriate to the gospel of God's free grace because it turns Christ into a condition apart from which God is unable to be gracious, and makes the church into the "broker" of God's kingdom, something Jesus refused to be. Such a claim is heretical and presumptuous.

Several functions of the term "only" in theological discourse are relevant to this discussion. (1) Characteristically, when Israel is said to be God's "only" love, this serves to remind Israel of God's commandment that justice be done to all those whom God loves. That is, Israel is singled out for service or called into judgment. "You only have I known of all the families of the earth; therefore I will punish you for all your iniquities" (Amos 3:2). Here God's gracious election of Israel is referred to in order to recall Israel to the way (*torah*) in which God wishes it to walk. This would be one appropriate way to refer to Jesus Christ as our "only savior." Another (2) meaning of "only" is discerned when we note that it can function to locate where and how the discernment of the grace of God occurred. This is the "locative" function of "only"; it serves to locate, not limit, the grace of God. It is a category blunder to confuse the locative with the limiting function of "only," a version of the fallacy of simple location, the view that something can be in one place only and nowhere else.[77] Or (3) "only" can be understood as expressing doxology and praise. We give praise and thanks to God for giving us Christ, our only savior. But if we turn doxology into definition, while forgetting that what we are defining is precisely doxology, then it becomes pernicious. Yet again (4), if christological statements are rightly understood as statements about God, "only" might function in such statements to make the claim that the God who disclosed God's self to us in Jesus Christ is the only God there is.

Jesus Christ the Gift

Everything we receive from the hands of God is a gift—a "free gift," theologians say, as if there could be another kind; but we are forced to be redundant because the point is so often missed. As a nineteenth-century theologian made the list: The gospel is a gift. Jesus Christ is a gift. The church is a gift. Justification is a gift. The Holy Spirit is a gift. The new and transformed life that we are given and called to lead is a gift. "Truly, we are saved by *grace*."[78] Exclusivist Christologies represent Christianity's failure to confess Jesus Christ to the glory of God and to remember that Jesus Christ is the gift to us of the God of Israel and of the Israel of God, without whom there would be no Jesus Christ. To believe this is to believe in Jesus Christ *with* the apostles, whose understanding of the faithfulness or faithlessness of others never allowed them to "nullify the faithfulness of God" (Rom. 3:3).

8

The God of Israel and of the Church

_____

> In the end, we know God—specifically in the Mes-
> siah—as No One other than the God of Israel.
>
> —*1977 Mennonite European Regional Conference*

In their post-*Shoah* teaching documents, the churches affirm that the
God whom Christians worship is the living God of the Bible, the God of
Israel, worshiped by Jews. They assert that Christians have come and still
come to know this God in Jesus Christ—that in, through, and by means
of Jesus Christ Christians are again and again confronted with the
promise and command of the God of Israel. That the God of Israel was
incarnate in Jesus Christ, the Jew from Nazareth, is a claim that further
makes it clear that the God of Israel "is not an isolated God without relationships, but a God who turns toward humankind and who is affected
by human destiny." God, who dwells not only in transcendence but in
the midst of God's people, is subject to distress and persecution "as
Lord, Father, Companion and Redeemer."[1] The covenantally related
God of Israel, whose covenant love *(hesed)* involves God in interacting
with all God's creatures and particularly with God's people, is here asserted against the church's tradition of construing God as in all respects
unrelated to and unaffected by events in the world.

Classical Christian Theism

Because the Christian tradition de-Judaized itself and interpreted itself as both anti- and better-than Jewish, its classical doctrine of God
tells us more about pre-Christian, Greek understandings of God than

202

about the living, covenantal God of the Bible. Greek theology (in the sense of a doctrine of God) was as antithetical to Israel's understanding of God as covenantally related as any alternative model for God could possibly be. The God of Greek theology was an impassible absolute, what Aristotle called the "unmoved mover," who effects all others but is in no way affected by them.[2] By contrast, Israel's story begins with God's being affected by the cry of the people for liberation from slavery ·in Egypt: "Out of their slavery their cry for help rose up to God. God heard their groaning, and God remembered his covenant with Abraham, Isaac, and Jacob. God looked upon the Israelites, and God took notice of them" (Ex. 2:23c-25). God was moved.

"Hellenic theology," declares Robert Jenson, "was an exact antagonist of biblical faith."[3] Greek thought regarded time, in the words of John Dewey, as "the tooth that gnaws; it is the destroyer."[4] The ultimate concern of Greek religion was to overcome time and the realities of chance and death that came in its wake. It attempted to do this by identifying God with timelessness as such. When the question is, What can save us from the ravages of time? the answer comes in the form of an escape from time by union or reunion with the God who is in all respects eternal and in no respects temporal. The defining characteristic of God becomes God's total exemption from time, history, becoming, and relationships. Hence God must be immutable and impassible, unsusceptible to change or to being affected, and these in all, not merely some, respects. "Whereas Yahweh was eternal by his faithfulness *through* time," says Jenson, "the Greek gods' eternity was their abstraction *from* time. Yahweh's eternity is thus intrinsically a relation to his creatures—supposing there are any—whereas the Greek gods' eternity is the negation of such relation."[5] The word "negation" in this sentence is important, because from this Hellenic understanding of God Christian "negative" theology derives. Greek theology of an utterly impassible deity is necessarily negative because all the metaphors or analogies that we might use to speak of God are drawn from the sphere of historical, social, and temporal life. They must be negated in order to be attributed as predicates to the atemporal, asocial, ahistorical deity of pure necessity. The God of Greek and classical Christian theism is defined negatively, as not finite (infinite), impassible, immutable, invisible, intangible, incorporeal, and so forth. God is also, therefore, not knowable (unknowable) and not utterable (ineffable). Power is ascribed to this asocial God, without noticing that power itself is a social concept. Precisely these Greek models for God became standard fare in the church and reflect its de-Judaization of itself.

The so-called negative theology is not a totally worthless effort from which we can learn nothing. We may distinguish two meanings of negative theology. The first is spelled out above, that God's being is in all respects immutable and hence the negative of all our relational, social understandings of being from which we might draw analogies with which to talk about God. A criticism of this theology is that, in spite of its denials, it claims to know altogether too much about God; for example, that God is impassible, absolute, eternal, and necessary, and these in all respects. The other meaning of negative theology is that all our models and metaphors, including the negative ones, are mere pointers to the God whose inexhaustibility and fullness of being relativize all our language. Any "knowledge" we have of God by way of our human constructs, however well argued, remains a *docta ignorantia*, a learned ignorance. This meaning of negative theology is prophetic and humbling and points to something affirmative (not merely negative in the first sense) about God. This second sense loosens up our ways of talking about God and makes us receptive to new ones that bid fair to uncover forms of God-talk obscured by the traditional dominance of the first sense of negative theology. Accepting this second bearing of negative theology, I want to argue that some ways of talking about the God of biblical faith are more appropriate than others and, within the limitations of our language, make more sense.

The conviction that we cannot know God because God is "both invisible and ineffable" gained ground early in church history. Clement of Alexandria quotes as his authorities on this point such writers as Plato, Orpheus, Solon, and Empedocles, and interprets the biblical witness to God in the light of their view of God. He argues from the premise of God's unknowability that God "is infinite not in the sense of measureless extension but in the sense of being without dimension or boundaries, and therefore without shape or name."[6] Our names for God function only to "point to the power of the Almighty."[7] Clement fails to note that on his grounds "power" can be only another pointer to the infinite mystery, making it an exception in order to turn it into that to which other metaphors point. Gregory of Nyssa utilized Plato's metaphor of "ascent from below" to talk about how we may arrive at "the ineffable knowledge of God."[8] A discipline of "total purification" is needed to approach the vision of intelligible reality, for we must transcend the realm of sense, and only those may seek this vision who have been chosen by their fellow Christians and deemed "able to grasp divine truth." These worthies will leave "the realm of phenomena behind entirely" to search for "the unseeable and the incomprehensible," the seeing of which consists in not seeing.[9]

As these examples show, traditional theism suffers both from internal strains and from an uneasy relation to the biblical witness in which God is said to disclose God's name to Moses and to condescend to us in the incarnation. Another example of this uneasy relation is Origen's answer to the question as to how God can be said by scripture to undergo a change of mind when we know, before we read scripture, that God does not do these things.[10] Although scripture on several occasions refers to God's repenting, Origen's commitment to God's foreknowledge of the future (an implicate of God's total immutability) means that this cannot be. Origen's way out of the dilemma is to distinguish God "as he is in himself" from God as involved with human affairs. In "himself," God does not repent or change; but to keep us from thinking that we are not free, God "acts as if he did not know the future in your case."[11] Whereas the covenant partners of Yahweh are both free and responsible, the freedom Origen is prepared to ascribe to them is merely "as if."

Augustine named God as "being itself" and defined being itself as "untouched by want or change," as befits sheer timelessness.[12] God is "that good which makes things good," and being as being is good; God's relation to the world of creatures is entirely one-way, a relation of "making." God's being is true and "immutable being."[13] God's name, disclosed to Moses at the burning bush, means "I Am Who I Am" and signifies the identity of God and being-itself. Augustine was keenly aware that self-contemplation leads one to a sense of transience, of being-toward-death. He knew, as Dewey later put it, "Time is the tooth that gnaws; it is the destroyer; we are born only to die and every day brings us one day nearer death."[14] This led him to seek in memory, the seat of our ability to transcend the temporal fragmentariness of existence, for an immediate awareness of God as Eternal, necessary being. The fear of God will "of necessity . . . lead us to the thought of our mortality and of our future death and will affix all our proud motions, as if they were fleshly members fastened with nails, to the wood of the cross."[15] Thus, for Augustine, the theological problematic focused on the antithesis of the changeless to the changing. *Bonum, verum, esse* (goodness, truth, and being) were defined in terms of their power to endure in spite of the vicissitudes of time. Our salvation from time was located in our capacity for self-transcendence in memory and anticipation and in our power to contemplate immediately realities that do not change. Because the character of the world was defined as its corruptibility, its liability to be destroyed by time, Augustine's advice on seeking truth and God was to turn inward: "Thine is truth itself; embrace it."[16] The goal of theology is to unveil the ground of being, of truth, and of goodness. On Augustine, Tillich remarks, "No changeable or conditioned good can overcome the fear that it may be lost. Only in the Unchangeable can be found the *prius* of all goodness."[17]

That God can in no respect be affected and is in all respects immutable and impassible exacted a high price from the church. We see this most sharply in Anselm's question to God: "But, how art thou compassionate, and, at the same time, passionless?" Noting that if God is passionless God cannot feel sympathy, Anselm wonders "whence cometh so great consolation to the wretched?" His answer is reminiscent of Origen's explanation of God's repentance: "Thou art compassionate in terms of our experience, and not compassionate in terms of thy being." While we "experience the effects of compassion, . . . thou dost not experience the feeling."[18] God is not only not related but unrelatable to the world and history, the meaning and value of which are downplayed because they only "seem" to matter to God.

The doctrine of God as in all respects absolute, necessary, and eternal, yet as also being said, incoherently, to know and love the creatures, became virtually axiomatic in theology. Biblical or theological justifications for it are seldom proferred. Yet there is a world of difference between biblical talk of God's unchangeableness as God's faithfulness, as God's unfailing involvement *with* the covenant people, and ontological claims about God's impassibility, impassivity, and indifference *to* the fortunes of God's creatures. The former is a comment on God's character, the latter on God's being. God's total immutability represents, says Jaroslav Pelikan, "a more subtle and more pervasive effect of" de-Judaization than does the treatment of Judaism in the *adversus Judaeos* tracts.[19] Whereas Judaism saw God's immutability "as the trustworthiness of his covenanted relation to his people," in the developed "Christian doctrine of God, immutability assumed the status of an axiomatic presupposition for the discussion of other doctrines. Hence the de-Judaization of Christian thought contributed, for example, to the form taken by the christological controversy."[20]

The classical doctrine of God developed in the church understood God along the lines of what Langdon Gilkey calls "the transcendent absolute of much speculative philosophy: necessary, impersonal, unrelated, independent (*a se*), changeless, eternal."[21] God was considered as *in all respects* (not merely in some) unrelated, eternal, changeless, independent, and incapable of being affected by the fate of the creatures. It is one thing to say that God's being is necessary, that God cannot fail to be and to be God, quite another that God's experience or knowledge of the contingent and accidental affairs of the world is necessary and that God must have eternally foreknown the conditional details of the future. No account is given of how God could necessarily foreknow the accidental and contingent, yet the tradition affirmed God's impassibility in all respects.

Although the Christian tradition wanted to affirm that God is related to us, genuinely responsive to creaturely needs, involved in history, the model of God as totally impassible stressed that God is absolutely noncontingent, "changeless in the sense of participating in and relating to no change, purely spiritual instead of in any fashion material, unaffected and thus seemingly unrelated and even unrelateable to the world." Such a God could relate to the world only by intervening in it supernaturally; the rest of the time God is absent and, for all practical purposes, powerless. If changelessness, lack of becoming, and relatedness *define* the supremely real, then no wonder that along with this went a progressive loss of the sense of the "reality, value, or meaning of the changing, temporal, material world, and of earthly human and historical life in time."[22] That such a view of God is inappropriate to the gospel of God's love for each and all is beyond dispute. That an impassible absolute is poles removed from the covenant God of Israel and the church, a God who loves and has a purpose for the world, is beyond doubt.

The understanding of God as both immutable and all-powerful (except for the limit imposed by the law of noncontradiction), besides reflecting the church's de-Judaization of itself and failing to articulate a model of God that can give voice to God's covenant love, has other deficiencies. One is otherworldliness, which results from the emphasis of classical theism on salvation as escape from the transience of this world.[23] There is truth in this understanding of salvation, but it is lost when theology devalues this world by contrasting it with what is "really real" and when the latter is devoid of change, becoming, and relationality. This world *is* transient, yet that observation only raises the question as to what justifies our efforts to spread in the world the love of God and neighbor. What would justify that would be the claim that this world matters to God who is engaged in pathos with what happens here. In denying this of God, classical theism promotes otherworldliness, despite its claim that God loves the world.

Another deficiency of classical theism is its sponsorship of the worship of power. The God who is omnipotent, capable of doing anything not involving self-contradiction, is devoid of sensitivity and sympathy, and has no capacity to feel with the creatures. We saw in classical Christology how both the Arian and Athanasian parties, agreeing on divine immutability, placed a buffer between the suffering of the Jew Jesus on the cross and the immutable Logos who cannot suffer. Arius denied that God was incarnate in Jesus, drawing a line between God and the incarnation. Athanasius drew a line within Jesus between his two natures. Both reflect pre-Christian understandings of God as impervious to time and suffering. Whitehead charged the church with ignoring the revelation that God had given it in Jesus Christ, allowing the "brief Galilean vision of humility" to flicker uncertainly throughout the ages while rendering "unto God the attributes which belonged exclusively to Caesar."[24] Today the influence of "patriarchy" is seen in the projection onto God of the attributes of the strong, stoically unmovable male. Such a doctrine reflects and reinforces coercive forms of power in all aspects of human relationships. At its best, immutability results in an understanding of God's *agape* love as lacking real affection, being dispassionate; at its worst, it becomes punitive, as reflected in traditional understandings of atonement and their requirement of a worthy victim to pay the price exacted by God's justice.[25] Seldom noticed is that the impact of understanding of God as power devoid of sympathy on the doctrine of atonement is works-righteous: someone has to perform the good work of setting things right between us and God. Jesus Christ as our atonement is no longer God's sheer gift to us, but the one who makes it possible for God to relate to us, apart from whom God would not have this possibility. Jesus Christ becomes a condition upon the grace of God, apart from which God is not free to be gracious. By contrast, God's sympathetic goodness, the goodness of God's covenant love, underwrites a solid doctrine of the grace of God.

After the Holocaust, another difficulty besetting the traditional doctrine of God is that if God has the *kind* of power traditionally attributed to God, God cannot avoid being thought of as the "sanctioner of the status quo."[26] God as unchangeable absolute has established an unchangeable order for the world and as controlling power wills the existence of this order. If God is omnipotent, able to intervene and change the course of events, but does not do so, the conclusion is that God intends for things to be the way they are. This problem becomes more acute if one posits that God knows what is going on with the world and intends that things go well with the world. Were one to claim, with Aristotle, that an unmoved God does not know what goes on with the world, or with Jung that God has a "dark side," one would have a different problem. But these claims seldom find a home, at least in their pure form, in Christian thought. We cannot avoid observing that the classical doctrine of God as all powerful underrates the power of evil; it grants to God a kind of control of worldly events that is far from evident.

Post-*Shoah* Jewish Thinking About God

There has been considerable discussion of the meaning of the word *God* in Jewish theology "after Auschwitz." The most famous is that of Richard L. Rubenstein, who rejected altogether the notion of the omnipotent God active in history. Such a view, he concluded, means that there is no tenable alternative to the notion "that it was God's will that Hitler had exterminated the Jews." Rubenstein chose to stand with Albert Camus in preferring human solidarity to ideology, even if this meant an "inability to accept the God of the Judaeo-Christian tradition in the face of the suffering of the innocent and his [Camus'] choice of an absurd cosmos." He parts company with Camus only at the point of

Camus's atheism, choosing instead "to share the tragic fatalities of the God of nature."[27] Like a twentieth-century Spinoza, Rubenstein thinks of God as nature in its cycles of creation and destruction and of religion as empathy with nature.

Rubenstein's criticism of traditional theism is shared by many contemporary theologians seeking more appropriate and adequate ways to talk of God. Yet what is particularly difficult with regard to Rubenstein's approach to God "after Auschwitz" is to comprehend how it could serve either the Jewish or Christian tradition as a vital source of faith and life for contemporary people. Rubenstein's views appear to be a return to pre-Jewish occupation with those powers of nature personified by Baal and Astarte, and hence an abandonment of Jewish tradition. That such a view almost amounts to a desertion of Judaism is reason not to consider it further.

Another option in contemporary Jewish theology is Harold Schulweis' "predicate theology," according to which the term *God* names no actual entity. Rather, "Godliness is discovered within humanity, within nature, and within history by the human subject." Schulweis uses Wittgenstein to argue that the "ontological bewitchment of language" occurs when a grammatical subject (in this case, God) is converted into a metaphysical "substance."[28] God should not be regarded as an existing subject. Instead, God should be sought in the predicates, the attributes, usually uttered of God. God is justice, love, kindness, all the things that we ought to be and manifest in our behavior. Schulweis' "predicates" are modeled on John Dewey's "ideals," which Dewey regarded as the pragmatic equivalent of God; God is our ideals. Dewey associates the quality of being "religious" with faith in "the unification of the self through allegiance to inclusive ideal ends, which imagination presents to us and to which the human will responds as worthy of controlling our desires and choices." For Dewey, "God" signifies not an existing divine being but, instead, the unity of the ideal possibilities that we can actualize through intelligence and action.

> We are in the presence neither of ideals completely embodied in existence nor yet of ideals that are mere rootless ideals, fantasies, utopias. For there are forces in nature and society that generate and support the ideals. They are further unified by the action that gives them coherence and solidity. It is this *active* relation between ideal and actual to which I would give the name "God."[29]

The problem faced by such a view of God, which owes as much to certain metaphysical assumptions about naturalism as it does to a pragmatic understanding of meaning and truth, is that in making our ideals God, in rendering them ultimate, it fails to take sufficiently into account two things. First, our ideals are always the ideals of flawed, ambiguous, and sinful selves; they are ideals subject to systemic distortion by all the forces (psychological, economic, the struggle for power) that require us to exercise a hermeneutic of suspicion on them. Second, our ideals undergo revision over time, sometimes are made more inclusive, at other times jettisoned because what once looked ideal ("a car in every garage") now looks pernicious ("a source of air pollution"). One function of God is to save us from our ideals and to transform them in more inclusive and authentic directions. "Predicate theology" pays too little attention to the role of God as redeemer.

The Biblical, Jewish Criticism of Omnipotence

Jon D. Levenson, a scholar of the Hebrew Bible, argues that the traditional doctrine of God's omnipotence combined with the doctrine of the creation of the world *ex nihilo* (out of absolute nothingness) results both in and from a failure to give due regard to "the formidability and resilience of the forces counteracting creation" and leads "to a neglect of the role of humanity in forming and sustaining the world order." Nor do omnipotence and *creatio ex nihilo* deal adequately with the biblical understanding of "God as lord in covenant." One cannot read traditional understandings of creation out of nothing from the Genesis creation stories without first reading them in. The waters are not created and "are most likely primordial," as are the other divine beings to whom God proposes the creation of humanity: "Let us make humankind in our image, according to our likeness" (Gen. 1:26). The story of the flood (Genesis 8–9) shows that God's ordering of reality was not complete. It "manifests a profound anxiety about the givenness of creation, a keen sense of its precariousness." God promises to preserve the order of creation, but "does so only after having ended a state of chaos that began with his announcing that he regretted having ever authored creation in the first place." Levenson notes that between the creation and the flood, which returned creation to the chaos with which God was initially presented, there was neither human righteousness "nor God's intrinsic unchangeability (which this and many other biblical stories belie), but only God's covenantal faithfulness, his respect for the solemn pledge that he makes to Noah." Creation is sustained by God's covenantal faithfulness, the divine *hesed*. God's creative activity limits, but does not eliminate, chaos and evil; the world remains innately precarious. When Israel's experience made belief in God's command over evil most perplexing, Israel extolled God's victory over it:

God's mythic victory must be interpreted in the light of the historical experience of the torching of his cult sites, the absence of miracles, the blaspheming of his sacred name, the defeat of his partners in covenant, and the general collapse of his mastery over the world.[30]

Biblical literature displays what Tillich called a "belief-ful realism," a dialectic of hope and realism.[31] Its understanding of God's omnipotence is proleptic: "So long as Israel's ancient and by now archetypical enemy endures, YHWH is not altogether YHWH, and his regal power is not yet fully actualized. Rather, he is the omnipotent cosmocrator only *in potentia*."[32] In later Jewish understandings of the "evil impulse," which reflect the biblical view that the evildoer needs a new heart ("Create in me a clean heart, O God, and put a new and right spirit within me" [Ps. 51:10; see Jer. 31:31–34]), "we hear the Augustinian rather than the Pelagian accents of ancient Judaism."[33] Judaism is not an unqualifiedly optimistic faith; it is, instead, a redemptive faith; we need less a new resolve on the part of a flawed heart than a new heart. God is not wholly in control of chaos and cannot coerce the human heart into doing good: "Rabbi Hanina said: 'Everything is in the hand of heaven [God] except the fear of heaven.'"[34] God does not exercise total dominance over the created order or the human heart. The Hebrew Bible does not tell a fairy tale of goodness and order only to have to face evil and disorder.

What guarantees that evil and disorder will not finally triumph is God's eternal and unconditional covenant, made with Noah (the "covenant of friendship" or "peace" of Isa. 54:10) and David, covenants in which the utterly promissory commitment of God's faithfulness predominates. With the Sinai covenant, the bilateral character of ancient treaties is evident, emphasizing both God's grace and Israel's free response, the free will with which Israel enters the covenant. Israel serves God in freedom, and this freedom separates "covenantal theonomy from theocratic tyranny."[35] God depends on God's covenant partners for the actualization of God's purposes in the world and for the restraint and overcoming of evil. In this relationship, God and the people interact with one another.

In Levenson's account we gain two important insights. First, we have an interpretation of the power of God as inherently social and entailing freely given service on the part of God's covenant partners if evil and disorder are to be restrained. Such an understanding of God will prove more adequate in a post-Holocaust situation than a restatement of the traditional doctrine of God that had enough difficulties with evil before the Holocaust. Second, we have a strong argument (and this was Levenson's point) that precisely such an understanding of God is appropriate to the witness of the biblical and Jewish traditions. Indeed, Levenson's contentions confirm the biblical warrants of the ways in which process theology speaks of God.

Mending the World

Since the medieval period there has been an alternative in Judaism to the understanding of God in classical theism; this alternative, which arose from medieval Jewish mysticism, is regarded by some contemporary theologians as articulating a doctrine of God that is more religiously accessible, more appropriate to the Jewish understanding of God as related to the Israel of God, and more affirmative of the importance of the command of God that God's covenant partners take up the task of mending the world (*tikkun olam*).

Not only Christian doctrines of God, but also Jewish ones as well, were influenced by Hellenic theology's negative approach to God, an approach dictated by the assumption that God is in all respects unlike the temporal, social, and relational realities of life and history. In their monumental dismantling of traditional doctrines of God, Charles Hartshorne and William L. Reese label Philo of Alexandria (c. 20 B.C.E.–54 C.E.), an older contemporary of Jesus, as the "founder" of classical theism.[36] For Philo, God is utterly independent of the world and history; he interprets the *Shema*'s affirmation that God is one to deny complexity altogether in God. Philo's God is incorporeal, immutable, hidden, and One of whom no positive affirmations can be made, utterly unvarying, having no future and no relations. God's relation to the world is in all respects active, in none passive; God does not interact with or socially relate to God's creatures. Says Philo: "The living god, inasmuch as he is living, does not consist in relation to anything; for he himself is full of himself, and he is sufficient for himself, . . . for he is immovable and unchangeable, having no need of any other thing or being whatever, so that all things belong to him, but, properly speaking, he does not belong to anything."[37] Philo does not make a biblical argument for this understanding of God.

Maimonides (1135–1204) consummated the tradition of classical theistic reflection on God in Judaism. In his *Guide of the Perplexed* he argued for God's utter indescribability (in spite of the religious need to "describe" God as knowing, caring, willing, etc.), for God's immutable perfection, and God's utter simplicity. Our talk of God is purely negative. Says Maimonides: "[The question is] . . . whether some real relation exists between God and any of the substances created by Him, by which He could be described? That there is no correlation between Him and any of

His creatures can easily be seen." There can be no relations in God because God is "a simple essence." Relations posited of God "exist only in the thoughts of men."[38] Such a totally unrelated God is wholly abstract.

The absolute simplicity of God articulated by medieval Jewish thinkers led them to adopt a theology of negation "in which one can only say what God is not, never what He is."[39] The resultant austerity in talking about God led to the passion for a direct, mystical relation to God. Kabbalistic mysticism formulated a doctrine that distinguished between God as the *En Sof*, God as God is in God's self, and the *Sefirot*, God as God reveals God's self or God in God's emanations. In the later Kabbalah of Isaac Luria (the sixteenth-century mystic known as the *Ari*, the Lion), we find a system of thought created out of response to the questions: How can there be a world at all if God is everywhere? How can God create out of nothing if there is no nothing? Isaac Luria answered "with the doctrine of *Tzimtzum* ('withdrawal'), i.e., that God 'withdrew from Himself into Himself' in order to leave room for the world."[40] Luria modified Kabbalistic doctrine by teaching that, whereas in traditional Kabbalah the *Sefirot* are emanations of God, what really takes place is that God's first impulse is to withdraw that the world might be created, and only after that do the *Sefirot* emanate from God. After God's withdrawal, what was left was "empty space," not a literal empty space, because space itself had not been created, but a primordial emptiness into which the emanations from God and space and time consequently developed. From these emerged in turn the "primordial human being" (*Adam Kadmon*). In the process of creation, the "lights" that preceded from the *Adam Kadmon* were unable to be contained by the "vessels" of the *Sefirot*, the result being the cosmic catastrophe known as "the breaking of the vessels" that allowed for the rise of the demonic aspect of existence. The rise of the demonic was necessary for people to be able freely to choose between good and evil. In the process, the light of God the *En Sof* became fragmented and everything is in disarray. The task of human beings is to reclaim and release the "holy sparks" by returning them to their Source. This is known as *tikkun olam*, mending the world; complete redemption will come to Israel and the world only when the task of mending the world is complete. Then God will be one and the world one. Meanwhile, human beings who mend the world by doing good deeds (*mitzvot*) affect God as well as the world.

The views of Isaac Luria are mythological and have affinities with Gnosticism; yet they affirm the reality and unity of God while accounting not only for the diversity of the world but also for human freedom and responsibility as well as the divine capacity to be affected by what happens in the world. In our time, the Lurianic option has been developed by Hans Jonas as one possible response to the suffering and evil of the Holocaust. Jonas' revision of the doctrine of God after Auschwitz has the dual advantage of *retrieving* an option in the history of Jewish thought and *restating* the doctrine of God in a way that promises to be credible in the light of the fires of Auschwitz.

Jonas proposes a "tentative myth" for consideration:[41] God "chose" in the beginning to give God's self "over to the chance and risk and endless variety of becoming," entering into the adventure of space and time. God effaced God's self for the world, renouncing "His own being, divesting Himself of His deity—to receive it back from the Odyssey of time weighted with the chance harvest of unforeseeable temporal existence: transfigured or possibly even disfigured by it." The world can enrich the experience of God or contribute to God's pathos. As a result of God's decision to commit God's self to the adventure of becoming, there arose life, mortality, human beings, knowledge, freedom, and the advent of good and evil. "To the promise and risk of this agency the divine cause, revealed at last, henceforth finds itself committed; and its issue trembles in the balance." Henceforth, God accompanies our human doing "with the bated breath of suspense . . . while not intervening in the dynamics of his worldly scene."[42] God has deliberately become vulnerable to the lavishness and sternness of becoming and history. This is a divine adventure with the world; God does not create the world by fiat (although God *does* create the world), but leads it by beckoning it into novel possibilities of becoming. God takes a great risk in doing so, because God does not know, once the risk has been taken, how it will come out.

As Jonas extrapolates the theological implications of his myth, God is a *suffering* God. That God is related to the world (and not merely the world to God) requires an understanding that God suffers as *only* God can suffer. God is a *becoming* God. The notion of God as in all respects nontemporal, impassible, immutable, and unqualifiedly omnipotent is dropped. God is affected by what happens in the world, experiences it; God is engaged in pathos with the world. God's "continuous relation . . . to the creation" means that God's "own being is affected by what goes on in it." God is a *caring* God—"not remote and detached and self-contained but involved with what He cares for." Not omnipotent, God has "left something for the other agents to do and thereby made his care dependent upon them." God is endangered and at risk. Were this not so, the world should be permanently perfect. Thus, God is *not omnipotent*. The very concept of power "is a relational concept and requires relation." The idea of one being having all the power is "senseless." Power not limited by another would have no object on which to exercise its power; power having another to overpower would not be total. Here is a case where "'all' equals 'zero.'" Power that is not socially shared is no power. Jonas rejects divine omnipotence as compatible with divine goodness only at the cost of complete divine inscrutability. Arguing that divine goodness is not compatible with notions of omnipotence, omniscience, omnibenevolence, and the fact of evil except at the cost of claiming that God is totally enigmatic, Jonas affirms God's goodness: "Goodness is inalienable from the concept of God."[43] After Auschwitz we have to choose between omnipotence on God's part or goodness, and Jonas chooses goodness.

The ethical conclusions that ensue from Jonas' myth are as follows. First is "the transcendent importance of our deeds."[44] Because we affect God, for good or ill, our responsibility is not measured in human terms alone. God, not human beings, is the measure, and it is to God that we are responsible. What happens matters, and matters ultimately, because it matters to the One who is ultimate. Although Jonas calls this an ethical consequence, it is more accurate to call it "meta-ethical"; it is the final reason why we should be moral.[45] Another ethical conclusion is that God has given God's self wholly to the world; "God has no more to give."[46] It is our turn to give to God and to one another. The future of the divine adventure is in our hands; we must not fail God and one another. When things go wrong, there is "weeping in the heights at the waste and despoilment of humanity." Such is the result of Jonas' attempt to push "further the old Jewish idea of the *tzimtzum*, the contraction of divine being as the condition for the being of the world."[47]

More recently, Jonas has reaffirmed his earlier conclusions out of the conviction that the cries of people like his mother, who died in Auschwitz, "be not denied to them." He restates his earlier view, noting two further matters: that his unorthodox speculations are not so wayward when seen in the company of the Kabbalah and its idea of a "divine fate bound up with the coming-to-be of a world," and that the idea that it is "we who can help God rather than God helping us" has been found among some of the Auschwitz victims themselves.[48] Jonas discovered it in Etty Hellesum's prayers, where her "God is one to whom she makes promises, but of whom she expects and asks nothing."[49] She prayed:

> I shall try to help you, God, to stop my strength ebbing away, though I cannot vouch for it in advance. But one thing is becoming increasingly clear to me: that You cannot help us, that we must help You to help ourselves. . . . Alas, there does not seem to be much You Yourself can do about our circumstances, about our lives. Neither do I hold You responsible. You cannot help us, but we must help You and defend Your dwelling-place in us to the last.[50]

Myth is the vehicle for Jonas' "concept." "All this is but stammering." Nor were the words of the prophets and psalmists any more than "stammers before the eternal mystery." Although Jonas' answer differs from Job's, it is an answer to Job, "that in him God himself suffers."[51]

Christian Theological Reconstruction

In the most significant Christian theological response to the reality of the Israel of God to date, Paul M. van Buren has recourse to the Lurianic myth to articulate a doctrine of God conversant with the Jewish tradition and the realities of evil and suffering after the Holocaust. He comments that Luria's notion "of the *tsimtsum* (the divine contraction) may appear purely speculative, but Scholem argues that it was part of his response to the inordinate suffering of the Jewish people that followed upon their mass expulsion from Spain in 1492." Van Buren speaks of God's self-determination in the act of creating the world as a "free act of love" in which God determined to create the world "as a place for the free display of and free response to his love."[52] God's decision to create the world as a world of free creatures was a freely chosen step in the divine self-determination after which "things will *never* be the same for that agent."[53] Van Buren spells out the consequences of his decision to take up the Lurianic option in a radically revised doctrine of God. The *omnipotence* of God undergoes significant reinterpretation. Now it is seen "as God's truly unlimited freedom to *not* act even when those most dear to him are threatened and cry to him to intervene."[54] Omnipotence is "an act of praise, a liturgical ascription, not a definition." The power of God is "made perfect in weakness" (2 Cor. 12:9), hence "opposite to what human beings mean by power." It is "nonviolent, as opposed to violent or military, political power." Indeed, the "power that is specific to God" is the power to bear with the creation in its suffering and to lead to "an inclusive view of God's part in human suffering." God's way of "slowly winning us to himself," God's way of exercising power on us, "is by sharing our very life with us." What we should have learned from Golgotha, we may learn from Auschwitz: "that God's omnipotence is such that God can and does enter into the pain and suffering of his children."[55]

Van Buren rejects the classical notion of God's immutability. The orthodox Christian "inability to go so far as to say that God was directly, personally, and immediately involved in the suffering of Jesus becomes unbearable when we reflect on the suffering of the Jewish men, women, and children in the Holocaust." He notes that both the Arian and Athanasian Christologies were "burdened . . . by the concept of the impassibility of God." God had "no place in that last bitter and final struggle" of Jesus' suffering and death; "thus the tradition leaves the Church with its primary symbol working against its own faith." God's covenantal self-determination to have a world of free creatures means that God has "God's own history," that we can "no longer see changelessness as a necessary attribute of God." Instead, God depends upon God's "human partners to take responsibility for how . . . [God's] plan and purpose shall look" and, instead of being aloof from the world's pain, "suffers on the cross, suffering more hellishly in the gas chambers of the camps and the mass murders of the *Einsatz* teams." In place of immutability, we find an "intimacy between God and Israel," even an "intimacy in failure."[56]

With omnipotence and immutability out of the picture, God is no longer thought of as "the absolute," because "absolute" means devoid of real or internal relationships. To think of God as "absolute" is to absolve God from the covenantal relationship: "The Absolute ultimately cannot suffer with its 'children,' cannot finally have 'children,' be they nailed to a cross or gassed and burned in death camps. The Absolute cannot bind itself to a particular people and submit to human history, much less to Jewish history." Whereas the absolute is unrelatable to a free and contingent world, absolutely powerful and absolutely unmoved and unmovable, van Buren understands God to be engaged "in a game in which his moves depend on ours," and in which God can be "surprised or displeased by what his creatures do," in which God "can grasp with pleasure new opportunities presented by human initiatives." God is "more committed to process and give-and-take persuasion," in contrast to traditional theism, which sees God as the only, because omnipotent actor. God is capable of change, of "novelty as well as continuity." God responds to God's creation, acts upon and is acted upon by it, and so understanding God "is a metaphysical alternative that appears more congenial to the covenant context of Christ" than classical theism. God's free decision to be covenantally self-determined results in a "compromised God," a God *with promise*, no longer omnipotent, immutable, and absolute. Covenant becomes the controlling metaphor, the way after Auschwitz to speak of God: "It is God's own expression of God's own self . . . God's way of being for his creation. . . . God is not a being in and for himself. God is love, grace, self-giving, self-binding to others, and God is this in his very being."[57]

Let us note three formal features of van Buren's understanding of God. First, it attempts to state the doctrine of God in a manner *appropriate* to the central symbols of the Christian faith. It criticizes the traditional doctrine of God for undercutting these symbols. Second, it represents the *triumph of grace* in van Buren's doctrine of God, according to which covenant making *is* God's way of being gracious (a central biblical and Jewish insight) and grace is what God *is* (a central insight of the Reformation). Third, it attempts to rethink the doctrine of God in a manner conversant with Jewish efforts to talk appropriately of God in the face of Jewish suffering, even if these efforts constitute a minority voice in Judaism itself. It is mindful of Greenberg's maxim: "No statement, theological or otherwise, should be made that would not be credible in the presence of the burning children."[58]

John K. Roth and Richard L. Rubenstein find van Buren's "suggestions about God's relations to Auschwitz . . . less credible than his estimates about how to reconceive the relations between Christians and Jews." They reproach him for not asserting a traditional understanding of God's power to intervene in human history: "At the very core of Christianity . . . is the assertion that God's divine power far exceeds anything that human beings can do."[59] This echoes Roth's understanding of God: "If God raised Jesus from the dead, he had the might to thwart the Holocaust long before it ended."[60] Van Buren's mistake, as they see it, is that he tries to make God's goodness "as great as God's suffering" and God's "love as vast as God's freedom."[61] The problem is that by so doing van Buren robs God of God's power to intervene in history and thwart the Holocaust.

It is difficult to know quite what to make of this criticism, particularly because its proponents do not claim that God intervened in history to thwart the Holocaust and because Rubenstein previously abandoned the idea of an omnipotent God who could have stopped the Holocaust but did not. We have seen his claim that an omnipotent God cannot be saved from the conclusion "that it was God's will that Hitler had exterminated the Jews."[62] On that point, Rubenstein's logic is that if God has all the power, the inescapable conclusion is that whatever happens takes place either because God does or allows it. In either case, God is responsible and indictable for evil. Against such a God it makes no sense to work for the amelioration of injustice or the limitation of evil, for it is more difficult to fight omnipotence than city hall. Even less does it make sense, as Roth wishes to do, to protest with God (if God is omnipotent, whence comes the power even to protest?) because God is heedless of protest (immutability being heedless by definition). Rubenstein's rejection of precisely the view of God's power that Rubenstein and Roth together (somehow) assert nullifies their criticism of van Buren.

The strengths of van Buren's revisionist doctrine of God are that it seeks to express such a doctrine that befits the suffering love of God revealed in the cross of Christ, seeks to express a doctrine of God as gracious, and seeks to adhere to Greenberg's maxim of not saying anything that could not be said in the presence of the burning children. A God having the power to intervene, but who does not, cannot answer Abraham's question: "Shall not the Judge of all the earth do what is just?" (Gen. 18:25). That God could intervene to obstruct evil but does not is not what is revealed in the cross of Christ, does not bespeak a gracious God, and is not something that one can say in the presence of the burning children.

Nonetheless, van Buren's doctrine of God's self-limitation might lend credibility to Roth and Rubenstein's criticism, despite the disagreement between them. When van Buren introduced his discussion of God's "freely chosen" act of creation, he said: "Thereafter, things will *never* be the same for that agent."[63] The question is, What is the force of this "never"? It could be understood as saying that once God has got a pluralistic universe of diverse and partially self-determining agents, then there is no more possibility of God's intervening in things, period. If God is self-determined to be covenantally related and creates creatures who are in turn free and self-determining, then "after" this decision power is genuinely social, genuinely shared, and the exercise of unilateral power no longer possible. But van Buren sometimes speaks as if God's freedom is a freedom "to *not* act," as though God, having once withdrawn to create freedom, could withdraw the withdrawal and intervene. This seems to be what he has in mind when he speaks of God's "failure to act."[64] It is only meaningful to speak of a failure to act if the possibility of acting remains open. That God "fails" to act grants Roth and Rubenstein's criticism of van Buren some credibility on the grounds of the internal coherence of van Buren's position if not in relation to experience broadly and fairly construed. That we can think (as opposed to imagine) of God intervening without regarding God a finite being, who can be alternately present and absent, seems impossible. In what sense can a universal agent intervene? If absent, where is God? That experience broadly and fairly construed allows us to talk of God as both good and capable of coercive intervention seems unlikely. If God can literally feed five thousand people with a few loaves and fishes, what is God doing today when thirty children per minute starve to death? To say that God can act in this situation, but "fails" to do so, raises an insuperable problem of evil. Another way to put this problem is to say that some ways of talking of God's freedom are decidedly unhelpful. For example, if God in a literal sense freely chooses to be gracious, but retains the possibility of freely choosing not to be gracious, then we had better start appeasing God. But to do so misses the point involved in asserting that God is gracious. The way that will be taken out of this problem, here, is by going all the way with van Buren's insight that an understanding of God in terms of process, relationality, and give-and-take persuasion is "more congenial to the covenantal context of Christ" than the traditional option. I intend to develop van Buren's insight because, of the various post-Holocaust reflections on God from Christian theologians, it is the most convincing.

A Process-Relational Model of God

A process-relational model of God is more appropriate to the living, covenantally related God of the Bible and more adequate to the needs of a vital faith after the Holocaust than either traditional theism or various recent attempts to redefine God out of all recognition. Ancient Greek thought, which the early church found all-too-convincing with regard to God, regarded objects of ordinary perception as paradigmatic cases of reality. In this way, an object such as a gray stone came to exemplify the two basic categories of interpretation of classical thought. "Gray" was understood as an attribute or property of the underlying reality of the stone, which in turn was conceived in terms of "substance" or "being." Hence, reality was understood in terms of unrelated substances undergoing external and accidental adventures of change as indicated by alterations in their attributes. God was thought of as a substance in the perfect, immutable sense of whom we can know only the attributes.

The process-relational model of God begins with a different starting point, taking our awareness of our own existence as experiencing subjects as the basis of our fundamental models and metaphors. Unlike the notion of substances, which are nontemporal and nonrelated, the "very being of the self is relational or social; and it is nothing if not a process of change involving the distinct modes of present, past, and future."[65] Always embodied (there are no disembodied selves), by means of the body the self both is affected by and affects, interacts with, a much larger whole of reality. Because it both affects and is affected by others who change and differ, the self is temporal and social. A process-relational self can be spoken of as in, of, and with its worldly neighbors as they, in turn, are in, of, and with it.

If we develop a model of God from this social-temporal awareness of the self, we would understand God to be genuinely social and temporal, effecting (creating) others as well as being affected by them, and utterly "different from the wholly timeless and unrelated Absolute of traditional theism."[66] The categorically unique status of God, categorically unique because understood to be the perfect exemplification of such categories as relationality and freedom, means that God would not be thought of as being utterly immutable and static but as being the only One capable of undergoing influence from all others and the only One capable of influencing all others.[67] Whereas every finite agent is capable of relating only to *some* others and to each inadequately, God relates to *all* others and to each perfectly. Yet God is affected by no agent whom God has not previously effected. Whereas the human self is incarnate in the world, it is so in a highly circumscribed way, interacting with a limited context. God's "body is the whole universe of nondivine beings," with each of which God's relation is immediate and direct.[68] That God's experience is ever enriched, even if tragically, is why God is thought of on this model as "the self-surpassing surpasser of all."[69] Hence, God's perfection is not utterly static and asocial, but the unique, perfect instance of creative becoming and relationality.

A chief liability of traditional theism is that it leaves us with an insuperable problem of evil. Its view of God as coercive, omnipotent benevolence, who could at any moment intervene in the course of worldly affairs but fails to do so, falters at every point. Evil was always a difficulty for Christian theism, with its dual emphases on God's unsurpassed goodness and God's possession of all power. With the rise of the late modern worldview, with its understanding of natural entities as having no inherent power of their own, together with the Reformation's stress on voluntaristic theologies that accorded all power to God and none to God's creatures, the problem of evil became even more critical. If people have no power in relation to God with which they could frustrate God's purposes for and with them, how is it possible for them to sin? The problem of evil, defined as the apparent contradiction between God's coercive yet omnipotent benevolence and the experienced reality of evil, constitutes the single most important reason for the decline of belief in God. That half the Jews born into the world in the last eight hundred years have been killed, that population expulsion and elimination have become problem-solving mechanisms for ruthless governments in the twentieth century, that 1,800 children per hour die for lack of simple nutrition and fifty cents' worth of vaccine in their veins—these are all, at best, difficult to render coherent with the existence of an all-powerful, omnibenevolent God.

On the alternative model developed in process-relational theology, God does several things. First, God creates everything that is. Because process thought regards actuality as composed of events of becoming and of each event as "called" into being and becoming by God's primordial envisagement of the realm of possibility, it claims that without God there would be nothing. The doctrine of creation out of nothing is taken to mean that without God there would be nothing, certainly nothing other than God: "Apart from God, the remaining formative elements [creativity and the realm of possibility] would fail in their functions. There would be no creatures."[70] The traditional view that there was a "time" before time began when God existed in isolated grandeur surrounded by "nothing" is a literalized myth that process theology rejects. When Whitehead first began to write about God, he did so because he concluded that the final metaphysical analysis at which he had arrived left him with the same problem faced by Plato: if the world is finally analyzable into the ongoing flux of creativity and a realm of potentiality, there is no way for them to be brought together so that something actual happens. What is required is some agent. Whitehead understood each new event as having to take into account a new past actual world, on which it needed a new perspective. But this new perspective could not, by definition, come from the past. Nor could the new occasion generate it, because that occasion could itself arise only from this new perspective. Therefore, Whitehead introduced God into his metaphysical reflection, referring to God as the "principle of concretion," that is, the principle by means of which concrete actuality was created.[71] Later, Whitehead would change this formulation in the light of his "ontological principle" and argue that God is an actual entity, an agent, who envisages the possibilities and orders them in relevance to the course of the world so that novel finite occasions can arise.[72] At this point, creativity becomes a category that is actual only in virtue of its accidents and which itself does nothing. Possibilities themselves have to be accounted for in terms of the ontological principle, rendering them dependent on God's creative envisaging of them. It is important to note that for process theology there would be nothing without God, to avoid the misimpression that the socially related God of process thought is subject to an *independently* existing universe. God is affected by all others in process theology, and perfectly so, but God is affected by nothing that God has not previously effected.

What is at stake in the doctrine of creation out of nothing is not the claim that up until a particular time God existed in unrestricted seclusion, and that at that time God created, by fiat, a universe. That is a literalized myth that cries out to be deliteralized. It also distorts, as Levenson carefully argued, the biblical witness. What is at stake, rather, is Paul's proclamation, "There is one God, the Father, from whom are all things and for whom we exist" (1 Cor. 8:6), that we say of God, "from him and through him and to him are all things" (Rom. 11:36). God is the ground (from whom) and end (to whom) of all things, the Alpha and the Omega, without whom nothing would be or be redeemed. God alone is "the universal necessary cause of all other existence that, being wholly contingent, depends on the Deity for its being and worth."[73]

Second, when God's creative activity is understood as offering the aim at becoming around which events are enabled to arise, we see that God calls each new moment into being and enables these new occasions to appropriate the richness of accumulated value that is the past. God is the ground of our relation to all that has gone before. The depth of experience, its thickness, the way in which the past is present in contemporary experience, is owed to God. As process theology sees matters, new occasions do not arise, establish a perspective upon their past actual worlds, and then permit themselves to be influenced by God. No, without God, there would be no creatures. What happens is the reverse: God calls forth the new occasion by offering it an aim at a value around which it can arise and that at the same time enables it to establish a perspective upon its past actual world, which is never quite the same past inherited by any other occasion. The more of the past we can appreciate, the richer our present experience, the greater our range of future possibilities, and the more significant our freedom.

Third, God not only creates the creatures but creates them as free, partially self-creating creatures. Process thought stipulates that indeterminacy and self-determination are general characteristics descriptive of all true individuals (as distinct from mere aggregates, such as stones).[74] We experience ourselves as free and realize that freedom is unavoidable, even if we paradoxically seek leave of the responsibility that comes with freedom. To be a human being is to decide how to understand and how to constitute oneself. If no possibilities were offered us other than what the automatic consequences of the past necessitated, we would be cogs in a cosmic mechanism, which in the worldview of modernity we were. But this contradicts our experience as free to constitute ourselves, albeit always in relation to a context. Because God in each moment calls us forward into God's promised future for us, "it is by virtue of the presence of God that I experience a call to be more than I have been and more than my circumstances necessitate that I be." In other words, "it is by God's grace that I am free."[75] Thus, in process thought, the *kind* of power God exercises upon the creatures is referred to as "persuasive." The point is not that God exercises no efficacy upon the creatures (God effects the creatures' creation as partially self-constituting creatures). The point is that once the momentary actual occasion is set on its way, it is free to decide how to constitute itself. Process theology seeks not only to make grace and freedom compatible with each other, thus overcoming a dilemma that plagued classical theism, but also to argue that grace makes freedom possible. If so, God's mode of creating by calling the creatures forward into their own becoming means that God would be split against God's self were God to intervene coercively in God's own way of doing things. That the creatures are free and responsible means that God is only one among many actors, even if the indispensable one, and that responsibility for the course of events is genuinely pluralistic. God requires the free cooperation of God's covenant partners if God's reconciling purposes in history are to be served. Absent this cooperation, God's purposes can be frustrated and obstructed, but God is far from the only one responsible for the resultant evil. The creatures bear their share of responsibility as does God. God's chief responsibility is that of having brought forth free and possibly uncooperative creatures. Because each creature has its own God-given power of self-creation, God is the necessary but not the sufficient cause of any event.

God is the ground and end of our being and becoming, without whom neither we nor anything else would be at all; God is the ground of our relation to the past; God is the ground of our freedom. One more thing must be said, by way of emphasis, about what God does. Because God is genuinely, not merely apparently, social, God not only acts upon but interacts with all others. Not only is God unsurpassably active in the sense of "doing all that could conceivably be done by any one individual for all others," but also God is "unsurpassably passive, being open to all that could be conceivably done or suffered by anyone as something that is also done to God."[76] We may *trust* God unqualifiedly because God is always doing for us everything that it is possible and appropriate for God to do. God may not always do for us everything that we want God to do, but that is another matter. It is only appropriate to ask God to do for us those things that only God can do; the rest is up to us. The rule is: if an action *can* be undertaken by God's covenant partners, it is they who will have to do it. And if some things should be done, *we should* do them. Here the moral issue appears. Not all actions that God's covenant partners can do *should* be done in a moral sense. There are many appropriate options in most situations, not all (or any) of which should be done in the sense that *not* to do them is immoral. Moral reflection is indispensable to God's covenant partners. The covenantally related God does for God's covenant partners everything possible and necessary for God to do for them. The things that the covenant partners can do are left up to them. We may be unqualifiedly *loyal* to God because God, by accepting us and all others into God's everlasting life, redeems our lives from sin, transience, and insignificance. How we decide to understand and constitute ourselves, who we are and what we do, matters because it matters to God. Our faith in the meaningfulness and worthwhileness of who we are and what we do is the faith that is justified by God's gracious acceptance of us. God is Redeemer as well as Creator, Omega as well as Alpha, "not the unmoved mover of Aristotle, but the most moved mover of the prophets and rabbis."[77]

In these functions of God we see the relation between justice and faith. God regards each and all of God's creatures as of intrinsic value and desires that each actualize its highest possibilities. God desires that each enjoy the greatest possible richness of experience. God intends that each be free and self-determining. God promises that each one is loved, everlastingly taken into the divine life, saved, redeemed. Because God unfailingly undergoes whatever happens to each of the creatures, what we do or fail to do to others we do or fail to do to God. Faith demands justice because God demands justice. "There is just one sphere of action, this-world-in-God."[78] God redeems us from insignificance, and by promising that we are justified by grace through faith offers us the freedom to love our neighbors as ourselves, to cease being closed in upon ourselves. God does everything for each and all of us that God can possibly do, leaving it up to us to do all those things that only we can do if they are to be done at all.

Such a view of God as exercising a categorically excellent form of relational power, interacting with God's creatures and covenant partners, is arguably appropriate to the biblical witness and the covenantal context of Christ. Part of the case for this view was made by Levenson's criticism of traditional theism for the inadequacy of its understanding of God and creation to the biblical witness, another part by van Buren's arguments from the reality of evil and the covenantal context of Christ, and yet another through the references to Paul's statements to the effect that all things are from and to God. Further, one cannot fail to note that one of the favorite biblical prepositions used in relation to God is the word *with*. God promises Joshua that "as I was with Moses, so I will be with you" (Josh. 1:5); the psalmist can put aside certain kinds of fear because of the realization that "you are with me" (Ps. 23:4). The name of Jesus was "Emmanuel, which means 'God is with us'" (Matt. 1:23). The eschatology of fulfillment with which the Bible ends promises that in the new heaven and the new earth, God "will dwell with them as their God" (Rev. 21:3). The universal, omnipresent God who interacts with God's creatures, who is not in all respects immutable, finds biblical warrant. On the other hand, various modern efforts to redefine God as identical with our moral ideals avoid involving God with the messiness of history and evil not only by denying God's traditional omnipotence but by identifying God with moral ideals themselves. Yet such a drastic redefinition of God answers to nothing in the tradition and fails to understand God as the One who is the standard and measure of our moral ideals. To define God as our ideals is to deny that God is actual and to capitulate to modernity's ban on theism.

The Triune God

The doctrine of the Trinity is the church's way of asserting that the God it worships is the God of Israel and of the Israel of God. Of all the propositions articulated in this book, this one will strike many readers, Jews particularly, as the most outrageous. Some Christians will regard it as obvious; others will be puzzled. Jews regard Christians as monotheists, yet do so in spite of the "strange mixture" (*shituf*) which, in their view, the Trinity introduces into monotheism. For their part, Christians have always claimed (although sometimes this was a counterclaim against the denial of the same point by other Christians) to worship the same God whom Jews worship. Yet the most distinctively Christian thing that Christians have had to say about the God whom Israel declares to be one is that this God is a Trinity. The problem for Christians is that when they say that they worship the God of the Jews, they give Jews a voice in whether this is recognizably the case. Jews tend to respond that it would be more obviously so if Christians just politely kept quiet about the Trinity and affirmed the oneness of God. The traditional *adversus Judaeos* retort to Jews on this point varied. Sometimes it asserted that Jews could see that Christians worship the same God as do they if they were not willfully blind. At others, the affirmation of the doctrine of the Trinity and the denial of Monarchy (the church fathers' term for monotheism) was interpreted as the great difference between Christianity and Judaism, which difference the Monarchists were accused of denying. Tertullian, who coined the Western Trinitarian expression *tres personae in una substantia*, made exactly this argument.[79] Hence, the affirmation that the doctrine of the Trinity is the church's way of asserting that it worships the God of Israel faces some heavy sledding. We will articulate this affirmation by a two-step process. Step one will be to identify and set aside some problems that inhibit reflection on the doctrine of the Trinity. Step two will be to state the *point* of the doctrine of the Trinity.

Several problems both dog understanding of the doctrine of the Trinity on the part of Christians and frustrate conversations between Jews and Christians on the topic of God. Among them is one that surfaced early in this chapter, and that is the classical Christian assumption about immutability of the divine. An immutable God needs a mediator in order to relate to humanity, because by definition what is immutable is unrelated. Yet because what is eternally immutable remains eternally unrelatable, to recognize the need for a mediator starts a process of infinite regress that cannot be stopped. Who will mediate between the mediator and the unmediatable God? And that mediator who is said to be incarnate in Jesus Christ, however much associated with God, always carries with it the hint of being a different God because the hint of subordinationism can never be completely erased. If one is eternally begetting and the other eternally begotten, the latter seems to be less divine than the former and subordinate to because dependent on the former. The "begotten" is not as immutable as the "begetter." Hence protestations about the unity, coeternity, and consubstantiality of the two are less than convincing. The church paid a price for hanging on to the doctrine of the total immutability of God, both in its Christology and its doctrine of God as triune. Although we will restrict ourselves to the *point* of the doctrine of the Trinity, it is worth noting that among contemporary theologians the view is widely held that only a relational understanding of God will be of help in formulating a doctrine of God appropriate to the living God of the biblical witness and adequately Trinitarian.[80]

Second, it is wise to remember that the doctrine of the Trinity developed slowly in the early church and was not formulated by an ecumenical council until Nicaea in 325. Even here the doctrine was so stated, with its use of *homoousion* (of the same being or substance), that it set off a conflict that raged for another fifty years until it could be resolved at the Council of Constantinople in 381, where *homoousios* was interpreted to make it plain that oneness of essence did not preclude distinctions among members of the Trinity. *Homoousios* created a fuss because it had been a favorite term of the Sabellians who argued that each of the three "persons" was simply God in a different mode or wearing a different "mask," the Latin term *persona* (*sona* = sounding, *per* = through) referring to the mask worn by an actor in a play, through which the actor spoke. Those who denied the Trinity liked the term *homoousios*, and those who wanted to make distinctions within the Trinity disliked it. After Constantinople, the theological debate shifted from the Trinity to Christology and the question of the relation of the divine and the human to each other in Christ. But Trinitarian reflection did not end in the fourth century; it remains vital today with new formulations constantly being offered. The doctrine of the Trinity is consequent upon other, prior matters. It is historically consequent, developing late and taking the form it did because of a wide variety of factors—intellectual, cultural, and political. Thus, it could have developed differently. It is religiously consequent upon a more primary datum, the awareness of the Gentile church that salvation had been made available to it through Jesus Christ. The church developed a doctrine of the Trinity because it believed that in Jesus Christ the God of Israel, creator and redeemer of heaven and earth, graciously met with it.

The third difficulty of the doctrine of the Trinity, particularly but not only in the conversation between Christians and Jews, is that a lot of the language used to discuss it promotes the understanding that what is being affirmed is a modified polytheism, a tritheism in which the three "persons" or "hypostases" of the one God form a divine committee. Though this is not the intent of the doctrine, it would be less than honest not to admit that when one hears discussions of the doctrine of the Trinity, one hears a lot of the language of polytheism. For those for whom every distinction is a separation, the Trinity almost inevitably becomes a tripartite God. One reason for this may be that the classical term "person" (*persona*), meaning that which supports a character, has almost no currency in recent times, so that it is heard as an analogue to a discrete human person with a center of consciousness. Hence, the Trinity is thought of as three centers of consciousness yet somehow one. All this is very difficult, if not impossible, and may indicate that the doctrine needs a new set of terminology if it is to be usefully discussed. One of the sadder aspects of the confusion and debilitude that beset the doctrine of the Trinity today is that when we understand the heart of the doctrine, the question at issue, we learn, has *nothing* to do with a numbers game. In this discussion, we will leave the numbers to one side.

The *point* of the doctrine of the Trinity will be discussed in terms of three issues with which the early church had to deal. First, if we say that God was in Christ reconciling the world to God's self, that it is God before whom we are laid bare when we encounter Jesus Christ, of which God are we speaking? *Who* was active in Jesus Christ? Second, if we say that salvation and reconciliation occur through Jesus Christ, how is this possible unless God is operative both in and through Jesus Christ and in and upon us? Can we be "saved" by any other and any less than God? Third, if we say that this God saves us, is our savior, what do we mean by so speaking of God? We will consider each of these questions in turn and, in doing so, formulate the point of the doctrine of the Trinity. The ideas that will be a key to this construal of the point of the doctrine of the Trinity are two: that the good news of God in Jesus Christ is that we are justified by God's free grace, by no work of our own, and that the God who justifies us is the One who covenantally interacts with all others empowering even their faithful response to God's free grace.

In a nutshell, Christian thought about God is inherently Trinitarian because of the presumption that in all our relationships with God the *initiative* lies with God's grace. In every revelation of God in the Bible, the God of Israel gives God's self, discloses God's self, to the recipients of that revelation. The God of Israel, Yahweh, is the *giver*. The God of Israel is the *gift*. And it is God operating upon and in our spirits that opens us to the reception of the gift, so it is the God of Israel who is the *giving*. Yahweh is the giver, Yahweh is the gift, Yahweh is the giving. One God known as giver, gift, and giving or as lover, love, and loving.

First, then, what God was active in Jesus Christ? Students of the history of Christian thought have long known that when Gentiles started coming into the church from the variety of religions and religiophilosophical cults of the ancient world, they brought many of their assumptions and practices with them. Paul's correspondence with the Corinthian congregation describes a Hellenistic Gentile religious cult which, as Paul sees matters, has misunderstood a range of points involving questions as diverse as Baptism, the Eucharist, religious enthusiasm, and the Christian life. It would be surprising if such Gentile converts did not also bring along a variety of notions about God or, more precisely, about which of the many gods of their acquaintance really is God and which of them is made known to us in Jesus Christ. Indeed, Paul, as we have had occasion to note before, had to remind his Gentile followers that although there "may be so-called gods in heaven or on earth—as in fact there are many gods and many lords—yet for us there is one God, the Father, from whom are all things and for whom we exist, and one Lord, Jesus Christ, through whom are all things and through whom we exist" (1 Cor. 8:5–6). The "many, so-called gods" are all those gods in whom we erroneously place our ultimate trust and confidence; in this sense there are indeed "many gods and many lords." Yet the one God, from and to whom are all things, is the One who is God and whom we serve. Paul here deals with a problem that would become more and not less severe in the Gentile churches. The problem was that many Gentiles thought that some god whom they knew from Gentile religion was superior to the God of the Jews. Marcion, Montanus, and the Gnostics agreed with such an extreme anti-Jewish Gentile as Saturninus, who said: "Christ came to destroy the god of the Jews."[81]

The argument over the question of which God we know in Jesus Christ began long before Arius came upon the scene. The Trinitarian discussion has its context in a prior debate between the anti-Gnostic thinkers of the church and their Gnostic opponents who sought to introduce new ideas into the Christian tradition, ideas that included the notion that the god who meets us in Jesus Christ is *not* the God of the Jews but a new, different, and better god. This new and better god was said to save us out of this material world, which the inferior god of the Jews created and in which we are trapped, and to save us to and for a reunion with the Supreme God on high. Jesus came into this material world, "seemed" to, but did not really, take on a body, and offers salvation by making available to us the passwords necessary if we are to move through the various "eons" who guard the way to the Supreme God. Salvation is differently defined. Whereas with Jesus and Paul it could never be disengaged from a promised future for *this* world, now it consists in abandoning hope for this world in exchange for a purely "spiritual" salvation found in reunion with the source of our spirits, which, otherwise, would remain trapped in matter and earth. Also, only an "elite" are eligible for salvation. Of the three classes of human beings—the physical, psychical, and spiritual—only the latter are guaranteed salvation. Members of the psychical type may go either way, whereas the physical people, being irredeemably carnal, are beyond hope. The connection between Gnosticism and racism, expressed in a doctrine of privilege and elitism with respect to salvation, is clear. The claim that the god who meets us in Jesus Christ is not the God of the Jews is also a claim that salvation is different from what Jews and early Christians had thought it to be, and that what it means to call God "savior" differs as well.

The doctrine of the Trinity, then, has to do with the issue of how we are to *identify or name* the God who is incarnate in Jesus Christ and with whom the risen Christ continues to confront us in the witness of the church. The claim of the doctrine of the Trinity, hammered out by the anti-Gnostic thinkers, is that the God who saves us through Jesus Christ is the God of Israel, maker and redeemer of heaven and earth, that this God is one, and that this God who is one is the one and only God. The chief purpose of the doctrine of the Trinity is to name God and to see to it that Christians name God properly: the God whom we encounter in Jesus Christ is the God who redeemed Israel from bondage, led Israel through the wilderness, revealed God's self to Israel in history and through the law and the prophets, and it is this God and no other who is made known by Jesus Christ, through the church, to Gentiles. The first point of the doctrine of the Trinity was and is to reject any and all claims about the relation of Jesus Christ to God that themselves deny or contradict Jesus' own relationship to God, a relationship expressed in Jesus' name *Yahweh is salvation* and a God proclaimed by the early witness's recollection of Jesus' repetition of the *Shema*: "Hear, O Israel: The LORD IS our God, the LORD alone." No other and certainly no better god, whether of Marcion, Montanus, or Saturninus, is made manifest in Christ and the church. The God made known to us in Jesus Christ is the one God, the God of Israel. That assertion of the identity of God is the first point of the doctrine of the Trinity.

Second, how is God operative in and through Jesus Christ? The doctrine of the Trinity was developed in order to claim and to understand what is involved in claiming that salvation takes place through Jesus Christ. The key insight is utterly biblical: that God is the author of our salvation, that, as Jesus' name has it, *Yahweh is salvation*; that *if* we are saved through Jesus Christ, *then* God must be salvifically operative in Jesus Christ. We can be saved, re-created, by none other than our creator, redeemed by none other than the One who redeemed Israel from bondage. Salvation is by the grace and initiative of the God of Israel.

In saying this much we already verge on an inherently Trinitarian structure of thought. *God* saves us. God saves us *through* Jesus Christ. God through Jesus Christ saves *us*. The knowledge of God is a *saving*, transforming knowledge, a point on which both traditional and revisionist understandings of Christology agree, and a saving knowledge of God requires that we know God in, through, and by means of some *medium* of revelation (Jesus Christ) and that our ability to appropriate this saving knowledge of God is itself the gracious gift of God's efficacy upon the human spirit (the Holy Spirit). This is what the church has insisted upon as long as it has claimed that the church is a creation of the Holy Spirit (Acts 2). We cannot "know" God apart from some construal of God through a finite medium of the divine ground and end of our being and becoming, nor can we know God by any innate or natural human ability to do so apart from God's gracious direction. Hence the salvific self-disclosure of God happens both through Jesus Christ and the Spirit of God. The internal framework of Christian faith is Trinitarian. The characteristically Christian knowledge of the God of a singular promise and a singular command is ministered historically by the event of Jesus Christ. Its actual occurrence, its happening in and to a human being, is made possible by the work of the Spirit and by no work of our own. Its inner logic is shaped by the symbols of Jesus and the Spirit. We cannot be saved except by God. We cannot come to a saving knowledge of the circumambient mystery of God apart from some finite medium and construal of God. God must be operative both in that finite medium and in us if we are to be brought to a saving knowledge of God, because we cannot save ourselves. As none less and none other than God is at work in Jesus Christ, so none less and other than God is at work in us enabling us to apprehend (not comprehend) God in Jesus Christ. These two claims mark out the major steps in the development of the Trinitarian doctrine in the ancient church: none other and no less than God, maker and redeemer of heaven and earth, is salvifically operative in Jesus Christ (Nicaea's affirmation that the Logos is consubstantial with the Father), and none other and no less than God is efficacious upon us through the Spirit (Constantinople's affirmation that the Holy Spirit "proceeds from the Father").

So far, we have argued that there are two points involved in the doctrine of the Trinity: that the God whom we know in Jesus Christ is the God of Israel, maker and redeemer of heaven and earth, the one God; and that it is this God who is efficacious for our salvation in Jesus Christ and in our appropriation of this salvation through the Holy Spirit. The doctrine of the Trinity developed as the church sought to give voice to its conviction that in, through, and by means of Jesus Christ and by virtue of the grace of God's Spirit, it had known salvation, that the God whom it knew to be its savior was the God of Israel, operative in Jesus Christ and in the appropriation of faith in Christ on the part of the church.

Third, what do we mean by saying that God saves us? The assumption is that by salvation what is meant, at least in part, is authentic self-understanding (what the tradition termed deliverance from "ignorance"), and that to understand one's self authentically is to understand oneself in any ultimate sense in terms of and only in terms of the love of God freely offered and the dual command of God that those who so understand themselves in turn must love God with all their selves and their neighbors as themselves. (Note: Unless one bifurcates the individual and the community, one will not find talk of individual or personal self-understanding to be privatistic.) The further claim is that the possibility of such a self-understanding is not something that comes "naturally" to human beings but that it is "given" by God, or that the weight of the biblical witness is such that we there find ourselves called and claimed by the unfathomable love and demanding justice of God.

Jesus Christ confronts us with the singular call and claim, promise and command, of the God of Israel, and we interpret and so understand God in terms of the ministry, resurrection, and continuing efficacy of Jesus Christ in and upon the church. The situation, as far as I can see, is dialectical: Jesus Christ is God's gracious gift to us, to be accepted gratefully and not boastfully; and Jesus Christ gives God to us, in the sense that he is the one through whom by the witness of the church we Gentiles are faced with the radical call and total claim of the God of Israel. Jesus Christ both points us beyond himself to God ("Whoever believes in me believes not in me but in him who sent me," John 12:44) and, as the contemporary Jesus present to the church through word and sacrament, bodies forth the presence of God. God as Spirit, present and immanently active in the lives of people, opens us to the efficacy of Christ and the transforming power of the knowledge of God available through Christ. The Holy Spirit is the spirit of Christ in the further sense that the activity of the Spirit does now what Christ did then—confronts his followers with the extraordinary promise and command of the God of Israel. Any and all claims that this, that, or the other is the work of the Spirit are to be tested by reference to Jesus Christ.

The God whom Christians identify as the Trinity, then, is the God of a unique promise and a unique command, of an unfathomable love and total claim, and Christians may dare to say that God is not other than God is known to be in Jesus Christ. This understanding and construal of God neither displaces nor improves upon the biblical and hence Jewish understanding of God precisely because it celebrates the grace of God who operates everywhere and particularly in the history and life of the Israel of God in the same way in which God operates through Jesus Christ and in the Spirit. The whole Christian understanding of the Trinity is an attempt to think out what it means for Gentile Christians to claim that *Yahweh is salvation* and that we have known this saving God through Christ and the Spirit. God is a gracious, salvific God who ever intends to be God with and for God's creatures.

In summary, the point of the doctrine of the Trinity is itself "trinitarian" in structure: (1) the one God whom we know in Jesus Christ is the God of Israel; (2) through Jesus Christ and in the Spirit this God graciously saves us and creates in and with us a community of the Spirit; and (3) God is nowhere and never other than the gracious savior of all God's creatures.

9

The Doctrine of the Church

————·—·——·——·——·—

The Church of Christ is rooted in the life of the People
Israel.

—*Faith and Order Study Group on Christian-Jewish Relations*
of the National Council of Churches, 1973

When the doctrine of the church is expounded, it is customary to find
an outline of the classic "marks" or "notes" of the church—its unity,
holiness, catholicity, and apostolicity—and a discussion of the Reformation claim that the church exists where the Word is rightly preached
and the sacraments rightly administered. Such issues can hardly be ig-
nored in a doctrine of the church, and we will return to them later in
this chapter.

What must first be taken into account in a post-Holocaust church
theology is the underside of Christian teaching on the church, how the
marks of the church were systematically distorted by the anti-Jewish, supersessionist connotations with which they were endowed. We are familiar with the usual Christian image of Judaism: blind to Christian truth,
unable to understand its own scriptures, old, sterile, carnal; inferior in
worship, ethics, and way of life to Christianity, which is new, fruitful,
spiritual, and superior. A dead faith, Judaism and the synagogue are particularistic, ethnocentric, and guilty of killing Christ, whereas the church
is alive, universal (catholic), Gentile, and faithful to the Christ whom
Jews condemn to death.

These images of the church and synagogue appear in Christian art as
the figures of two women, *Ecclesia* and *Synagoga*.[1] They show up in medieval churches in statuary, stained glass, and illuminated manuscripts.
These churches still function as places of worship and tourist attractions,

and Ecclesia and Synagoga make their silent witness every time people encounter them at the front doors or in the windows of these houses of worship. A symbol stands for something not itself a symbol. Christians—meeting Synagoga and Ecclesia at the door of a cathedral, depicted in a stained-glass window, or adorning an illuminated manuscript—receive a voiceless confirmation of their understanding of the victorious church and the defeated synagogue. In previous ages, Synagoga represented to Christians their daily experience of Jewish degradation.[2]

At the south transept of the Strasbourg Cathedral we find the best example of these symbols. Carved between 1230 and 1240, Synagoga and Ecclesia face each other across the portal. Their poses are repeated in every other occurrence of the pair. Ecclesia stands upright, a crown placed triumphantly on her head; she holds in her right hand a standard topped by the cross and in her left a chalice. In some versions, both figures stand under a crucifix, with blood flowing from Jesus' wounded side directly into Ecclesia's chalice. The figure and lines of Ecclesia are vertical and strong, her stride steady and purposeful.

In contrast, Synagoga sways backward, away from Ecclesia's strong gaze. In her right hand, Synagoga holds a spear for wounding, which is broken (sometimes into several pieces) and does not support her figure; she totters and falls away from Ecclesia. Her other hand, fallen to her side, holds the "Old Testament." Synagoga's eyes are blindfolded, unable to read the book. Stung by Ecclesia's rebuke, she is submissive, ready for exile. Ecclesia is strong, indomitable; Synagoga weak and vanquished. Full of hate and obduracy, guilty of deicide, Synagoga awaits her deserved fate at the hands of the upright and victorious church. The image is a powerful one for Christians to see as they enter the cathedral. In the Middle Ages, cathedrals were "the Bible in stone and glass" for congregants who could not read; their art remains today, for better and for worse, a guide to the Christian faith. Albertus Magnus (c. 1200–1280) described the pair this way:

> To the right of the Crucified, a maiden is portrayed with a joyful expression and beautiful face and crown: it is Ecclesia, who reverently received the blood of Christ in the chalice . . . whereas on the left stands a figure with eyes blindfolded, a sad expression and bowed head from which the crown falls; it is Synagoga, who has spilled this same blood and still despises it.[3]

These portrayals of the church and synagogue express visually what Christian theologians stated verbally in many of their treatments of the church.

The Church as the Exclusive Ark of Salvation

In their tracts against the Jews and doctrines of the church, Christian theologians traditionally interpreted the church as the exclusive bearer of salvation and the sign of God's rejection of the Jews. The more universalistic the doctrine of the church became, the more anti-Jewish it was. In our discussion of supersessionist interpretations of the covenant, we attended to ways in which the church was understood as a new people with whom God had replaced the Israel of God. David Patrick Efroymson terms the doctrine of the church in Tertullian (and the patristics generally) the "'payoff' symbol, the point at which the 'cash value' of the anti-Judaism of the other symbols is redeemed." His point is not that Tertullian's doctrine of the church is more anti-Jewish than his other doctrines, but that in it we have to do with Tertullian's "understanding of himself and his community."[4] The church is a community of Gentiles, not Jews; is universal, not particularistic; spiritual, not carnal; superior in all ways to the inferior Jews and, above all, Tertullian's own people. Efroymson develops a typology for describing the anti-Judaism of Tertullian's doctrine of the church according to which the church is a *replacement* people, a *gentile* and *universal* people, a *superior* people and, of most importance, *us.* Because it is so apt, we will here use his typology.

The church is "a *replacement* people."[5] The old, fleshly, idolatrous, and rebellious Jewish people have been replaced by a new, spiritual, faithful, and obedient people, Gentile Christians, who now receive God's grace. All the biblical prophecies of promise apply to us, the prophecies of rejection to the Jews. Tertullian speaks of God "transferring his favor" from the Jews to the church, justifying the church's claim to possession of the "scriptures, history, and legitimacy" of the Jews. The replacement people are "more faithful" than the Jews, capable of a more complete discipline.[6] In his discussion with Marcion, Tertullian agrees that "a new *ordo*, a new law, and a new people" have appeared. Whereas Marcion argued also for a new god, Tertullian preserves the God of the Bible at the expense of the people of the Bible by shifting the blame to the Jewish people, citing their sinfulness, their stubborn clinging to what is old and gone, and by arguing the superiority of the church with its commitment to what is new, different, and better. Israel was replaced because of its sinfulness and the church elected because of its switch from idolatry to faithfulness. Tertullian interprets the gospel passages that tell of Jesus' rejection of his mother and brothers by regarding his mother as "a figure of the synagogue" and his brothers as a figure "of the Jews." Once inside, Jews now find themselves outside. Grace "comes to an end" for Jews when Christianity "begins."[7] The mother and brothers, figures of the synagogue and the Jews, remain outside the room in which Jesus speaks, his true disciples inside.

That the church is a *replacement* people is the theme of numerous paragraphs in Cyprian's *Three Books of Testimonies Against the Jews*.[8] The "first circumcision" was made void and the "former law" made to cease, with a second circumcision "of the spirit" and "a new law" to be given. A new dispensation, covenant, and baptism replace their older counterparts, as a new yoke, new pastors, and a new temple supplant their shadowy predecessors. The ancient sacrifices, priesthood, and prophet (Moses) have been displaced by the Eucharist and Christ. The newer, younger people take the place of the older.[9] Cyril (c. 315–386), bishop of Jerusalem from about 349, tightly linked his understanding of the church as a catholic people "spread through the whole world" to his view of it as a *replacement* people. Because "the Jews have fallen out of favour because of their conspiring against the Lord, . . . the Saviour has built up from among the gentiles a second assembly or Church." Cyril found support for his view in Psalm 26:5, which he interpreted as David's prediction that the church of the Jews would be cast off: "I hate the company of evildoers" (Ps. 26:5). He read in the final verse of the psalm, "In the great congregation I will bless the LORD" (Ps. 26:12), a description of the church of the Gentiles. Also, according to Cyril, Malachi spoke of the church of the Jews when he said, "I have no pleasure in you," and of the Gentiles as their replacement in stating "from the rising of the sun to its setting my name is great among the nations" (Mal. 1:10–11).[10] To this "second" church, after the rejection of the first, God has given apostles, prophets, teachers, and miracles.[11] Cyril reiterates this point throughout his lectures, where he interprets the prophets as saying that "the grace of life will no longer abide in Israel, but among the Gentiles." This is so because the "people whom he had freed from Egypt and often from other places kept shouting against Him: 'Away with him! Away with him! Crucify him!' Why, O you Jews? Because He healed your blind?"[12] Lactantius (c. 240–c. 320) argued that because of the repeated impieties of the Jewish people God quit sending prophets to them for their correction and, instead, "ordered [Christ] to come down from heaven that He might transfer the holy religion of God to the nations, that is, to those who knew not God, and teach them the justice which the perfidious people had cast aside."[13] Christianity is thus a transferred religion. Augustine used Paul's metaphor of the olive tree to argue the opposite of its point, that "the unbelieving pride of the native branches is broken away from the living patriarchal root, and, by the grace of divine goodness, the faithful humanity of the wild olive is ingrafted," thus turning even Paul's assertion that the church is rooted in the life of Israel into an argument that it is, instead, a replacement people. The people of God is "now the Christians." The vineyard has now been let out to "other vine-dressers." Gentiles have been elected, Jews "cast off."[14]

For Tertullian, the church is a *gentile* and *universal* people. The terms *gentile* and *Christian* are virtually synonymous for Tertullian. "Our" people are gentiles, those who once were committed to the service of idols; God "adopts the gentiles, while the Jews make a mockery of his patience." "We" are adopted by God, "they" are rejected. Tertullian frequently uses the biblical metaphor of the "two peoples," one older, one younger, or the older and younger brothers, claiming that the older (as in the case of Esau) is a "type" of the Jews, the younger (Jacob) a type of "God's later and more honorable people, that is, of ourselves."[15] Jews who were inside the house of God, "found themselves outside when they were thrown out because of their sins," whereas the Gentiles, who were outside, took advantage of the offer of salvation that the Jews refused.[16]

Cyprian, too, elucidates the identity of the replacement people as gentile. Using the two peoples allegory, he contends that wherever two peoples are mentioned, or an older and younger brother, or Jacob's two wives Leah and Rachel, we have types of the synagogue and the church, of Jews and Gentiles: "The elder Leah, with weak eyes, [is] a type of the synagogue; the younger the beautiful Rachel a type of the Church, who also remained long barren, and afterwards brought forth Joseph, who also was himself a type of Christ." The church, which had been barren, has brought forth "more children from among the Gentiles than what the synagogue had before." It is they who now believe in Christ, and therefore in God, whereas Jews do not.[17] Ambrose (c. 339–397) inventively interpreted the story of Naaman the Syrian, who was told by a "maiden from among the captives" of a prophet in Israel who could cure him of his leprosy, as a story about the church. The maiden of the captives "is . . . the younger generation of the Gentiles" who were previously captives of sin but who now believe the word of prophecy which they once doubted. As Naaman the Syrian was healed, so "now all are healed, or at least one Christian people *alone*."[18] For Augustine, Gentiles are the substitute people replacing Jews; the church is being filled up "with the increasing plenitude of the Gentiles." The new covenant is with Gentiles, whereas the Jews "have remained stationary in useless antiquity." This "old" Israel is "natural," "Israel according to the flesh," and, because blind to the signs of the times, are now the "enemies" of God.[19]

The emphasis elsewhere in Tertullian is on the *universality* of the gentile church. The replacement people come from "every race and people and place."[20] All peoples receive God's revelation. Christ takes all nations captive, whereas David ruled over only one. Christ blesses all peoples, whereas Solomon blessed only one. Cyril of Jerusalem claims that the gentile, catholic church "alone bears sway in all the world, and knows no bounds."[21] This gentile church is a church of "all peoples which are under heaven," as Lactantius puts it.[22] That the new, gentile church is a universal church, except for its rejection of Jews, is asserted by Augustine when he claims that the God who delivered the church "shall be called the God of all the earth."[23]

Tertullian claimed that the replacement, gentile, universal people is a *superior* people, "more honorable," more obedient, more ready to accept God's discipline, who give Christ a "better acceptance." Christians have a better liturgy, "new" ceremonies different from the "old," "Jewish," and "legalistic" rites. Christians are able to pray to God, whereas Jews cannot, because the Father is known through the Son and Jews do not know the Son; hence, says Tertullian, "they never really knew the Father." Jewish hands, red with the blood of Christ, cannot be raised to God in prayer, nor can Jews ever be clean; "we, however, enter the font once, and our sins are washed away."[24] Our worship is spiritual, theirs carnal; our sabbaths eternal, theirs temporal. Jewish "carnality" results in blindness to the promises of the Eucharist and Baptism. Christians are *morally* superior to Jews, possessing a spiritual freedom denied to "legalistic" Jews, which results in a Christian "severity" that surpasses Jewish "laxity." The superiority of Christian to Jewish sacraments for Irenaeus consists partly in that Christian sacraments are currently efficacious, whereas Jewish ones are not, partly in that Jews did not make their offerings rightly but, like Cain, "murdered the righteous one," so that "their hands are full of blood." The sacrifice is sanctified by the pure disposition of those offering it.[25] Cyril of Jerusalem agrees that the sacraments of the "old" covenant have "come to an end," which was reflected in the Jews' inability to understand Christ when he spoke to them of eating his flesh and drinking his blood.[26] John Chrysostom argues the inferiority of Jewish sacraments on the grounds that "in the days of the old covenant, . . . men were at a much more imperfect stage," and God was ready to accept blood that they offered to idols, but "now he has provided in its place a more awesome and glorious way of worship."[27] Ambrose of Milan contended that whereas God had rained manna on the Jews, God has granted to the church sacraments that "are more ancient than those of the synagogue and more excellent than manna is."[28] The flesh of Christ is "more excellent" than the bread of angels, so that when the Jews drink of their sacrament they remain thirsty; "when you drink, you will not be able to be thirsty; that was in a shadow, this is truth."[29] Unlike Jews who disbelieved when God spoke to them of earthly things, and proved doubly faithless when God spoke to them of heavenly things, the gentile church is a faithful and superior people. Unsurprisingly, the prototypical Jew is

Judas, who "strangled himself with the halter of his own wickedness." In Judas, the betraying Jews "did violence to two things, more preeminent than all, to faith and duty, and in both to Christ the Author of faith and duty." Hence Jews are children "of iniquity, . . . of pestilence, and . . . of the Devil, as Scripture testifies."[30] Augustine argues that the sacraments and offerings of the Jews are inferior to those of the church, and further contends both that God "refuses to receive a gift from your [the Jews'] hands" and that, in any case, Jews "do not offer Him a gift with your hands," because the only place where they have been commanded to do so is in the church.[31]

The payoff of all this anti-Judaism is that it "describes" Tertullian's church, Tertullian's people, and Tertullian himself. The benefits of the work of Christ are bestowed upon the members of the church who, in contrast to Jews, are blessed, saved, redeemed, and set upon a superior course of life. The ideological character of Tertullian's teachings on the church is too evident to warrant comment. Christianity wins; Judaism loses. We [Christians] are the ultimate beneficiaries of anti-Judaism, because we did the "good work" of switching from idolatry to the worship of God. That this point of view is works-righteous at its heart, that it takes the sheer gift of God's grace in Jesus Christ and turns it into a condition apart from which God is not free to be gracious, is clear. That it plays a significant role in establishing a sense of Christian identity—a way of answering the question "who are we?" by convincing Christians that they are not only other than Jewish, but anti-Jewish, better-than-Jewish, and those with whom God displaces Jews—is also clear. Unfortunately, this way of establishing a sense of Christian identity achieved an incredible success. Cyprian ensures that the payoff is not lost on his readers, calling to their attention the fact that we are the replacement people: scripture speaks of a new people "which should consist of us." We gain what the Jews missed: "That the Jews would lose while we should receive the bread and the cup of Christ and all His grace," that "the Gentiles rather than the Jews attain to the kingdom of heaven."[32] Cyprian is famous for his claim that extra ecclesiam nulla salus, "outside the church there is no salvation." Although his target with this remark was Novatian and the rigorist movement, his understanding that those who are not in the church can neither be loved by Christ nor benefit from his grace clearly applies to Jews as well.[33] Saint Basil (c. 330–379) makes it clear that because "no one considers the people of the Jews blessed," this must refer to "that people which was chosen according to merit from all the peoples." We are this meritorious people: "we are the nation of whom the Lord is our God; we are also the people whom He chose as an inheritance for Himself." Nor will Israel be saved when "all the Gentiles have come in," as Paul had it. Rather, "not just anyone will be saved, but only the remnant which is according to the election of grace." Israel missed its calling in failing to accept Jesus Christ and is properly regarded as "the fool [who] hath said in his heart: 'There is no God.'" Hence, the name of Israel "is not written in the book of the living nor counted with the Church of the first-born which is numbered in heaven." We were elected when they were "cast off." After Christ, the habitation of the Jews was made desolate, and we are those to whom God refers when he says "other sheep I have that are not of this fold."[34] Lactantius agrees that Christ through his death "makes us heirs of the eternal kingdom from which the Jewish people have been debarred and disinherited." Christ has now recognized "us as the heirs of His heavenly kingdom."[35]

The anti-Jewish deformation of the doctrine of the church does not cease with the patristics, but continues through the Reformation era and into the present, although in the present there are also Christian theologians who seek to understand the church in ways appropriate to the gospel and corrected by the covenantal loyalty of Jesus of Nazareth.[36] We may thank God for these recent efforts to redirect Christian theology onto its proper path, but must first take into account the fact that they are a minority voice on the current scene and that we continue to have a problem with the doctrine of the church. The problem stems from the fact that in the Reformation era the Reformers projected onto Jews and Judaism the negative attitudes that they held toward the medieval church, and interpreted both Jesus and Paul as opposing in the first century what the Reformers resisted in the sixteenth. The modern heirs of the Reformers, the liberal and neo-orthodox Protestant theologians of the last two centuries and their analogues in the Roman Catholic Church, persist in this strategy, which we saw clearly in an earlier chapter in Adolf Harnack.

Thomas Müntzer likened opposition to the gospel in his day to the scribes' rejection of Jesus in their day:

> Accordingly the scribes refused him . . . , as they are still accustomed to do today. Verily in fact they have been reenacting the Passion with him, ever since the pupils of the apostles died. They have taken the Spirit of Christ for laughingstock and do indeed as it is written in Psl 69 (11f.). They have quite openly stolen him like the thieves and murderers (John 10:1). They have robbed Christ's sheep of the true voice and have made the true crucified Christ into an utterly fantastic idol. How has this happened? Answer: They have rejected the pure handiwork of God and set in his place a pretty little golden statue of deity, before which the poor peasants slobber, as Hosea has clearly said (ch. 4:8–10) and Jeremiah in Lamentations (ch. 4:5).[37]

That Müntzer fuses past and present, Jews and his current opponents, becomes clear when he says that "all the unbelieving Turks, pagans, and

Jews have very cheaply ridiculed us and held us for fools."[38] Similarly, John Denck regarded Jews as typifying the wrongheaded understanding of salvation to which his understanding of the Christian faith was opposed: "If you believe in a fleshly salvation, then you will have also a fleshly felicity. In this sense Paul [in dealing] with the Jews used the word of Moses about the ways of the perverse, saying [Rom. 10:5]: The man who keeps the commandments shall live by them—as though Paul wished to say: You keep the commandments only outwardly, therefore also you lead no more than a superficial life." Denck's opponents make the same mistake made long before; as "all perverse Jews do and have done," they deny "the law which God has written with his finger on their hearts and sought it [instead] in the book written by human hands."[39]

Dietrich Philips, in outlining the Mennonite understanding of the church, its creation and restoration, its true ordinances, and its ten marks, systematically contrasts it with the people Israel. Starting from the story of Cain and Abel, he claims:

> from that time on there were two kinds of people, two kinds of children, two kinds of congregations on earth, namely the people of God and the devil's people, God's children and the devil's children, God's congregation and the synagogue or assembly of Satan, and that the children of God had to suffer persecution from the children of the devil, and that the congregation of Christ must be suppressed, hunted, and put to death by Antichrist's assembly.

With Christ, Gentiles came into the church, "figures had an end, but the true realities came into being." At this point "did Jerusalem arise and shine," because the light shone upon her and the true knowledge of God appeared. Only through Christ can one enter the kingdom of God and attain the knowledge of God; the law, given to Jews, suffices only to reveal sin. Jews, like Cain, persecute the church (as the Mennonites were persecuted in Philips' time): "Annas and Caiaphas, together with the bloodthirsty Jews, gather together and hold counsel against him, nor can they cease until they have killed him and force Pilate to do their will."[40] Ulrich Stadler conflates his "enemies," the Roman Catholic Church, with the Jews: "For the Babylonian whore who sits on the dragon with seven heads, I mean the Roman church, a synagogue of the living devil, spews out all the children of God and only drives them into the wilderness."[41]

The Protestant Reformation did not reject Cyprian's claim that outside the church there is no salvation, affirming (as, for example, in the Second Helvetic Confession) that "none can live before God who do not communicate with the true church of God, but separate themselves from the same. For as without the ark of Noah there was no escaping when the world perished in the flood; even so do we believe that without Christ, who in the Church offers himself to be enjoyed of the elect, there can be no certain salvation."[42] Although the Confession qualifies this claim by observing that the church is not limited by its signs, the qualification clearly applies to Christians who lack or fail to participate in all the marks of the church. Nor did this exclusivist understanding of salvation disappear in the era of nineteenth-century liberal theology, where we still find Schleiermacher claiming that "the Church alone saves," that "the world, so far as it is outside this fellowship of Christ, is always, in spite of . . . [its] original perfection, the place of evil and sin."[43] Part of the church's animus against the Israel of God reflected its deep anxiety over the question whether God had enough grace to spread it around freely. If not, and if the issue is of ultimate importance, then it is critical that the church stake its claim to salvation, even at the cost of denying it to others and, particularly, to Jews who otherwise have the advantage of having been God's first love.

For Luther's supersessionist and exclusivist understanding of the church, we do not have to turn to his late and scatological anti-Jewish diatribes but find it in his treatment of the doctrine of the church. His 1539 "Sermon in Castle Pleissenburg" deals with the church and was preached when Leipzig joined the Reformation. To open his sermon, Luther comments on the apostles' misunderstanding of Jesus, how they held "fleshly and Jewish notions" and "were hoping for a worldly kingdom of the Lord Christ" and wanted to be rulers in it.[44] It remains the case "to this day" that "Jews have this same attitude and hope for an earthly messiah." To the apostles in the person of Judas Luther attributes the notion that the revelation of God in Christ is to be "meager," including only Jews. This "false Jewish delusion" is why Jesus has to say "no" to Judas. When Jesus claims in John 14 that he will be with those who keep his commandments, he is saying that he will "dwell" with them, which means that "he is prophesying and forgetting the dwelling of Jerusalem, of which all the prophets said: Here will I dwell forever. This dwelling the Lord Christ pulls down and erects and builds a new dwelling, a new Jerusalem, not made of stones and wood, but rather: If a man loves me, and keeps my Word, there shall be my castle, my chamber, my dwelling." Hence the "true church," the "new church is a different dwelling from that of Jerusalem." Jesus Christ "tears down all the prophecies concerning Jerusalem, as if Jerusalem were nothing in his eyes, and he builds another dwelling, the Christian church."[45] Sadly, Luther's utterly appropriate insight, that the church is wherever God's Word is kept, was marred by Luther's anti-Judaism. Luther could not conceive that Jews might keep God's Word.

The Jewish "No"

The church must come clean on the matter of the Jewish "no" to the church's proclamation; this "no" is a proper and faithful response to the church's distortion of the gospel. It has been inherited orthodoxy to interpret the Jewish "no" as a simple and straightforward "no" to Jesus Christ, and to argue that this "no" constitutes the reason for the early and categorical separation of the church and synagogue from each other. Neither claim is true. Initially, Jews were the only people who said "yes" to Jesus Christ, and they did so without entertaining any thought of thereby leaving Judaism. Paul the apostle said of himself two generations after the resurrection that he was "a member of the people of Israel, of the tribe of Benjamin, a Hebrew born of Hebrews" (Phil. 3:5). Until Sabbatai Zvi in the seventeenth century (the last in a long line of messianic claimants), numerous Jews were thought by some of their fellow Jews to be the messiah, yet so to believe never turned their followers into non-Jews.[46] In the most famous case, Rabbi Akiba (ca. 50–135 C.E.) believed that bar-Kochba was the messiah.[47] Yet Akiba remains an authoritative Talmudic rabbi. Nor does an early and categorical separation of Christianity and Judaism from each other seem to have happened. Chrysostom preached his series of sermons "against the Judaizers" in Antioch in 386 and 387 to stop his people's practice of socializing with Jews and attending the synagogue.[48] Well into the Middle Ages, the church published and republished laws trying to ban social intercourse between Jews and Christians.

The Jewish "no" is quite real, but it was a "no" to a displacement ideology of the covenant; a "no" to a spiritualized and dehistoricized understanding of redemption emptied of its this-worldly promises of the end of oppression, war, and injustice; and a "no" to the claim that salvation was now the property of Gentiles and accessible to Jews only on condition that they turn their backs on the God of the Exodus and Sinai. Of the God who displaces Jews with Gentiles and abrogates the covenant made with Israel, Martin Buber comments: "When I contemplate this God I no longer recognize the God of Jesus."[49] The Jewish "no" was a "no" to an invitation to join a church that defined itself as a gentile (not a Jewish) people, as a universal (not a particular, Jewish) people, as a spiritual (not a carnal, Jewish) people, as a replacement (not a replaced, Jewish) people, and as a superior (not an inferior, Jewish) people. This Jewish "no" to the Gentile church's ideological distortion of its own gospel results from a firm decision to remain faithful to the God who had liberated Israel from oppression and who promised someday so to liberate and redeem not only Israel but all the world. Jews could only reject a church whose message denied the validity of the

covenant of Sinai and the importance of a dual fidelity to that covenant—
the fidelity of Israel to Torah and covenant and the fidelity of the God of
Israel to the Israel of God and to God's gracious promise.

The *adversus Judaeos* tradition of the church interprets this Jewish
"no" as a willful "no," a willful "blindness" to the gospel, the truth of
which Jews refuse to see because they always "trifle" when Christians
present to them arguments supporting the Christian faith.[50] Yet Jews,
from the apostle Paul to Martin Buber, have consistently contended that
the Jewish refusal to see the truth of the Christian claim results not from
a voluntary obstinacy but from an *inability* to see the Christian point.
Paul put this down to God's doing, refusing to blame Jews for it, credit-
ing it instead with the fact that the knowledge of the God of Israel had
come to the Gentiles (Rom. 11:25). Because of God's action in hardening Israel, Israel is *unable*, not unwilling, to see the significance of Jesus
Christ. Buber argues: "The church rests on its faith that the Christ has
come, and that this is the redemption which God has bestowed on
mankind. We, Israel, *are not able* to believe this." Rather, says Buber:
"We know more deeply, more truly, that world history has not been
turned upside down to its very foundations—that the world is not yet
redeemed. We *sense* its unredeemedness."[51]

This Jewish "no," as Paul Tillich insisted, is the most profound question that can be put to Christianity. Tillich tells the story of some Polish
Jews hiding out in a graveyard to escape the roundups for Auschwitz. In
one of the graves a young woman gave birth to a boy, assisted by an old
grave-digger. When the child was born, "the old man prayed: 'Great
God, hast Thou finally sent the Messiah to us? For who else than the
Messiah can be born in a grave?' But after three days [he] saw the child
sucking his mother's tears because she had no milk for him." Whereas
Christians talk too readily of redemption having come into the world in
Jesus Christ, the old Jewish grave-digger knew better: "For him, the im-
measurable tension implicit in the expectation of the Messiah was a reality, appearing in the infinite contrast between the things he saw and the
hope he maintained."[52] That tension means that *if* Christians continue to
insist on calling Jesus "the messiah," they cannot do so except in a
sharply dialectical way in which the "not yet" of liberation is consistently
laid alongside the "already" of the gracious knowledge of God to which
Jesus Christ has led some of the Gentiles. I say "if," because there is good
reason to articulate the significance of Jesus Christ without using the title
"*the* messiah." In one sense, it says too much about Jesus Christ, and the
Jewish inability to see this "too much" gives us fair warning that the liberation for which Jews wait on behalf of themselves and all the world lies
still ahead of us, a point of which Paul was poignantly aware when he declared, again two generations *after* the resurrection, "I consider that the

sufferings of this present time are not worth comparing with the glory about to be revealed to us" (Rom. 8:18). Paul almost wholly avoids speaking of Jesus as "the" messiah. In another sense, use of the title "messiah" says too little. Were Jesus simply the liberator of Israel from oppression, not only would that have been the end of the story, but also it would have been to say considerably less of him than the church came to say throughout the process of creedal formulation in Nicaea, Chalcedon, and Constantinople, through which process it struggled to express its conviction that in and through Jesus Christ it had been confronted with the promise and command of the God of Israel, creator and redeemer of heaven and earth.[53]

The Teaching of Respect for Judaism

Another point on which the church needs to come clean is to recognize that its self-understanding is inherently tied up with its understanding of "the other," specifically the Jewish other. The church needs to rid itself of all vestiges of its traditional "teaching and practice of contempt" for Jews and Judaism and in its place put a "teaching of respect" and a theological theory of Jews and Judaism in which Jews can recognize themselves.

By a theological theory of Jews and Judaism that Jews can acknowledge as one in which they are fairly represented, I intend a new criterion of verification for use by Christian theologians and preachers. It is inappropriate for talk of Jews and Judaism to serve the purpose of the self-aggrandizement of Christianity. There must be a twofold criterion: whether such a description serves the purposes of the gospel (the spread in the world of the love of God and the love of the neighbor, including the Jewish neighbor) and whether such a description is one to which those neighbors are willing to give their consent as one in which they find themselves understood. I intend no "philoJudaism" or an unrealistic idealization of Jews and Judaism, but a corrective to the tradition of contempt and to the stereotypes with which that tradition is reinforced.[54]

All religions are ambiguous, Judaism no less than any other; in a nutshell, this is the message of the prophets. But these ambiguities do not serve to distinguish one religion from another. Christians have consistently described Judaism as *essentially* legalistic, hypocritical, works-righteous, judgmental, committed to the letter rather than the spirit of faith. Jews are said to be legalistic and works-righteous if they keep the law, hypocritical if they do not. The church has put them in a no-win situation. By contrast, Christianity is gracious, committed to love and acceptance, and spiritual, everything new and good that Judaism, being old and bad, can never be. Yet legalism, works-righteousness, judgmentalism, and literalism amply characterize the Christianity with which I am familiar.

The church should get out of the business of defaming Jews and Judaism. Jews must have an Anti-Defamation League because for two millennia the church has served as the Defamation League. One way to express the church's newfound sense of responsibility to the Israel of God would be for the church to take over the task of standing up to protect and defend the rights of Jews as of all other persecuted minorities, thus, in effect, putting the Anti-Defamation League out of business.

De-Centering the Church

The church must learn to understand and define itself anew in the light of the good news of God made known to us in Christ Jesus, the word of the promise given to the church of the love of God freely offered to each and all and of the command of God that, in turn, we are to love God with all our selves and our neighbors as ourselves.

The church needs to understand itself in relation to God, the maker and redeemer of heaven and earth, the God of Israel; in relation to Jesus Christ, through whom it comes to the saving and transforming knowledge of the God of a singular promise and a singular command; in relation to the neighbor, the people and creatures of this fragile planet, whom we are commanded to love and to whom we are commanded to do justice; and in relation to the future to which God calls us forward. The church needs to see that its reality can only appropriately be understood and stated in a way that takes the church out of the center of the picture and in place of itself sees there, instead, God, Christ, the neighbor, and God's promise of what is yet to come. What is called for is both a de-ideologizing of the inherited form of the doctrine of the church and a new way of configuring what we understand the church to be given and called to be and do in and for the world. The need for de-ideologizing arises from awareness of the ways in which the church has framed its doctrines, including its doctrine of the church, to justify and reinforce its power. Joseph Haroutunian alerted us to this fact:

> There is no doctrine in orthodox Christian theology that is not in line with the purposes and interests of the ecclesiastical establishments called churches. These establishments have been "the arks of salvation," or places outside of which there is no salvation. Hence, not only the doctrine of salvation but also the other doctrines have been so stated and elaborated as to function in the rationale of these establishments and their practices.[55]

Gustavo Gutierrez proposes a de-centering of the church, turning it away from its "ecclesiocentrism" toward an existence that is not "for itself" but "for others." Although he manifests no particular awareness of it, the *adversus Judaeos* interpretation of the church is one of the severest instances of its ecclesiocentrism and a sign of its readiness to endorse dehumanizing situations. But he rightly contends that were the church to understand itself in relation to God, the gospel, and the neighbor, and so no longer in an ecclesiocentric way, it would discover that it now has to "criticize every sacralization of oppressive structures to which the Church itself might have contributed."[56]

By transcending and eliminating ecclesiocentrism, what is meant is that Christians are not called to believe *in* the church. The ancient creeds of the church, as Hans Küng has made clear, talk of believing *in* God, *in* Jesus Christ, *in* the Holy Spirit, but *not* of believing in the church.[57] Instead the ancient creeds say simply "I believe the church" (*credo ecclesiam*). The absence of the preposition "in" signifies that although the church believes *in* God, Christ, and the Holy Spirit, it can hardly in the same sense be said to believe *in* itself. To do so would confuse the church with that which is ultimate and absolute. The church is *not* God, and to believe that the church is, explicitly or tacitly, is to commit idolatry. The term *church* means community, and the community, which we constitute, can hardly be said to believe in itself. We are a sinful people ever in need of the gracious love of God and of the reminder that God graciously calls us to be the church in order to serve God's larger purpose of the reconciliation of the world to itself and to God. We "believe the church" because it is here, in this context, that we have been and ever and again are laid bare before the promise and command, the call and claim of the God of Israel. Here we learn of God's friendliness toward us, and here we are called to be friends of the Friend of the world.

When we believe *in* the church, as the *adversus Judaeos* tradition obviously does, we believe too much about the church. The problem posed for contemporary theology would be simpler if this were our only difficulty. Unfortunately, we also have the opposite problem that many believe too little about the church. The significant number of people in contemporary America who feel that they can be fully religious without any relation to a religious community is a signal that many Christians find the church dispensable. So far as churches have failed to attend to "the one thing necessary," helping people understand themselves in relation to God and the neighbor, they have encouraged this tendency to relativize themselves and their importance. Another sign of believing too little about the church is found in those forms of church life that foster the idea that the church is merely a voluntary association organized for the purpose of meeting the needs of individuals and families for therapy and lodgelike activities. Relativism and individualism are as significant a deviation from what the church is about as are institutionalism and ecclesiocentrism.[58] "De-centering" the church is not a proposal for subjecting it to the relativism and individualism that tempt it today. Rather, it is a call to understand the church in the light of the critical principle, which Tillich explains as the "protest against any absolute claim made for a relative reality, even if this claim is made by a Protestant church."[59] This absolutistic mistake is made when the church forgets that it is *not* the kingdom of God.

The Purpose of the Church

The church is that community of human beings called into existence by God, through the Holy Spirit, to live from and by the gospel of God, witnessing to the grace and command of the gospel as the call and claim of the God of Israel offered to all the world and hence to the church in Jesus Christ, and doing so both to remind itself of what it is about, and, on behalf of the world, that it might, one day, reflect the glory of God.

Such a definition, hardly incorrigible, is not an attempt to describe the churches in empirical terms but a stab at identifying the indispensable character of the ecclesial community. The churches manifest their indispensable character only fragmentarily and ambiguously.[60] Yet they are not reducible to a sociological description, because, however ambiguous and oppressive they may be, they never cease to risk teaching, proclaiming, and studying the Word of God. Hence they are always in danger of raising up their own critics, and running this risk is a sign of faithfulness. Nor do they fail to pray "forgive us our sins," thus recognizing, albeit often faintly and tacitly, that the church has a lot for which it needs to be forgiven. Nothing about the church is perfect or finished; nor is God done with it. The Reformation understanding of the church de-centered it by bringing it under the norm *ecclesia reformata et semper reformanda* (the church reformed and always reforming). This norm applies to the Reformers themselves, as it does to such proposals as this. Theology, bringing the church to self-understanding and self-criticism, is always unfinished.

The church would do well to understand that it lives from and by the grace of God, that it is given and called to be a grateful community. The proper response to grace is gratitude, not the arrogance and works-righteousness typical of inherited and assumed attitudes toward the church. The core problem with the *adversus Judaeos* understanding of the church was that at its heart lay a works-righteousness which claimed that those in the church were saved because they had done the good work of believing in Jesus Christ, whereas the Jews (and everybody else for that matter) were condemned because they had not done this good work. There is something ugly about smugness.

Just as every aspect of the church's life is to be understood in the light of and to reflect the gracious promise of the love of God freely offered to each and all, so the church is to understand itself as claimed by the command of God that it love God with all its self and its neighbors as itself. The church is to find its center in the love of God and neighbor and its task in spreading abroad love of God and neighbor in the world. It is called to become theo-centric and neighborcentric. The sense of exclusivism and privilege that dog historical formulations of the church's self-understanding must give way to a sense of service to God and to the neighbor.

The church is called to live out a transfigured style of human peoplehood, a transpersonal existence. Transpersonal is neither impersonal nor privatistic. It points to the reality that human life is life in community, that persons become who they are in the transactions between and among themselves. The manner in which community takes shape and persons are formed in the church should be consonant with the gospel, involving respect for one another, love between and among one another, justice (as the social form of love) toward one another. Transpersonal human beings are caught up in the awareness of a growing and dynamic community of loyalty to one another, a loyalty that extends to all God's creatures. The church should reflect that universal community in which human beings in all their variety are taken seriously as children of God for whom Christ died. The tendency to regard everybody who is different, inside or outside the community, as an alienated other onto whom we project our fears, loathings, and mistrust holds no constructive promise for the future. It is an unredeemed form of human relationship, not the unambiguous community of faith and love, unity, and universality that the church is given and called to become.

Rooted in the Jewish people, the church remains essentially related to the Jewish people today and to the synagogue across the street. By "essentially related" I mean that the being, the *esse*, of the church is unintelligible apart from the God of Israel and the Israel of God. The church lives by bearing witness to the grace of the God of Israel made known to it in the Jew, Jesus, who is a gift to it from the God of Israel and from the Israel of God. The church lives by bearing witness to the singular command of the God of Israel, that in response to God's unmerited love for us we are to understand ourselves in any ultimate sense in terms of and only in terms of the love of the God of Israel graciously offered to us and in terms of the command of that same God that we do justice to our neighbors and thereby also love God with all our hearts.

In a way in which Karl Barth did not mean it, the people Israel and the synagogue perform a service for the church, even though they perform this service outside the church. This assistance is *not* that of showing forth in their sufferings the fate of those who rejected Christ; they are *not* the paradigm of divine judgment. The people Israel and the synagogue serve the church by constituting a reminder to it, sometimes audible but more often primarily visible, but always a pertinent and timely reminder that all forms of idolatry are to be resisted. By defining itself as over and against Judaism, better than Judaism, as a new, superior, gentile, and universal people with a better religion and a better God, the church risked defining itself simply as another form of idolatry and oppression that a true witness to the God of Israel must always resist. The mere existence of the Jewish people and the synagogue, entirely apart from the question of the faithfulness and morality of individual Jews (who can sin as boldly as any Christian), reminds the church that its existence stands as a challenge to all gods that are absolutizations of might, race, country, imperialism, gender, injustice, oppression, or the substitution of demonic ecstasy for faith and love. Given our history, it is clear that the church *needs* the synagogue and the people Israel. It would be an act of maturity and repentance to recognize and confess that need and celebrate our inherent relatedness to the people Israel.

The purpose of the church is to make known in the world the promise and command, the call and claim, of the God of Israel, to spread abroad the love of God and of the neighbor. It is to do this through words and deeds, neither words alone nor deeds uninterpreted by words, but both. Words separated from deeds are empty; deeds separated from words are blind. The mission of the church is one that it shares *with* the people Israel, not one that it is to take *to* the people Israel. Its mission is its call from God to bear witness before the world of the promise and command, the grace and task, of God. This mission is itself a gracious gift to the church from the God of Israel, as is Israel's mission of being a "light to the Gentiles" a gracious gift to Israel from the God of Israel. The relationship of the church to the Jewish people today is based on the fact that both have been graciously and irrevocably called and claimed by God. Hence, the church has no conversionary mission to the Israel of God. Its mission to the people Israel is one of service (*diakonia*), not one of proclamation (*kerygma*). Its service may be critical; there may be times when Christians will want to call Jews *back* to faithfulness to the God of Israel, but its service is never to call Jews to convert *from* the God of Israel. Jews, too, may serve the church critically by reminding it of what it is all too prone to forget, that it is called and claimed by the God of Israel.

The idea of a conversionary mission to the Jews is premised upon the theologically absurd notion that Jews are unacquainted with the

God of the Bible. The idea of a conversionary mission to the Jews results, more than anything else, from a Christian resentment at being "younger" brothers and sisters, at being "members" with Jews in the household of God (Eph. 2:19). The *adversus Judaeos* ideology was no longer content with Paul's concern that his Gentile converts be accepted in the church on equal terms with Jews, but chose, instead, to take complete control of the house of God and set conversionary terms for Jewish admission.

Christians need to think carefully about this issue of a conversionary mission to the Jewish people. The pertinent New Testament literature offers no warrant for such a mission. Paul understood himself as an apostle to the Gentiles, claiming that God revealed Jesus Christ to him "that I might proclaim him among the Gentiles" (Gal. 1:16), a theme reiterated in all accounts of Paul's encounter with the risen Christ in the Book of Acts. Paul refers to Jesus Christ who "was declared to be Son of God with power according to the spirit of holiness by resurrection from the dead, Jesus Christ our Lord, through whom we have received grace and apostleship to bring about the obedience of faith among all the Gentiles for the sake of his name" (Rom. 1:4–5). Jesus' last appearance to the disciples in Luke finds him saying "that repentance and forgiveness of sin is to be proclaimed in his name to all the Gentiles [*panta ta ethne*]" (24:47; translation mine). Luke-Acts ends with the claim that the mission to the Jews is over, the time for it passed, and that the gospel will now go to the Gentiles (Acts 28:28). In Matthew, the risen Christ closes the gospel by commissioning the apostle to "make disciples of all the Gentiles [*panta ta ethne*], baptizing them in the name of the Father and of the Son and of the Holy Spirit, and teaching them to obey everything that I have commanded you" (28:19–20; translation mine). The claim that the mission of the church is to "all the peoples" in the sense of all the Gentiles (*ethne*) gains in force from the argument put forward by several biblical scholars that the words *ethnos* and *ethne* in the gospels and the words *goyim* and *ethne* in Jewish sources from the time have the technical meaning of "Gentiles." Hence the Great Commission in Matthew "does not include the nation of Israel." For Matthew, argue these scholars, "the *ethne* and Israel are two distinct entities in salvation history. Although the divine plan required that the gospel be preached first to the Jews (10:5; cf. 15:24, 26), for Matthew the time for the mission to Israel as Israel is over."[61]

Christian mission is a *shared* mission, one in which both the church and synagogue are called to be witnesses of the God of Israel before the world and each other. That common mission has as its goal the hallowing of God's name in the world, the struggle for human dignity, the active pursuit of peace and justice, and the obligation to be signs of hope in

God's future. Israel is commissioned by God to be a light to the Gentiles. So far as the people Israel is concerned, the church's responsibility to it is so to comport itself vis-à-vis Israel as to make clear God's "Yes" to the permanent election of Israel. Unless the church is reconciled with the Israel of God, it is difficult to see how it can claim to be reconciled with the God of Israel.

The Kingdom of God

The church's self-understanding must be relativized in relationship to the kingdom of God as a primary reference point for understanding the church. Feminists object to the term *kingdom* as sexist and patriarchal, and there is no cause to be oblivious to this protest. Two reasons, however, suggest that it might be wise to retain the term *kingdom*. First, no better alternative is available, not one that suggests both a sense of place (somewhere where God rules) and the promise/hope for God's eventual rule over human life. Second, the nature of "rule" or "kingship" in Christian thought that is appropriate to the gospel of Jesus Christ is redefined against all forms of oppression: "You know that among the Gentiles those whom they recognize as their rulers lord it over them, and their great ones are tyrants over them. But it is not so among you; but whoever wishes to become great among you must be your servant, and whoever wishes to be first among you must be slave of all" (Mark 10:42–44; see also Matt. 20:25–27; Luke 22:25–27).

The extent to which the church has felt satisfied that it had overcome and transcended Judaism was identical to the extent to which it was satisfied with itself in its present form. Christianity as the perfect, true, "fulfilled" version of religion was a vast improvement on what preceded it and, in turn, identical with what God had promised. Any sense of disappointment on God's part, at having wanted the kingdom of God and having gotten the church instead, was missing. In short, the church often confuses itself with the "kingdom" of God. This stupefaction results from thinking too highly of the church and is another sign of ecclesiocentrism. At times, it identifies the church and kingdom with each other. At times, it defines the kingdom as the extent to which the world has come under the influence of the church. At other times, it claims that the church is the "present" form of the kingdom, as distinct from the latter's future actualization. These confusions indicate nothing more than theological chaos and institutional self-justification. In two ways did the church congratulate itself: that it had supplanted the Jews in God's favor and transcended Judaism in the claim to the status of perfect religion. Paul's intense awareness, two generations after the resurrection, that the agonies of the present age were not worth comparing to the glory of God *yet* to be revealed (Rom. 8:18), that salvation remains ahead of us (Rom. 13:11), was lost on the church as it de-Judaized itself.

Just as the Torah and the prophets never let the people Israel rest in self-satisfaction, so Jesus Christ calls the church forward to the rule of God that is ahead of it. The wonderful nonending of the Gospel of Mark tells the story of the women followers of Jesus who were asked to "go, tell his disciples and Peter that he is going ahead of you to Galilee" (16:7). Christ transcends the church as much by being "ahead" of it as "above" it, and continues to point it to the kingdom ahead of it.

Nonetheless, the fact that the church constantly repeats the Lord's prayer and petitions God to let God's kingdom come, God's will be done on earth, is a sign of a continuing faithfulness in the church and an awareness on the church's part, however vague, that the kingdom of God relativizes the church. In the light of the promised kingdom, all church structures and organizations are temporary and makeshift. Nor, thank God, is God limited to the church in manifesting God's will in the world. Indeed, because the church idolatrously identifies itself with the kingdom and with the final form in which God's reign will appear on earth, God's rule has often had to make itself visible outside the church and in opposition to the church. Lack of attention to the coming reign of God on the part of the church, which reign was the absorbing passion of Jesus, is part of the reason church people seem massively indifferent to the ambiguities of the churches themselves and to the injustices, brutalities, and wars that are the way of the world. In contrast to this perspective stands the Bible, which is utterly realistic about the world in which we live and proclaims the kingdom of God as a *coming* reality.

What the church needs to be and become in a world where systemic injustices reign over people—where sexism, militarism, racism, classism, ecocide, and the struggle for power predominate—is an honest institution, a sane asylum. A sane asylum is a place where, in the midst of the insanity of the world and its way of going about its business, human beings can understand who they are and what they are called to be and do in the light of the gospel of God. The church as a sane asylum is a place where we can tell each other the truth about oppression, killing, injustice, and prejudice, and preserve each other from the temptation of understanding ourselves inauthentically and acting immorally. The church as an honest institution would be one in which we are encouraged to uncover the liabilities and defects of our political and social life and bring the structures of church and society under the criticism of the kingdom of God. Instead, all too often the church draws a stained-glass curtain between itself and the world (God's first love) in the interest of the privatization of religion. Thus the church is distorted, and it functions to divert attention from the situation of human beings in the world to realms of otherworldly fulfillment.

With the loss of a sense of contrast between the present realities of life and the hoped-for kingdom of God, the church was free to aggrandize itself at the expense of Judaism and the Jewish people. Whereas for the people Israel we cannot separate, and can even hardly distinguish, the coming of the Messiah from the coming of the "days of the Messiah" (the kingdom of God), the church managed to settle comfortably into the present, with its victory in the Constantinian-Theodosian empire, and identify the kingdom of God with the church's reign on earth. From Jesus' sermon on the plain ("Blessed are you who are poor, . . . Blessed are you who are hungry now, . . . Blessed are you who weep now" [Luke 6:20–21]) to the Book of Revelation's vision of the new Jerusalem, the New Testament is dominated by a sense of the contrast between present reality and the promised reign of God:

> See, the home of God is among mortals.
> He will dwell with them as their God;
> they will be his peoples,
> and God himself will be with them;
> he will wipe every tear from their eyes.
> Death will be no more;
> mourning and crying and pain will be no more,
> for the first things have passed away.
>
> (Rev. 21:3–4)

The church's self-satisfied forgetting of the kingdom of God, which allows it to disparage Jews and Judaism as still awaiting that which it grandly proclaims has already arrived, is simply contradicted by Jesus' commitment to the coming eschatological reign of God and by the Book of Revelation's awareness that in the new Jerusalem there will be no mourning and no death. The Book of Revelation describes a reality different from the persecution suffered by its community. The promise of and hope for God's rule on earth lies ahead of both church and synagogue, remaining in the future of Christians and Jews. The purpose of the church and synagogue in relation to each other is to serve as signs of hope in God's future, in the days of the Messiah, the kingdom of God, yet to come, when human dignity, peace, justice, and a sustainable way of life are available for all people. Jews have a keen sense of the unredeemedness of the world. Were Christians to develop an equally keen sense of the provisionality, the incompleteness of the church relative to the kingdom of God, that would constitute a great step forward in taking up our joint mission with the people Israel at the behest of the God of Israel.

The Means of Grace

What the church has traditionally called the "means of grace" (God's word, Baptism, and the Eucharist) are all ways in which Christians are again and again confronted with the promise and command of the God of Israel. Jesus Christ, as preached in the church and present in the sacraments, does today what he did in his lifetime: he confronts his followers with the call and claim of the God of Israel. The singular promise of the love of God freely offered to each and all (God's *hesed*) and the singular command of God that we in turn love God and do justice to all our neighbors are the heart and soul of the word of God and of the sacraments of the church.

The word of God and the sacraments are called "means of grace" because in, through, and under them God effectively acts to confront us again and again with this unique promise and command. God is immediately and effectively active and present in the means of grace because the living God who acts in the present is the One who is the ground and end of all being and therefore present to us in, through, and by means of any and all actualities. Historically, the *adversus Judaeos* tradition of the church claimed that the sacraments were the *only* means of grace, that grace was "channeled," and that apart from the means of grace controlled by the church, grace was not available. The church was the broker of the grace of God, in spite of Jesus' proclamation that God's grace and reigning presence is "among you," if only you want it. A post-Holocaust theology must insist, to the contrary, that there is no reason to limit the means of grace and no reason to deny that the God of Israel encounters God's followers just as effectively through the synagogue. Indeed, this latter must be fully affirmed. Because God is the One who interacts with all others, anything may be a means of grace or sacrament (these terms are used synonymously) provided it is grasped as such. Without the sacramental character of the world as such, that is, of the *sacramentalia*, there can be no great sacraments. The more the Protestant tradition denies the *sacramentalia*, the less significant its great sacraments become and the less frequently they are observed. Yet the means of grace in the Christian sense are defined by the event of Jesus Christ. So, the word (written and oral) is a means of grace, as are Baptism in the name of the Trinity, and the breaking of bread. The means of grace are the modes of activity of the Holy Spirit, because the Holy Spirit is the Spirit of Christ.

The "word" as a means of grace is the self-disclosure of God's love graciously offered to each and all (and therefore commanding that justice be done to each and all) in the form of an *announcement*. This announcement can only be appropriated in faith. It confronts us with the necessity of deciding whether we will understand ourselves in any ultimate sense in terms of and only in terms of God's love freely offered to us. In other words, the basic appropriation of the word takes the form neither of theoretically accepting a doctrine nor of noting that the word expresses certain "religious experiences." Rather, the word tells us who God is, who we are, and what the meaning of Jesus Christ is as the one by whom, through the preaching of the church, we are laid bare before the God of Israel, maker and redeemer of heaven and earth. Preaching as *announcement*, proclamation, is a means whereby we can come to understand ourselves in relationship to God and to the neighbor. It is a word that bears repeating because none of us does not frequently need to "return" to God or to be reminded who it is that we are given and commanded to be. When the word is properly heard, it is heard as the voice of God speaking to us.

The word as a means of grace is a sure and living word. It is sure in the sense that its meaning is clear—it is the word of God who is the God of a unique promise and a unique command—the promise of God's grace lovingly offered to us, and the command to love our neighbors as ourselves, thus fulfilling all the *torah*. It is sure in the sense that it encapsulates the structure of biblical faith (the structure of promise and command, proclamation and paranesis, the indicative [what God has done for us] and the imperative [therefore what we are to do]). It is a living and lively word because it bespeaks the grace of God who is the nurturing and enlivening ground and end of our being. It lives in preaching and teaching, in oral tradition and *kerygma*. The written word(s) of scripture come to life as means of grace when so appropriated. Or, alternatively, we come to life when we appropriate the words of scripture as the Word of God.

The task of preaching is to enable each generation to hear that the word of God is a living and pertinent word, to interpret the events and insights, problems and dilemmas, of that generation in the light of the tradition and to reinterpret prior Christian tradition in the light of the contemporary situation. For example, the church is belatedly coming to realize that the expression "God's love for each and all" includes women as part of the "all," that doing justice to women includes affirming and sharing their struggle to be liberated from a male-dominated and male-defined culture. Insofar as preaching does its job, proclamation is itself a living word of God, necessary to the life of the church. The word of God comes to us as law and as gospel, command and promise. The promise without the command is cheap grace; the command without the promise is works-righteousness. The gospel is not a circle with one center, but an ellipse with two foci. Taken together, both promise and command are the word of God; separated, neither is.

A discussion on the word of God as means of grace would be incomplete without reference to the Hebrew Bible. The "scriptures," which is the New Testament term for the canonical writings of Israel, are every bit as much word of God as are the writings of the first-century church. Whenever in the history of the church the connection between the two was severed, as in Gnosticism, the relation of redemption to creation and of faith to history was also cut, resulting in radical misinterpretations of redemption that privatized it and freed it from the need to engage in the struggle of the neighbor for justice.

The breaking of bread as a means of grace conveys the self-bestowal of God's love—the identical love met with in the word as announcement—in the form of *action*. The function of the sacraments is precisely the same as that of the word of God. They confirm, proclaim, and seal the promise of God to be gracious and are not means of grace in the sense that the grace of God is exclusively channeled through them. Rather, they show and ratify what is given to us by the grace of God. They proclaim, but do not procure, the grace of God. Grace is what God is. It is God's free and unfailing resolve, God's faithfulness (*hesed*), to be for all God's creatures, even us, despite our failure to be for God and for the neighbor. Grace is not one attribute of God among others (such as wrath), with which it alternates. Rather, it is God acting out of God's deepest being. This grace is the cause of faith, and we encounter grace or God in the word of God and in the other means of grace.

For centuries, particular sacraments were defended on the grounds that they had been "instituted" by Jesus of Nazareth. Roman Catholics argued, for example, that when Jesus told his disciples to feed his sheep, he instituted ordination to the priesthood as a sacrament. Many Christians still refer Baptism to the Great Commission (Matt. 28:18–20), which they take as Jesus' "institution" of it. It is not likely, in light of present findings of New Testament scholarship, that Jesus instituted any sacrament. As Alfred Loisy put it: "Jesus foretold the Kingdom, and it was the Church that came."[62] What makes Baptism and the Lord's Supper constitutive factors in the life of the church is their meaning, not our ability to determine exactly when and where, historically, they originated within the church. From early on they have been part of the life of the church, but the church's observance of them (as well as the form of that observance) developed at different speeds in different times and places. Baptism and the Lord's Supper are sacraments because they provide, in the form of action, a comprehensive expression of the central content of the gospel and are organically connected to the church's witness to the significance of Jesus Christ as the one by whom, through the church's action, the promise and command of the God of Israel are again and again re-presented to us. God's love is concretely re-presented in Baptism and the Lord's Supper, which are no mere historical institutions but actions of continuing divine grace.

The significance of the sacraments is not that without them God's grace cannot be communicated or God's love apprehended. As with everything else connected with God's grace, they are a *gift*, and we may not turn the gift into a condition apart from which God is not free to be gracious. Their significance does not lie in the fact that they mediate some kind of grace other than that which is announced to us in the gospel. Their importance lies in the fact that in them the central core of the good news meets us in a concentrated way in the form of an act. The sacraments are a "visible word" (*verbum visibile*), in which the word is not only heard but seen as dramatically acted out.

So-called realistic and symbolic interpretations of the sacraments are two polar misconceptions that live in a parasitic symbiosis with each other. On the realistic (Latin: *re(s)* = "thing" + *alis* [suffix]) interpretation, God's grace becomes a "substance" and works in a physical way and on a level below personal relationships and existential appropriation. Ignatius' reference to the Eucharist as a "medicine" exemplifies this. On this view, the gift received in the sacrament is something other and less than the self-communication of God's grace, God's deepest *self-disclosure*. The "symbolic" (simple memorial) view arose chiefly to deny the realistic view, and it denies the actual as well as real presence of God, thus placing all the emphasis on the human activity of faith and causing the sacrament to lose its character as divine gift and grace.

"Really" is best understood to mean "truly," that Christ is truly present at the Eucharist. That is the way it will be taken here. The Lord's Supper is an action of Christ, of the living Lord present in the Lord's Supper. There is no more essential point to be made about it. Its significance lies in the fact that it is an act of Christ. If it is not so understood, it is reduced to a memorial of what once happened, a remembrance of grace past. Its present significance, then, is constituted entirely by our contemporary piety and not by the grace and command of God confronting us anew in Jesus Christ. As Christ was present at the last supper and at the meals shared with his disciples, so Christ in the supper is *with* his disciples "always, to the end of the age" (Matt. 28:20). In the supper, Christ is re-presented to the church and serves it. Christ is the "celebrant" of the supper, the host of the banquet. When he says to us, "This is my body, broken for you, this is my blood, shed for you," the ever-present reality of God's grace is rendered concrete and vivid.

Christ re-presents the same grace of God that had earlier been re-presented to the people Israel and that continues to be re-presented in the synagogue. Hence, we must understand the grace of God in Christ in the light of God's continuous faithful dealing with the Israel of God. The bread of the supper re-presents the bread that the Hebrew people ate in the exodus from slavery in Egypt, the unleavened bread that had to be baked in haste. This is the bread of freedom, the bread of liberation from every form of slavery, oppression, exploitation, and subjugation. When the bread broken in the Eucharist loses its rootedness in Israel's story, it is wrongly and badly spiritualized, de-spiritualized. The "bread of heaven" theme of John 6 (subtracting its anti-Jewish animus) recalls the manna graciously given by God to the people in the wilderness. It is the bread that kept them from starving, reminding us that God is the nurturing ground of our being, and reminding us that we are to keep the neighbor from starving.

Baptism and the Eucharist must be understood in terms of God's covenant-making grace and covenant faithfulness freely offered to the Israel of God and to the church. Baptism introduces a person into the covenant and the covenantal community. In Communion, God renews with us the covenant into which we were inaugurated at Baptism. Neither Baptism nor the breaking of bread conveys any different or "better" kind of grace than is available to Jews through the synagogue and family. The waters of Baptism recall the waters of freedom through which the Israelites passed at the Exodus; the bread and wine of Communion recall the bread and wine of the Passover-Unleavened bread observances that Jews reenact every Passover. Baptism and the Eucharist re-present the death and resurrection of Jesus Christ. At Baptism we are buried with him in death and rise to newness of life. At the Eucharist we remember, in the sense of making present (*anamnesis*), the gracious love of God manifest in the cross and resurrection. The Exodus/Sinai and cross/resurrection complexes remind us that torture, evil, oppression, coercive power, and brutality are all too real, but that they are not the last reality, not the last word on the subject. God has the last word, and it bespeaks life, liberation, goodness, and righteousness.

The chief gift offered us in the Eucharist is communion with God's self, the self-disclosure of God's loving grace. All other gifts affiliated with the supper are embraced in this offering of God's own self-disclosure. These other gifts are justification by grace through faith, a new and transformed life, and salvation. Protestants have so tended to interpret the gospel simply as justification, rendered as "forgiveness," that they overemphasize the gift of forgiveness of sins and suppress its meaning. By reducing the gospel in effect to a circle with one center, forgiveness, they are reluctant to talk of the gift of the supper as "life," despite the early church's strong emphasis on the gift of new life in the supper ("I am the bread of life" [John 6:48]). The constriction of meaning that results is reflected in the negative understanding of forgiveness as a remission of guilt and punishment. To understand the new and transformed life to which God calls us as a gift, however, enables us to see that God demands nothing of us that God's grace does not enable us to do.

This new life of salvation (understanding oneself appropriately in relation to the promise and command of God and living a new and transformed life in the light of that understanding *is* salvation) is never one that we simply and directly possess amid the conditions of sin and death that characterize our human condition. No talk of newness of life may undialectically ignore the realities of sexism, racism, militarism, terracide, anti-Judaism, exploitation, oppression, and bureaucratic manipulation that mark life on earth. This new life of salvation occurs only under the sign of promise and hope. The gift of salvation in the supper is a foretaste of "the life of the world to come," a present but fragmentary reality.

The Marks of the Church

The marks of the church, classical and reformed, must be reconceived that they might reflect the singular promise and command of the God of Israel made known to us in Christ Jesus and that they might lead the church to understand itself and to act as an agent of justice and liberation in the world.

We have described how the marks of the church in the classical tradition were distorted by the heavily anti-Jewish interpretation given them. The church's catholicity was understood in part in terms of its being a gentile people and in no sense a Jewish people; its universality (catholicity) was set in sharp contrast to Jewish particularism. Its holiness was misunderstood as an empirical holiness descriptive of the church's superiority to the old, inferior Jews, and its apostolicity taken to mean that it had a better God to whom to witness and a better witness to that God to offer than had the Jews.

These are not the only criticisms that may be offered of distortions that came into historical understandings of the marks of the church. Cyprian transformed the understanding of the church's unity by locating it in a line of bishops (instead of in Christ or in the body of Christ), thus bureaucratizing the unity of the church and identifying it with the lineage passed down from generation to generation of the hierarchy. Not to be missed is that he also identified the unity of the church with a line of male clergy. There were misgivings and qualifications in the tradition, but Cyprian settled the distinctive features of Western ecclesiology for more than a millennium. The unity of the church could take on an oppressive character when so tightly linked with bishops who had the power to excommunicate any who might disagree or want to put things differently.

Where the unity of the church is defined by a dynasty of successor male bishops, unity becomes oppressive of diversity and plurality. Laity (the *laos theou*, the people of God) are not truly or fully the church but dependent on, and infantilized by, the bishop whose church it is. Women are infantilized by being forever marginalized in and by the church and are the only members of the church forever stuck in this childlike condition. Men could become bishops; women could not. Children could not be bishops, but they could grow up and become bishops (unless they were little girls). Women were not allowed to grow up.

The apostolicity of the church and its unity were closely connected in this pattern. Apostolicity was precisely a matter of the succession of one male bishop by another all the way back to Peter. Hence apostolicity became construed as clericalism of the worst sort (having nothing to do with the laity's actively bearing witness to the gospel) and hierarchalism or patriarchy. When catholicity is interpreted as the spread throughout the world of the sway of a church whose unity and apostolicity are so construed, the difficulties are compounded.

Where the holiness of the church was identified with certain empirical characteristics that the church possesses (or claims to possess), it tended to marginalize and oppress as sinners all who did not share these traits and/or to absolutize relative forms of behavior. Often in the more sectarian forms of the holiness movement in the church, holiness seems to become little more than clinging to culturally relative modes of dress and transportation. In the churches in which many of us grew up, holiness seemed to have most to do with not going to the movies on Sunday or playing the pinball machine in the corner drugstore. One problem with identifying holiness with an empirical description of communal characteristics is trivializing it.

The classic Reformation marks of the church were and are not any more free from ambiguity and distortion than were the marks of the ancient church. "Where the word is rightly preached" depends on what one understands by the "word" or "rightly," and the incredible splintering of Protestantism into hundreds of denominations testifies to the zeal and ferocity with which people can absolutize different understandings of what constitutes right preaching of the word. The same observation applies with more force to the other Reformation criterion, "where the sacraments are rightly administered." Nothing in all Christian history has been more divisive than different interpretations of the Eucharist. One hardly knows whether to laugh or cry when the Eucharist is defined as the "sacrament of unity." Certainly it should be. But in fact, nothing else has generated as much hostility and division among Christians as disagreement over the Lord's Supper. As the 1529 Marburg colloquy between Luther and Zwingli illustrates, every peace colloquy during the Thirty Years' War broke up over failure to agree on the last item on the agenda—the interpretation of the Lord's Supper.[63]

The first point to be seen is that the marks of the church cannot be taken as simply describing the churches. Instead, the attributes of the church must be taken as what their name implies: tributes, *gifts* to the church from God and expectations placed on it by God. The church can never boast of these attributes because they are more God's gift to it than its attainments and because they always stand ahead of the church beckoning it to become what it is given and commanded to be. Because of the church's awareness that it is not what it is given and called to be, it prays "forgive us our sins."

The unity of the church is more a statement about God than about the church. The church is one because it is grounded in the unity of God, the Holy Spirit, who calls the community into being, creating it out of a wide diversity of peoples, cultures, traditions, races, and languages (Acts 2). Such a community is humanly inconceivable and becoming more so in the late twentieth century. The unity of the church is an ontological unity, having to do with the very being, the *esse* of the church; essentially, the church is one. Empirically, the church is not only many but a divided, jostling, and competing plurality. Genuine unity does not exclude and oppress diversity and plurality in the church any more than it does in a healthy family, which is unfeignedly one but in which the diversity and individuality of its members are prized and respected. Genuine unity is identical with creative plurality, and the mark of creative plurality is that the various members of the plurality remain bound to one another in bonds of love and conversation. Destructive plurality occurs where affection is allowed to die and conversation ceases. Then plurality is not mutually enriching but impoverishing, learning from one another is replaced by ignorance of and hostility toward one another, and diversity becomes simple division.

Such unity occurs in the church, fragmentarily but really, where the diverse members of the body of Christ are aware of and appreciate their essential relatedness to each other, where they love one another with the kind of love with which they have been loved. Where unity is actual, it is a matter of the whole people of God having room in their hearts for one another. What unity then is, finally, is our realizing that God's love for all, including even us, is the only way in which we can appropriately understand ourselves, and that God's command that we love our neighbors as ourselves includes even those different and disagreeable neighbors in the church.

The church also needs to find creative ways to celebrate and affirm its unity with the Jewish people and the synagogue. This unity cannot take the form of attempts to "include" Jews in the church for fear that the church appear "exclusive" of Jews. This is a case where Jews would regard contemporary Christian desires to be inclusive as an all too familiar and oppressive Christian tendency. What is called for is appreciation of Judaism precisely for its differences from and disagreements with Christianity as differences and disagreements in conversation with which Christians might learn something of an alternative understanding of biblical faith. Appreciating the Jewish "no" to Christianity can help Christians not only affirm and celebrate their unity-in-disagreement with the synagogue but can also help them better understand the Christian "yes" to Jesus Christ, who was himself God's "yes" to the covenants and the promises. Odd as it sounds, it just may be that in rediscovering their unity with the Israel of God, Christians might be helped to rediscover their unity with each other. They do seem to have lost both.

Catholicity must be understood in terms of God's love for *all* God's creatures, not only those in the church, and fundamentally as a statement about God's love and the church's mission to spread in the world the love of God and neighbor. This latter it does by proclaiming and working for the liberation of the neighbor from oppression. No longer is it possible to define catholicity as the attempt on the part of the church to enroll every last human being on the earth in membership in the church. No longer can catholicity entail an effort to eliminate from Planet Earth every other faith-tradition in which people find meaning and guidance for the task of being human. No longer can catholicity mean an effort to eradicate Jews and Judaism from the earth through the spiritual genocide of converting all of them. The church's "universality" is eschatologically ahead of it, because this catholicity points to the church's hope in God's promise that all people and the earth itself will be liberated from oppression, abuse, hunger, ignorance of the promise and command of God, and manipulation.

With regard to the people Israel, the church's catholicity takes the form of recognizing that the church's life *is* grounded in the Israel of God, and not just in the life of the people Israel in the past, but of the Jewish people today. Genuine catholicity is compatible with covenantal pluralism when and where it recognizes that catholicity itself is a way of talking first and last about *God's* all-inclusive love. One clue to the genuine meaning of catholicity is the memory of Dietrich Bonhoeffer, who protested against the decision by the "German Christians" (who were followers of Hitler) to remove the word "catholic" from the creed.

The church's holiness, too, is a gift to it from God because the church is created by the Holy Spirit. It is as well a demand of God laid upon the church, as understanding itself in terms of God's love for each and all lays upon Christians the awareness that they are called to live a new and transformed life of love and service to the neighbor. Like genuine unity and catholicity, holiness remains also an eschatological concept. The church is a communion of sinners as much as of saints, as much a *communio peccatorum* as a *communio sanctorum* or of sinners called to be saints. Christians who have trouble with the idea of being called to lead a new and transformed life have a far too de-Judaized understanding of Christianity. The fact that God gives the church a distinctive word to say to the world, and a distinctive witness to make to it with its life as well as its statements, means that the church will be and look "different" to the extent to which it carries out its witness. Christians cannot convert this proposition to make it say that the odder they seem, the more faithful to God's mission they are. Yet fear of being "different" from the surrounding culture is probably what, more than anything else, deters contemporary churches from taking seriously the command of God that we work for justice for our neighbors. Further, holiness is to be understood as deriving from the indwelling of God's Spirit in the church, not from the attainment or worthiness of Christians. Holiness is what is at stake in heeding Jesus' comment to his followers: "You are the light of the world" (Matt. 5:14).

Last, apostolicity is an essential trait of a community that understands itself in terms of the gospel of God's love freely offered to each and all and God's command that they in turn love God by loving and seeking justice for each and all of God's beloved. A community that lives from and by this word, that takes the risk of hearing and studying it and seeks in turn to witness to it before other people as the only ultimate way in which they believe that human beings may authentically understand themselves will of necessity be an apostolic community. The entire community is apostolic because it is given an apostolic message to bear (the gospel), because it is called to an apostolic function (spreading in the world the love of God and of the neighbor), and because in every generation it is characterized by the gift to and presence in it of the apostolic truth.

Apostolicity also has to do with the need of the church in every generation to have authoritative (*not* authoritarian) preachers and teachers of the Christian faith. Here the point is diametrically opposite to Cyprian's authoritarianism and hierarchalism. The apostolic teaching functions of the church can and should be carried out by any Christians who care enough to prepare themselves to do so, which should be the only criterion for whether one can be set aside (ordained) by the church for that purpose. It is not the case that only the ordained should be allowed to teach the Christian faith. But it is the case that those who cannot teach the Christian faith should not be ordained. The church ordains people, not to assign to them a higher status, but to see to it that the church is nowhere without an authoritative teacher of the faith. Apostolicity also calls the church to participate in service (*diakonia*), service that bears witness to the love of neighbor and the love of God, and not only in the formal teaching functions of the church.

The church is apostolic in Paul's sense where it understands and makes clear that the news of God's grace that justifies the ungodly is true for both Jews and Gentiles, and where it makes clear that the command of God that we love God and one another applies both to Gentiles and Jews.

Endings and Beginnings

In the beginning, Jesus of Nazareth led a movement committed to the restoration of the Jewish people and, especially, to the lost sheep of the house of Israel, an inclusive movement opposed to the drawing of lines within the people of God. Later, Paul the apostle pressed this inclusive logic further, arguing for the legitimacy of his Gentile converts and their right to participate as equals in the church without having to observe Jewish identity markers. The promise to Abraham, he said, was confirmed, and Gentiles along with Jews are children of Abraham. That promise could not be ratified without Gentile inclusion. Judaism without Gentiles was not the final form of the people of God.

Neither, therefore, is a Gentile church, separate from the Israel of God, the final form of the people of God. In the beginning and in the apostolic witness to that beginning, there is authorization for a mission to the Gentiles in the work of the risen Jesus and the apostolate of Paul, but there is no New Testament warrant for the existence of a Gentile church separate from the Israel of God. If the numbers of the children of Abraham could not be filled up without including Gentiles, how today can the church be oblivious to its own incompleteness, its lack of any vital relation to the Israel of God?

God is not yet done with the church and the synagogue. In an age when ecumenism seems on the wane, when disputatiousness grows as much within as between denominations, thinking that God has yet some future in store for the synagogue and the church together is nothing short of a pipe dream, ridiculous. But, then, the promise to Abraham, aged seventy-five, and Sarah, barren, that their offspring would be as numerous as the sands of the sea and that through them the Gentiles would be blessed, was equally preposterous. Biblical faith itself is preposterous, yet true.

At the heart of the Jesus movement and the theology of Paul was a denunciation of every effort to place limits and conditions on the gracious love of God. That God justifies the ungodly, that this is true for all "others" if it is true for Christians, that it is not their place to instruct God as to the limits to be put on the divine grace, that God can and will do new things that none of us can either imagine or anticipate—all this is at the heart of Christianity's apostolic witness. So we may dream the pipe dream of some future changed relationship between the church and the Jewish people, and work toward it, when the first schism within the people of God will be overcome, when both church and synagogue will look different from the way they do now, when the church's days of wandering in the wilderness of exclusivist anti-Judaism finally come to an end and we all enter into God's promise to the children of Abraham.

Notes

_·—·—·—·—·—·—·—·_

Chapter 1: Theology After the _Shoah_

1. Some scholars prefer the term _Shoah_ to "Holocaust," because the latter has biblical connotations referring to an offering made by fire unto the Lord. Hence "Holocaust" is inappropriate when applied to the Nazi "final solution of the Jewish problem," because nothing could have been further from Nazi intentionality than to make an offering to the God of Israel. However, the term "holocaust" has become so well established that it communicates better than _Shoah._

2. See, for example: David E. Demson, "Israel as the Paradigm of Divine Judgment: An Examination of a Theme in the Theology of Karl Barth," _Journal of Ecumenical Studies,_ 26 no. 4 (1989), 611–627; Judith Plaskow, "Christian Feminism and Anti-Judaism," _Cross Currents_ 28 (1978), 306–309; Susannah Heschel, "The Denigration of Judaism as a Form of Christian Witness," in _A Mutual Witness,_ ed. Clark M. Williamson (St. Louis: Chalice Press, 1992), pp. 33–47; Clark M. Williamson, "Christ Against the Jews: A Review of John Sobrino's Christology," in _Christianity and Judaism: The Deepening Dialogue,_ ed. Richard W. Rousseau, S.J. (Scranton, Pa.: Ridge Row Press, 1983), pp. 145–154.

3. Sally A. Smith, "Tried and Condemned," _The Disciple_ 17 (March 1990), 35.

4. For an explanation of how anti-Judaism is learned by participation in church life, see Rodney Stark et al., _Wayward Shepherds_ (New York: Harper & Row, 1971).

5. Of the sixteen uses of "hypocrite(s)" in the New Testament, thirteen occur in Matthew, all directed at Jews. The tendency of Christians to think of Jews as essentially hypocritical is something for which we have Matthew to thank.

6. Auschwitz was one of six "killing centers" operated by the Nazis. Other concentration camps, such as Theresienstadt and Dachau, were

not killing centers, although 90 percent of the Jews assigned to them were slaughtered. Because more Jews were killed there than anywhere else, Auschwitz has become a symbol for the Nazi program to rid the world of Jews. For a discussion of the death factories, see Raul Hilberg, *The Destruction of the European Jews* (New York: Harper & Row, 1979), pp. 555–635.

7. Although the later Barth's position seems to have changed, in ways discussed in Chapter 5, his earlier views were particularly dreadful. See Karl Barth, *Church Dogmatics,* vol. 2, pt. 2, trans. G. W. Bromiley et al. (Edinburgh: T. & T. Clark, 1957), pp. 206–236.

8. Johann-Baptist Metz, *The Emergent Church,* trans. Peter Mann (New York: Crossroad, 1981), p. 29.

9. "Supersessionism" comes from two Latin words: *super* (on or upon) and *sedere* (to sit), as when one person sits on the chair of another, displacing the latter. Supersessionist theology is also called displacement theology for its claim that Christians replace Jews in the covenant with God.

10. Rosemary Ruether, *Faith and Fratricide* (New York: Seabury Press, 1974), pp. 117–182.

11. David Patrick Efroymson, "Tertullian's Anti-Judaism and Its Role in His Theology" (Ph.D. diss., Temple University, 1976), pp. 223, 224.

12. On this point, see Gregory Baum, "The Holocaust and Political Theology," in *The Holocaust as Interruption,* ed. Elisabeth Schüssler Fiorenza and David Tracy (Edinburgh: T. & T. Clark, 1984), p. 35.

13. Ruether, *Faith and Fratricide,* p. 183.

14. For a list of some canon and state laws, see Clark M. Williamson, *Has God Rejected His People?* (Nashville: Abingdon Press, 1982), pp. 106–112.

15. Augustine, *Reply to Faustus,* in *Disputation and Dialogue,* ed. Frank E. Talmage (New York: KTAV, 1975), pp. 28–32.

16. See Williamson, *Has God Rejected His People?,* pp. 114–118.

17. See Gustavo Gutierrez, *A Theology of Liberation,* trans. Sister Caridad Inda and John Eagleson (Maryknoll, N.Y.: Orbis Books, 1983), p. 15.

18. Peter von der Osten-Sacken, *Christian-Jewish Dialogue,* trans. Margaret Kohl (Philadelphia: Fortress Press, 1986), p. 135. This point is confirmed in any standard history of Christian thought.

19. See the excerpt from the *Malleus Maleficarum* in *Women and Religion,* ed. Elizabeth Clark and Herbert Richardson (New York: Harper & Row, 1977), pp. 116–130, and Leon Poliakov, *The History of Anti-Semitism,* trans. Richard Howard (New York: Schocken Books, 1974), pp. 137–153.

20. *The Gospel of Mary,* ed. Douglas M. Parrott, in James M. Robinson, gen. ed., *The Nag Hammadi Library* (San Francisco: Harper & Row, 1977), p. 472.

21. Alan T. Davies, "The Aryan Christ," *Journal of Ecumenical Studies* 12, no. 4 (Fall 1975), 571.

22. Sandra M. Schneiders, "Does the Bible Have a Postmodern Message?" in *Postmodern Theology,* ed. Frederic B. Burnham (San Francisco: Harper & Row, 1989), p. 67.

23. A. Roy Eckardt, *Black—Woman—Jew: Three Wars for Human Liberation* (Bloomington: Indiana University Press, 1989), p. 3.

24. Ibid., p. 15.

25. Ronald J. Allen and I have addressed these issues in a practical theology for preaching: *A Credible and Timely Word* (St. Louis: Chalice Press, 1991).

26. An interesting example of such an approach is Jane Schaberg's *The Illegitimacy of Jesus* (San Francisco: Harper & Row, 1987). Schaberg's concern for fatherless children and husbandless women is entirely commendable, but does Jesus have to have been illegitimate in order for us to be responsible?

27. David Tracy suggests that historical-critical inquiry into the earliest witnesses to Jesus can perform this function. See his *The Analogical Imagination* (New York: Crossroad, 1981), pp. 237–241. The term "empirical-historical Jesus" is Schubert M. Ogden's. See his *The Point of Christology* (San Francisco: Harper & Row, 1982), pp. 56, 58, 59–64, 87.

28. John Bowden, *Jesus: The Unanswered Questions* (London: SCM Press, 1988), p. 8.

29. This point was well made by George Foot Moore, "Christian Writers on Judaism," *Harvard Theological Review* 14 (1921), 197–254; it has been made more recently by Robert L. Wilken, *The Myth of Christian Beginnings* (Garden City, N.Y.: Doubleday, 1971), p. 17.

30. Jeffrey Stout, *Ethics After Babel* (Boston: Beacon Press, 1988), p. 164.

31. Charles Hartshorne, *Omnipotence and Other Theological Mistakes* (Albany: SUNY Press, 1984), p. 98.

32. George Lakoff and Mark Johnson, *Metaphors We Live By* (Chicago: University of Chicago Press, 1980), p. 4.

33. Henry Nelson Wieman, *The Source of Human Good* (Carbondale: Southern Illinois University Press, 1946), pp. 58–61.

34. Paul Tillich, *Systematic Theology*, vol. 3 (Chicago: University of Chicago Press, 1963), p. 234.

35. Wieman, *The Source of Human Good*, pp. 64, 55–65.

36. David Tracy, *Plurality and Ambiguity* (San Francisco: Harper & Row, 1987), p. 18.

37. Karl Barth, *The Humanity of God*, trans. J. N. Thomas and Thomas Wieser (Richmond: John Knox Press, 1960), p. 32.

38. Irving Greenberg, "Cloud of Smoke, Pillar of Fire," in *Auschwitz: Beginning of a New Era?* ed. Eva Fleischner (New York: KTAV, 1977), p. 23.

39. Elie Wiesel, *Night* (New York: Avon Books, 1969), p. 76.

40. In this sense, John T. Pawlikowski, O.S.M., speaks of the re-Judaization of Christianity in *Sinai and Calvary* (Beverly Hills: Benziger, 1976), pp. 222–229.

41. Gary L. Comstock coined the term "pure narrative theology" in "Two Types of Narrative Theology," *Journal of the American Academy of Religion* 55 (Winter 1987), 688.

42. Among the "postliberal" theologians are George Lindbeck, *The Nature of Doctrine* (Philadelphia: Westminster Press, 1984), Stanley Hauerwas, *Against the Nations* (Minneapolis: Winston Press, 1985), and Hans Frei, "Eberhard Busch's Biography of Karl Barth," in *Karl Barth in Re-View*, ed. H. Martin Rumscheidt (Pittsburgh: Pickwick Press, 1981).

43. Lindbeck, *The Nature of Doctrine*, p. 22.

44. Stanley Hauerwas, *A Community of Character* (Notre Dame: University of Notre Dame Press, 1981), p. 37; for Hauerwas, "truthfulness" means both telling the story accurately and living it out in concrete discipleship.

45. Comstock, "Two Types of Narrative Theology," p. 688.

46. Schneiders, "Does the Bible Have a Postmodern Message?" p. 65.

47. See Ogden, *The Point of Christology*, p. 94.

48. Gregory Baum, "Catholic Dogma After Auschwitz," in *Anti-Semitism and the Foundations of Christianity*, ed. Alan T. Davies (New York: Paulist Press, 1979), p. 141.

49. Ronald F. Thiemann, *Revelation and Theology: The Gospel as Narrated Promise* (Notre Dame: University of Notre Dame Press, 1985).

50. Michael Goldberg, "God, Action, and Narrative: *Which* Narrative? *Which* Action? *Which* God?" *Journal of Religion* 68 (January 1988), 43, 44.

51. Ibid., pp. 47 (emphasis Goldberg's), 48, 51, 54–55.

52. Jack Dean Kingsbury, *Matthew as Story* (Philadelphia: Fortress Press, 1986), pp. vii, 3–5, 7–8, 10.

53. Ibid., pp. 10, 19, 23, 127, 128.

54. Wilken, *The Myth of Christian Beginnings*, pp. 21, 25, 36.

55. Ibid., pp. 158, 197.

56. Cited in ibid., pp. 48, 60.

57. Delwin Brown, "Struggle till Daybreak: On the Nature of Authority in Theology," *Journal of Religion* 65 (January 1985), 15–16. Here I follow Brown's analysis.

58. Ibid., p. 21.

59. Cited in ibid.

60. Ibid., pp. 23, 27, 32.

61. Judith Plaskow, "'It Is Not in Heaven': Feminism and Religious Authority," *Tikkun* 5 (March/April 1990), 39, 40.

62. For accounts of the "German Christian" movements and their intellectual leadership, see James A. Zabel, *Nazism and the Pastors* (Missoula, Mont.: Scholars Press, 1976), and Robert P. Ericksen, *Theologians Under Hitler* (New Haven: Yale University Press, 1985).

63. Karl Barth, *Church Dogmatics*, vol. 1, pt. 1, trans. G. T. Thompson (Edinburgh: T. & T. Clark, 1936), p. 1.

64. Schubert M. Ogden so formulates the relationship between the church's making of the Christian witness and the theologian's critical reflection on that witness. See his *On Theology* (San Francisco: Harper & Row, 1986), pp. 1–21.

65. "Canonical criticism" is a technical term coined by James A. Sanders to refer to his proposal for scriptural authority. See his *Canon and Community* (Philadelphia: Fortress Press, 1984). I have discussed this proposal in relation to other efforts to ground a norm of appropriateness in "The Authority of Scripture After the *Shoah*," in *Faith and Creativity*, ed. George Nordgulen and George W. Shields (St. Louis: CBP Press, 1987), pp. 125–142.

66. Alfred North Whitehead, *Process and Reality*, corrected ed., ed. David R. Griffin and Donald W. Sherburne, (New York: Free Press, 1978), p. 15.

67. Rowan D. Williams, "Postmodern Theology and the Judgment of the World," in *Postmodern Theology*, ed. Frederic B. Burnham (San Francisco: Harper & Row, 1989), pp. 93, 94.

68. Sanders, *Canon and Community*, p. 52.

69. Ibid., p. 53.

70. Marinus de Jonge, *Christology in Context* (Philadelphia: Westminster Press, 1988), p. 72.

71. Sanders, *Canon and Community*, p. 43.

72. Ibid., p. 28.

73. Alfred North Whitehead, *Religion in the Making* (New York: Macmillan, 1926), pp. 29, 31, 30.

74. H. Richard Niebuhr, *The Meaning of Revelation* (New York: Macmillan, 1941), pp. 93, 94.

75. Friedrich Schleiermacher, *The Christian Faith*, trans. H. R. Mackintosh and J. S. Stewart (Edinburgh: T. & T. Clark, 1928), pp. 83–85, proposition 17.

76. Ibid., pp. 112–118, proposition 27.

Chapter 2: The Church and the Jewish People

1. To name certain writings "anti-Jewish" is to give them the name they took for themselves, as in Augustine's *Tractatus Adversus Judaeos (Tract Against the Jews)*.

2. Summaries of these and other canon laws can be found in Williamson, *Has God Rejected His People?*, pp. 107–110, and *When Jews*

and Christians Meet (St. Louis: CBP Press, 1989), pp. 61–62. A large catalogue is available in James H. Parkes, *The Conflict of the Church and the Synagogue* (New York: Atheneum, 1977), pp. 379–391. All the canons of Elvira are found in Jan L. Womer, ed., *Morality and Ethics in Early Christianity* (Philadelphia: Fortress Press, 1987), pp. 75–82.

3. Helga Croner, comp., *Stepping Stones to Further Jewish-Christian Relations* (New York: Stimulus Books, 1977), p. 48.

4. Clark M. Williamson and Charles Blaisdell, "Disciple Contributions and Responses to Mainstream Theology: 1880–1953," in *A Case Study of Mainstream Protestantism*, ed. D. Newell Williams (Grand Rapids: Eerdmans, 1991), pp. 129–137.

5. Alan Brockway et al., *The Theology of the Churches and the Jewish People* (Geneva: WCC Publications, 1988), pp. 112, 5–8, 23, 42.

6. Statements from the Swiss Protestant Church Federation, in ibid., pp. 86–87; and from the Norwegian Bishops' Conference, in ibid., p. 91.

7. Brockway et al., *The Theology of the Churches and the Jewish People*, pp. 93, 98, 103.

8. This phrase is Alice L. Eckardt's name for the new confessions being written by councils, synods, and assemblies of the church on relations between Jews and Christians. See Alice L. Eckardt, "A Christian Problem: Review of Protestant Documents," in *More Stepping Stones to Jewish-Christian Relations*, comp. Helga Croner (New York: Paulist Press, 1985), p. 19.

9. "The Ten Points of Seelisberg," in Croner, *More Stepping Stones*, pp. 32–33.

10. This important declaration can be found in Walter M. Abbott, S.J., ed., *The Documents of Vatican II* (New York: America Press, 1966), pp. 660–668.

11. See J. L. Austin, *Philosophical Papers*, ed. J. O. Urmson (Oxford: Oxford University Press, 1961), pp. 220–239, for a discussion of "performative utterances."

12. Whitehead, *Process and Reality*, pp. 259, 187.

13. The "call forward" is John B. Cobb's name for one way that God works efficaciously in the world. See his *God and the World* (Philadelphia: Westminster Press, 1969), pp. 45–66.

14. 1980 Roman Catholic German Bishops' Conference; in Croner, *More Stepping Stones*, p. 140.

15. Statement of the 1987 General Assembly of the Presbyterian Church (U.S.A.); in Brockway et al., *The Theology of the Churches and the Jewish People*, p. 115.

16. Ibid., pp. 115, 100, 92–93, 90–91.

17. Ibid., pp. 66–69, 62.

18. Ibid., pp. 40, 36, 5–11.

19. Croner, *Stepping Stones*, p. 20.

20. The 1967 Belgian Protestant Council on Relations Between Christians and Jews; in Croner, *More Stepping Stones*, p. 195.

21. Croner, *More Stepping Stones*, pp. 229–230, 2, 141, 31, 87.

22. Croner, *Stepping Stones*, p. 46.

23. A study by the Council of the Evangelical Church in Germany, 1975; in ibid., p. 138.

24. Croner, *Stepping Stones*, p. 1.

25. "Joint Catholic Protestant Statement to Our Fellow Christians, 1973"; in ibid., p. 152.

26. 1977 Mennonite European Regional Conference; in Croner, *More Stepping Stones*, p. 205.

27. 1967 Belgian Protestant Council on Relations Between Christians and Jews; in ibid, p. 194.

28. 1982 Texas Conference of Churches; in ibid., p. 186.

29. 1984 National Conference of Brazilian Bishops; in ibid., p. 152.

30. 1987 General Assembly of the Presbyterian Church (U.S.A.); in Brockway et al., *The Theology of the Churches and the Jewish People*, p. 110.

31. 1977 Central Board of the Swiss Protestant Church Federation; in ibid., pp. 84–85.

32. Central Committee of Roman Catholics in Germany, 1979; in Croner, *More Stepping Stones*, p. 113.

33. Croner, *More Stepping Stones*, p. 161.

34. Brockway et al., *The Theology of the Churches and the Jewish People*, p. 38.

35. 1980 Roman Catholic German Bishops' Conference; in Croner, *More Stepping Stones*, p. 139.

36. "A Statement to Our Fellow Christians," National Council of Churches (U.S.A.), 1973; in Croner, *Stepping Stones*, p. 155.

37. 1975 Council of the Evangelical Church in Germany; in ibid., p. 141.

38. Belgian National Catholic Commission for Relations Between Christians and Jews, 1973; in ibid., pp. 57–58.

39. Statement of Christian-Jewish Coordinating Committee of Vienna, 1968; in ibid., p. 42.

40. Synod of the Evangelical Church of the Rhineland, 1980; in Brockway et al., *The Theology of the Churches and the Jewish People*, p. 93.

41. Franklin H. Littell, *The Crucifixion of the Jews* (New York: Harper & Row, 1975), pp. 29–32.

42. Synod of the Evangelical Church of the Rhineland, 1980; in Brockway et al., *The Theology of the Churches and the Jewish People*, p. 94.

43. 1975 Guidelines of the Galveston-Houston Archdiocese; in Croner, *More Stepping Stones*, p. 67.

44. 1980 Roman Catholic German Bishops Conference; in ibid., p. 125.

45. Diocesan Synod [Roman Catholic] of Vienna, published in the *Handbuch der Synode*, 1969–1970; in Croner, *Stepping Stones*, p. 46.

46. British Working Group for World Council of Churches Consultation on the Church and the Jewish People, 1977; in Croner, *More Stepping Stones*, p. 162.

47. Croner, *Stepping Stones*, pp. 13, 50, 51–52, 32, 90.

48. Brockway et al., *The Theology of the Churches and the Jewish People*, p. 66.

49. Statement of the Synod of the Evangelical Church of the Rhineland, 1980; in Brockway et al., *The Theology of the Churches and the Jewish People*, p. 93. According to Alice L. Eckardt, the authors of the statement insist that the text is meant to refer to Jesus Christ as the Messiah *from*, not *of*, Israel. See Eckardt, "Review of Protestant Documents," in Croner, *More Stepping Stones*, p. 21.

50. 1985 Roman Catholic Commission for Religious Relations with the Jews; in Croner, *More Stepping Stones*, pp. 226–227.

51. Council of the Evangelical Church in Germany, 1975; in Brockway et al., *The Theology of the Churches and the Jewish People*, p. 76.

52. 1969 Suggestions for the application of *Nostra Aetate*, Rome; in Croner, *Stepping Stones*, p. 9.

53. 1973 French Bishops' Committee for Relations with Jews; in ibid., p. 62.

54. 1970 Pastoral Council of the Roman Catholic Church in the Netherlands; in ibid., p. 53.

55. Vatican Commission for Religious Relations with the Jews; in ibid., p. 13.

56. Guidelines for Catholic-Jewish Relations, U. S. National Conference of Catholic Bishops, 1967; in ibid., p. 20. See also 1969 Joint Protestant-Catholic Statement; in ibid., pp. 152–153.

57. 1968 Christian-Jewish Coordinating Committee of Vienna; in ibid., p. 45.

58. 1973 National Catholic Commission for Relations Between Christians and Jews, Belgium; in ibid., p. 57.

59. 1973 French Bishops' Committee for Relations with Jews; in ibid., p. 62.

60. 1979 Ecumenical Commission, Archdiocese of Detroit; in Croner, *More Stepping Stones*, p. 88.

61. 1985 Roman Catholic Commission for Religious Relations with the Jews; in ibid., p. 227.

62. 1968 Christian-Jewish Coordinating Committee of Vienna; in Croner, *Stepping Stones*, pp. 37, 43.

63. 1970 Synod of the Reformed Church, Holland; in ibid., p. 98.

64. 1973 "Statement to Our Fellow Christians"; in ibid., p. 151.

65. 1979 Central Committee of Roman Catholics in Germany; in Croner, *More Stepping Stones*, p. 116.

66. Brockway et al., *The Theology of the Churches and the Jewish People*, p. 93.

67. 1984 Synod of the German Evangelical Church; in Croner, *More Stepping Stones*, p. 218.

68. 1975 Lutheran World Federation; in Croner, *Stepping Stones*, p. 127.

69. 1979 Central Committee of Roman Catholics in Germany; in Croner, *More Stepping Stones*, p. 117. See also the 1975 study of the Council of the Evangelical Church in Germany; in ibid., p. 133.

70. 1977 Roman Catholic Study Outline on the Mission and Witness of the Church; in ibid., p. 45.

71. Reformed Church of Holland, 1980; in Croner, *Stepping Stones*, p. 91.

72. WCC Considerations on Dialogue, 1982; in Brockway et al., *The Theology of the Churches and the Jewish People*, p. 39.

73. General Assembly of the Presbyterian Church (U.S.A.), 1987; in ibid., p. 109.

74. Ibid, p. 112.

75. The Commission on Faith and Order, 1967; in ibid., p. 24.

76. Ibid., p. 41.

77. Ibid., pp. 112–114.

78. 1977 Study Outline on the Mission and Witness of the Church; in Croner, *More Stepping Stones*, pp. 44, 47.

79. Roger Cardinal Etchegaray of Marseilles at a Plenary Session of the Synod of Bishops on Reconciliation, Rome, 1983; in ibid., p. 62.

80. Brockway et al., *The Theology of the Churches and the Jewish People*, p. 102.

81. General Assembly of the Presbyterian Church (U.S.A.); in ibid., p. 118.

82. See the declaration of the Baden Provincial Synod of the German Evangelical Church, 1984; in Croner, *More Stepping Stones*, p. 219. Numerous Roman Catholic statements as well as those of the Bristol Report, the United Methodist Church, and the American Lutheran Church call attention to the mutual commitment of Jews and Christians to promote social welfare.

83. Texas Conference of Churches, 1982; in Brockway et al., *The Theology of the Churches and the Jewish People*, p. 98.

84. See, for example, the Pastoral Recommendations of the Pastoral Council of the Roman Catholic Church in the Netherlands, 1970; in Croner, *Stepping Stones*, pp. 48–55.

85. Clark M. Williamson and Ronald J. Allen, *Interpreting Difficult Texts: Anti-Judaism and Christian Preaching* (Philadelphia: Trinity Press International; London: SCM Press, 1989), pp. 9–27.

86. See Stark et al., *Wayward Shepherds.*

87. Ecumenical Commission of the Archdiocese of Detroit; in Croner, *More Stepping Stones,* p. 90.

88. Notes on the Correct Way to Present the Jews and Judaism in Preaching and Catechesis in the Roman Catholic Church; in ibid., p. 230.

89. See Williamson and Allen, *Interpreting Difficult Texts,* pp. 112–120.

Chapter 3: Jesus of Nazareth

1. Howard Clark Kee, *Jesus in History: An Approach to the Study of the Gospels* (San Diego: Harcourt Brace Jovanovich, 1977), p. 83.

2. Paula Fredriksen, *From Jesus to Christ* (New Haven: Yale University Press, 1988), p. vii.

3. See George Foot Moore, *Judaism in the First Centuries of the Christian Era,* 3 vols. (Cambridge: Harvard University Press, 1927–30); E. P. Sanders, *Paul and Palestinian Judaism* (London: SCM Press, 1977); Charlotte Klein, *Anti-Judaism in Christian Theology,* trans. Edward Quinn (Philadelphia: Fortress Press, 1978).

4. Norman Perrin, *Rediscovering the Teaching of Jesus* (New York: Harper & Row, 1976), pp. 15–16. See also Kee, *Jesus in History,* p. 299.

5. Perrin, *Rediscovering the Teaching of Jesus,* pp. 39, 43.

6. Ibid., p. 92.

7. Ibid., p. 94 (emphasis mine). For E. P. Sanders' criticism of Perrin on this point, see his *Jesus and Judaism* (Philadelphia: Fortress Press, 1985), pp. 200–204.

8. Perrin, *Rediscovering the Teaching of Jesus,* p. 94.

9. Norman Perrin, *The New Testament: An Introduction* (New York: Harcourt Brace Jovanovich, 1974), pp. 195–196.

10. E. P. Sanders, *Judaism: Practice and Belief 63 BCE–66 CE* (Philadelphia: Trinity Press International, 1992), p. 233.

11. Joachim Jeremias, *New Testament Theology*, trans. John Bowden (New York: Charles Scribner's Sons, 1971), p. 227.

12. Hans Küng, *On Being a Christian*, trans. Edward Quinn (Garden City, N.Y.: Doubleday, 1976), pp. 211–212, 337.

13. Williamson, *Has God Rejected His People?*, p. 12.

14. Ludwig Wittgenstein, *Philosophical Investigations* (Oxford: Basil Blackwell, 1958), sec. 19.

15. Paul M. van Buren, *A Theology of the Jewish-Christian Reality*, Part 3: *Christ in Context* (San Francisco: Harper & Row, 1988), p. 29. Similarly, Marinus de Jonge contends that Jesus' identity can be known only in context. See his *Christology in Context*, p. 10.

16. John P. Meier, *A Marginal Jew: Rethinking the Historical Jesus* (New York: Doubleday, 1991), p. 172.

17. D. G. A. Calvert, "An Examination of the Criteria for Distinguishing the Authentic Words of Jesus," *New Testament Studies* 18 (1971–72), 211–212.

18. James H. Charlesworth, *Jesus Within Judaism* (New York: Doubleday, 1988), p. 45. Peter von der Osten-Sacken agrees, saying that a Jesus who emerged from the criterion of dissimilarity would be a "shadow," a docetic and anti-Jewish Jesus. See his *Christian-Jewish Dialogue*, p. 42.

19. The criticism of traditional Christology for depicting Jesus as a "visitor," who "entered into this place where we are, but . . . was not grounded in this place as we are," was offered by the early Paul M. van Buren in *The Secular Meaning of the Gospel* (New York: Macmillan, 1963), p. 40.

20. Kee, *Jesus in History*, p. 295.

21. Fredriksen, *From Jesus to Christ*, p. 6.

22. Calvert, "An Examination of the Criteria," pp. 212–213.

23. Ibid., pp. 214–216.

24. Ibid., pp. 216–217.

25. Kee, *Jesus in History*, p. 294.

26. Gerhard Kittel, ed., *"Abba,"* in *Theological Dictionary of the New Testament*, vol. 1, trans. G. W. Bromiley (Grand Rapids: Eerdmans, 1964), p. 6. For Kittel's support of Hitler, see his *Die Judenfrage* (Stuttgart: Verlag von W. Kohlhammer, 1933).

27. Joachim Jeremias, *The Prayers of Jesus*, trans. John Bowden, Christoph Burchard, and John Reumann (London: SCM Press, 1967), ch. 1.

28. James D. G. Dunn, *Unity and Diversity in the New Testament* (Philadelphia: Westminster Press, 1977), p. 187.

29. Jeremias, *The Prayers of Jesus*, p. 57 (emphasis mine); on the same page, Jeremias makes the further claim "*that Jesus constantly addressed God as 'my Father'* . . . *and that in so doing he used the Aramaic form 'Abba'*" (emphasis Jeremias').

30. Dunn, *Unity and Diversity in the New Testament*, p. 187.

31. James Barr, "Abba Isn't 'Daddy,'" *Journal of Theological Studies* 39 (1988), 28–47; Ernst Haenchen, *Der Weg Jesu* (Berlin: Topelmann, 1966), p. 492; J. C. G. Greig, "Abba and Amen: Their Relevance to Christology," in F. L. Cross, ed., *Studia Evangelica: The New Testament Message*, vol. 5, pt. 2 (Berlin: Akademie-Verlag, 1968), pp. 3–13; Ernst Käsemann, *An die Römer* (Tübingen: J. C. B. Mohr, 1973), pp. 219–220; Herbert Braun, *Spätjudisch-häretischer und frühchristlicher Radikalismus* (Tübingen: J. C. B. Mohr, 1969), pp. 127–128.

32. See the discussion in Charlesworth, *Jesus Within Judaism*, pp. 113–114.

33. Fredriksen, *From Jesus to Christ*, p. 91.

34. Geza Vermes, *Jesus the Jew* (New York: Macmillan, 1973), p. 211.

35. Hanan, *bTaan* 23b; cited in ibid., p. 211.

36. Meier, *A Marginal Jew*, p. 174.

37. Clemens Thoma, *A Christian Theology of Judaism*, trans. Helga Croner (New York: Paulist Press, 1980), p. 95.

38. Joseph A. Grassi, "*Abba*, Father (Mark 14:36): Another Approach," *Journal of the American Academy of Religion* 50 (September 1982), 455. This use of *abba* is found in some Targums in use at the time of Jesus; see Thoma, *A Christian Theology of Judaism*, pp. 92–96.

39. Charlesworth, *Jesus Within Judaism*, p. 167.

40. Ibid., p. 5 (emphasis Charlesworth's). E. P. Sanders agrees with this general criticism of the dissimilarity criticism. See his *Jesus and Judaism*, pp. 16–17.

41. H. J. Cadbury, *Jesus: What Manner of Man?* (London: SPCK, 1962), p. 57.

42. Schubert M. Ogden's claim that we "can only compare one kerygma with another, never kerygma with historical material" recognizes the truth that the gospel tradition is the witness of faith all the way down. See Ogden, *The Point of Christology*, p. 55.

43. Charlesworth, *Jesus Within Judaism*, pp. 5–6. See also Markus Barth, *Jesus the Jew*, trans. Frederick Prussner (Atlanta: John Knox Press, 1978).

44. Fredriksen, *From Jesus to Christ*, p. 6.

45. Sanders, *Jesus and Judaism*, p. 11.

46. Gerald Downing, *Jesus and the Threat of Freedom* (London: SCM Press, 1987), pp. 151f.

47. Bowden, *Jesus: The Unanswered Questions*, p. 41.

48. Scholars have long argued that "it appears not unlikely that the incorporation of John into the Christian picture was a deliberate and studied attempt by early Christians to vanquish an embarrassing rival." Morton Scott Enslin, *Christian Beginnings* (New York: Harper & Brothers, 1956), p. 152.

49. See the excellent discussion of this tendency in James Breech, *The Silence of Jesus* (Philadelphia: Fortress Press, 1983), pp. 22–24, and in Fredriksen, *From Jesus to Christ*, pp. 97–98.

50. John Dominic Crossan, *The Historical Jesus* (San Francisco: HarperSanFrancisco, 1991), p. 232.

51. Walter Wink, *John the Baptist in the Gospel Tradition* (Cambridge: Cambridge University Press, 1968), p. 26.

52. Ibid., p. 17.

53. Ibid., p. 41.

54. For further discussion, see Clark M. Williamson, *Baptism: Embodiment of the Gospel* (St. Louis: CBP Press, 1987), pp. 22–23.

55. Fredriksen, *From Jesus to Christ*, p. 77.

56. Hendrikus Boers, *Who Was Jesus?* (San Francisco: Harper & Row, 1989), p. 39.

57. Josephus, *Jewish Antiquities*, 18.117–118; cited in Vermes, *Jesus the Jew*, p. 50.

58. Boers, *Who Was Jesus?*, pp. 42, 44, 45.

59. Crossan, *The Historical Jesus*, pp. 259, 283.

60. Sanders, *Jesus and Judaism*, pp. 11, 326–327.

61. Emil Schürer, *A History of the Jewish People in the Time of Jesus*, ed. N. Glatzer (New York: Schocken Books, 1961), p. 198.

62. Leo Trepp, *A History of the Jewish Experience* (New York: Behrman House, 1973), p. 44.

63. Gerard S. Sloyan, *Jesus on Trial* (Philadelphia: Fortress Press, 1973), p. 21.

64. A summary of problems with the historical authenticity of the trial can be found in Williamson, *Has God Rejected His People?*, pp. 39–41.

65. Hendrikus Boers, *Who Was Jesus?*, pp. 67–68.

66. Sanders, *Jesus and Judaism*, pp. 298–300.

67. Fredriksen, *From Jesus to Christ*, p. 117.

68. John T. Townsend, "The New Testament, the Early Church and Anti-Semitism," in *From Ancient Israel to Modern Judaism*, vol. 1, ed. Jacob Neusner, Ernest S. Frerichs, and Nahum M. Sarna (Atlanta: Scholars Press, 1989), p. 177.

69. Fredriksen, *From Jesus to Christ*, p. 119.

70. See the discussion in Williamson, *Has God Rejected His People?*, pp. 41–46.

71. Sanders, *Judaism*, pp. 12, 83; see also pp. 491–493.

72. James D. G. Dunn, *The Partings of the Ways* (Philadelphia: Trinity Press International, 1991), p. 32.

73. Fredriksen, *From Jesus to Christ*, p. 120. John T. Townsend comments that the simple ascription to Jesus of the title "Messiah" "would have invited condemnation by Rome." See his "The New Testament, the Early Church, and Anti-Semitism," p. 178.

74. Sanders, *Jesus and Judaism*, pp. 206, 203.

75. Ibid., p. 204 (emphasis mine).

76. See the discussion in Boers, *Who Was Jesus?*, pp. 51–52.

77. Richard A. Horsley, *Sociology and the Jesus Movement* (New York: Crossroad, 1989), p. 121, comes to the same conclusion: "In such contexts the Jesus movement may well have attracted some socially disreputable or despised people such as 'toll collectors,' although the evidence is weak and problematic. It has been suggested that many (even the majority) of Jesus' followers were from some particular groups in Palestinian

society, such as 'tax collectors' and 'prostitutes.' Aside from such people not being identifiable social *groups*, there is little or no evidence that Jesus himself ministered to or associated with such people as tax collectors or prostitutes." See also Horsley's fuller discussion in *Jesus and the Spiral of Violence* (San Francisco: Harper & Row, 1987), pp. 212–223.

78. Henry J. Cadbury argued that the charge that Jesus was a "friend of tax collectors and sinners" served the evangelists' "purpose of showing how willfully the Jews rejected God's spokesmen. There is little reason to think that when the [evangelists] were under the influence of such a purpose they were peculiarly faithful to historical fact." See his "Mixed Motives in the Gospels," *Proceedings of the American Philosophical Society* 95 (April 1951), 120.

79. Perrin, *The New Testament*, p. 150.

80. Dunn, *The Partings of the Ways*, p. 114.

81. Joachim Jeremias, *Jesus' Promise to the Nations*, trans. S. H. Hooke (Naperville, Ill.: Alec R. Allenson, 1958), p. 29.

82. Sanders, *Jesus and Judaism*, p. 220.

83. Vermes, *Jesus the Jew*, p. 49.

84. Bernard J. Lee, S.M., *The Galilean Jewishness of Jesus* (New York: Paulist Press, 1988), p. 67. See also Dunn, *The Partings of the Ways*, p. 23.

85. Dunn, *The Partings of the Ways*, p. 115.

86. Crossan, *The Historical Jesus*, p. 340.

87. Lee, *The Galilean Jewishness of Jesus*, p. 66.

88. Ibid., p. 67.

89. Horsley, *Sociology and the Jesus Movement*, pp. 109, 111.

90. Horsley, *Jesus and the Spiral of Violence*, p. 193.

91. Ibid., p. 195; Charlesworth, *Jesus Within Judaism*, pp. 16–17. For a defense of the authenticity of the "exclusivity logion," see Amy-Jill Levine, *The Social and Ethnic Dimension of Matthean Social History* (Lewiston, N.Y.: Edwin Mellen Press, 1988).

92. Horsley, *Jesus and the Spiral of Violence*, p. 200.

93. Dunn, *The Partings of the Ways*, pp. 98–116.

94. Richard A. Horsley, with John S. Hanson, *Bandits, Prophets, and*

Messiahs (San Francisco: Harper & Row, 1985), pp. xviii, 3. Throughout this section I am dependent on Horsley's work.

95. Ibid., p. 9.

96. van Buren, *Christ in Context* [Part 3 of *A Theology of the Jewish-Christian Reality*], p. 168.

97. Horsley, *Bandits, Prophets, and Messiahs*, p. 11; see also his *Sociology and the Jesus Movement*, pp. 72–80.

98. Josephus, *Jewish Antiquities*, 17.32–45 (Loeb Classics 8, pp. 387–393).

99. Philip Culbertson, "Fish, Taxes, and Civil Disobedience" (Unpublished paper), p. 23.

100. See Walter Brueggemann's *The Land: Place as Gift, Promise, and Challenge to Biblical Faith* (Philadelphia: Fortress Press, 1977) for a discussion of land as "storied space."

101. Sanders, *Judaism*, p. 168.

102. Horsley, *Jesus and the Spiral of Violence*, pp. 232, 240.

103. Ibid., p. 300.

104. Fredriksen, *From Jesus to Christ*, pp. 112–113.

105. Gerard S. Sloyan, *Jesus in Focus* (Mystic, Conn.: Twenty-Third Publications, 1983), p. 92.

106. John Chrysostom, *Homilies on the Gospel of Matthew*, 68.1; cited in Aaron A. Milavec, "A Fresh Analysis of the Parable of the Wicked Husbandmen in the Light of Jewish-Catholic Dialogue," in *Parable and Story in Judaism and Christianity*, ed. Clemens Thoma and Michael Wyschogrod (New York: Paulist Press, 1989), p. 83.

107. Brad H. Young, *Jesus and His Jewish Parables* (New York: Paulist Press, 1989), pp. 318, 319.

108. Clemens Thoma, "Literary and Theological Aspects of the Rabbinic Parables," in *Parable and Story in Judaism and Christianity*, ed. Clemens Thoma and Michael Wyschogrod (New York: Paulist Press, 1989), p. 30.

109. Philip Culbertson, "Reclaiming the Matthean Vineyard Parables," *Encounter* 49, no. 4 (Autumn 1988), 261, 264, 267.

110. David Flusser, "Aesop's Miser and the Parable of the Talents,"

in *Parable and Story in Judaism and Christianity*, ed. Clemens Thoma and Michael Wyschogrod (New York: Paulist Press, 1989), p. 20.

111. Pinchas Lapide and Karl Rahner, *Encountering Jesus—Encountering Judaism*, trans. Davis Perkins (New York: Crossroad, 1987), p. 52.

112. Flusser, "Aesop's Miser and the Parable of the Talents," p. 10.

113. Thoma, "Literary and Theological Aspects of the Rabbinic Parables," p. 38.

114. I owe my awareness of the link between the story of the temptation and Deuteronomy to my colleague J. Gerald Janzen.

115. Leonard Swidler, "Why Christians Need to Dialogue with Jews and Judaism About Jesus," in Leonard Swidler, Lewis John Eron, Gerard Sloyan, and Lester Dean, *Bursting the Bonds?* (Maryknoll, N.Y.: Orbis Books, 1990), p. 15.

116. See Sanders, *Jesus and Judaism*, pp. 55–56, 268.

117. Lewis John Eron, "A Response to Leonard Swidler," in Swidler et al., *Bursting the Bonds?*, p. 68.

118. See Perrin, *The New Testament*, p. 171, and Krister Stendahl, *The School of St. Matthew* (Philadelphia: Fortress Press, 1968), p. xi. Rudolf Bultmann long ago pointed out that the church increasingly tended "to clothe its dominical sayings, its views and its fundamental beliefs in the form of controversy dialogue." Rudolf Bultmann, *The History of the Synoptic Tradition*, trans. John Marsh (New York: Harper & Row, 1963), p. 51.

119. Mekilta *Shab* 1.

120. Bowden, *Jesus: The Unanswered Questions*, p. 7.

121. Meier, *A Marginal Jew*, p. 218.

122. Vermes, *Jesus the Jew*, pp. 134–140. See also the discussions in Thoma, *A Christian Theology of Judaism*, pp. 59–64; de Jonge, *Christology in Context*, p. 28; and Marinus de Jonge, "The Use of the Word 'Anointed' in the Time of Jesus," *Novum Testamentum* 8 (1966), 132–148.

123. Jacob Neusner, *Messiah in Context* (Philadelphia: Fortress Press, 1984), p. ix.

124. Ibid., pp. xi, xiii.

Chapter 4: The Triumph of Grace in Paul's Theology

1. See Lloyd Gaston, "Paul and the Torah," in *Anti-Semitism and the Foundations of Christianity,* ed. Alan T. Davies (New York: Paulist Press, 1979), pp. 48–71, and *Paul and the Torah* (Vancouver: University of British Columbia Press, 1987). See also John G. Gager, *The Origins of Anti-Semitism* (New York: Oxford University Press, 1983).

2. E. P. Sanders, *Paul and Palestinian Judaism,* and *Paul, the Law, and the Jewish People* (Philadelphia: Fortress Press, 1983).

3. Heikki Räisänen, *Paul and the Law* (Philadelphia: Fortress Press, 1986).

4. James D. G. Dunn, *Jesus, Paul, and the Law* (Louisville: Westminster/John Knox Press, 1990), and *Romans 9–16,* Word Biblical Commentary 38b (Dallas: Word Books, 1988); Alan F. Segal, *Paul the Convert: The Apostolate and Apostasy of Saul the Pharisee* (New Haven: Yale University Press, 1990); Fredriksen, *From Jesus to Christ,* pp. 165–176.

5. This essay is "Paul and Israel," in Ernst Käsemann, *New Testament Questions of Today,* trans. W. J. Montague (Philadelphia: Fortress Press, 1969), pp. 183–187.

6. Ibid., p. 183. Käsemann accepts the authenticity of this verse. Since F. C. Baur in 1830, several critics have maintained that it is an interpolation. A history of the argument over 1 Thessalonians 2:13–16 is found in R. F. Collins, *Studies on the First Letter to the Thessalonians* (Louvain: University Press, 1984), pp. 93–135.

7. Ibid., pp. 184, 186, 185.

8. Ibid., p. 185 (emphasis mine).

9. Ibid., pp. 185–187.

10. Matthew Black, *Romans* (London: Marshall, Morgan & Scott, 1973), pp. 47–48. Calvin L. Porter first suggested seeing Black's commentary as exemplifying the traditional paradigm for reading Paul. See his "A New Paradigm for Reading Romans," *Encounter* 39 (Summer 1978), 257–272.

11. Black, *Romans,* p. 65.

12. Lester Dean, "The Problem of a Jew Talking About Paul," in Swidler et al., *Bursting the Bonds?,* p. 129; cf. Moore, "Christian Writers on Judaism," p. 197.

13. Moore, "Christian Writers on Judaism," pp. 197–198.

14. Ibid., pp. 221–222.

15. Klein, *Anti-Judaism in Christian Theology.*

16. Sanders, *Paul and Palestinian Judaism*, pp. 47, 427.

17. C. G. Montefiore, *Judaism and St. Paul* (London: Max Goschen, 1914), pp. 29–30, 42, 78.

18. H. J. Schoeps, *Paul: The Theology of the Apostle in the Light of Jewish Religious History* (Philadelphia: Westminster Press, 1961), pp. 188, 213.

19. Lester Dean, "Paul's 'Erroneous' Description of Judaism," in Swidler et al., *Bursting the Bonds?*, pp. 136–140.

20. J. Christiaan Beker, *Paul the Apostle* (Philadelphia: Fortress Press, 1980), pp. 339, 340.

21. Fredriksen, *From Jesus to Christ*, p. 161. Lloyd Gaston points out that what most bothers Jewish scholars about Paul is less his invective "than his ignorance. For anyone who understands rabbinic Judaism, Paul's attacks are not merely unfair—they miss the mark completely." See his "Paul and the Torah," p. 51.

22. Gaston, "Paul and the Torah," p. 51.

23. Fredriksen, *From Jesus to Christ*, pp. 160–161.

24. This approach was first articulated by Krister Stendahl, *Paul Among Jews and Gentiles* (Philadelphia: Fortress Press, 1976). It has been developed by Gaston, "Paul and the Torah" and *Paul and the Torah*, as well as by Gager, *The Origins of Anti-Semitism*, esp. pp. 197–264. An able popular treatment of it has been provided by Philip A. Cunningham, *Jewish Apostle to the Gentiles: Paul as He Saw Himself* (Mystic, Conn.: Twenty-Third Publications, 1986).

25. Two excellent treatments of the question of the historical-critical reliability of the Pauline portion of Acts are provided by Dixon Slingerland: "'The Jews' in the Pauline Portion of Acts," *Journal of the American Academy of Religion* 54, no. 2 (Summer 1986), 305–321, and "The Composition of Acts: Some Redaction-Critical Observations," *Journal of the American Academy of Religion* 56, no. 1 (Spring 1988), 99–113.

26. Krister Stendahl's essay "The Apostle Paul and the Introspective Conscience of the West," in *Paul Among Jews and Gentiles*, pp. 78–96, convincingly argues that a romantic, psychologizing interpretation of Paul leads us astray from Paul's intent. Whenever Paul introduces "justification" in his letters, it is in the context of a *social* problem in the congregation being addressed.

27. Stendhal, *Paul Among Jews and Gentiles*, p. 9.

28. A scholar who supports a "commissioning/conversion" understanding of Paul's encounter with the risen Christ is Alan F. Segal in *Paul the Convert:* "Paul was both converted and called," contends Segal, pointing to the "enormous transformation" that Paul underwent from persecutor to apostle, to the contrasts Paul draws between his past and present life, as well as to his understanding of himself as an apostle (pp. 3–14).

29. Gaston, "Paul and the Torah," p. 55.

30. Ibid., p. 56. So, says Gaston, "Paul's converts were all Gentiles"; see *Paul and the Torah*, p. 8.

31. Gaston, "Paul and the Torah," p. 61 (emphasis Gaston's).

32. Gaston, *Paul and the Torah*, p. 10.

33. Gaston, "Paul and the Torah," p. 62.

34. Gaston, *Paul and the Torah*, p. 14.

35. Markus Barth, "Was Paul an Anti-Semite?" *Journal of Ecumenical Studies* 5 (1968), 78–104.

36. The following six propositions are found in fuller form in Gager, *The Origins of Anti-Semitism*, pp. 200–201.

37. Ibid., p. 201 (emphasis mine).

38. Francis H. Agnew, "Paul's Theological Adversary in the Doctrine of Justification by Faith," *Journal of Ecumenical Studies* 25, no. 4 (Fall 1988), 549. Agnew does not present his position as a variation on the Gaston/Gager hypothesis, but I am regarding it here as such because according to Agnew what Paul rejects is Judaizing and Judaizers, any further opponents being "fictive."

39. Jeffrey S. Siker, *Disinheriting the Jews: Abraham in Early Christian Controversy* (Louisville: Westminster/John Knox Press, 1991), pp. 71–73.

40. Gager, *The Origins of Anti-Semitism*, pp. 205, 206.

41. Fredriksen, *From Jesus to Christ*, p. 162.

42. Gaston, *Paul and the Torah*, p. 9.

43. Gager, *The Origins of Anti-Semitism*, p. 202.

44. Ibid., pp. 210–211.

45. Sanders, *Paul and Palestinian Judaism*, p. 552.

46. Ibid., p. xi for Sanders' purpose.

47. Ibid., p. 17 (emphasis Sanders').

48. Agnew, "Paul's Theological Adversary," p. 545.

49. Stephen Westerholm, *Israel's Law and the Church's Faith* (Grand Rapids: Eerdmans, 1988), p. 48.

50. *Deut.R.*, Wa'ethanan, II, I; cited in C. G. Montefiore and H. Loewe, eds., *A Rabbinic Anthology* (New York: Schocken Books, 1974), p. 91.

51. *Lamentations Rabbah*, III, 60, on 3:43; cited in Montefiore and Loewe, eds., *A Rabbinic Anthology*, p. 316.

52. Sanders, *Paul and Palestinian Judaism*, p. 157.

53. Ibid., p. 552.

54. Fredriksen, *From Jesus to Christ*, p. 164; see also Gager, *The Origins of Anti-Semitism*, p. 203.

55. See, for example, Gager, *The Origins of Anti-Semitism*, pp. 203–204.

56. Sanders, *Paul, the Law, and the Jewish People*, p. 197.

57. Räisänen, *Paul and the Law*, pp. 83, 82.

58. Ibid., pp. 118–119, 199.

59. Ibid., p. 200.

60. Ibid., pp. 200–201, 268.

61. Ibid., pp. 187, 189–191.

62. Norman Perrin and Dennis C. Duling, *The New Testament: An Introduction*, 2d ed. (San Diego: Harcourt Brace Jovanovich, 1982), p. 147.

63. Ibid., p. 149.

64. Dunn, *Jesus, Paul, and the Law*, p. 186. Dunn's views are articulated, defended, and nuanced in this book and in his Word Biblical Commentary, *Romans 9–16*. Here for the sake of brevity I will follow the argument in "The New Perspective on Paul," chapter 7 of *Jesus, Paul, and the Law*.

65. Ibid., p. 190. Here and elsewhere I avoid a term Dunn regularly uses, as when he refers to the belief of Paul's opponents that "Jews as a *race*

are God's covenant people" (emphasis mine). It would have been preferable to stick to the notion of a "people." Paul's opponents admitted that "converts" could be added to the people, an admission incompatible with what moderns hear when the term "race" is used for Jews.

66. Ibid., pp. 191, 190.

67. See Segal, *Paul the Convert*, p. 169; Sanders makes the same point in *Paul, the Law, and the Jewish People*, pp. 84, 113.

68. Dunn, *Jesus, Paul, and the Law*, p. 192.

69. Ibid., p. 194.

70. Segal, *Paul the Convert*, pp. 129–130, 202, 204, 211.

71. Dunn, *Jesus, Paul, and the Law*, pp. 194–197.

72. It is important to note here that Dunn is not making a distinction between ritual and ethical commandments in general, nor claiming that Paul did. It is questionable whether Paul or other Jews would find such a distinction intelligible: is the commandment against committing idolatry a ritual or ethical commandment?

73. Ibid., p. 198. Similarly, Fredriksen argues that *"Paul denationalizes Jewish restoration theology."* See Fredriksen, *From Jesus to Christ*, p. 172.

74. Dunn, *Jesus, Paul, and the Law*, pp. 200–201.

75. See Dunn, *Romans 9–16.*

76. Dunn, *Jesus, Paul, and the Law*, p. 202.

77. On this, see R. David Kaylor, *Paul's Covenant Community: Jew and Gentile in Romans* (Atlanta: John Knox Press, 1988), p. 171.

78. Segal, *Paul the Convert*, p. 263.

79. Williamson, *Has God Rejected His People?*, p. 48. See Segal, *Paul the Convert*, p. 262.

80. Segal, *Paul the Convert*, pp. 262, 282.

81. J. Reynolds and R. Tannenbaum, *Jews and God-fearers at Aphrodisias: Green Inscriptions with Commentary* (Cambridge: Cambridge University Press, 1987), pp. 56–58; cited in Fredriksen, *From Jesus to Christ*, p. 149.

82. Fredriksen, *From Jesus to Christ*, p. 166.

83. Perrin and Duling, *The New Testament*, p. 80.

84. Segal, *Paul the Convert*, p. 26.

85. Fredriksen, *From Jesus to Christ*, p. 166.

86. Wayne A. Meeks, *The First Urban Christians* (New Haven: Yale University Press, 1983), p. 112 (emphasis mine).

87. Fredriksen, *From Jesus to Christ*, p. 167.

88. Ibid., pp. 167–168.

89. This list is compiled by Dunn, *Jesus, Paul, and the Law*, p. 133; see also Williamson, *Has God Rejected His People?*, pp. 36–39.

90. Williamson, *Has God Rejected His People?*, p. 38.

91. Dunn, *Jesus, Paul, and the Law*, pp. 134–135.

92. Ibid., p. 135.

93. Segal, *Paul the Convert*, pp. 150, 223. Antiochus also showed contempt for the law on unclean foods by sacrificing a swine on the Temple altar; see Dunn, *Jesus, Paul, and the Law*, p. 137.

94. Dunn, *Jesus, Paul, and the Law*, p. 136.

95. Ibid., p. 138.

96. Dunn, *Romans 9–16*, p. 522.

97. See the discussion in Williamson, *Has God Rejected His People?*, pp. 59–60.

98. Clemens Thoma regards this as a significant possibility. See his *A Christian Theology of Judaism*, p. 157.

99. von der Osten-Sacken, *Christian-Jewish Dialogue*, p. 20.

100. Although much of what Karl Barth wrote about the people Israel appalls Christians whose work focuses on the conversation between Jews and Christians, it is still the case, as Paul M. van Buren points out, that Barth, contradicting almost the entirety of the Christian tradition, "insisted that the Jewish people today are Israel, as Jews themselves have always said." It was Barth who taught contemporary theologians to speak of "the church and Israel." See Paul M. van Buren, "The Church and Israel: Romans 9–11,." *The Princeton Seminary Bulletin*, Supplementary Issue, no. 1 (1990), 7.

101. von der Osten-Sacken, *Christian-Jewish Dialogue*, p. 24.

102. Dunn, *Romans 9–16*, p. 526.

103. von der Osten-Sacken, *Christian-Jewish Dialogue*, p. 28.

104. Ibid., p. 22.

105. Ibid., p. 29.

106. Dunn, *Romans 9–16*, p. 534.

107. Karl Barth, "The Jewish Problem and the Christian Answer," in *Against the Stream* (London: SCM Press, 1954), p. 200.

108. See J. Christiaan Beker, "Romans 9–11 in the Context of the Early Church," *The Princeton Seminary Bulletin*, Supplementary Issue, no. 1 (1990), 47; and Otfried Hofius, "All Israel Will Be Saved," *The Princeton Seminary Bulletin*, Supplementary Issue, no. 1 (1990), 36–37.

109. David Satran, "Paul Among the Rabbis and the Fathers," *The Princeton Seminary Bulletin*, Supplementary Issue, no. 1 (1990), 105.

Chapter 5: Covenant

1. Karl Barth, *Church Dogmatics* IV.3.1, trans. G. W. Bromiley (Edinburgh: T. & T. Clark, 1961), p. 374.

2. That Hebrews is a supersessionist argument is not really disputable. Alexander C. Purdy speaks of the Melchizedek priesthood in Hebrews as "destined to supersede" the Levitical order and of the first covenant as having "been superseded by the sacrifice of Christ." Purdy, "Introduction" to the Epistle to the Hebrews, *The Interpreter's Bible*, vol. 11 (Nashville: Abingdon Press, 1955), p. 578. Purdy speaks of Judaism both as having been "abolished" and as having been "fulfilled" (ibid., p. 589). Here is the logic of traditional Christian claims vis-à-vis Judaism: what is to be fulfilled must first be emptied of salvific significance.

3. Gerhard Kittel, ed., *Theological Dictionary of the New Testament*, vol. 2, trans. G. W. Bromiley (Grand Rapids: Eerdmans, 1964), p. 124.

4. Alan Richardson, ed., *A Theological Dictionary of the Bible* (New York: Macmillan, 1950), p. 118.

5. Barnabas, *The Epistle of Barnabas*, in *The Ante-Nicene Fathers*, vol. 1, trans. and ed. Alexander Roberts and James Donaldson (Grand Rapids: Eerdmans, 1979), pp. 138, 139.

6. Ibid., pp. 138–141.

7. W. D. Davies, *The Gospel and the Land* (Berkeley: University of California Press, 1974), p. 368.

8. *The Epistle of Barnabas*, pp. 145, 146.

9. Ibid., pp. 146–147.

10. This is a frequent theme of the Gospel According to John, that Jews search the scriptures but, being blind, never "see" that they bear witness to Christ (e.g., John 5:37–40).

11. Tertullian, *An Answer to the Jews*, in *The Ante-Nicene Fathers*, vol. 3, trans. S. Thelwall, ed. Alexander Roberts and James Donaldson (Grand Rapids: Eerdmans, 1978), pp. 151–152, 154–155, 157.

12. Numerous anti-Jewish tracts make essentially the same points with regard to the doctrines of the covenant and the church. In his classical study, A. Lukyn Williams examines the role of anti-Judaism in some seventy theologians of the early and medieval church. See his *Adversus Judaeos* (Cambridge: Cambridge University Press, 1935).

13. Cyril of Jerusalem, *Catechetical Lecture 18, 22–7*, in *Documents in Early Christian Thought*, ed. Maurice Wiles and Mark Santer (Cambridge: Cambridge University Press, 1975), pp. 166–168.

14. Irenaeus, *Against the Heresies IV, 17.5–18.6*, in Wiles and Santer, eds., *Documents in Early Christian Thought*, pp. 184, 185 (emphasis mine), 186.

15. Louis Finkelstein, *The Jews: Their History* (New York: Schocken Books, 1970), p. 158.

16. Justin Martyr, *Dialogue with Trypho the Jew*, in *The Ante-Nicene Fathers*, vol. 1, trans. and ed. Alexander Roberts and James Donaldson (Grand Rapids: Eerdmans, 1979), pp. 179, 184, 202–203.

17. Irenaeus, *Against All Heresies*, in *The Ante-Nicene Fathers*, vol. 1. trans. and ed. Alexander Roberts and James Donaldson (Grand Rapids: Eerdmans, 1979), p. 466.

18. David Patrick Efroymson, "The Patristic Connection," in *Anti-Semitism and the Foundations of Christianity*, ed. Alan T. Davies (New York: Paulist Press, 1979), p. 99.

19. Tertullian, *An Answer to the Jews*, p. 174.

20. Origen, *Against Celsus*, in *The Ante-Nicene Fathers*, vol. 4, trans. and ed. Alexander Roberts and James Donaldson (Grand Rapids: Eerdmans, 1979), p. 433.

21. Augustine, *Reply to Faustus*, pp. 28–32.

22. Ibid., p. 32.

23. Augustine, *The City of God,* trans. Marcus Dods (New York: Random House, 1950), pp. 140, 141, 204, 602.

24. Ibid., pp. 654, 656–657.

25. Edward H. Flannery, *The Anguish of the Jews* (New York: Macmillan, 1965), p. 126.

26. Wellhausen's major work considered here is his *Prolegomenon to the History of Ancient Israel,* Preface by W. Robertson Smith (Gloucester, Mass.: Peter Smith, 1973; originally published 1886). An excellent overview of numerous scholars reflecting Wellhausen's approach is found in Klein, *Anti-Judaism in Christian Theology.*

27. Herbert F. Hahn, *The Old Testament in Modern Research* (Philadelphia: Fortress Press, 1966), p. 14.

28. Roger Brooks, *The Spirit of the Ten Commandments* (San Francisco: Harper & Row, 1990), p. 7.

29. Georg Fohrer, *Studien zur alttestamentlichen Theologie und Geschichte, 1949–66* (Berlin: Walter de Gruyter, 1969), p. 37.

30. Georg Fohrer, *History of Israelite Religion* (Nashville: Abingdon Press, 1972), p. 49.

31. Hans Werner Bartsch, "Die Bedeutung Jerusalems für das jüdische Volk und die Stadt unter Besatzung, Materialen zum Nahostkonflikt, 47," *Evangelischer Arbeitskreis Kirche und Israel in Hessen und Nassau,* pp. 2, 4; cited in Klein, *Anti-Judaism in Christian Theology,* p. 19.

32. Jeremias, *New Testament Theology,* p. 227.

33. Jon Sobrino, *Christology at the Crossroads,* trans. John Drury (Maryknoll, N.Y.: Orbis Books, 1978), pp. 146–147.

34. Ibid., p. 206.

35. William F. Buggert, "The Christologies of Hans Küng and Karl Rahner: A Comparison and Evaluation of Their Mutual Compatibility" (Ph.D. diss., The Catholic University of America, 1978), p. 109.

36. Karl Barth, cited in Pinchas Lapide, "Christians and Jews—A New Protestant Beginning," *Journal of Ecumenical Studies* 12, no. 4 (Fall 1975), 485.

37. Barth, *Church Dogmatics,* vol. 2, pt. 2, p. 236.

38. Barth, "The Jewish Problem and the Christian Answer," p. 200.

39. Barth, *Church Dogmatics,* vol. 2, pt. 2, pp. 206–209.

40. Barth, *Church Dogmatics*, vol. 4, pt. 1, trans. G. W. Bromiley (Edinburgh: T. & T. Clark, 1959), p. 3.

41. Karl Barth, *Dogmatics in Outline*, trans. G. T. Thompson (New York: Harper & Brothers, 1959), p. 74, 76–78.

42. Ibid., p. 81.

43. The Justinian Code, issued in 534 C.E., retained and left intact older bans in canon law against building new synagogues and repairing old ones, the purpose being partly to make the practice of Jewish faith difficult and partly to ensure that the physical appearance of synagogues would give evidence of their "spectral" character. See Williamson, *Has God Rejected His People?*, p. 111.

44. Lloyd Gaston, "Paul and the Torah," in *Anti-Semitism and the Foundations of Christianity*, ed. Alan T. Davies (New York: Paulist Press, 1979), p. 55.

45. Barth, *Against the Stream*, p. 200.

46. Gerhard von Rad, *Moses* (New York: Association Press, 1959), p. 29.

47. Jon D. Levenson, *Sinai and Zion* (San Francisco: Harper & Row, 1985), p. 37.

48. Ibid., p. 50.

49. Ibid., p. 77.

50. Abraham J. Heschel, *The Prophets*, vol. 1 (New York: Harper & Row, 1962), pp. 25–26.

51. Frederick Holmgren, *The God Who Cares* (Atlanta: John Knox Press, 1979), p. 48.

52. William Klassen, *The Forgiving Community* (Philadelphia: Westminster Press, 1966), p. 73.

53. Brooks, *The Spirit of the Ten Commandments*, pp. 28–30.

54. Horace D. Hummel, "Law and Grace in Judaism and Lutheranism," in *Speaking of God Today: Jews and Lutherans in Conversation*, ed. Paul D. Opsahl and Marc H. Tannenbaum (Philadelphia: Fortress Press, 1974), p. 16.

55. B. D. Napier, *Exodus* (London: SCM Press, 1963), p. 70.

56. Ben Zion Bokser, "Witness and Mission in Judaism," in *Issues in the Jewish-Christian Dialogue: Jewish Perspectives on Covenant, Mission*

and Witness, ed. Helga Croner and Leon Klenicki (New York: Paulist Press, 1979), p. 90.

57. "Covenant," *Encyclopaedia Judaica,* vol. 5, ed. Cecil Roth (New York: Macmillan, 1971), p. 1019.

58. Cited in Montefiore and Loewe, eds., *A Rabbinic Anthology,* p. 91.

59. Cited in ibid., p. 91.

60. Cited in ibid., p. 89.

61. Cited in Solomon Schechter, "God, Israel and Election," in *Understanding Jewish Theology,* ed. Jacob Neusner (New York: KTAV, 1973), p. 70.

62. Manfred Vogel, "Covenant and the Interreligious Encounter," in *Issues in the Jewish-Christian Dialogue,* ed. Helga Croner and Leon Klenicki (New York: Paulist Press, 1979), p. 75.

63. Cited in Schechter, "God, Israel, and Election," p. 72.

64. The *Schulchan Aruch* is an authoritative, Sephardic-oriented code of Jewish law and custom compiled by the Talmudic scholar Joseph Caro (1488–1575) and published in Vienna in 1565.

65. Cited in David Ellenson, "Jewish Covenant and Christian Trinitarianism," in *Jewish Civilization: Essays and Studies,* ed. Ronald A. Brauner (Philadelphia: Reconstructionist Rabbinical College, 1985), p. 88.

66. Cited in Frank Ephraim Talmage, "Christianity and the Jewish People," in *Disputation and Dialogue,* ed. Frank Ephraim Talmage (New York: KTAV, 1975), p. 245.

67. Cited in Culbertson, "Reclaiming the Matthean Vineyard Parables," p. 281.

68. Mary Potter Engel, "Calvin and the Jews: A Textual Puzzle," in *The Princeton Seminary Bulletin,* Supplementary Issue, no. 1 (1990), 123.

69. These points are all made by Engel, ibid., p. 119, and can also be found in John Calvin, *Institutes of the Christian Religion,* vol. 1, trans. Ford Lewis Battles, ed. John T. McNeill (Philadelphia: Westminster Press, 1960), pp. 428–449.

70. Ibid., p. 120; for what it is worth, Engel has persuaded me of the inadequacy of my earlier view of Calvin; see ibid., p. 121, and Williamson, *Has God Rejected His People?,* p. 102.

71. Calvin, *Institutes of the Christian Religion,* vol. 1, p. 434.

72. Ibid., pp. 428–430.

73. Ibid., pp. 431–432, 437.

74. Ibid., pp. 450, 453–454, 456, 458, 460–461.

75. R. E. Clements, "Covenant," in *The Westminster Dictionary of Christian Theology* (Philadelphia: Westminster Press, 1983), p. 128.

76. The Westminster Confession in *Creeds of the Churches*, ed. John H. Leith (Richmond: John Knox Press, 1973), pp. 202–203 (emphasis mine).

77. Ibid., p. 203.

78. William Ames, *The Marrow of Theology*, trans. and ed. John D. Eusden (Durham: Labyrinth Press, 1968), pp. 202, 204–206. Ames, virtually unknown today, was an influential Puritan theologian, particularly in New England, although he never left Europe.

79. Charles Wesley, "Love Divine, All Loves Excelling," in *Hymnbook for Christian Worship* (St. Louis: Bethany Press, 1970), p. 297.

80. Barth, *Church Dogmatics* IV.3.1., pp. 368–369. Sin has three forms in Barth's theology: in contrast to the humility of Christ, it is pride; in contrast to the majesty of Christ, it is sloth; in contrast to the truth of Christ, it is a lie: "Epigrammatically, and to be taken *cum grano salis,* we might say that falsehood is the specifically Christian form of sin." Ibid., p. 374. These three are not separable forms of sin: "Proud and slothful, he [the human being] is necessarily false as well." Ibid., p. 372.

81. Ibid., p. 435.

82. Robert T. Osborn, "The Christian Blasphemy: A Non-Jewish Jesus," in *Jews and Christians,* ed. James H. Charlesworth (New York: Crossroad, 1990), p. 214. In the rest of his article, Osborn lays out various forms of what he considers to be the Christian "blasphemy," a brush that he wields too freely, tarring some who had the courage to resist Hitler (e.g., Tillich). My appreciation of Osborn's insight does not imply agreement with all the ways in which he develops it.

Chapter 6: The Authority of Scripture

1. See the discussion in Jack T. Sanders, *The Jews in Luke-Acts* (London: SCM Press, 1987), p. xvi.

2. Norman A. Beck, in *Mature Christianity* (London and Toronto: Associated University Presses, 1985), pp. 21–30, speaks of "polemic";

Luke T. Johnson, in "The New Testament's Anti-Jewish Slander and the Conventions of Ancient Polemic," *Journal of Biblical Literature* 108, no. 3 (1989), 419–441, uses both terms and rejects anti-Semitism as anachronistic, arguing that it "derives from the contemporary Jew-Christian polarity," and downplays, although uses, "anti-Jewish" (pp. 422–423).

3. For a summary of Marcion's views, see Justo L. Gonzalez, *A History of Christian Thought*, vol. 1 (Nashville: Abingdon Press, 1970), pp. 140–144.

4. See Robert M. Grant and David Tracy, *A Short History of the Interpretation of the Bible* (Philadelphia: Fortress Press, 1984), pp. 40–41.

5. Perrin, *The New Testament*, p. 331.

6. Cyril C. Richardson, "Introduction to Early Christian Literature," in *Early Christian Fathers*, vol. 1 of the Library of Christian Classics (Philadelphia: Westminster Press, 1953), pp. 24–25. Gnostics also appear to have been the first "to provide relatively systematic exegesis of the New Testament"; see Grant and Tracy, *A Short History of the Interpretation of the Bible*, p. 54.

7. I have learned the sound of one hand clapping; it is the reaction of a Jewish woman to the news that the New Testament is no longer sexist, but still anti-Jewish.

8. My colleague Ronald J. Allen and I have written on the subject of the teaching of the Bible in the churches in *The Teaching Minister* (Louisville: Westminster/John Knox Press, 1991).

9. See Williamson, *Has God Rejected His People?*, pp. 64–83.

10. See Jon Levenson's discussion of Kaufmann on this point in *Sinai and Zion*, p. 109. Norman A. Beck also points out the role of polemic in the Hebrew Bible in his *Mature Christianity*, pp. 21–23. Levenson's fuller argument about the role of polemic in the Hebrew Bible is found in his article "Is There a Counterpart in the Hebrew Bible to New Testament Anti-Semitism?" *Journal of Ecumenical Studies* 22 (1985), 242–260.

11. Levenson, *Sinai and Zion*, p. 110.

12. Beck, *Mature Christianity*, p. 22.

13. Ibid., pp. 23–27.

14. See Johnson, "Anti-Jewish Slander," pp. 419–441.

15. Ibid., pp. 419, 423–424.

16. See Slingerland, "'The Jews' in the Pauline Portions of Acts,"

pp. 305–321, and "The Composition of Acts," pp. 99–113.

17. Johnson, "Anti-Jewish Slander," pp. 429, 431, 433–435.

18. Ibid., p. 439.

19. Cited in ibid., p. 440.

20. Ibid., p. 441.

21. Samuel Sandmel, *Judaism and Christian Beginnings* (New York: Oxford University Press, 1978), p. 4.

22. Wayne A. Meeks and Robert L. Wilken, *Jews and Christians in Antioch* (Missoula, Mont.: Scholars Press, 1978), pp. 87–89.

23. J. Christiaan Beker, "The New Testament View of Judaism," in *Jews and Christians,* ed. James H. Charlesworth (New York: Crossroad, 1990), p. 65.

24. Perrin and Duling, *The New Testament,* pp. 79–81, 242, 263–266, 293–296.

25. See Sanders, *The Jews in Luke-Acts,* p. 97.

26. Werner Kelber, *The Oral and the Written Gospel* (Philadelphia: Fortress Press, 1983), pp. 130–131. Using a much less complicated argument than does Kelber, Lindsey P. Pherigo agrees that for Mark "the view of Jesus among the conservative Jewish Christians is unsatisfactory to the Gentile Christian church." "The Gospel According to Mark," in *The Interpreter's One Volume Commentary on the Bible* (Nashville: Abingdon Press, 1971), p. 644. What Pherigo here calls "Gentile Christian," Perrin designates as the Hellenistic Jewish Gentile Mission church; deeply concerned with Gentiles, this church was still Jewish, but different from the traditional Jesus followers.

27. Raymond E. Brown, *The Community of the Beloved Disciple* (New York: Paulist Press, 1979), pp. 63–88.

28. Ibid., p. 22; see John T. Townsend, "The Gospel of John and the Jews: The Story of a Religious Divorce," in *Antisemitism and the Foundations of Christianity,* ed. Alan T. Davies (New York: Paulist Press, 1979), pp. 84–88; and Beck, *Mature Christianity,* pp. 248–251.

29. David A. Tracy, "Religious Values After the Holocaust: A Catholic View," in *Jews and Christians After the Holocaust,* ed. Abraham J. Peck (Philadelphia: Fortress Press, 1982), pp. 96–97.

30. Lloyd Gaston, "Jesus the Jew in the Apostolic Writings," *Religion & Intellectual Life* 3 (1986), 58, 59.

31. Van Buren does contend that Paul the apostle can help us affirm the *sola scriptura* "which he himself affirmed, the Scriptures of Israel, and so learn to read and interpret our so-called New Testament writings always in the light of and with reference to the Scriptures which fed Paul, not to speak of his Lord and ours." Van Buren, "The Church and Israel," p. 16. That the New Testament must be read "in the light of and with reference to" the Hebrew Scriptures does not imply that it is without its own authority for Christians, only that that authority will never be correctly interpreted except in the light of the whole of the biblical witness. Also, it is the case for van Buren that Paul and (the witnessed-to) Jesus are authoritative for Christians.

32. This review of Gaston's position may be unfair, because it scrutinizes one essay, and a short one at that. Let us take what is said of Gaston's supposed views here, then, as representing a "type," one possible response to the issue of the authority of the New Testament post-Holocaust.

33. For an account of the scope of this revolution, see Ellis Rivkin, *A Hidden Revolution* (Nashville: Abingdon Press, 1978).

34. Arthur F. Glasser, "Truth as Revealed in Scripture," *Religion & Intellectual Life* 3 (1986), 65, 67–68.

35. Ibid., pp. 68–69; for a recent articulation of the theory of scriptural inerrancy, see John H. Gerstner, "A Protestant View of Biblical Authority," in *Scripture in the Jewish and Christian Traditions: Authority, Interpretation, Relevance,* ed. Frederick E. Greenspahn (Nashville: Abingdon Press, 1982), pp. 41–63.

36. Paul Tillich, *Perspectives on 19th and 20th Century Protestant Theology* (New York: Harper & Row, 1967), p. 227.

37. Glasser, "Truth as Revealed in Scripture," p. 71 (emphasis mine).

38. See Edward Farley and Peter C. Hodgson, "Scripture and Tradition," in *Christian Theology: An Introduction to Its Traditions and Tasks,* ed. Peter C. Hodgson and Robert H. King (Philadelphia: Fortress Press, 1985), pp. 61–87. In what follows, I summarize their account.

39. Ibid., pp. 63, 65.

40. Ibid., pp. 65–66.

41. See Rivkin, *A Hidden Revolution,* pp. 209–311.

42. On Tertullian's reaction to the idea of a canon, see Bruce L. Shelley, *Church History in Plain Language* (Waco, Tex.: Word Books, 1982), p. 80.

43. Farley and Hodgson, "Scripture and Tradition," p. 68.

44. *B. Menah,* 29b, cited in Frederick E. Greenspahn, ed., *Scripture in the Jewish and Christian Traditions* (Nashville: Abingdon Press, 1982), p. 87.

45. Jacob Neusner, "Scripture and Mishnah: Authority and Selectivity," in *Scripture in the Jewish and Christian Traditions,* ed. Frederick E. Greenspahn (Nashville: Abingdon Press, 1982), p. 65.

46. Ibid., p. 66.

47. Ibid., pp. 67–69, 71.

48. Michael Fishbane, "Jewish Biblical Exegesis: Presuppositions and Principles," in *Scripture in the Jewish and Christian Traditions,* ed. Frederick E. Greenspahn (Nashville: Abingdon Press, 1982), pp. 96–97.

49. Neusner, "Scripture and Mishnah," p. 71.

50. Ibid., pp. 75, 77–79.

51. Ibid., p. 66.

52. James Barr, *The Scope and Authority of the Bible* (Philadelphia: Westminster Press, 1980), p. 58.

53. See Avery Dulles, S.J., "The Authority of Scripture: A Catholic Perspective," in *Scripture in the Jewish and Christian Traditions,* ed. Frederick E. Greenspahn (Nashville: Abingdon Press, 1982), p. 33.

54. David H. Kelsey, "Protestant Attitudes Regarding Methods of Biblical Interpretation," in *Scripture in the Jewish and Christian Traditions,* ed. Frederick E. Greenspahn (Nashville: Abingdon Press, 1982), p. 137.

55. Luther argued that the scriptures had to be understood "in favor of Christ, not against him. For that reason they must either refer to him or must not be held to be true Scriptures." *Theses Concerning Faith and Law,* thesis 41 in *Luther's Works* (Philadelphia: Muhlenberg Press, 1960), 34:112.

56. Jaroslav Pelikan, *Luther the Expositor* (St. Louis: Concordia, 1959), p. 67.

57. *Luther's Works,* 35:396.

58. Ibid., 35:166.

59. See, for example, Luther's tract *The Freedom of a Christian* in John Dillenberger, ed., *Martin Luther: Selections from His Writings* (Garden City, N.Y.: Doubleday Anchor Books, 1961), pp. 42–85.

60. Schubert M. Ogden, "The Authority of Scripture for Theology," *Interpretation* 30 (1976), 245; Ogden's essay is also available in his *On Theology*, pp. 45–68.

61. Ibid., p. 246.

62. Ibid., p. 250.

63. Ibid., p. 252.

64. Ibid., p. 257.

65. Ogden, *The Point of Christology*, p. 63.

66. Schubert M. Ogden, *The Reality of God* (New York: Harper & Row, 1966), pp. 201–203.

67. Schubert M. Ogden, *Christ Without Myth* (New York: Harper & Row, 1961), pp. 142–143, 145.

68. Ibid., p. 144.

69. Ogden, "The Authority of Scripture for Theology," pp. 260–261.

70. It was Bultmann who understood the relation of the Old and New Testaments to each other, respectively, as question and answer. This understanding, I submit, was part and parcel of his failure to carry through his program of demythologizing and existential interpretation consistently and without remainder. Ogden, who corrected Bultmann on this in his *Christ Without Myth*, should, therefore, not follow Bultmann in his understanding of the New Testament as the "answer" to the Old Testament's "question."

71. James A. Sanders, *Canon and Community*, pp. xv, 31, 27–28.

72. Ibid., pp. 52–53.

73. Ibid., pp. 66–67.

74. Ibid., p. 58.

75. Schubert M. Ogden, "Toward a New Theism," in *Process Philosophy and Christian Thought*, ed. Delwin Brown, Ralph E. James, Jr., and Gene Reeves (Indianapolis: Bobbs-Merrill, 1971), p. 173.

Chapter 7: Christology

1. Ruether, *Faith and Fratricide*, p. 246.

2. One can trace this whole line of christological anti-Judaism as it is developed in the roughly one hundred *adversus Judaeos* tracts analyzed

by A. Lukyn Williams in his *Adversus Judaeos* or see it developed in the intensive analysis of one theologian, as in the excellent study of the anti-Judaism present in twenty-seven of Tertullian's thirty-two extant works provided by David Patrick Efroymson, "Tertullian's Anti-Judaism and Its Role in His Theology."

3. One of the better recent treatments is that of Carl E. Braaten in *Christian Dogmatics,* vol. 1, ed. Carl E. Braaten and Robert W. Jenson (Philadelphia: Fortress Press, 1984), pp. 465–569.

4. Irenaeus, *Against All Heresies,* vol. 1, bk. 5, p. 526.

5. Athanasius, *On the Incarnation of the Word,* in *Christology of the Later Fathers,* vol. 3 of the Library of Christian Classics, ed. Edward Rochie Hardy (Philadelphia: Westminster Press, 1954), p. 55.

6. Ibid., pp. 59., 62–63.

7. Ibid., pp. 65, 67.

8. Ibid., p. 71. Athanasius reiterates this theme of the divine impassibility of the Logos in his *Orations Against the Arians,* in *The Christological Controversy,* trans. and ed. Richard A. Norris, Jr. (Philadelphia: Fortress Press, 1980), pp. 92–93.

9. Ibid., p. 72.

10. Ibid., p. 87.

11. That the earliest *adversus Judaeos* literature was intended to distinguish Christianity from Judaism rather than to constitute an overt attack on Judaism itself is argued by Robert S. MacLennan in *Early Christian Texts on Jews and Judaism* (Atlanta: Scholars Press, 1990). That anti-Judaism constituted an attempt to provide a social identity for Christians as other and better than Jewish is clear from reading the *adversus Judaeos* literature. That it largely succeeded in that attempt is part of our continuing problem.

12. Athanasius, *On the Incarnation,* p. 89.

13. Ibid., pp. 90–92.

14. Ibid., p. 93.

15. Gregory of Nyssa, *Catechetical Oration 37,* in Wiles and Santer, eds., *Documents in Early Christian Thought,* pp. 194–196.

16. Walter Lowe, "Christ and Salvation," in *Christian Theology: An Introduction to Its Traditions and Tasks,* ed. Peter C. Hodgson and Robert H. King (Philadelphia: Fortress Press, 1985), p. 232.

17. Jaroslav Pelikan shows that the immutable God of classical theology was simply assumed by the church fathers and never argued biblically or theologically, yet governed the development of the christological dogma. See his *The Christian Tradition*, vol. 1: *The Emergence of the Catholic Tradition (100–600)*(Chicago: University of Chicago Press, 1971), pp. 228–232.

18. See Schubert M. Ogden's telling criticism of modern revisionist Christologies on these issues in *The Point of Christology*, pp. 111–112.

19. Jeremias, *New Testament Theology*, p. 227.

20. Adolf Harnack referred to this as "a *pharmacological* process" of salvation in *What Is Christianity?*, trans. Thomas Bailey Saunders (New York: Harper & Brothers, 1957), p. 232.

21. Immanuel Kant, *"What Is Enlightenment?"* trans. and ed. L. W. Beck (Chicago: University of Chicago Press, 1955), p. 286.

22. Immanuel Kant, *Religion Within the Limits of Reason Alone*, trans. Theodore M. Greene and Hoyt H. Hudson (New York: Harper & Brothers, 1960), pp. 95–96.

23. Ibid., pp. 116–117.

24. Ibid., pp. 74, 118.

25. Ibid., pp. 119, 155.

26. See Richard Kroner, "Hegel's Philosophical Development," in *Friedrich Hegel, On Christianity: Early Theological Writings*, trans. T. M. Knox (New York: Harper & Brothers, 1961), p. 9.

27. Ibid., pp. 9–10.

28. Ibid., pp. 68–69.

29. Ibid., pp. 78, 177–178, 185–188, 191, 193.

30. Ibid., p. 265.

31. Ibid., pp. 285–286, 281, 268–269, 253, 240–241, 212, 205, 179.

32. Friedrich Hegel, *The Phenomenology of Mind*, trans. James B. Baillie (London: George Allen & Unwin, 1949), p. 366.

33. Friedrich Hegel, *Lectures on the Philosophy of Religion*, vol. 2, trans. E. B. Speirs and J. Burdon Sanderson (London: Routledge & Kegan Paul, 1895), pp. 208–219, see esp. 209, 210–211, 216.

34. For a discussion of Hegel's impact on modern Christologies in this regard, see Colin E. Gunton, *Yesterday and Today: A Study of Conti-*

nuities in Christology (Grand Rapids: Eerdmans, 1983), pp. 16–17.

35. Schleiermacher, *The Christian Faith*, pp. 12, 31, 33, 37, 60–62, 380–385, 425.

36. For an excellent discussion of Schleiermacher and Jews of his time, see Joseph W. Pickle, "Schleiermacher on Judaism," *Journal of Religion* 60, no. 2 (April 1980), 115–137.

37. Friedrich Schleiermacher, *The Life of Jesus*, trans. S. Maclean Gilmour, ed. Jack C. Verheyden (Philadelphia: Fortress Press, 1975), pp. 316–317.

38. Ibid., pp. 102, 107–108.

39. Adolf Harnack, *The Mission and Expansion of Christianity*, trans. and ed. James Moffatt (New York: Harper & Row, 1961), pp. 36, 43.

40. Ibid., p. 65–67, 69–70.

41. Adolf Harnack, *What Is Christianity?*, pp. 7, 19, 30–31, 11.

42. Ibid., pp. 35 (emphases mine), 38, 47–48.

43. Cited in G. Wayne Glick, *The Reality of Christianity* (New York: Harper & Row, 1967), p. 187.

44. Harnack, *What Is Christianity?*, p. 47.

45. Ibid., pp. 48, 50–51.

46. Ibid., pp. 56, 63, 91, 103, 72.

47. Ibid., pp. 144, 128, 175.

48. Joao Dias de Araujo, "Images of Christ in the Culture of the Brazilian People," in *Faces of Jesus*, trans. Robert R. Barr, ed. Jose Miguez-Bonino (Maryknoll, N.Y.: Orbis Books, 1984), pp. 32–37.

49. Saul Trinidad and Juan Stam, "Christ in Latin American Protestant Preaching," in Miguez-Bonino, ed., *Faces of Jesus*, pp. 40–43.

50. Georges Casalis, "Jesus—Neither Abject Lord nor Heavenly Monarch," in Miguez-Bonino, ed., *Faces of Jesus*, p. 73.

51. Ibid., p. 74.

52. Trinidad and Stam, "Christ in Latin American Protestant Preaching," in Miguez-Bonino, ed., *Faces of Jesus*, p. 50.

53. Ignacio Ellacuria, "The Political Nature of Jesus' Mission," in Miguez-Bonino, ed., *Faces of Jesus*, p. 81.

54. Jose Miranda, *Being and the Messiah*, trans. John Eagleson (Mary-knoll, N.Y.: Orbis Books, 1977), pp. 53, 80–81, 84.

55. Jon Sobrino, *The True Church and the Poor*, trans. Matthew J. O'Connell (Maryknoll, N.Y.: Orbis Books, 1984), p. 128.

56. J. Severino Croatto, "The Political Dimension of Christ the Liberator," in Miguez-Bonino, ed., *Faces of Jesus*, pp. 103, 104 (emphasis mine), 105, 106.

57. Ibid., pp. 107, 110 (emphasis Croatto's).

58. Ibid., p. 113. Croatto states the same position in his *Exodus: A Hermeneutic of Freedom*, trans. Salvator Attanasio (Maryknoll, N.Y.: Orbis Books, 1981), pp. 52, 64.

59. Croatto, "The Political Dimension of Christ the Liberator," p. 119.

60. Küng, *On Being a Christian*, p. 212.

61. Niebuhr, *The Meaning of Revelation*, pp. viii–ix.

62. Paul Tillich, *Systematic Theology*, vol. 2 (Chicago: University of Chicago Press, 1957), p. 114.

63. Ibid., p. 98; once in a conversation with me, Tillich revised his position to contend that estrangement had to be overcome in the life of Jesus as imagined by the apostles.

64. Paul Tillich, *Systematic Theology*, vol. 1 (Chicago: University of Chicago Press, 1951), p. 133.

65. Crossan, *The Historical Jesus*, Part 3: "Brokerless Kingdom."

66. Tillich, *Systematic Theology*, vol. 2, p. 134.

67. Ibid., p. 135.

68. This is precisely the burden of Elisabeth Schüssler-Fiorenza's *In Memory of Her* (New York: Crossroad, 1983), pp. 105–159, in which she struggles mightily to describe a Jesus liberating women from patriarchy, without falling into anti-Judaism. Why Jesus has to do this is made clear on p. 334: unlike patriarchy, which "cannot claim the authority of Jesus for its own Christian praxis," a more inclusive vision can lay claim to Jesus' authority. That Jesus *is* the authority is not argued theologically.

69. See the discussion of this point in Barth's Christology by Demson, "Israel as the Paradigm of Divine Judgment," p. 623.

70. This term was coined by Alfred North Whitehead and has been

used in more than one way to criticize traditional and modern Christologies. See Ogden, *The Point of Christology,* pp. 28–29, and Rita Nakashima Brock, *Journeys by Heart* (New York: Crossroad, 1988), p. 68.

71. David R. Griffin, *A Process Christology* (Philadelphia: Westminster Press, 1973), p. 12.

72. See the discussion in Clark M. Williamson, *God Is Never Absent* (St. Louis: Bethany Press, 1977), p. 91.

73. James A. Sanders, *Canon and Community,* p. 59.

74. van Buren, *Christ in Context* [Part 3 of *A Theology of the Jewish-Christian Reality*] (San Francisco: Harper & Row, 1988), p. 80.

75. Ibid., p. 37.

76. Cyprian, *Letter 69, 1–5,* in Wiles and Santer, eds., *Documents in Early Christian Thought,* p. 160.

77. Whitehead, *Process and Reality,* p. 137.

78. Alexander Campbell, *The Christian System* (Cincinnati: H. S. Bosworth, 1866), p. 34.

Chapter 8: The God of Israel and of the Church

1. Statement of the 1979 Central Committee of Roman Catholics in Germany; in Croner, *More Stepping Stones,* p. 117.

2. See Aristotle, *The Works of Aristotle,* trans. and ed. J. A. Smith and W. D. Ross (Oxford: Clarendon Press, 1912), sec. 17.

3. Robert W. Jenson, "The Triune God," in *Christian Dogmatics,* vol. 1, ed. Robert W. Jenson and Carl E. Braaten (Philadelphia: Fortress Press, 1984), p. 115.

4. John Dewey, "Time and Individuality," in *Philosophers of Process,* ed. Douglas Browning (New York: Random House, 1965), p. 208.

5. Jenson, "The Triune God," p. 116.

6. Clement of Alexandria, *Miscellanies 5, xii, 78–82,* in Wiles and Santer, eds., *Documents in Early Christian Thought,* p. 6.

7. Ibid., p. 7.

8. Gregory of Nyssa, *The Life of Moses II,* in Wiles and Santer, eds., *Documents in Early Christian Thought,* p. 12.

9. Ibid., p. 15.

10. Origen, *Homilies on Jeremiah 18*, in Wiles and Santer, eds., *Documents in Early Christian Thought*, p. 7.

11. Ibid., p. 10.

12. Augustine, *On the Psalms 134*, in Wiles and Santer, eds., *Documents in Early Christian Thought*, p. 18.

13. Ibid., p. 19.

14. Dewey, "Time and Individuality," p. 208.

15. Augustine, *On Christian Doctrine*, trans. D. W. Robertson, Jr. (Indianapolis: Bobbs-Merrill, 1958), p. 38.

16. Cited by Paul Tillich, "The Two Types of Philosophy of Religion," in *Theology of Culture*, ed. Robert C. Kimball (New York: Oxford University Press, 1959), p. 13.

17. Ibid., p. 14.

18. Anselm, *Basic Writings*, trans. S. N. Deane (La Salle, Ill.: Open Court, 1962), p. 13.

19. Pelikan, *The Christian Tradition*, vol. 1, pp. 21–22.

20. Ibid., p. 22.

21. Langdon Gilkey, "God," in *Christian Theology: An Introduction to Its Traditions and Tasks* (Philadelphia: Fortress Press, 1985), p. 90.

22. Ibid., p. 93.

23. Charles Hartshorne, *The Divine Relativity* (New Haven: Yale University Press, 1948), pp. 148–149; here I am following Hartshorne for this list of deficiencies of classical theism.

24. Whitehead, *Process and Reality*, p. 342.

25. This has been nicely shown by Brock, *Journeys by Heart*, pp. 53–57.

26. This phrase was coined by John B. Cobb, Jr., and David R. Griffin in *Process Theology: An Introductory Exposition* (Philadelphia: Westminster Press, 1976), p. 9.

27. Richard L. Rubenstein, *After Auschwitz* (Indianapolis: Bobbs-Merrill, 1966), pp. 65, 67–68.

28. Harold M. Schulweis, *Evil and the Morality of God* (Cincinnati: Hebrew Union College Press, 1984), pp. 125–126.

29. John Dewey, *A Common Faith* (New Haven: Yale University Press, 1934), pp. 33, 50–51.

30. Jon D. Levenson, *Creation and the Persistence of Evil* (San Francisco: Harper & Row, 1988), pp. xiii., xiv, 4, 14, 19.

31. Paul Tillich, *The Protestant Era,* trans. James Luther Adams (Chicago: University of Chicago Press, 1948), pp. 66–68.

32. Levenson, *Creation and the Persistence of Evil,* p. 38.

33. Ibid., p. 39.

34. Cited in Montefiore and Loewe, *A Rabbinic Anthology,* p. 285.

35. Levenson, *Creation and the Persistence of Evil,* p. 141.

36. Charles Hartshorne and William L. Reese, *Philosophers Speak of God* (Chicago: University of Chicago Press, 1953), p. 76.

37. Philo as quoted in ibid., p. 78.

38. Maimonides as cited in ibid., pp. 113–114.

39. Louis Jacobs, *A Jewish Theology* (New York: Behrman House, 1973), p. 27.

40. Ibid., p. 32.

41. Hans Jonas, "The Concept of God After Auschwitz," in *Out of the Whirlwind,* ed. Albert H. Friedlander (New York: Schocken Books, 1976), p. 468.

42. Ibid., pp. 465–468.

43. Ibid., pp. 469–471.

44. Ibid., p. 473.

45. For a rigorous argument that precisely such a panentheistic understanding of God is the only adequate ground for moral theory, see Franklin I. Gamwell, *The Divine Good* (San Francisco: HarperCollins, 1990).

46. Jonas, "The Concept of God After Auschwitz," p. 474.

47. Ibid., pp. 475, 473.

48. Hans Jonas, "The Concept of God After Auschwitz: A Jewish Voice," *Journal of Religion* 67, no. 1 (January 1987), 1, 12.

49. Cited in ibid., p. 13, n. 8.

50. Quoted in ibid.

51. Ibid.

52. Paul M. van Buren, *A Theology of the Jewish-Christian Reality,* Part 2: *A Christian Theology of the People Israel* (New York: Seabury Press, 1983), pp. 63–64.

53. Ibid., p. 62 (emphasis mine).

54. van Buren, *Christ in Context* [Part 3 of *A Theology of the Jewish-Christian Reality*], p. 167.

55. Ibid., pp. 166, 175–176, 165.

56. Ibid., pp. 165, 240, 172–174.

57. Ibid., pp. 177, 185–186, 217–218, 227.

58. Greenberg, "Cloud of Smoke, Pillar of Fire," p. 23.

59. Richard L. Rubenstein and John K. Roth, *Approaches to Auschwitz* (Atlanta: John Knox Press, 1987), pp. 297–298.

60. John K. Roth, "A Theodicy of Protest," in *Encountering Evil,* ed. Stephen T. Davis (Atlanta: John Knox Press, 1981), p. 14.

61. Rubenstein and Roth, *Approaches to Auschwitz,* p. 298.

62. Rubenstein, *After Auschwitz,* p. 65.

63. van Buren, *A Christian Theology of the People Israel* [Part 2 of *A Theology of the Jewish-Christian Reality*], p. 62 (emphasis mine).

64. van Buren, *Christ in Context* [Part 3 of *A Theology of the Jewish-Christian Reality*], p. 167.

65. Ogden, *The Reality of God,* p. 57.

66. Ibid., p. 58.

67. That God's uniqueness is to be thought of not as the chief exception to but as the perfect exemplification of all our most general concepts is an insight owed to Alfred North Whitehead, *Process and Reality,* p. 343; that this perfect exemplification can be articulated in terms of the distinctions between the modifiers "all," "some," and "none" is a contribution of Charles Hartshorne, *A Natural Theology for Our Time* (La Salle, Ill.: Open Court, 1967), pp. 34–43.

68. Ogden, *The Reality of God,* p. 60.

69. Hartshorne, *The Divine Relativity,* p. 20.

70. Whitehead, *Religion in the Making,* p. 100.

71. Alfred North Whitehead, *Science and the Modern World* (New York: New American Library, 1925), p. 160.

72. This set of changes is in accord with Whitehead's ontological principle "that actual entities are the only *reasons;* so that to search for a reason is to search for one or more actual entities." *Process and Reality,* p. 24.

73. David R. Peel, "Is Schubert M. Ogden's 'God' Christian?" *Journal of Religion* 70, no. 2 (April 1990), 148.

74. This is Whitehead's "category of freedom and determination," according to which each occasion "is internally determined [self-determined] and is externally free." *Process and Reality,* p. 27. However much an occasion may be determined by its context, there is always some "remainder" to be decided by that occasion in its act of self-constitution.

75. John B. Cobb, Jr., *Talking About God* [with David Tracy] (New York: Seabury Press, 1983), p. 53.

76. Schubert M. Ogden, "The Metaphysics of Faith and Justice," *Process Studies* 14, no. 2 (Summer 1985), 96.

77. Susannah Heschel, "The Changing Face of Europe," *Perkins Journal* 48 (July/October 1990), 10.

78. Hartshorne, *The Divine Relativity,* p. 152.

79. Tertullian, *Against Praxeas,* in *The Ante-Nicene Fathers,* vol. 3, trans. S. Thelwall, ed. Alexander Roberts and James Donaldson (Grand Rapids: Eerdmans, 1979), p. 627.

80. See, for example, Jürgen Moltmann, *The Crucified God,* trans. R. A. Wilson and John Bowden (New York: Harper & Row, 1974); Eberhard Jüngel, *Gott als Geheimnis der Welt,* 2d ed. (Tübingen: J. C. B. Mohr, 1977); and Heribert Mühlen, *Die Veränderlichkeit Gottes als Horizont einer zukünftigen Christologie* (Munich: Aschendorff, 1969). All of these doctrines of the Trinity move away from understanding God or Being as immutable toward a redefinition involving sociality, becoming, and interpersonal relationship.

81. Cited in Robert M. Grant, *Gods and the One God* (Philadelphia: Westminster Press, 1986), p. 107.

Chapter 9: The Doctrine of the Church

1. The best study of *Synagoga* and *Ecclesia* is found in Wolfgang S. Seiferth, *Synagogue and Church in the Middle Ages: Two Symbols in Art*

and Literature, trans. L. Chadeayne and P. Gottwald (New York: Frederick Ungar, 1970). Numerous examples of the pair are shown in Gertrude Schiller, *Iconography of Christian Art,* vol. 2, trans. Janet Seligman (Greenwich, Conn.: New York Graphic Society, 1972); see illustrations 364–367, 371, 373, 385, 424, 427, 432–433, 438, 442, 446, 448, 450–452, 507, 527–531, 555, 570.

2. That the two depict the power-relations between the church and the synagogue and between the church and the state is well argued by Schiller, *Iconography of Christian Art,* vol. 2, p. 111.

3. Albertus Magnus, cited in Seiferth, *Synagogue and Church in the Middle Ages,* p. 102.

4. Efroymson, "Tertullian's Anti-Judaism and Its Role in His Theology," p. 197. In Chapter 5, in the discussion of election, we discussed Tertullian's *An Answer to the Jews* in some detail. In this discussion of Tertullian, I am following Efroymson's discussion of Tertullian's doctrine of the church throughout the bulk of Tertullian's extant writings. Notes in this discussion of Tertullian are to quotations from Tertullian in Efroymson, unless otherwise noted.

5. Ibid., p. 198.

6. Ibid., p. 199.

7. Ibid., pp. 200–201.

8. Cyprian, *Three Books of Testimonies Against the Jews,* in *The Ante-Nicene Fathers,* vol. 5, ed. Alexander Roberts and James Donaldson (Grand Rapids: Eerdmans, 1978), pp. 507–528.

9. Ibid., pp. 510–512.

10. Cyril of Jerusalem, *Catechetical Lecture 18, 22–7,* in Wiles and Santer, eds., *Documents in Early Christian Thought,* p. 167. (Cyril's translation of the biblical texts is used here.)

11. Ibid., p. 168.

12. Cyril of Jerusalem, *The Works of Saint Cyril of Jerusalem,* vol. 2, trans. Leo P. McCauley, S.J., and Anthony A. Stephenson (Washington, D.C.: Catholic University of America Press, 1970), pp. 9, 15.

13. Lactantius, *The Divine Institutes,* trans. Sister Mary Francis McDonald, O.P. (Washington, D.C.: Catholic University of America Press, 1964), p. 267.

14. Augustine, "In Answer to the Jews," in *Saint Augustine: Treatises on Marriage and Other Subjects,* ed. Roy J. Deferrari (New York:

Fathers of the Church, 1955), pp. 393–394, 399, 408; see also pp. 412–413.

15. Efroymson, "Tertullian's Anti-Judaism and Its Role in His Theology," p. 202.

16. Tertullian, *Prescriptions Against Heretics,* in *Early Latin Theology,* ed. S. L. Greenslade (Philadelphia: Westminster Press, 1956), pp. 36–37.

17. Cyprian, *Three Books of Testimonies Against the Jews,* pp. 512–514.

18. Ambrose, *Theological and Dogmatic Works,* trans. Roy J. Deferrari (Washington, D.C.: Catholic University of America Press, 1963), pp. 10–11, 13.

19. Augustine, "In Answer to the Jews," pp. 400, 403.

20. Efroymson, "Tertullian's Anti-Judaism and Its Role in His Theology," p. 203.

21. Cyril of Jerusalem, *Catechetical Lecture 18, 22–7,* in Wiles and Santer, eds., *Documents in Early Christian Thought,* p. 168.

22. Lactantius, *The Divine Institutes,* p. 270.

23. Augustine, "In Answer to the Jews," p. 411.

24. Efroymson, "Tertullian's Anti-Judaism and Its Role in His Theology," pp. 205–206.

25. Irenaeus, *Against the Heresies IV, 17.5–18.6,* in Wiles and Santer, eds., *Documents in Early Christian Thought,* pp. 185–186.

26. Cyril of Jerusalem, *On the Mysteries 4 and 5,* in Wiles and Santer, eds., *Documents in Early Christian Thought,* p. 188.

27. John Chrysostom, *Homilies on 1 Corinthians 24:1–2,* in Wiles and Santer, eds., *Documents in Early Christian Thought,* p. 198.

28. Ambrose, *Theological and Dogmatic Works,* p. 21.

29. Ibid., p. 23; see also pp. 273–328.

30. Ibid., pp. 177, 198, 255.

31. Augustine, "In Answer to the Jews," p. 410.

32. Cyprian, *Three Books of Testimonies Against the Jews,* pp. 512, 514.

33. Cyprian, *Letter 69, 1–5,* in Wiles and Santer, eds., *Documents in Early Christian Thought,* p. 161.

34. Saint Basil, *Exegetic Homilies,* trans. Sister Agnes Clare Way,

C.D.P. (Washington, D.C.: Catholic University of America Press, 1963), pp. 241, 322–323, 336–337, 198.

35. Lactantius, *The Divine Institutes,* pp. 299–300.

36. See, for example, Chapter 11 of van Buren, *A Christian Theology of the People Israel* [Part 2 of *A Theology of the Jewish-Christian Reality*], pp. 320–352.

37. Thomas Müntzer, *Sermon Before the Princes,* in *Spiritual and Anabaptist Writers,* ed. George H. Williams and Angel M. Mergal (Philadelphia: Westminster Press, 1957), p. 52.

38. Ibid.

39. John Denck, *Whether God Is Cause of Evil,* in Williams and Mergal, eds., *Spiritual and Anabaptist Writers,* pp. 93, 98.

40. Dietrich Philips, *The Church of God,* in Williams and Mergal, eds., *Spiritual and Anabaptist Writers,* pp. 231, 233–235, 252.

41. Ulrich Stadler, *Cherished Instructions on Sin, Excommunication, and the Community of Goods,* in Williams and Mergal, eds., *Spiritual and Anabaptist Writers,* pp. 282–283.

42. *The Second Helvetic Confession,* in Leith, ed., *Creeds of the Churches,* p. 147.

43. Schleiermacher, *The Christian Faith,* p. 527.

44. Luther, "Sermon in Castle Pleissenburg," in *Martin Luther: Selections from His Writings,* ed. Dillenberger, p. 240.

45. Ibid., p. 241.

46. Jewish literature contains many accounts of Sabbatai Zvi, one of which can be found in Trepp, *A History of the Jewish Experience,* pp. 245, 256.

47. Trepp also relates the story of Rabbi Akiba and bar Kochba, ibid., pp. 47, 56, 71.

48. See the discussion and Chrysostom's first sermon in this series in Meeks and Wilken, *Jews and Christians in Antioch,* pp. 87–89, 90–100.

49. Martin Buber, *Two Types of Faith,* trans. Norman P. Goldhawk (New York: Harper & Row, 1961), p. 89.

50. That Jews are "trifling" when it comes to seeing the truth of Christian arguments for the truth of Christianity was Athanasius' claim. See his *On the Incarnation,* p. 93.

51. Martin Buber, *Der Jude und sein Judentum* (Cologne: J. Melzer, 1963), p. 562, cited in Jürgen Moltmann, *The Way of Jesus Christ*, trans. Margaret Kohl (San Francisco: HarperCollins, 1990), p. 28.

52. Paul Tillich, *The Shaking of the Foundations* (New York: Charles Scribner's Sons, 1948), pp. 164–168.

53. Paul M. van Buren has called to my attention the fact that Friedrich-Wilhelm Marquardt was the first to argue that Christians will not overcome our Christian anti-Judaism until we make something theologically positive of the Jewish "no" to Christianity. See Marquardt's *Verwegenheiten* (Munich: Chr. Kaiser Verlag, 1981).

54. I try to provide some fleshing out of what this entails in *When Jews and Christians Meet*.

55. Joseph Haroutunian, *God with Us* (Philadelphia: Westminster Press, 1965), p. 279.

56. Gutierrez, *A Theology of Liberation*, pp. 256–261, 267–269.

57. Hans Küng, *The Church*, trans. Ray and Rosaleen Ockenden (New York: Sheed & Ward, 1967), pp. 53–59.

58. See, for example, Edward Farley, *Ecclesial Man* (Philadelphia: Fortress Press, 1975), pp. 182–185.

59. Tillich, *The Protestant Era*, p. 163.

60. Tillich, *Systematic Theology*, vol. 3, pp. 165–172.

61. Douglas R. A. Hare and Michael Harrington, "'Make Disciples of All the Gentiles' (Mt. 28:19)," *Catholic Biblical Quarterly* 37 (1975), 359–369.

62. Alfred Loisy, *The Gospel and the Church*, trans. C. Home (New York: Charles Scribner's Sons, 1909), p. 4.

63. See, for example, Williston Walker, *A History of the Christian Church* (New York: Charles Scribner's Sons, 1918), p. 370.

Bibliography

Abbot, Walter M., S.J., ed. *The Documents of Vatican II*. New York: American Press, 1966.

Agnew, Francis H. "Paul's Theological Adversary in the Doctrine of Justification by Faith." *Journal of Ecumenical Studies* 25, no. 4 (Fall 1988), 538–554.

Ambrose. *Theological and Dogmatic Works*. Translated by Roy J. Deferrari. Washington, D.C.: Catholic University of America Press, 1963.

Ames, William. *The Marrow of Theology*. Translated and edited by John D. Eusden. Durham: Labyrinth Press, 1968.

Anselm. *Basic Writings*. Translated by S. N. Deane. La Salle, Ill.: Open Court, 1962.

Aristotle. *The Works of Aristotle*. Translated and edited by J. A. Smith and W. D. Ross, sec. 17. Oxford: Clarendon Press, 1912.

Athanasius. *On the Incarnation of the Word*. In *Christology of the Later Fathers*. Vol. 3 of the Library of Christian Classics, edited by Edward Rochie Hardy, pp. 55, 110. Philadelphia: Westminster Press, 1954.

———. *Orations Against the Arians*. In *The Christological Controversy*, translated and edited by Richard A. Norris, Jr., pp. 83–101. Philadelphia: Fortress Press, 1980.

Augustine. *The City of God*. Translated by Marcus Dods. New York: Random House, 1950.

———. "In Answer to the Jews." In *Saint Augustine: Treatises on Marriage and Other Subjects*, edited by Roy J. Deferrari, pp. 391–414. New York: Fathers of the Church, 1955.

———. *On Christian Doctrine*. Translated by D. W. Robertson, Jr. Indianapolis: Bobbs-Merrill, 1958.

———. *Reply to Faustus*. In *Disputation and Dialogue*, edited by Frank E. Talmage, pp. 28–32. New York: KTAV, 1975.

Austin, J. L. *Philosophical Papers*. Edited by J. O. Urmson. Oxford: Oxford University Press, 1961.

Barnabas. *The Epistle of Barnabas*. In *The Ante-Nicene Fathers*. Vol. 1, translated and edited by Alexander Roberts and James Donaldson, pp. 137–149. Grand Rapids: Eerdmans, 1979.

Barr, James. "Abba Isn't 'Daddy.'" *Journal of Theological Studies* 39 (1988), 28–47.

———. *The Scope and Authority of the Bible*. Philadelphia: Westminster Press, 1980.

Barth, Karl. *Church Dogmatics*. Vol. I, pt. 1. Translated by G. T. Thompson. Edinburgh: T. & T. Clark, 1936.

———. *Church Dogmatics*. Vol. II, pt. 2. Translated by G. W. Bromiley et al. Edinburgh: T. & T. Clark, 1957.

———. *Church Dogmatics*. Vol. IV, pt. 1. Translated by G. W. Bromiley. Edinburgh: T. & T. Clark, 1956.

———. *Dogmatics in Outline*. Translated by G. T. Thompson. New York: Harper & Brothers, 1959.

———. *The Humanity of God*. Translated by J. N. Thomas and Thomas Wieser. Richmond: John Knox Press, 1960.

———. "The Jewish Problem and the Christian Answer." In *Against the Stream*, pp. 193–202. London: SCM Press, 1954.

Barth, Markus. *Jesus the Jew*. Translated by Frederick Prussner. Atlanta: John Knox Press, 1978.

———. "Was Paul an Anti-Semite?" *Journal of Ecumenical Studies* 5 (1968), 78–104.

Bartsch, Hans Werner. "Die Bedeutung Jerusalems für das jüdische Volk und die Stadt unter Besatzung, Materialen zum Nahostkonflikt, 47." *Evangelischer Arbeitskreis Kirche und Israel in Hessen und Nassau*, i.

Basil, Saint. *Exegetic Homilies*. Translated by Sister Agnes Clare Way, C.D.P. Washington, D.C.: Catholic University of America Press, 1963.

Baum, Gregory. "Catholic Dogma After Auschwitz." In *Anti-Semitism and the Foundations of Christianity*, edited by Alan T. Davies, pp. 137–150. New York: Paulist Press, 1979.

———. "The Holocaust and Political Theology." In *The Holocaust as Interruption*, edited by Elisabeth Schüssler Fiorenza and David Tracy, pp. 34–42. Edinburgh: T. & T. Clark, 1984.

Beck, Norman A. *Mature Christianity*. London and Toronto: Associated University Presses, 1985.

Beker, J. Christiaan. "The New Testament View of Judaism." In *Jews and Christians*, edited by James H. Charlesworth, pp. 60–69. New York: Crossroad, 1990.

———. *Paul the Apostle*. Philadelphia: Fortress Press, 1980.

———. "Romans 9–11 in the Context of the Early Church." *The Princeton Seminary Bulletin*, Supplementary Issue, no. 1 (1990), 40–55.

Black, Matthew. *Romans*. London: Marshall, Morgan & Scott, 1973.

Boers, Hendrikus. *Who Was Jesus?* San Francisco: Harper & Row, 1989.

Bokser, Ben Zion. "Witness and Mission in Judaism." In *Issues in the Jewish-Christian Dialogue: Jewish Perspectives on Covenant, Mission and Witness,* edited by Helga Croner and Leon Klenicki, pp. 89–107. New York: Paulist Press, 1979.

Bowden, John. *Jesus: The Unanswered Questions.* London: SCM Press, 1988.

Braaten, Carl E. *Christian Dogmatics.* Vol. 1. Edited by Carl E. Braaten and Robert W. Jenson. Philadelphia: Fortress Press, 1984.

Braun, Herbert. *Spätjudisch-häretischer und frühchristlicher Radikalismus.* Tübingen: J. C. B. Mohr, 1969.

Breech, James. *The Silence of Jesus.* Philadelphia: Fortress Press, 1983.

Briggs, Sheila. "Images of Women and Jews in Nineteenth and Twentieth-Century German Theology." In *Immaculate and Powerful,* edited by Clarissa W. Atkinson, Constance H. Buchanan, and Margaret R. Miles, pp. 226–259. Boston: Beacon Press, 1985.

Brock, Rita Nakashima. *Journeys by Heart.* New York: Crossroad, 1988.

Brockway, Alan, Paul van Buren, Rolf Rendtorff, and Simon Schoon. *The Theology of the Churches and the Jewish People: Statements by the World Council of Churches and Its Member Churches.* Geneva: WCC Publications, 1988.

Brooks, Roger. *The Spirit of the Ten Commandments.* San Francisco: Harper & Row, 1990.

Brown, Delwin. "Struggle till Daybreak: On the Nature of Authority in Theology." *Journal of Religion* 65 (January 1985), 15–32.

Brown, Raymond E. *The Community of the Beloved Disciple.* New York: Paulist Press, 1979.

Brueggemann, Walter. *The Land: Place as Gift, Promise, and Challenge to Biblical Faith.* Philadelphia: Fortress Press, 1977.

Buber, Martin. *Two Types of Faith.* Translated by Norman P. Goldhawk. New York: Harper & Row, 1961.

Buggert, William F. "The Christologies of Hans Küng and Karl Rahner: A Comparison and Evaluation of Their Mutual Compatability." Ph.D. diss., The Catholic University of America, 1978.

Bultmann, Rudolf. *The History of the Synoptic Tradition.* Translated by John Marsh. New York: Harper & Row, 1963.

Cadbury, Henry J. *Jesus: What Manner of Man?* London: SPCK, 1962.

———. "Mixed Motives in the Gospels." *Proceedings of the American Philosophical Society* 95 (April 1951), 117–124.

Calvert, D. G. A. "An Examination of the Criteria for Distinguishing the Authentic Words of Jesus." *New Testament Studies* 18 (1971–72), 209–218.

Calvin, John. *Institutes of the Christian Religion.* Vol. 1. Edited by John T. McNeill. Translated by Ford Lewis Battles. Philadelphia: Westminster Press, 1960.

Campbell, Alexander. *The Christian System.* Cincinnati: H. S. Bosworth, 1866.

Casey, Maurice. *From Jewish Prophet to Gentile God*. Louisville: West-minster/John Knox Press, 1991.

Charlesworth, James H. "Exploring Opportunities for Rethinking Rela-tions Among Jews and Christians." In *Jews and Christians*, edited by James H. Charlesworth, pp. 35–53. New York: Crossroad, 1990.

——. *Jesus Within Judaism*. New York: Doubleday, 1988.

Clark, Elizabeth, and Herbert Richardson, eds. *Women and Religion*. New York: Harper & Row, 1977.

Clements, R. E. "Covenant." In *The Westminster Dictionary of Christian Theology*, pp. 127–129. Philadelphia: Westminster Press, 1983.

Cobb, John B., Jr. *God and the World*. Philadelphia: Westminster Press, 1969.

——. *Talking About God* [with David Tracy]. New York: Seabury Press, 1983.

Cobb, John B., Jr., and David R. Griffin. *Process Theology: An Introduc-tory Exposition*. Philadelphia: Westminster Press, 1976.

Collins, R. F. *Studies on the First Letter to the Thessalonians*. Louvain: University Press, 1984.

Comstock, Gary L. "Truth or Meaning: Ricoeur versus Frei on Biblical Narrative." *Journal of Religion* 66 (April 1986), 117–140.

——. "Two Types of Narrative Theology." *Journal of the American Academy of Religion* 50 (1987), 687–717.

Croatto, J. Severino. *Exodus: A Hermeneutic of Freedom*. Translated by Salvator Attanasio. Maryknoll, N.Y.: Orbis Books, 1981.

Croner, Helga, comp. *More Stepping Stones to Jewish-Christian Relations*. New York: Paulist Press, 1985.

——. *Stepping Stones to Further Jewish-Christian Relations*. New York: Stimulus Books, 1977.

Crossan, John Dominic. *The Historical Jesus*. San Francisco: HarperSan-Francisco, 1991.

Culbertson, Philip. "Fish, Taxes, and Civil Disobedience." Unpublished paper.

——. "Reclaiming the Matthean Vineyard Parables." *Encounter* 49, no. 4 (Autumn 1988), 257–283.

Cunningham, Philip A. *Jewish Apostle to the Gentiles: Paul as He Saw Himself*. Mystic, Conn.: Twenty-Third Publications, 1986.

Cyprian. *Three Books of Testimonies Against the Jews*. In *The Ante-Nicene Fathers*. Vol. 5, edited by Alexander Roberts and James Donaldson, pp. 507–528. Grand Rapids: Eerdmans, 1978.

Cyril of Jerusalem. *The Works of Saint Cyril of Jerusalem*. Vol. 2. Trans-lated by Leo P. McCauley, S.J., and Anthony A. Stephenson. Wash-ington, D.C.: Catholic University of America Press, 1970.

Davies, Alan T. "The Aryan Christ." *Journal of Ecumenical Studies* 12, no. 4 (Fall 1975), 569–579.

Davies, W. D. *The Gospel and the Land.* Berkeley: University of California Press, 1974.

———. *Jewish and Pauline Studies.* Philadelphia: Fortress Press, 1984.

———. *Paul and Rabbinic Judaism.* Philadelphia: Fortress Press, 1980.

de Jonge, Marinus. *Christology in Context: The Earliest Christian Response to Jesus.* Philadelphia: Westminster Press, 1988.

———. "The Use of the Word 'Anointed' in the Time of Jesus." *Novum Testamentum* 8 (1966), 132–148.

Demson, David E. "Israel as the Paradigm of Divine Judgment: An Examination of a Theme in the Theology of Karl Barth." *Journal of Ecumenical Studies* 26, no. 4 (1989), 611–627.

Dewey, John. *A Common Faith.* New Haven: Yale University Press, 1934.

———. "Time and Individuality." In *Philosophers of Process,* edited by Douglas Browning, pp. 208–224. New York: Random House, 1965.

Downing, Gerald. *Jesus and the Threat of Freedom.* London: SCM Press, 1987.

Dulles, Avery, S.J. "The Authority of Scripture: A Catholic Perspective." In *Scripture in the Jewish and Christian Traditions: Authority, Interpretation, Relevance,* edited by Frederick E. Greenspahn, pp. 13–40. Nashville: Abingdon Press, 1982.

Dunn, James D. G. *Jesus, Paul, and the Law.* Louisville: Westminster/John Knox Press, 1990.

———. *The Partings of the Ways.* Philadelphia: Trinity Press International, 1991.

———. *Romans 9–16.* Word Biblical Commentary 38b. Dallas: Word Books, 1988.

———. *Unity and Diversity in the New Testament.* Philadelphia: Westminster Press, 1977.

Eckardt, A. Roy. *Black—Woman—Jew: Three Wars for Human Liberation.* Bloomington: Indiana University Press, 1989.

———. "Christians and Jews: Along a Theological Frontier." In *Christianity and Judaism: The Deepening Dialogue,* edited by Richard W. Rousseau, S. J., pp. 27–48. Scranton, Pa.: Ridge Row Press, 1983.

Eckardt, Alice L. "A Christian Problem: Review of Protestant Documents." In *More Stepping Stones to Jewish-Christian Relations,* compiled by Helga Croner, pp. 16–23. New York: Paulist Press, 1985.

Efroymson, David Patrick. "The Patristic Connection." In *Anti-Semitism and the Foundations of Christianity,* edited by Alan T. Davies, pp. 98–117. New York: Paulist Press: 1979.

———. "Tertullian's Anti-Judaism and Its Role in His Theology." Ph.D. diss., Temple University, 1976.

Ellenson, David. "Jewish Covenant and Christian Trinitarianism." In *Jewish Civilization: Essays and Studies*, edited by Ronald A. Brauner, pp. 85–100. Philadelphia: Reconstructionist Rabbinical College, 1985.

Engel, Mary Potter. "Calvin and the Jews: A Textual Puzzle." *The Princeton Seminary Bulletin*, Supplementary Issue, no. 1 (1990), 106–123.

Enslin, Morton Scott. *Christian Beginnings*. New York: Harper & Brothers, 1956.

Ericksen, Robert P. *Theologians Under Hitler*. New Haven: Yale University Press, 1985.

Farley, Edward. *Ecclesial Man*. Philadelphia: Fortress Press, 1975.

Farley, Edward, and Peter C. Hodgson. "Scripture and Tradition." In *Readings in Christian Theology*, edited by Peter C. Hodgson and Robert H. King, pp. 61–87. Philadelphia: Fortress Press, 1985.

Finkelstein, Louis. *The Jews: Their History*. New York: Schocken Books, 1970.

Fishbane, Michael. "Jewish Biblical Exegesis: Presuppositions and Principles." In *Scripture in the Jewish and Christian Traditions: Authority, Interpretation, Relevance*, edited by Frederick E. Greenspahn, pp. 91–110. Nashville: Abingdon Press, 1982.

Flannery, Edward H. *The Anguish of the Jews*. New York: Macmillan, 1965.

Flusser, David. "Aesop's Miser and the Parable of the Talents." In *Parable and Story in Judaism and Christianity*, edited by Clemens Thoma and Michael Wyschogrod, pp. 9–25. New York: Paulist Press, 1989.

Fohrer, Georg. *History of Israelite Religion*. Nashville: Abingdon Press, 1972.

———. *Studien zur alttestamentlichen Theologie und Geschichte, 1949–66*. Berlin: Walter de Gruyter, 1969.

Fredriksen, Paula. *From Jesus to Christ*. New Haven: Yale University Press, 1988.

Frei, Hans. "Eberhard Busch's Biography of Karl Barth." In *Karl Barth in Re-View*, edited by H. Martin Rumscheidt, pp. 95–116. Pittsburgh: Pickwick Press, 1981.

Gager, John G. *The Origins of Anti-Semitism*. New York: Oxford University Press, 1983.

Gamwell, Franklin I. *The Divine Good*. San Francisco: HarperCollins, 1990.

Gaston, Lloyd. "Jesus the Jew in the Apostolic Writings." *Religion & Intellectual Life* 3 (1986), 55–59.

———. *Paul and the Torah*. Vancouver: University of British Columbia Press, 1987.

———. "Paul and the Torah." In *Anti-Semitism and the Foundations of Christianity*, edited by Alan T. Davies, pp. 48–71. New York: Paulist Press, 1979.

Gerstner, John H. "A Protestant View of Biblical Authority." In *Scripture in the Jewish and Christian Traditions: Authority, Interpretation, Relevance*, edited by Frederick E. Greenspahn, pp. 41–63. Nashville: Abingdon Press, 1982.

Gilkey, Langdon. "God." In *Christian Theology: An Introduction to Its Traditions and Tasks*, pp. 88–113. Philadelphia: Fortress Press, 1985.

Glasser, Arthur F. "Truth as Revealed in Scripture." *Religion & Intellectual Life* 3 (1986), 65–71.

Glick, G. Wayne. *The Reality of Christianity*. New York: Harper & Row, 1967.

Goldberg, Michael. "God, Action, and Narrative: *Which* Narrative? *Which* Action? *Which* God?" *Journal of Religion* 68 (January 1988), 39–56.

Gonzalez, Justo L. *A History of Christian Thought*. Vol. 1. Nashville: Abingdon Press, 1970.

Grant, Robert M. *Gods and the One God*. Philadelphia: Westminster Press, 1986.

Grant, Robert M., and David Tracy. *A Short History of the Interpretation of the Bible*. Philadelphia: Fortress Press, 1984.

Grassi, Joseph A. "*Abba*, Father (Mark 14:36): Another Approach." *Journal of the American Academy of Religion* 50 (September 1982), 449–458.

Greenberg, Blu. "The Holocaust and the Gospel Truth." *Holocaust and Genocide Studies* 4, no. 3 (1989), 273–282.

Greenberg, Irving. "Cloud of Smoke, Pillar of Fire." In *Auschwitz: Beginning of a New Era?* edited by Eva Fleischner, pp. 7–55. New York: KTAV, 1977.

Greenspahn, Frederick E., ed. *Scripture in the Jewish and Christian Traditions: Authority, Interpretation, Relevance*. Nashville: Abingdon Press, 1982.

Greig, J. C. G. "Abba and Amen: Their Relevance to Christology." In *Studia Evangelica: The New Testament Message*. Vol. 5, pt. 2, edited by F. L. Cross, pp. 3–13. Berlin: Akademie-Verlag, 1968.

Griffin, David R. *A Process Christology*. Philadelphia: Westminster Press, 1973.

Gunton, Colin E. *Yesterday and Today: A Study of Continuities in Christology*. Grand Rapids: Eerdmans, 1983.

Gutierrez, Gustavo. *A Theology of Liberation*. Translated by Sister Caridad Inda and John Eagleson. Maryknoll, N.Y.: Orbis Books, 1983.

Haenchen, Ernst. *Der Weg Jesu: Eine Erklärung des Markus-Evangeliums und der kanonischen Parallelen.* Berlin: Topelmann, 1966.

Hahn, Herbert F. *The Old Testament in Modern Research.* Philadelphia: Fortress Press, 1966.

Hare, Douglas R. A., and Michael Harrington. "'Make Disciples of All the Gentiles' (Mt. 28:19)." *Catholic Biblical Quarterly* 37 (1975), 359–369.

Harnack, Adolf. *The Mission and Expansion of Christianity.* Translated and edited by James Moffatt. New York: Harper & Row, 1961.

———. *What Is Christianity?* Translated by Thomas Bailey Saunders. New York: Harper & Brothers, 1957.

Haroutunian, Joseph. *God with Us.* Philadelphia: Westminster Press, 1965.

Hartshorne, Charles. *The Divine Relativity.* New Haven: Yale University Press, 1948.

———. *A Natural Theology for Our Time.* La Salle, Ill.: Open Court, 1967.

———. *Omnipotence and Other Theological Mistakes.* Albany: SUNY Press, 1984.

Hartshorne, Charles, and William L. Reese. *Philosophers Speak of God.* Chicago: University of Chicago Press, 1953.

Hauerwas, Stanley. *Against the Nations.* Minneapolis: Winston Press, 1985.

———. *A Community of Character.* Notre Dame: University of Notre Dame Press, 1981.

Hegel, Friedrich. *Lectures on the Philosophy of Religion.* Translated by E. B. Speirs and J. Burdon Sanderson. London: Routledge & Kegan Paul, 1895.

———. *On Christianity: Early Theological Writings.* Translated by T. M. Knox. New York: Harper & Brothers, 1961.

———. *The Phenomenology of Mind.* Translated by James B. Baillie. London: George Allen & Unwin, 1949.

Heschel, Abraham J. *The Prophets.* Vol. 1. New York: Harper & Row, 1962.

Heschel, Susannah. "The Changing Face of Europe: Antisemitism and the Role of the Church in the Holocaust Era and Now." *Perkins Journal* 48 (July/October, 1990), 7–13.

———. "The Denigration of Judaism as a Form of Christian Mission." In *A Mutual Witness,* edited by Clark M. Williamson, pp. 33–47. St. Louis: Chalice Press, 1992.

Hilberg, Raul. *The Destruction of the European Jews.* New York: Harper & Row, 1979.

Hofius, Otfried. "'All Israel Will Be Saved': Divine Salvation and Israel's Deliverance in Romans 9–11." *The Princeton Seminary Bulletin*, Supplementary Issue, no. 1 (1990), 19–39.

Holmgren, Frederick. *The God Who Cares.* Atlanta: John Knox Press, 1979.

Horsley, Richard A. *Jesus and the Spiral of Violence.* San Francisco: Harper & Row, 1987.

———. *Sociology and the Jesus Movement.* New York: Crossroad, 1989.

Horsley, Richard A., with John S. Hanson. *Bandits, Prophets, and Messiahs.* San Francisco: Harper & Row, 1985.

Hummel, Horace D. "Law and Grace in Judaism and Lutheranism." In *Speaking of God Today: Jews and Lutherans in Conversation*, edited by Paul D. Opsahl and Marc H. Tannenbaum, pp. 15–30. Philadelphia: Fortress Press, 1974.

Irenaeus. *Against All Heresies.* In *The Ante-Nicene Fathers.* Vol. 1, translated and edited by Alexander Roberts and James Donaldson, pp. 315–567. Grand Rapids: Eerdmans, 1979.

Jacobs, Louis. *A Jewish Theology.* New York: Behrman House, 1973.

Jenson, Robert W. "The Triune God." In *Christian Dogmatics.* Vol. 1, edited by Robert W. Jenson and Carl E. Braaten, pp. 79–191. Philadephia: Fortress Press, 1984.

Jeremias, Joachim. *Jesus' Promise to the Nations.* Translated by S. H. Hooke. Naperville, Ill.: Alec R. Allenson, 1958.

———. *New Testament Theology: The Proclamation of Jesus.* Translated by John Bowden. New York: Charles Scribner's Sons, 1971.

———. *The Parables of Jesus.* Translated by S. H. Hooke. New York: Charles Scribner's Sons, 1954.

———. *The Prayers of Jesus.* Translated by John Bowden, Christoph Burchard, and John Reumann. London: SCM Press, 1967.

Johnson, Luke T. "The New Testament's Anti-Jewish Slander and the Conventions of Ancient Polemic." *Journal of Biblical Literature* 108, no. 3 (1989), 419–441.

Jonas, Hans. "The Concept of God After Auschwitz." In *Out of the Whirlwind*, edited by Albert Friedlander, pp. 465–476. New York: Schocken Books, 1976.

———. "The Concept of God After Auschwitz: A Jewish Voice." *Journal of Religion* 67, no. 1 (January 1987), 1–13.

Josephus. *Jewish Antiquities.* 17.32–45; 18.117–118.

Jüngel, Eberhard. *Gott als Geheimnis der Welt.* 2d edition. Tübingen: J. C. B. Mohr, 1977.

Justin Martyr. *Dialogue with Trypho the Jew.* In *The Ante-Nicene Fathers.* Vol. 1, translated and edited by Alexander Roberts and James Donaldson, pp. 179–270. Grand Rapids: Eerdmans, 1979.

Kant, Immanuel. *Religion Within the Limits of Reason Alone.* Translated by Thedore M. Greene and Hoyt H. Hudson. New York: Harper & Brothers, 1960.

———. *"What Is Enlightenment?"* Translated and edited by L. W. Beck. Chicago: University of Chicago Press, 1955.

Käsemann, Ernst. *An die Römer.* Tübingen: J. C. B. Mohr, 1973.

———. *New Testament Questions of Today.* Translated by W. J. Montague. Philadelphia: Fortress Press, 1969.

Kaylor, R. David. *Paul's Covenant Community: Jew and Gentile in Romans.* Atlanta: John Knox Press, 1988.

Kee, Howard Clark. *Jesus in History: An Approach to the Study of the Gospels.* San Diego: Harcourt Brace Jovanovich, 1977.

Kelber, Werner H. *The Oral and the Written Gospel.* Philadelphia: Fortress Press, 1983.

Kelsey, David H. "Protestant Attitudes Regarding Methods of Biblical Interpretation." In *Scripture in the Jewish and Christian Traditons: Authority, Interpretation, Relevance,* edited by Frederick E. Greenspahn, pp. 133–161. Nashville: Abingdon Press, 1982.

Kingsbury, Jack Dean. *Matthew as Story.* Philadelphia: Fortress Press, 1986.

Kittel, Gerhard. *Die Judenfrage.* Stuttgart: Verlag von W. Kohlhammer, 1933.

Kittel, Gerhard, ed. *"Abba."* In *Theological Dictionary of the New Testament.* Vol. 1, translated by G. W. Bromiley, pp. 5–6. Grand Rapids: Eerdmans, 1964.

———. *Theological Dictionary of the New Testament.* Vol. 2, translated by G. W. Bromiley, p. 124. Grand Rapids: Eerdmans, 1964.

Klassen, William. *The Forgiving Community.* Philadelphia: Westminster Press, 1966.

Klein, Charlotte. *Anti-Judaism in Christian Theology.* Translated by Edward Quinn. Philadelphia: Fortress Press, 1978.

Küng, Hans. *The Church.* Translated by Ray and Rosaleen Ockenden. New York: Sheed & Ward, 1967.

———. *On Being a Christian.* Translated by Edward Quinn. Garden City, N.Y.: Doubleday, 1976.

Lactantius. *The Divine Institute.* Translated by Sister Mary Francis McDonald, O.P. Washington, D.C.: Catholic University of America Press, 1964.

Lakoff, George, and Mark Johnson. *Metaphors We Live By.* Chicago: University of Chicago Press, 1980.

Lapide, Pinchas. "Christians and Jews—A New Protestant Beginning." *Journal of Ecumenical Studies* 12, no. 4 (Fall 1975), 485–492.

Lapide, Pinchas, and Ulrich Luz. *Jesus in Two Perspectives.* Translated by Lawrence W. Denef. Minneapolis: Augsburg, 1985.

Lapide, Pinchas, and Karl Rahner. *Encountering Jesus—Encountering Judaism.* Translated by Davis Perkins. New York: Crossroad, 1987.

Lee, Bernard J., S.M. *The Galilean Jewishness of Jesus.* New York: Paulist Press, 1988.

Leith, John H., ed.. *Creeds of the Churches.* Richmond: John Knox Press, 1973.

Levenson, Jon D. *Creation and the Persistence of Evil.* San Francisco: Harper & Row, 1988.

———. "Is There a Counterpart in the Hebrew Bible to New Testament Anti-Semitism?" *Journal of Ecumenical Studies* 22 (1985), 242–260.

———. *Sinai and Zion.* San Francisco: Harper & Row, 1985.

Levine, Amy-Jill. *The Social and Ethnic Dimensions of Matthean Social History.* Lewiston, N.Y.: Edwin Mellen Press, 1988.

Lindbeck, George. *The Nature of Doctrine: Religion and Theology in a Postliberal Age.* Philadelphia: Westminster Press, 1984.

Littell, Franklin H. *The Crucifixion of the Jews.* New York: Harper & Row, 1975.

Loisy, Alfred. *The Gospel and the Church.* Translated by C. Home. New York: Charles Scribner's Sons, 1909.

Lowe, Walter. "Christ and Salvation." In *Christian Theology: An Introduction to Its Traditions and Tasks,* edited by Peter C. Hodgson and Robert H. King, pp. 222-248. Philadelphia: Fortress Press, 1985.

Luther, Martin. *The Freedom of a Christian.* In *Martin Luther: Selections from His Writings,* edited by John Dillenberger, pp. 42–85. Garden City, N.Y.: Doubleday Anchor Books, 1961.

———. *Luther's Works.* Vol. 34, *Career of the Reformer IV.* Vol. 35, *Word and Sacrament I.* Philadelphia: Muhlenberg Press, 1960.

MacLennan, Robert S. *Early Christian Texts on Jews and Judaism.* Atlanta: Scholars Press, 1990.

Marquardt, Friedrich-Wilhelm. *Verwegenheiten.* Munich: Chr.Kaiser Verlag, 1981.

Meeks, Wayne A. *The First Urban Christians.* New Haven: Yale University Press, 1982.

Meeks, Wayne A., and Robert L. Wilken. *Jews and Christians in Antioch.* Missoula, Mont.: Scholars Press, 1978.

Meier, John P. *A Marginal Jew: Rethinking the Historical Jesus.* New York: Doubleday, 1991.

Metz, Johann-Baptist. *The Emergent Church.* Translated by Peter Mann. New York: Crossroad, 1981.

————. "Facing the Jews: Christian Theology After Auschwitz." In *The Holocaust as Interruption*, edited by David Tracy and Elisabeth Schüssler Fiorenza, pp. 26–33. Edinburgh: T. & T. Clark, 1984.

Miguez-Bonino, Jose, ed. *Faces of Jesus*. Translated by Robert R. Barr. Maryknoll, N.Y.: Orbis Books, 1984.

Milavec, Aaron A. "A Fresh Analysis of the Parable of the Wicked Husbandmen in the Light of Jewish-Catholic Dialogue." In *Parable and Story in Judaism and Christianity*, edited by Clemens Thoma and Michael Wyschogrod, pp. 81–117. New York: Paulist Press, 1989.

Miranda, Jose. *Being and the Messiah*. Translated by John Eagleson. Maryknoll, N.Y.: Orbis Books, 1977.

Moltmann, Jürgen. *The Crucified God*. Translated by R. A. Wilson and John Bowden. New York: Harper & Row, 1974.

————. *The Way of Jesus Christ*. Translated by Margaret Kohl. San Francisco: HarperCollins, 1990.

Montefiore, C. G. *Judaism and St. Paul*. London: Max Goschen, 1914.

Montefiore, C. G., and H. Loewe, eds.. *A Rabbinic Anthology*. New York: Schocken Books, 1974.

Moore, George Foot. "Christian Writers on Judaism." *Harvard Theological Review*, 14 (1921), 197–254.

————. *Judaism in the First Centuries of the Christian Era*. 3 vols. Cambridge: Harvard University Press, 1927–30.

Mühlen, Heribert. *Die Veränderlichkeit Gottes als Horizont einer zukünftigen Christologie*. Munich: Aschendorff, 1969.

Napier, B. D. *Exodus*. London: SCM Press, 1963.

Neusner, Jacob. *Messiah in Context*. Philadelphia: Fortress Press, 1984.

————. "Scripture and Mishnah: Authority and Selectivity." In *Scripture in the Jewish and Christian Traditions*, edited by Frederick E. Greenspahn, pp. 64–85. Nashville: Abingdon Press, 1982.

Neusner, Jacob, William Scott Green, and Ernest S. Frerichs. *Judaisms and Their Messiahs at the Turn of the Christian Era*. New York: Cambridge University Press, 1987.

Niebuhr, H. Richard. *The Meaning of Revelation*. New York: Macmillan, 1941.

Ogden, Schubert M. "The Authority of Scripture for Theology." *Interpretation* 30 (1976), 242–261.

————. *Christ Without Myth*. New York: Harper & Row, 1961.

————. "The Metaphysics of Faith and Justice," *Process Studies* 14, no. 2 (Summer 1985), 87–101.

————. *On Theology*. San Francisco: Harper & Row, 1986.

————. *The Point of Christology*. San Francisco: Harper & Row, 1982.

————. *The Reality of God*. New York: Harper & Row, 1966.

————. "Toward a New Theism." In *Process Philosophy and Christian*

Thought, edited by Delwin Brown, Ralph E. James, Jr., and Gene Reeves, pp. 173–187. Indianapolis: Bobbs-Merrill, 1971.

Origen. *Against Celsus*. In *The Ante-Nicene Fathers*. Vol. 4, translated and edited by Alexander Roberts and James Donaldson, pp. 395–669. Grand Rapids: Eerdmans, 1979.

Osborn, Robert T. "The Christian Blasphemy: A Non-Jewish Jesus." In *Jews and Christians*, edited by James H. Charlesworth, pp. 211–238. New York: Crossroad: 1990.

Parkes, James H. *The Conflict of the Church and the Synagogue*. New York: Atheneum, 1977.

Pawlikowski, John T., O.S.M. *Christ in the Light of the Christian-Jewish Dialogue*. New York: Paulist Press, 1982.

———. *Sinai and Calvary*. Beverly Hills: Benziger, 1976.

Peck, Abraham J., ed. *Jews and Christians After the Holocaust*. Philadelphia: Fortress Press, 1982.

Peel, David R. "Is Schubert M. Ogden's 'God' Christian?" *Journal of Religion* 70, no. 2 (April 1990), 147–166.

Pelikan, Jaroslav. *The Christian Tradition*. Vol. 1, *The Emergence of the Catholic Tradition (100–600)*. Chicago: University of Chicago Press, 1971.

———. *Luther the Expositor*. St. Louis: Concordia, 1959.

Perrin, Norman. *The New Testament: An Introduction*. New York: Harcourt Brace Jovanovich, 1974.

———. *Rediscovering the Teaching of Jesus*. New York: Harper & Row, 1976.

Perrin, Norman, and Dennis C. Duling. *The New Testament: An Introduction*. 2d ed. San Diego: Harcourt Brace Jovanovich, 1982.

Pherigo, Lindsey P. *The Interpreter's One Volume Commentary on the Bible*. Nashville: Abingdon Press, 1971.

Pickle, Joseph W. "Schleiermacher on Judaism." *Journal of Religion* 60, no. 2 (April 1980), 115–137.

Plaskow, Judith. "Christian Feminism and Anti-Judaism." *Cross Currents* 28 (1978), 306–309.

———. "'It Is Not in Heaven': Feminism and Religious Authority." *Tikkun* 5 (March/April 1990), 39–40.

Poliakov, Leon. *The History of Anti-Semitism*. Translated by Richard Howard. New York: Schocken Books, 1974.

Porter, Calvin L. "A New Paradigm for Reading Romans," *Encounter* 39 (Summer 1978), 257–272.

Purdy, Alexander C. "Introduction" to the Epistle to the Hebrews. *The Interpreter's Bible*. Vol. 11, pp. 577–595. Nashville: Abingdon Press, 1955.

Räisänen, Heikki. *Paul and the Law*. Philadelphia: Fortress Press, 1986.

Reynolds, J., and R. Tannenbaum. *Jesus and God-fearers at Aphrodisias: Green Inscriptions with Commentary*. Cambridge: Cambridge University Press, 1987.

Richardson, Alan, ed. *A Theological Dictionary of the Bible*. New York: Macmillan, 1950.

Richardson, Cyril C. "Introduction to Early Christian Literature." In *Early Christian Fathers*. Vol. 1 of the Library of Christian Classics, pp. 15–26. Philadelphia: Westminster Press, 1953.

Rivkin, Ellis. *A Hidden Revolution*. Nashville: Abingdon Press, 1978.

Robinson, James M., gen. ed. *The Nag Hammadi Library*. San Francisco: Harper & Row, 1977.

Roth, John K. "A Theodicy of Protest." In *Encountering Evil*, edited by Stephen T. Davis, pp. 7–22. Atlanta: John Knox Press, 1981.

Rubenstein, Richard L. *After Auschwitz*. Indianapolis: Bobbs-Merrill, 1966.

Rubenstein, Richard L., and John K Roth. *Approaches to Auschwitz*. Atlanta: John Knox Press, 1987.

Ruether, Rosemary. *Faith and Fratricide*. New York: Seabury Press, 1974.

———. *To Change the World: Christology and Cultural Criticism*. New York: Crossroad, 1983.

Sanders, E. P. *Jesus and Judaism*. Philadelphia: Fortress Press, 1985.

———. *Judaism: Practice and Belief 63 BCE—66 CE*. Philadelphia: Trinity Press International, 1992.

———. *Paul and Palestinian Judaism: A Comparison of Patterns of Religion*. London: SCM Press, 1977.

———. *Paul, the Law, and the Jewish People*. Philadelphia: Fortress Press, 1983.

Sanders, Jack T. *The Jews in Luke-Acts*. London: SCM Press, 1987.

Sanders, James A. *Canon and Community: A Guide to Canonical Criticism*. Philadelphia: Fortress Press, 1984.

Sandmel, Samuel. *Judaism and Christian Beginnings*. New York: Oxford University Press, 1978.

Satran, David. "Paul Among the Rabbis and the Fathers: Exegetical Reflections." *The Princeton Seminary Bulletin*, Supplementary Issue, no. 1 (1990), 90–105.

Schaberg, Jane. *The Illegitimacy of Jesus*. San Francisco: Harper & Row, 1987.

Schechter, Solomon. "God, Israel, and Election." In *Understanding Jewish Theology*, edited by Jacob Neusner, pp. 65–72. New York: KTAV, 1973.

Schiller, Gertrude. *Iconography of Christian Art*. Vol. 2. Translated by Janet Seligman. Greenwich, Conn.: New York Graphic Society, 1972.

Schleiermacher, Friedrich. *The Christian Faith.* Translated by H. R. Mackintosh and J. S. Stewart. Edinburgh: T. & T. Clark, 1928.

———. *The Life of Jesus.* Translated by S. Maclean Gilmour. Edited by Jack C. Verheyden. Philadelphia: Fortress Press, 1975.

Schneiders, Sandra M. "Does the Bible Have a Postmodern Message?" In *Postmodern Theology,* edited by Frederic B. Burnham, pp. 56–73. San Francisco: Harper & Row, 1989.

Schoeps, H. J. *Paul: The Theology of the Apostle in the Light of Jewish Religious History.* Philadelphia: Westminster Press, 1961.

Schulweis, Harold M. *Evil and the Morality of God.* Cincinnati: Hebrew Union College Press, 1984.

Schürer, Emil. *A History of the Jewish People in the Time of Jesus.* Edited by N. Glatzer. New York: Schocken Books, 1961.

Schüssler Fiorenza, Elisabeth. *In Memory of Her.* New York: Crossroad, 1983.

Segal, Alan F. *Paul the Convert: The Apostolate and Apostasy of Saul the Pharisee.* New Haven and London: Yale University Press, 1990.

Seiferth, Wolfgang S. *Synagogue and Church in the Middle Ages: Two Symbols in Art and Literature.* Translated by L. Chadeayne and P. Gottwald. New York: Frederick Ungar, 1970.

Shelley, Bruce L. *Church History in Plain Language.* Waco, Tex.: Word Books, 1982.

Siker, Jeffrey S. *Disinheriting the Jews: Abraham in Early Christian Controversy.* Louisville: Westminster/John Knox Press, 1991.

Slingerland, Dixon. "The Composition of Acts: Some Redaction-Critical Observations." *Journal of the American Academy of Religion* 56, no. 1 (Spring 1988), 99–113.

———. "'The Jews' in the Pauline Portion of Acts." *Journal of the American Academy of Religion* 54 no. 2 (Summer 1986), 305–321.

Sloyan, Gerard S. *Jesus in Focus.* Mystic, Conn.: Twenty-Third Publications, 1983.

———. *Jesus on Trial.* Philadelphia: Fortress Press, 1973.

Smith, Sally A. "Tried and Condemned." *The Disciple* 17 (March 1990), 35–36.

Sobrino, Jon. *Christology at the Crossroads.* Translated by John Drury. Maryknoll, N.Y.: Orbis Books, 1978.

———. *The True Church and the Poor.* Translated by Matthew J. O'Connell. Maryknoll, N.Y.: Orbis Books, 1984.

Stark, Rodney, Bruce D. Foster, Charles Y. Glock, and Harold E. Quinley. *Wayward Shepherds: Prejudice and the Protestant Clergy.* New York: Harper & Row, 1971.

Stendahl, Krister. *Paul Among Jews and Gentiles.* Philadelphia: Fortress Press, 1976.

————. *The School of St. Matthew*. Philadelphia: Fortress Press, 1968.

Stern, David. "Jesus' Parables from the Perspective of Rabbinic Litera-
ture." In *Parable and Story in Judaism and Christianity*, edited by
Clemens Thoma and Michael Wyschogrod, pp. 42–80. New York:
Paulist Press, 1989.

Stout, Jeffrey. *Ethics After Babel*. Boston: Beacon Press, 1988.

Swidler, Leonard, Lewis John Eron, Gerard Sloyan, and Lester Dean.
Bursting the Bonds? Maryknoll, N.Y.: Orbis Books, 1990.

Talmage, Frank Ephraim. "Christianity and the Jewish People." In
Disputation and Dialogue, edited by Frank Ephraim Talmage,
pp. 240–253. New York: KTAV, 1975.

Tertullian. *Against Praxeas*. In *The Ante-Nicene Fathers*. Vol. 3, translated by S. Thelwall; edited by Alexander Roberts and James Donaldson, pp. 597–627. Grand Rapids: Eerdmans, 1978.

————. *An Answer to the Jews*. In *The Ante-Nicene Fathers*. Vol. 3, translated by S. Thelwall; edited by Alexander Roberts and James Donaldson, pp. 151–173. Grand Rapids: Eerdmans, 1978.

————. *Prescription Against Heretics*. In *Early Latin Theology*, edited by
S. L. Greenslade, pp. 25–64. Philadelphia: Westminster Press, 1956.

Thackeray, H. St. J. *The Relation of St. Paul to Contemporary Jewish
Thought*. London: Macmillan, 1900.

Thiemann, Ronald F. *Revelation and Theology: The Gospel as Narrated
Promise*. Notre Dame: University of Notre Dame Press, 1985.

Thoma, Clemens. *A Christian Theology of Judaism*. Translated by Helga
Croner. New York: Paulist Press, 1980.

————. "Literary and Theological Aspects of the Rabbinic Parables." In
Parable and Story in Judaism and Christianity, edited by Clemens
Thoma and Michael Wyschogrod, pp. 26–41. New York: Paulist
Press, 1989.

Tillich, Paul. *Perspectives on 19th and 20th Century Protestant Theology*.
New York: Harper & Row, 1967.

————. *The Protestant Era*. Translated by James Luther Adams.
Chicago: University of Chicago Press, 1948.

————. *The Shaking of the Foundations*. New York: Charles Scribner's
Sons, 1948.

————. *Systematic Theology*. Vols. 1–3. Chicago: University of Chicago
Press, 1951, 1957, 1963.

————. "The Two Types of Philosophy of Religion." In *Theology of Culture*, edited by Robert C. Kimball, pp. 10–29. New York: Oxford
University Press, 1959.

Townsend, John T. "The Gospel of John and the Jews: The Story of a
Religious Divorce." In *Antisemitism and the Foundations of Christianity*, edited by Alan T. Davies, pp. 72–97. New York: Paulist Press,
1979.

————. "The New Testament, the Early Church, and Anti-Semitism." In *From Ancient Israel to Modern Judaism*. Vol. 1, edited by Jacob Neusner, Ernest S. Frerichs, and Nahum M. Sarna, pp. 171–186. Atlanta: Scholars Press, 1989.

Tracy, David. *The Analogical Imagination*. New York: Crossroad, 1981.

————. *Plurality and Ambiguity*. San Francisco: Harper & Row, 1987.

————. "Religious Values After the Holocaust: A Catholic View." In *Jews and Christians After the Holocaust*, edited by Abraham J. Peck, pp. 87–107. Philadelphia: Fortress Press, 1982.

————. "Theological Method." In *Christian Theology: An Introduction to Its Traditions and Tasks*, edited by Peter C. Hodgson and Robert H. King, pp. 35–60. Philadelphia: Fortress Press, 1985.

Trepp, Leo. *A History of the Jewish Experience*. New York: Behrman House, 1973.

van Buren, Paul M. "The Church and Israel: Romans 9–11." *The Princeton Seminary Bulletin*, Supplementary Issue, no. 1 (1990), 5–18.

————. *The Secular Meaning of the Gospel*. New York: Macmillan, 1963.

————. *A Theology of the Jewish-Christian Reality*. Part 1: *Discerning the Way*. New York: Seabury Press, 1980.

————. *A Theology of the Jewish-Christian Reality*. Part 2: *A Christian Theology of the People Israel*. New York: Seabury Press, 1983.

————. *A Theology of the Jewish-Christian Reality*. Part 3: *Christ in Context*. San Francisco: Harper & Row, 1988.

Vermes, Geza. *Jesus and the World of Judaism*. Philadelphia: Fortress Press, 1983.

————. *Jesus the Jew*. New York: Macmillan, 1973.

Vogel, Manfred. "Covenant and the Interreligious Encounter." In *Issues in the Jewish-Christian Dialogue: Jewish Perspectives on Covenant, Mission and Witness*, edited by Helga Croner and Leon Klenicki, pp. 62–85. New York: Paulist Press, 1979.

von der Osten-Sacken, Peter. *Christian-Jewish Dialogue: Theological Foundations*. Translated by Margaret Kohl. Philadelphia: Fortress Press, 1986.

von Rad, Gerhard. *Moses*. New York: Association Press, 1959.

Walker, Williston. *A History of the Christian Church*. New York: Charles Scribner's Sons, 1918.

Wellhausen, Julius. *Prolegomenon to the History of Ancient Israel*. Preface by W. Robertson Smith. Gloucester, Mass.: Peter Smith Publisher, 1973; originally published 1886.

Wesley, Charles. "Love Divine, All Loves Excelling." In *Hymnbook for Christian Worship*. St. Louis: Bethany Press, 1970.

Westerholm, Stephen. *Israel's Law and the Church's Faith*. Grand Rapids: Eerdmans, 1988.

Whitehead, Alfred North. *Process and Reality.* Corrected edition, edited by David R. Griffin and Donald W. Sherburne. New York: Free Press, 1978; originally published by Macmillan, 1929.

———. *Religion in the Making.* New York: Macmillan, 1926.

———. *Science and the Modern World.* New York: New American Library, 1925.

Wieman, Henry Nelson. *The Source of Human Good.* Carbondale: Southern Illinois University Press, 1946.

Wiesel, Elie. *Night.* New York: Avon Books, 1969.

Wiles, Maurice, and Mark Santer, eds. *Documents in Early Christian Thought.* Cambridge: Cambridge University Press, 1975.

Wilken, Robert L. *The Myth of Christian Beginnings.* Garden City, N.Y.: Doubleday, 1971.

Williams, A. Lukyn. *Adversus Judaeos.* Cambridge: Cambridge University Press, 1935.

Williams, George, and Ingel M. Mergal, eds. *Spiritual and Anabaptist Writers.* Philadelphia: Westminster Press, 1957.

Williams, Rowan D. "Postmodern Theology and the Judgment of the World." In *Postmodern Theology,* edited by Frederic B. Burnham, pp. 92–112. San Francisco: Harper & Row, 1989.

Williamson, Clark M. "The Authority of Scripture After the *Shoah.*" In *Faith and Creativity,* edited by George Nordgulen and George W. Shields, pp. 125–142. St. Louis: CBP Press, 1987.

———. *Baptism: Embodiment of the Gospel.* St. Louis: CBP Press, 1987.

———. "Christ Against the Jews." In *Christianity and Judaism: The Deepening Dialogue,* edited by Richard W. Rousseau, S.J., pp. 145–154. Scranton, Pa.: Ridge Row Press, 1983.

———. *God Is Never Absent.* St. Louis: Bethany Press, 1977.

———. *Has God Rejected His People?* Nashville: Abingdon Press, 1982.

———. "The New Testament Reconsidered: Recent Post-Holocaust Scholarship." *Quarterly Review* 4, no. 4 (1984), 37–51.

———. "Postwar Reflections on the Holocaust from a Christian Point of View." In *Movements and Issues in World Religions,* edited by Charles Wei-hsun Fu and Gerhard E. Spiegler, pp. 515–539. New York: Greenwood Press, 1986.

———. "Process Hermeneutics and Christianity's Post-Holocaust Reinterpretation of Itself." *Process Studies* 12, no. 2 (1982), 77–93.

———. *When Jews and Christians Meet.* St. Louis: CBP Press, 1989.

Williamson, Clark M., and Ronald J. Allen. *A Credible and Timely Word.* St. Louis: Chalice Press, 1991.

———. *Interpreting Difficult Texts: Anti-Judaism and Christian Preaching.* Philadelphia: Trinity Press International; London: SCM Press, 1989.

———. *The Teaching Minister*. Louisville: Westminster/John Knox Press, 1991.

Williamson, Clark M., and Charles Blaisdell. "Disciple Contributions and Responses to Mainstream Theology: 1880–1953." In *A Case Study of Mainstream Protestantism,* edited by D. Newell Williams, pp. 129–137. Grand Rapids: Eerdmans, 1991.

Wilson, Marvin. *Our Father Abraham*. Grand Rapids: Eerdmans, 1989.

Wink, Walter. *John the Baptist in the Gospel Tradition*. Cambridge: Cambridge University Press, 1968.

Wittgenstein, Ludwig. *Philosophical Investigations*. Oxford: Basil Blackwell, 1958.

Womer, Jan L., ed. *Morality and Ethics in Early Christianity*. Philadelphia: Fortress Press, 1987.

Young, Brad H. *Jesus and His Jewish Parables*. New York: Paulist Press, 1989.

Zabel, James A. *Nazism and the Pastors*. Missoula, Mont.: Scholars Press, 1976.

Zeitlin, Irving M. *Jesus and the Judaism of His Time*. Cambridge: Polity Press, 1988.

Index, Including
Scripture References

Abba, 53–55
Abbott, Walter M., 273n10
Acts 2:33, 194; 4:33, 194; 9:2, 18:26, 14; 28:28, 251
Agnew, Francis H., 86, 89, 288n38, 289n48
Akiba, 243
Albertus Magnus, 234, 312n3
Allen, Ronald J., 269n25, 278n85, 298n8
Ambrose, 237–239, 313nn18, 28
Ames, William, 134, 297n78
Amos 3:2, 125, 200; 9:7, 128
Anselm, 205–206, 308n18
Antiochus IV Epiphanes, 100
apostolicity, 18–19
Aristotle, 203, 307n2
Arius, 229
Athanasius, 168–173, 303nn5, 8, 12, 314n50
Augustine, 6, 115–117, 205, 236–239, 268n15, 272n1, 293n21, 294n23, 308nn12, 15, 312n14, 313nn19, 23, 31
Auschwitz, 267n6
Austin, J. L., 31, 273n11

Barnabas, Epistle of, 110–112, 292n5, 293n8
Barr, James, 280n31, 301n52
Barth, Karl, 4, 12, 21, 105, 107, 119–122, 136, 138, 250, 268n7, 270n37, 271n63, 291n100, 292nn107, 1, 294nn36–39, 295nn40–41, 45, 297n80

Barth, Markus, 85, 288n35
Bartsch, Hans Werner, 118, 294n31
Basil, 239–240, 313n34
Baum, Gregory, 268n12, 271n48
Beck, Norman A., 297n2, 298nn10, 12, 299n28
Beker, J. Christiaan, 82–83, 287n20, 292n108, 299n23
Black, Matthew, 80, 286nn10, 11
Blaisdell, Charles, 273n4
Boers, Hendrikus, 58–61, 281nn56, 58, 282nn65, 76
Bokser, Ben Zion, 295n56
Bonhoeffer, Dietrich, 263
Bowden, John, 10, 269n28, 281n47, 285n120
Braaten, Carl E., 303n3
Braun, Herbert, 280n31
Breech, James, 281n49
Brock, Rita Nakashima, 307n70, 308n25
Brockway, Alan, 273n5, 274nn30, 34, 275nn40, 42, 48, 49, 276nn51, 66, 277nn72, 80, 83
Brooks, Roger, 294n28, 295n53
Brown, Delwin, 19, 271n57
Brown, Raymond E., 147–148, 299n27
Brueggemann, Walter, 284n100
Brunner, Emil, 4
Buber, Martin, 243–244, 314n49, 315n51
Buggert, William F., 294n35
Bultmann, Rudolf, 285n118, 302n70

337